COMMAND OF THE SEA

IN TWO VOLUMES

Volume One: To 1815

Volume Two: Since 1815

By Clark G. Reynolds

Command of the Sea:
  The History and Strategy of Maritime Empires

The Fast Carriers:
  The Forging of an Air Navy

Famous American Admirals

The Carrier War
  With the Editors of Time-Life Books

Carrier Admiral
  With Admiral J. J. Clark

The Saga of Smokey Stover
  With E. T. Stover

Clark G. Reynolds
COMMAND

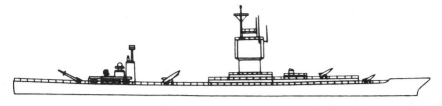

OF THE SEA

The History and Strategy of Maritime Empires

IN TWO VOLUMES

Volume One: To 1815

Volume Two: Since 1815

Robert E. Krieger Publishing Company
Malabar, Florida

Original Edition   1974
Reissued in Two Volumes w/new material 1983

Printed and Published by
ROBERT E. KRIEGER PUBLISHING COMPANY, INC.
KRIEGER DRIVE
MALABAR, FLORIDA 32950

Library of Congress Cataloging in Publication Data

Reynolds, Clark G.
    Command of the sea.

    Reprint. Originally published: New York : Morrow,
1974.
    Bibliography: p.
    1. Sea-power. 2. Naval strategy. 3. Naval history.
I. Title.
V25.R47   1983   359'.03'09   83-6129
ISBN 0-89874-630-2 (set)
ISBN 0-89874-628-0 (v. 1)
ISBN 0-89874-629-9 (v. 2)
10 9 8 7 6 5

To Theodore Ropp,
mentor

Preface

Study of the workings of the minds of the proved strategists stimulates, if it does not actually procreate, ideas. It opens up one's mental vision, it widens one's strategic horizon. . . . We see, in history, how the Masters of War have tackled their problems. Would it not be something approaching impudence to pretend that we can learn nothing from them, that we are self-sufficient in ourselves?

—SIR HERBERT RICHMOND, *c*. 1928

The contemplation of strategy in history does indeed open the mind—not only to the employment of military forces in wartime but to the essence of great power relationships at all times and indeed to the nature of nations themselves.

This writer's mind was opened by Theodore Ropp, whose unique intellect, courses and doctoral program in military history at Duke University between 1938 and 1982 challenged hundreds of students to ask new questions of the past. I learned as a graduate student there in the early 1960s. The other major influence in my intellectual development was William H. Russell, professor of history at the U.S. Naval Academy from 1946 to 1973 whose mind-stretching Seminar in Philosophy of War exposed me to fresh insights as a faculty member there in the mid-1960s. Both men developed their ideas through teaching seminars and directing student research rather than by the more usual means of active publishing. Both were brilliant at it, and I have been proud to draw upon their erudition for the present work.

What British historian Correlli Barnett in 1969 termed "strategic history" became the focus of my own research and teaching at the University of Maine between 1968 and 1976—not only in graduate seminars but undergraduate survey courses too; in my annual lectures at the Canadian Forces Staff College since 1974 and elsewhere; and in all my thinking about international relationships and patterns of national behavior. In the decade between the publication of the original one-volume edition and this updated two-volume edition, no historical scholarship or recent events—not the endless wars of the Third World nor the Falkland Islands War of 1982—have convinced me to change any of my strategic ideas or conclusions, with one exception. (Though I am indebted to Professor J. R. Bruijn of the University of Leiden for correcting some errors of fact about the Dutch navy.)

I believe that in all history only four true major maritime powers—thalassocracies—have existed: ancient Athens, Renaissance Venice and the Netherlands, and modern Great Britain. These I have defined as having had a common national mix: geographic and thus strategic insularity; politically liberal; economically mercantile and capitalistic; socially diversified with a dominant middle class; religiously tolerant; intellectually free and dynamic; and militarily oriented to the navy as the senior service. In 1973 I wanted to add the contemporary United States to this exclusive list of maritime states but had doubts, and my attempt was rejected as unconvincing by my excellent editor at William Morrow & Company, Howard Cady.

Even before the book appeared in 1974, I dug into the problem and erased any doubt in my mind about America's place on the list of true maritime imperial states—a conclusion which I presented in a trilogy of essays in honor of the U.S. Bicentennial: "American Strategic History and Doctrines: A Reconsideration," *Military Affairs* (December 1975), which won the Moncado Prize of the American Military Institute; "The British Strategic Inheritance in American Naval Policy, 1775–1975," in *The Atlantic World of Robert G. Albion* (Middletown, Conn., 1975), edited by B.W. Labaree; and "The Sea in the Making of America," *U.S. Naval Institute Proceedings* (July 1976).

The reader is not expected to accept uncritically the ideas and interpretations in this book. Rather, the work is intended as a point of departure, an introduction to the fascinating subject of the strategic impact of the sea on the peoples of the world throughout history. The facts are all here, perhaps too many of them, but they become comprehensible when utilized with the strategic projection maps—for, as Clausewitz said, geography is the bones of strategy.

C.G.R.

Contents

Introduction

From the days when we humans first began to use the seas, the great lesson of history is that the enemy who is confined to a land strategy is in the end defeated.

—MONTGOMERY OF ALAMEIN, 1958

"Sea power is indeed a great thing," Thucydides reminds us from his histories of that golden age of Greek learning from which Western civilization directly evolved. Why was it great then, during such an intellectually dynamic era? What were the political, economic and military dimensions of Greek commercial and war shipping? What considerations of strategy underlay the Athenian Empire and the employment of its navy? Indeed, how—if at all—did command of the sea make possible and even stimulate the monumental Greek art and thought of the fifth century B.C.? Upon what historical precedents did the thalassocracy of Athens build, and what legacies did that state leave for future nations that would be founded upon the sea?

Such questions are immense, but so important that they must be answered—the intent of the present work. Not only ancient Greece, but all maritime states and non-maritime-centered peoples who have⋅ plied the sea must be analyzed historically and strategically if sea power is to be appreciated, understood and applied in the future. The task is not a simple one, for it involves two methodological ingredients traditionally avoided by most historians: generalization and subjectivity. Historians, like other professionals, feel most secure in their own areas of specialization, and they jealously guard their specialties from generalizing pirates. Nevertheless, this writer believes that the painstaking labors behind a great many specialized studies can be synthesized into a meaningful overview of naval history. In contrast, strategists, by trade and definition, must analyze in order to understand principles, trends and any patterns in strategic thought and practice, which requires a large measure of subjective but informed opinion. Historical objectivity must then yield to such analysis if the notion of command of the sea is to have any real meaning.

This book consequently seeks to discover the strategic alternatives and constants governing navies and empires throughout the continuum of history by raising hypotheses to be tested by historical examination and by future action. It therefore examines the natural factors such as geography and topography, the political and economic aspects of empire building, the cultural and intellectual manifestations, technology and the tactical evolution of naval forces. Together, these elements define the concept of sea power—in the twentieth century A.D. as well as in the twentieth century B.C. Sea power, when applied to command of the major waterways of the world, indeed emerges as "a great thing"—in the past, today and for the foreseeable future.

PUBLISHER'S NOTE
The first 16 pages of Volume I **are**
repeated for introduction to this
volume, if used separately.

BOOK ONE

Command of the Sea—
and the Alternatives

. . . a vague feeling of contempt for the past, supposed to be obsolete, combines with natural indolence to blind men even to those permanent strategic lessons which lie close to the surface of naval history.

—ALFRED THAYER MAHAN

The primary aim of naval war is the command of the sea. Any other aim is an acceptance of the position of the inferior naval power, and the abnegation of all hopes of ultimate success.

—P. H. COLOMB

The sea covers 71 percent of the earth's surface; the remaining 29 percent is mostly land mass, generally occupied by human groupings in areas readily accessible either to the great saltwater oceans or to the many inland fresh-waterways, the major lakes and rivers. The seaborne communications between these settlements have often been a dominant force in the history of great nations. Thus, command of the sea and inland waterways has remained a key political and strategic concern of seagoing peoples throughout history.

Geography is the major determining factor in any nation's ability to utilize the sea commercially and to defend its political and economic

1

integrity from overseas attack. Thus, each nation tends to orient its political, economic and military life around the advantages of its geographical position vis-à-vis other nations. And history reveals that this orientation has usually favored either the ocean-maritime element or the continental. No nation has yet been able to afford the sheer expense of sustaining both a large army to control its continental frontiers and a large navy to maintain control over vast areas of water.

While immediately adjacent waters have been of constant concern to every nation, the specific waterways politically disputed throughout history have changed in emphasis with the growth and reach of Western civilization.

In the ancient and medieval periods of history, the Mediterranean Sea enclosed the areas of major political dispute. These were the Eastern Mediterranean, from the Aegean Sea and the Dardanelles in the north, to Cyprus and Crete islands in the center, to the Phoenician coast and Nile Delta in the south; the Central Mediterranean, from the Adriatic Sea and Italy in the north, to the Ionian and Tyrrhenian seas and Sicily in the center, to Carthage and Malta in the south; and the Western Mediterranean, the clockwise circle of southern France, Corsica, Sardinia, North Africa, Gibraltar, the Balearic Islands (Majorca and Minorca) and the Iberian peninsula.

In the modern period, roughly 1500 to 1900, maritime relations between nations were geographically governed by the so-called funnel of Europe, the sea lanes of the North Atlantic Ocean that passed through the narrow Strait of Dover and English Channel, connecting the North Sea nations with France, Spain and Portugal to the south. At the focus of this activity lay England, around which the major maritime events of this period revolved. Flanking this center of maritime activity and international rivalry were three virtual overseas lakes, all linked to the ever-lengthening European trade routes: the Baltic Sea to the north, the Mediterranean to the south and the Caribbean to the west. Secondary areas in this period were the South Atlantic, Indian and Pacific oceans, and the Black Sea.

In the contemporary period, the twentieth century, the rise of non-European powers has made the two great oceans, the Atlantic and Pacific, of equal importance. All the other oceans, seas, lakes and rivers are secondary in importance, although it must be recognized that international rivalry upon the seas has become global in this period.

Throughout history, the chances of a nation becoming a dominant power upon the sea, with a large merchant marine, overseas colonies and a strong navy to protect both, has been determined always by favorable geographic conditions. Insularity is of prime importance. Without land frontiers to defend, a maritime nation may minimize its army for home defense and simultaneously be able to project its commercial and naval strength overseas. Placed in the dominant geographic position relative to rival land powers, oceanic states such as ancient Athens, modern Great Britain or the contemporary United States have been able to emerge as dominant maritime nations. And their strategies have rested upon their ability to command the sea.

Nature must be kind to aspiring maritime nations by also providing them with many good bays and inlets, protected from storms and extreme tides, adverse winds and weather, yet deep enough and large enough to harbor many large ships. In the ancient period, smooth coastal waters were essential for the operation of rowed galleys between these harbors. In the modern period, favorable prevailing winds were essential to propel sailing ships from these ports. In addition, long and wide rivers with sizable outlets, deltas or bays opened oceanic trade and naval operations to and from the interior.

Without these strategic geographical assets, no nation has ever been able to achieve a lasting political and economic dominion over the seas. Continental powers so limited have had to adopt special measures or alternatives to compensate for their inherent geographical shortcomings. As a result, two separate strategic policies recur throughout history as great maritime and continental powers have confronted one another.

EMPIRES, NAVIES AND STRATEGY

Great powers have evolved to the height of their political prestige and might by becoming imperial nations, though they may not choose to accept this label. Though the meaning is forever debated among historians, *empire* may be generally defined as the supreme authority of a large and powerful nation over considerable territory beyond its immediate borders. *Imperialism* is the policy of extending that authority further, by acquiring colonies or dependencies. Though any sprawling nation may be (and many have been) considered *imperial,* common usage throughout history has tended to regard mostly those nations with overseas holdings as truly deserving of the label *imperial.* Nevertheless, landed rulers have often preferred the grandiose title of *emperor,* and occasionally they have deserved it in the political context of having far-flung subject peoples. But for purposes of convenience, historical accuracy and strategic analysis, real imperial powers may be considered as those great nations in history which have based their national political and economic policies and strategies chiefly on *maritime* activities: commercial trade, overseas possessions or dependencies, and naval forces. The other great powers, non-maritime by nature, may be simply labeled as continental, relying chiefly upon the produce and manufactures of the national homeland and whatever political or economic advantage it can gain from its continental neighbors. Lesser nations may vary in their orientations between livelihood on the sea and the soil, but their larger destinies are usually subject to the actions of the great *maritime/ imperial* and/or *continental* powers.

Maritime powers, vulnerable to external pressures on their food supply, raw materials and power sources and thus primarily interested in maintaining their economic wealth through overseas trade, have therefore sought to enforce a reasonable state of international order on the high seas, so that the economic lifeblood of their merchant economy should not be interrupted or threatened. They have consequently depended upon their navies to maintain that order by policing both the trade routes to their overseas markets and also the oceans of the world wherever their merchant vessels ply. The national interest of maritime powers has generally dictated a policy of either monopoly or the free use of the seas, whichever best profited their own economies. In addition, uninterrupted sea-borne communication among such a maritime people has tended to bind them politically and culturally as well as economically.

Domination of the seas by a great maritime power in the cause of economic and thus political stability has resulted in protracted periods of seeming "peace." Each so-called *Pax—Romana, Britannica* and *Americana*—has really been naval peace, where supremacy at sea provides a major deterrent against serious challenge by unfriendly opponents. In reality, *pax* or peace has been a misnomer, as true peace can exist only within a political vacuum. And political vacuums are—sad to say for "peace"-loving peoples—a virtual impossibility. Rather, periods of international stability and political orderliness are made possible by a precarious balance of tensions between two or more great powers. That the prolonged maintenance of such balances is difficult is evident in the multitude of "policing actions" and wars fought in the name of maintaining some balance of the great powers.

If one needs a working definition of the balance of power, it is the distribution of nearly equal political-military power between two competing nations or groupings of nations so that normal economic intercourse remains unrestrained—or, so that relations between nations remain "peaceful."

Maritime empires have been expensive to protect. A large navy is necessary to patrol the colonies and trade routes of the empire and, if necessary, the seas beyond them. Also required are police-type (pacification) ground forces to enforce internal order within the overseas possessions. But the biggest expense is ships, which are costly to build, arm, supply, man, keep up, repair and eventually replace. Still, the investment in a navy is an investment in political and economic security. Ignorance of this fact has led to strong internal political opposition to large naval budgets in all nations having warships. So necessary are the navy and constabulary troops to the welfare of a maritime empire that one may generalize that the stability, loyalty and trustworthiness of overseas colonies and dependencies are directly proportional to the strength of the mother navy.

Just as the navy helps to determine the political and economic destiny of great maritime nations, so too is it a dynamic force in the cultural and social aspects of the national life, for maritime nations or thalassocracies have two important social advantages over continental powers, stemming from the natural accident of their geographic location.

First, since maritime nations are usually insular, they enjoy what might be called national privacy. With no unfriendly powers poised on their borders, they enjoy something which continental peoples have always considered a luxury—no large standing army or national psychosis of impending attack. If maritime peoples can rely upon a formidable navy operating literally out of sight of their homeland to insure their insularity, they can ignore such culturally inhibiting forces as military frontiers and forts, military strongmen and despots, standing alliances, frequent invasions and wars, and the whole mosaic of problems involved in counterattacking, occupying, defeating and reconstructing an enemy nation. Such countries have had the advantage of *time* over their constantly embattled peers on the continents, time in which to develop their institutions and industries in relative peace. Maritime insularity, then, has been a key ingredient in intellectual ferment, the growth of applied technology, and the fostering of democracy. Isolated and thereby well-defended men have tended to be free men, free to think and to apply their ideas to machinery and to government.

The other advantage of the maritime nations over the continental, and closely related to this tendency of isolated peoples to promote free thought, is that by the very nature of their economic life such nations have placed a high premium on the worth and skills of the individual. Merchant traders on land or sea are an independent lot anyway, yet the growth of the merchant class has been more rapid and pronounced in countries that depend on overseas trade. Continental states have taken decades longer than their maritime counterparts to bridge or close the great gap between aristocracy and peasant class. Equally if not more significant has been the individual sailor. Life at sea is a high adventure, involving the wisdom and raw stamina of men against not only an enemy in battle but against nature. The spirit of great maritime peoples has been embodied in their naval heroes and their tireless explorers, who in the past conquered unknown frontiers overseas and in the contemporary period have been mastering the poles, the ocean depths, the skies and space beyond.

Navies especially have been a bedrock of individualism, while the naval profession nurtures this individualism by demanding the very qualities that shape great peoples—discipline, creativity and a high degree of practical intelligence. Discipline at sea is more than abiding by the orders issued from a rigid hierarchy of authority; it is also the self-discipline of the individual seaman in the face of constant danger. Practical common sense and the ability to improvise when short on doctrine or material are equally essential for survival at sea. Rugged and outspoken when in their own element, sailors have always possessed a large measure of tolerance and yet a keen sense of justice and fair play. They respect authority, but can be pushed to rebel against unreasonable commanders.

This thalassocratic individualism has remained an essential ingredient not only of effective navies but of great maritime nations. Small wonder, then, that such nations place such value on their seamen, merchant as well as naval. At one with the sea, which he must eternally battle to control in the struggle between man and the elements, the individual sailor develops a self-confidence and pride of service seldom equaled in armies. Relatively unaffected by shifting political winds ashore, the sailor fashions a hardened sense of duty and loyalty to his ship and his profession. Hence navies have usually been among the least political and most stable of institutions in maritime nations. A vital component of the democratic spirit, navies have remained a pillar in the support of free institutions, socially as well as strategically.

Politically, however, navies have always been weak in asserting themselves overtly. Sailors learn their professional skills at sea among a small ship's company, where administrative and political considerations are minimal. They are technical experts, skilled in the technology of service at sea and sensitive to the inherent fragility of their machines. And seamanship knows no politics. By contrast, land-oriented officers deal with vast administrative organizations of many men and large tracts of territory and are in constant physical association with the political organs of government. These army men are the most skilled administrators in any military operation involving both land and sea forces.

Naval officers have therefore lacked the political polish of the generals and have tended to remain aloof from politics or to adopt a seemingly safer, conservative approach. Even in political revolutions, navies tend to remain as nonparticipants. Broadly speaking, sea power works slowly and subtly, whereas generals, politicians and the people at large are impatient for direct, immediately apparent results, as with armies on the march. These elements of society therefore tend to view expensive navies with suspicion when confronted with often short-term or superficially more pressing domestic and diplomatic concerns. Resisting "liberals" out to cut the fleet, admirals tend to oppose changes to their service from which recovery will be difficult when the national mood again suddenly reverts to a frantic awareness of actual naval requirements. Thus sensitive to criticism by politicians and their constituents, flag officers usually fare rather badly when embroiled in broad political disputes.

Strategically, then, as well as politically, navies and their admirals tend to favor the *status quo*. They need *time* for their exercise of command over the seas to be felt, and they require an economically superior government to support their own needs for a superior fleet. Unlike armies, whose strength is built on manpower, navies depend more on the technology of their ships and weapons, which are infinitely more costly than the raising of armies. Furthermore, navies are intolerant of forces aimed at disrupting the order they enforce. Consequently, they have tended to regard interlopers into their imperial system as illegal enemies. Most outstanding of their "outlaw" foes throughout history have been rebels, smugglers and pirates.

Colonial settlers or subject peoples sooner or later develop a desire to share with the mother country the fruits of their labors. But if such empires persist in exploiting these areas and not sharing their wealth with such indigenous folk, they will likely be faced with revolt. The navy is then charged with the task of reestablishing order in the colonies, an expensive task that requires considerable effort and diversion of naval material from other pressing strategic activities. The rebels must be isolated from outside help, thus requiring warships to police the seas in the troubled area. Imperial troops must be sealifted to the place, then supported logistically by the navy and merchant marine. And once suppressed, the rebellious possession must then be closely watched by a garrison and the navy, which is dependent upon the area for its advanced base of operations. Thus navies, like their governments, regard any political upheaval as dangerous to imperial stability. Rebels cannot be tolerated if order (or "peace") is to prevail.

Pirates have generally been considered to be outlaws preying upon merchant shipping and the colonies. In the early ancient and early modern periods, before the advent of maritime empires based upon far-flung political and economic order, piracy and privateering (commissioned private raiders by an enemy) were considered to be more or less respectable professions. As civilization became more rigid and erected legal safeguards to protect the economic wealth of the nation-state, the pirate appeared increasingly as a violator of civilized international law upon the high seas. A "barbarian" (*i.e.*, uncivilized), this outlaw became such an outrage to imperial nations that he was effectively eliminated by them before the end of the modern period. In their role of policing the oceans of the realm, navies have always had to be able to suppress piracy effectively on the high seas. Without navies, pirates flourish.

Therefore, to maintain political and economic stability upon the oceans of the world and throughout their own empires, maritime nations have depended upon their navies. Their strategies have thus embodied the ability to deter rival powers from interfering with their own maritime activities, to suppress pirates and to police the trade routes and overseas possessions of their own empires. To do these things, such navies must be able to command the seas. Opponents of major maritime nations have been the competing maritime nations, major continental powers, or a combination of both.

Continental powers have been governed by very different geographical considerations, the result being that the naval or maritime aspects of these nations have generally been secondary in political and strategic importance. A systematic analysis of great land powers is not within the scope of this study, except as such nations have attempted to utilize waterborne economic power and military force in the face of strong maritime rivals. Generally speaking, continental powers have depended upon overland communications for their economic wealth and upon large armies and fortifications for their political and military security. Constantly exposed to and threatened by overland invasion, such nations have reduced their armies only at their peril. Agriculturally (and later industrially) based, these nations have depended mostly on manpower for defense—the mobilizing, disciplining and administration of large armies. The effect has been a general tendency toward authoritarian government, national regimentation and a servile population. In general, whereas the independent merchant class has typified maritime societies, a powerful landed aristocracy has dominated the life styles of continental powers until very recent times. Their political base has literally been the land. And their political goals have usually been obvious—defense against the invader—as opposed to nations which depend on more subtle goals to be gained through the application of sea power.

The attempt of continental powers to operate navies has consequently been frustrated not only by geographic limitations but by related political, cultural and social contradictions. Politically, the ruling landed aristocracy (or industrial managers in the contemporary period) is preoccupied with defending the *status quo* at home, preserving the government from internal upheaval and external attack. Such a class has little appreciation for expensive overseas enterprises and tends to be too rigid to adopt the techniques and innovations of the maritime powers.

So it invests primarily in the army, subordinating the navy to these continental objectives. Culturally and socially, such nations do not generally enjoy the spirit of individualism engendered by maritime adventurers, but rely rather upon their people as a mass. When in fact such land powers have attempted to create a maritime empire replete with a navy, as some have, their merchant mariners usually have emerged profitably, but the navy soon discovered itself outside the mainstream of internal politics and national life. This apolitical trait is consistent with the naval politics of maritime nations, except that eventually the continental navy finds itself manipulated into virtual extinction by the dominant army-supported class.

History indicates that the most viable solution a continental power can seek in its quest for a naval presence is—in addition to its own small navy—alliance with a maritime nation. Depending upon such an ally has proved risky, for obvious reasons, but alliance has probably been the most workable compromise solution to meet an otherwise almost impossible need.

So, strategically there have been great maritime nations and great continental nations. One type has shaped its strategy largely around the overseas thrust of its navy. The other has depended strategically upon the defensive stance and occasional offensive thrust of the standing army (and later, land-based air forces) overland. Despite exceptions throughout history, these distinctions between land and sea powers have generally held true for major peoples and nations.

STRATEGIC HISTORY

The history and strategy of maritime empires have been shaped not only by geography and men but by naval technology as well. Indeed, the fact that a navy exists is a sure indication of civilization and its growing technology. A full understanding of the technological element is thus crucial, because the misunderstanding of dominant weapons and other technical aspects of defense policy has often led historians and strategic analysts alike astray from the essential lasting principles of maritime power.

More so than armies, navies have required many years to evolve, due to the technological nature of their relatively more sophisticated equipment. Ships must be designed to incorporate the latest innovations in naval architecture and weaponry, then constructed over a number of years—up to four years for the largest warships of the modern and contemporary periods. These latter, often called capital ships, have usually been the yardstick of naval power, the ship-type around which the tactics of a fleet are formulated. Essential to evaluating the actual strength of such vessels, however, is an understanding of their cruising characteristics, the propulsion system and operating range, main and secondary armaments, defensive protection, signals communications and control over the ship's operation. Smaller vessels deserve equal attention as seagoing machinery. And the whole weapon (or weapons system, in recent parlance) depends on the skill and well-being of its operators. The officers and crew fashion the merchant ship and the vessel of war, so that a given naval technology is only as good as the training, experience, clothing, feeding, health and morale of the seagoing technicians.

Furthermore, naval technology and weaponry are utterly useless if the techniques of employing them prove wanting. Unfortunately, the inferior employment of potentially superior weapons has been an all too frequently repeated mistake of maritime and continental powers alike throughout history. This has been due largely to the very human assumption that the dominant weapon should determine the strategy and tactics of a given period. Often this has proved to be a sound assumption. But just as often, strategic and tactical realities change, rendering the apparently dominant weapon less effective or even downright obsolete.

This difficult strategic problem, of weighing the weapons technology of a given period against historical experience, has no simple solution. Indeed, strategic thought has tended to polarize into two general schools in the industrial nations of the late modern and contemporary periods. They are the material and historical schools of strategic analysis.

The *material* school rests upon the assumption that the dominant military hardware or weapon—the material strength—at a given time creates such an overwhelming superiority that it alone generally satisfies the nation's defense needs. This line of thinking is usually concerned primarily with waging or deterring *total war* between superpowers. It further includes a recognition that a technological ceiling has been reached, creating not only superior weaponry but perhaps also national superiority in overall technology, political and economic systems and culture. Such a weapons superiority in the Western world has given certain nations the power to dictate the course of international affairs or to balance off the weaponry of an equally strong power in a strategic stalemate. In either case, such a nation assumes the position of controlling the balance of political power. In the industrial and scientific environment since the early nineteenth century, such technological determinism has tended to dominate strategic thinking.

The *historical* school of strategy rejects this determinism by examining the past conduct of competing nations in order to understand all historical forces at work and thus the various alternative approaches to strategic problems. Along with the problems of waging or deterring total wars, historical strategists are also concerned with *limited war,* with the diplomatic and legal aspects and alternatives to conflict, and with the problems of combating primitive or undeveloped peoples who do not honor the technological assumptions of advanced Western nations.

In the search for simple solutions and panaceas in strategy, both schools of analysis have erred in overstating their respective cases. Many material strategists have viewed superweapons as a panacea, while strategic historians have often expected history to repeat itself, thus committing the folly of depending completely on the proverbial dead hand of precedent. The overconfidence of both groups has frequently led to unfortunate consequences throughout history.

The difficulty of adequately combining the military principles and ideas of both history and advanced technology in order to formulate strategy has been due partly to the sheer chance of historical timing. Until the mid-nineteenth century, each nation-state had been generally governed by the same constant factors—agricultural wealth, land-based aristocratic political institutions, and the extent of territory and raw materials under its control. The generally constant level of technology tended to limit the size of armies and navies, therefore making the strategic options open to great maritime and continental powers fairly predictable. Indeed, by the 1880s, the Old World seemed to have reached a state of eternal peace, or at least a political stability in which only limited wars could occur. At that time, however, a number of brilliant maritime-oriented strategic historians emerged to examine systematically the forces that had shaped their world. The leaders of this intellectual ferment were the American Mahan and the Britons Corbett and Richmond. Their penetrating questions, ideas and writings epitomized the historical school of strategy.

However, the pinnacle reached by the Old World and its strategic analysts was accompanied by the end of the modern period. With the advent of the twentieth century came advanced scientific thought, systematically applied to the new weapons of unprecedented power. In 1914, the Old World figuratively vanished as these weapons of the new technology were unleashed on the battlefields of Europe. Limited war and the relative peace also seemed to disappear in the new era of total technological war. So blinding was the new technology in its destructiveness that the Old World and its historical lessons were all but forgotten. In their place arose the material strategists such as the Italian Douhet, the Briton Trenchard and the American Mitchell who envisioned military success in the aerial superweapons of mass destruction. The events of this contemporary era, with its world wars, airborne nuclear weapons and resultant technological determinism, have dominated strategic thinking to the present. In fact, though, the efficacy of this school was finally revealed as wholly inadequate by the Cuban missile confrontation of 1962.

Indeed, by the 1970s, mankind has certainly reached a major historical watershed in all its activities—political relationships, communications, social habits, medicine, the need for control of unchecked technology, population and pollution—and in sheer scientific advancement, symbolized most dramatically by the landings on the Moon. Surely the time has come for new hypotheses and a fresh synthesis in strategic thinking as in the other aspects of human relations.

STRATEGIC APPLICATIONS OF NAVAL POWER

The examination of the strategic history of navies and maritime empires requires not only the analysis of evolving strategic principles of naval warfare but of the long and often slow development of tactics, logistics (supply), command and administrative control, communications, ships, weapons and other aspects of naval life and technology. Through studying the flow of history and navies in history, it is possible to discover both the impact of sea power upon history and the impact of historical forces upon navies, empires and strategy. Finally, along with the successful application of the strategic doctrine of command of the sea, an appreciation is possible of the strategic alternatives to such a policy.

As guidelines to this examination, a list of theoretical strategic applications of naval power is useful. Since no one type of nation has existed throughout history, however, there has been no one type of navy or naval strategy. The guidelines of applied naval power, therefore, are aimed at understanding three different types of navies, that of maritime or "blue-water" nations, that of continental nations and that of small nations.

For *maritime* nations, the navy has been the main strategic arm of the nation's defensive structure, dominating the defensive policies of the home government, maintaining a generally *offensive* stance, and operating mainly on the "blue water" of the high seas. The army of such a nation is usually small by contrast, so that for large-scale land operations, the maritime nation usually must depend upon a large continental ally. This navy has several functions, all of them geared to the principle of achieving *command of the sea:*

1. Maintain a superior fighting fleet either a) to seize command of the sea, or b) to deter an enemy from attempting to control the sea. In wartime, this fleet is used as the *active* force to seize, exercise and maintain control over disputed waters. The waters in question are usually the open ocean, but may also include coastal areas, lakes and rivers. In

periods when no declared war exists, this fleet acts as a *passive* force by demonstrating to competitor nations that it has the ability to dominate the seas; in this way, it deters aggression by its threat of seaborne retaliation.

2. Defend against invasion. A defensive requirement, this task calls upon the fleet to protect the shores of the home country either by destroying or otherwise neutralizing the enemy fleet in wartime or in "peacetime" by threatening a competitor navy with destruction.

3. Protect maritime commerce. Also a defensive need, this requires the fleet to keep open its own sea lanes for its merchant ships. It may utilize overseas bases and its own mobility either to escort merchant vessels or to clear the seas of enemy raiders, pirates or other interlopers.

4. Blockade the enemy coast. An offensive requirement of the fleet, the seas around the enemy coast must be denied the enemy for the use of his merchant marine, for neutral vessels trading with him and for his own vessels of war. As long as the enemy fleet survives, the blockade is generally *naval;* after the enemy fleet is destroyed or otherwise neutralized, the blockade is primarily *commercial,* aimed at stopping enemy trade. In either case, it may be a *direct* blockade, with the fleet actually remaining on station off the enemy ports, or it may be *indirect,* the fleet observing and thwarting enemy ship movements from a considerable distance away.

5. Engage in combined operations. Either in offensive or defensive situations, the blue-water fleet must be able to sealift ground forces, army and marines, to and from a disputed area, the goal being invasion and capture of an enemy's overseas possessions and bases. The fleet must be ready and able to invade the enemy's home country, in the event that a successful commercial blockade does not compel the enemy to submit. In all such amphibious landings, the fleet provides tactical bombardment to cover the assault, then logistical support of the beachhead. In such *sealift* and *support* operations, the navy cooperates with the ground forces (which in recent times have included land-based air forces) by keeping open their lines of communications, by policing coastal and inland waters, and by commanding the sea (and the air, in recent times).

6. Provide strategic bombardment. The ultimate expression of naval superiority comes when naval power can be projected inland against the vitals of the enemy homeland. This function is not always required, as an enemy may sue for peace or may surrender to the naval and commercial blockade first, or the army (and strategic air forces) may be better equipped for this task, which belongs essentially to a continental strategy. Nevertheless, recent technology has given the blue-water navy the capability to project its firepower well beyond the enemy coastline.

For *continental* powers, the army (and lately, in combination with the land-based air force) has been the main strategic arm of the nation's defense. For blue-water operations of a broad offensive nature, this nation will best rely upon an allied maritime power. Its own navy usually maintains a *defensive* strategic stance, governing its operations to enhance the strategic advantages of the army. This navy has several functions, all dictated by strategic needs on the continent:

1. Defend against invasion. This navy must augment coastal defenses to help repel an enemy fleet from the continental periphery, adjacent lakes and rivers, and overseas possessions for the purpose of not allowing the enemy to establish a bridgehead on the coast for an invasion or for small-scale raids.

2. Engage in combined operations. In *support* of the main strategic arm, the army, the continental navy may gain command of the sea by default, that is, by the combined effort of army and navy in capturing enemy ports mainly by overland attack, thus depriving the enemy fleet of its crucial bases. To do this, this navy should have a limited *sealift* capability, for transporting troops over short stretches of local waters. The magnitude of such offensive amphibious operations may vary from small raids to an actual mass expeditionary force invasion. But a major difficulty of such operations is that a continental navy usually lacks both command of the seas to carry out the assault and a sophisticated amphibious doctrine due to its lack of experience. The continental navy may also provide a complementary offensive capability by combining, in recent times, with the army or air force to project its firepower into the enemy interior. But such strategic bombardment remains under the control of the senior services, as it is still part of the continental strategy.

3. Attack enemy commerce. Using the technique of what the French call *guerre de course,* the continental navy operates small squadrons or single ship units to prey upon enemy commerce. If utilized in overwhelming strength, this offensive function may assume the proportions of an effective commercial *counterblockade,* preventing vital war supplies from reaching the maritime enemy's homeland.

4. Maintain an efficient second-class fighting fleet either a) to restrict enemy offensive action, or b) to deter an enemy from attempting to dominate local waters. These closely related objectives may be achieved by the construction of a force of sophisticated naval vessels, ship-for-ship at least slightly superior to their individual counterparts in the enemy navy. Such excellent warships deploying singly for sporadic operations can force their maritime adversary to deploy a significant number of his own ships to deal with them. Or such superior single units can be combined to present the appearance of a formidable fleet capable of blue-water operations. Loosely defined as a *fleet-in-being,* it can deter a maritime power from aggressive action, or in actual war it can tie down

the enemy blue-water fleet from other vital pursuits in order to keep track of its movements. (Correctly, however, a fleet-in-being seeks to hold the defensive until it is able to assume the offensive, a concept practiced more by hard-pressed maritime nations than continental ones.) A well-handled continental navy of superior vessels, though inferior quantitatively, can thus have a pronounced effect on restricting the actions of a blue-water navy against the continent. In the contemporary period, the possible use of such vessels for projecting their firepower strategically into the enemy homeland further increases their prestige in any continental strategy.

Thus, if such an effective continental navy is directed by enlightened leaders in the government and is blessed with a generally bungling blue-water adversary, it can win command of the sea vicariously. If such conditions are just right, it can in some measure neutralize the enemy fleet by keeping it off balance, cutting supply lanes to the enemy homeland with a counterblockade, and thus protecting its own coast and merchant marine. It can sealift ground forces over limited distances and possibly provide some measure of tactical and strategical bombardment. But as long as the enemy blue-water fleet exists in any real strength, the continental navy can never maintain control over the blue-waterways. Whatever brief command of the sea it may enjoy, that command is only temporary and must be exploited quickly in order to serve the ends of the continental strategy.

For *small* powers, armies and navies alike can usually only hope for major success by allying with a great continental or maritime power and adopting its particular strategy—that is to say, unless they are fighting an equally minor power, in which case their strategy is dictated by the strengths and weaknesses of their adversary, emphasizing appropriate ground or naval forces. In any case, the minor navy must concentrate on three immediate tasks:

1. Defend against invasion. Inshore craft and naval weapons can be used to augment the national army and allied navy to help thwart an overseas or overland enemy attack.

2. Police local waters. Inshore and river craft and occasional large cruisers are necessary to check pirates and high-handed maritime competitors in time of relative peace. In war, these forces are combined with the larger ally. Without such an ally, however, they have no hope for long-term success.

3. Attack enemy commerce. Utilizing their few cruisers as commerce raiders, small navies can impress major powers with their fighting prowess, but without a major ally they cannot hope seriously to alter the outcome of an open conflict by this technique.

These strategic guidelines for the application of naval power are admittedly broad and theoretical. But they represent the questions raised by nations throughout history aspiring to use navies. By utilizing these hypotheses based on the advantage of historical hindsight, we may arrive at a basis for understanding the strategic history of navies in all times. Without such guidelines, the roles of naval forces are obscured both for layman and naval professional alike, giving naval matters an aura of mystery, which is not only unnecessary but potentially dangerous.

BOOK FIVE

Pax Britannica

. . . industrial civilization . . . [tended] to underrate the significance of military strength as the basic framework that alone enabled it to attain its present pre-eminence. [This] development . . . was furthered by the peculiar nature of the deterrent force that throughout the nineteenth century did most to maintain the peaceful atmosphere in which capitalism could flourish. This was the British Navy, whose influence was exerted not so much by the actual exercise of its power as by its mere existence. Growing up under the shield of the silent presence of sea power, . . . the new industrial culture was geared to peace, rather than to war, in a way that the older civilizations had never been.

—HERBERT ROSINSKI

Just as the ordered world of the eighteenth century underwent monumental upheaval before the old order was restored, so too did the nineteenth century begin in the guise of tranquillity and peaceful intercourse between nations, only to be dramatically transformed by new historical forces already in motion by 1815. The Industrial Revolution, begun in Britain during the 1780s, spread to the continent and to North America to provide both the sources of unity and divisiveness that characterized that century. From about 1815 to 1860, free trade replaced the old mercantilism and fostered general acquiescence in Britain's lead in maritime and commercial matters. But concurrent forces of nationalism would combine with the new technological-industrial growth and lead—from the 1860s—to a return to the former pre-industrial urge to national economic self-sufficiency and concomitant trade barriers, arms races, colonial expansion and violent competition prerequisite to world war.

Despite these great changes wrought by applied science, even to weaponry, the British navy remained in undisputed command of the sea—by means of a superior number of ships, its judicious employment in support of free trade, and the staggering reputation gained from the long wars with France. The capital ships of the Royal Navy—from the sailing _Victory_s of 1815 through the steel _Dreadnought_s until 1914—commanded such respect that no nation or combination of nations dared challenge them. They were the prime, though subtle and usually invisible, deterrent to further world war. Their enormous prestige combined with other factors to sustain a new balance of power in Europe and throughout the world for one hundred years. To this era of outward stability and deceptive tranquillity historians have thus given the name _Pax Britannica_—the peace dominated by the British navy in the tradition of the navies of the fifth-century B.C. Athens, first-century A.D. Rome and fifteenth-century Venice. This peace, like all such "peaces," was actually the balancing of international tensions short of general war, though about midway during this century the balance began to deteriorate steadily.

During this transition century in which the wooden, then iron, then steel, warships of Great Britain policed the sea lanes of the world, the old political and human relationships succumbed to new forces unleashed by the industrial-technological revolution and by the American and French upheavals. The exclusiveness of oceanic peoples to monopolize wealth overseas—to explore, to trade, to colonize and to man navies—passed as the new technology enabled second-rate maritime nations to mechanize the elements of thalassocratic greatness where before skilled manpower had been the basic building block. From about mid-century, as each of these nations entered upon their industrial phases, the wealth enjoyed by the British Empire came to be shared, the British system envied, then coveted until eventually attacked. Thus as France, Germany, the United States, Russia and Japan adapted their technologies in order to imitate Britain's greatness, they came to face the same problems and responsibilities as their teacher. Indeed, though this phenomenon (particularly after 1870) sowed the seeds of general conflict, it more importantly bred a global cosmopolitanism that could only result in an at-first precarious unity of purpose among civilized peoples. If the Industrial Revolution bred competition among nations, it also continued the social trends begun in the Enlightenment—a wave of commercialism and humanitarianism that undermined the old monarchies which were based on control of land. Furthermore, all these nations so opened the non-Western world to these common problems and aspirations that no one nation or coalition would again be able to assert hegemony throughout the world.

Such a global cosmopolitanism was not anticipated, much less planned or even desired; it merely evolved from previous trends and historical accidents. Thus, the British Empire came to endorse the free trade formulas preached earlier by Adam Smith and used its naval might to insure that no other nation dared to erect trade barriers to inhibit this new formula for the accumulation of wealth and profit. Also, by this trend, Britain accepted the concept of "freedom of the seas" so long advocated by its maritime enemies into the mainstream of international law. This interpretation of international law met with such approval throughout the Western world that the era of *Pax Britannica* continued the legalism of the age of reason; nations not only endorsed Britain's new imposed maritime order, but expected it to eliminate the previous causes of war altogether. British customs upon the sea were universally accepted; the evolving admiralty courts codified maritime laws on the English model; and the system of marine insurance that had begun unobtrusively in London as Lloyd's Coffee House in 1688 came to monopolize world shipping in the nineteenth century as *Lloyd's Register of Shipping*. The legal reforms expressed an abhorrence of such activities upon the sea as piracy, the slave trade and smuggling, and even raised questions about the continuing efficacy of the legalized wartime practices of blockade and privateering. As a *Zeitgeist* of humanitarian reform developed against the excesses of industrial cities in England and the United States, so did it reach the ships that plied the sea. The lot of the seaman was slowly improved throughout the world and the activities of the slave traders curtailed progressively from the outlawing of that practice in 1807–14. Then when Britain outlawed slavery altogether in 1833—followed thirty years later by the United States—it was the policing warships of the Western world that had to enforce this new law.

The communications and transportation revolution, stimulated by the steamship at sea and the railroad on land, also helped to create a closer unity of spirit and cross-fertilization of ideas. Now nations with short coastlines and small fleets could afford to participate in the activities of and enjoy the benefits once monopolized by thalassocratic peoples. Britain remained the leader, of course, and her institutions—with those of the strategically insular United States—were still the most liberal, but the ideas once predominantly Anglo-American now came to be shared by other nations taking to the seas. The last unsailed waters were conquered, the barometer went to sea to give storm warnings, and the secrets of the ocean currents themselves were revealed in the oceano-graphic discoveries of the Briton James Rennell, the German Alexander von Humboldt and the American Matthew F. Maury. Early in the century the last remote regions of the Pacific were explored by such seamen as Frenchmen Louis C. de S. de Freycinet and Dumont d'Urville and the American Charles Wilkes, while even an Austrian frigate circum-navigated the globe on a scientific cruise in the 1850s. The Russians and Scandinavians probed the Arctic regions, especially the Russian Ferdi-nand P. von Wrangel in the 1820s, and the quest for the Northeast Passage from Atlantic to Pacific across the top of Russia was finally achieved by the Swede Nils Nordenskiöld in 1879. The Northwest Passage across the top of North America from East to West was dis-covered by the Briton Robert J. L. McClure in the 1850s and first sailed by the Norwegian Roald Amundsen in 1903–06. The voyages of partic-ularly the British explorer James C. Ross in the 1840s opened Antarctica to adventurers of several nations. The American Robert E. Peary reached the North Pole in 1909 and Amundsen the South Pole in 1911. These momentous events contributed only partly to the tremendous in-tellectual fervor of an age that came to be known for its intellectual cosmopolitanism and unity even in the midst of recurrent and divisive nationalism. Men from many lands thus helped to close the frontier of the sea in this century—yet, still within the strategic global hegemony governed by the *Pax Britannica.*

As the machines and ships of the West awakened the East and un-developed regions of the world (including the tropical interiors, deserts and mountains of South America, Africa and Asia), they were un-wittingly unleashing a whole new set of historical forces that created unprecedented problems. The colonial peoples, so exposed to Western culture and values, notably liberal ideals, eventually came to desire a share in the profits being gleaned in part from their own lands. The Western nations, especially Great Britain, were unsuspectingly Western-izing the rest of the world. As the nineteenth century ended, many of these peoples clamored for independence from colonial rule. Such a trend was incompatible with the neo-mercantilistic surge of this period, so that the overseas colonial powers—again led by the British example— had to exercise policing activities in the colonies. Naval patrols, in which the gunboat was the capital vessel, combined with professional imperial armies to control and keep pacified disgruntled subject natives. Closely related to anti-pirate and anti-slaving activities, these peace-keeping functions broadened the scope of the nineteenth-century *pax*. That the efforts of the old Western powers did not ultimately succeed would be borne out by the nationalistic "wars of liberation" in these regions dur-ing the mid-twentieth century.

SHIPS AND SEAFARING

The inventions that made the industrial age revolutionary naturally revolutionized naval technology—the first major change since the sailing galleon had begun to supplant the war galley in the sixteenth century. The desire for speed and efficiency in warships had led to sleeker 74s over heavier-gunned line-of-battle ships, which saw no significant improvement in the early nineteenth century, although the swift Yankee clipper ship briefly sped up the American merchant sailers. The advent of steam and the growing abundance of coal, however, in these years led to the total abandonment of all-sail warships by the last third of the century. For efficiency and protection to augment steam propulsion, applied scientific developments in metallurgy led to the concurrent use of iron-plating for armor on wooden vessels and eventually iron hulls, then the complete steel-armored and steel-hulled battleship by 1900. Advanced technology gave these new vessels unprecedentedly powerful ordnance. Stronger metals led to such improved smoothbore muzzle-loaders as the "soda-bottle" gun of the American John A. Dahlgren in 1850 and the huge breech-loading rifled guns of the Americans Robert Parrott and J. T. Rodman and Briton Sir William Armstrong during the 1860s. The gunnery principles embodied in these weapons underlay all subsequent developments in naval gunnery. Similarly, the fundamental inventions in explosives were made in this era, from the largely unsuccessful rockets of Sir William Congreve between 1812 and 1885 to the explosive shells introduced by the Frenchman Henry J. Paixhans and the smokeless powders especially of the Swedish inventor Alfred Nobel late in the century. Evolving naval weaponry thus resulted in the all-big-gun floating fortress epitomized by HMS *Dreadnought* in 1905.

The perfection and adaptation of these weapons over an entire century bear partial witness to the reluctance of particularly the British navy in accepting new techniques which would threaten the superiority of its standing fleet. This was particularly true of devices that came to threaten warships from beneath and above the surface of the water. The naval mines or torpedoes, with the vessels for employing them, represented such a major departure from accepted modes of war at sea that the Western nations initially assumed them to be uncivilized—a naive attitude and luxury surviving from the Enlightenment that moral distinctions could be made between various devices of death and destruction. Since weapons of underwater warfare appeared to be cheap substitutes for blue-water fleets, continental naval powers such as Russia and Austria turned to their development initially. But it was the Americans, from Bushnell and Fulton to Hunley, who most advanced the submarine mine and submersible vessel, first employing them fully in their Civil War. Then, in the 1870s, the floating mine and spar torpedo were replaced by the propelled auto-motive torpedo of the Scotsman Robert Whitehead in Austrian service, while experiments went forward in several countries, notably France, leading to surface torpedo boats and genuine submarines by 1900. Scarcely less revolutionary, but slower in development, was naval weap-onry from the air. Again, several nations supported experiments in manned balloons and heavier-than-air craft, but again the Americans seemed to prevail. As early as 1862, a military observation balloon was borne aloft from a barge in Virginia waters, and after the American Wright brothers invented the airplane in 1903 all industrial nations ex-perimented in its military and naval uses. As much promise as such weapons held, however, their actual development as major elements of naval power belong to the years after 1914.

Surprisingly, with such sweeping changes in naval technology, naval tactics did not change significantly over this century. The battle line not only survived the Napoleonic wars, but the British Admiralty as early as 1816 began to return to its rigid formalism of pre-Nelson days—no doubt due largely to stagnation from a dearth of pitched battles. Lack of tactical innovation combined with the general conservatism toward new weapons in resisting change. This attitude hurt the advent of steam-driven iron warships mounting a few heavy guns up to 300-pounders which caused a serious rent in traditional fleet composition—until the line-ahead formation was abandoned altogether in the 1860s. For two brief decades, well-armored warships were designed with underwater rams for line-abreast formations, tactics dormant since the last Mediter-ranean galley battles. The rise of the all-big-gun battleship in the 1890s, however, brought about a return to the line-ahead and conservative formalism in the Royal Navy and most of its imitators. Without full-scale world wars, tactical innovations could never occur with respect to combined amphibious operations, and throughout the long anti-pirate, pacification and other limited wars of the century small units improvised their own tactics. So-called naval brigades were formed from one or more ships' companies of sailors and marines with artillery to land and fight ashore. But some of these missions became so extensive that elements of, for instance, the Russian Naval Infantry and United States Marine Corps were often merged with their respective armies, and in 1862 the British Royal Marines were divided into the Royal Marine Light Infantry and the Royal Marine Artillery, a division which lasted until 1923. Tactical doctrine for nineteenth-century navies thus lacked the innovation typical of wartime.

The revolutions in science, industry and humanitarianism did, how-ever, together stimulate sweeping naval reforms which improved the life of the seaman in these years. In the field of naval health and diet, as in strategy, Britain led the way, but in such traditional areas as naval education and custom, like tactics, the British were less innovative than younger navies. For instance the United States, Japan and Germany all established four-year naval academies before Britain followed suit with Dartmouth in 1905, the same being true of advanced naval war colleges. Similarly, the British custom of the grog ration introduced in the mid-eighteenth century despite the alcoholism it bred survived the temperance crusaders of many decades (although it was cut in half in 1850). Whereas the United States Navy, for instance, abolished grog in 1862 and all alcohol on board in 1914, the Royal Navy kept its rum concoction till as late as 1970. Most importantly, however, Britain pioneered in the improvement of living conditions at sea. Largely due to American insistence, in 1815 the British agreed to abandon impressment (officially in 1833), meaning that enlistment became wholly voluntary and then the harsh discipline used to cow impressed sailors could be relaxed, with sailors being allowed shore leave without fear of their desertion. The latter change helped raise morale and reduce the sickness caused by continual confinement on board damp wooden men-of-war. Uneducated, rugged, fun-loving swabs still had to be disciplined and kept from deserting, but the popular mood of this democratic age spelled the end of flogging. This occurred by Act of the American Congress in 1850, in practice in the British and most other navies by the 1880s, and by British law finally in 1939. Continental navies continued to have their usual manpower problems, because of demands made by their armies. For example, Frenchmen living on the coast continued to be conscripted into the French navy, while the continental navies generally tended to lag behind the Anglo-American examples in maritime reforms.

The health and diet of the British tar and thus other navies by imitation improved with the introduction of canned foods in 1814, water stored in iron tanks rather than foul wooden casks in 1815, fresh vegetables, beef and bread ten years later, along with chocolate, sugar and tea, and preserved potatoes in 1850. Salt beef and salt pork became less frequent until the former was phased out in 1906, the latter finally by 1926. The health of the sailor naturally improved, but especially after steam made voyages of shorter duration and iron replaced disease-prone wood. More of the crew served in the fresh air of the new single upper gun deck, thus recreating the healthful conditions of the open-air galleys of antiquity. Finally, the last tropical diseases of malaria and yellow fever were conquered by modern medicine between 1866 and 1900. These events, along with the appearance of contracts, pensions, popular naval journals and religious activities, all combined to raise the common seaman of most navies and merchant marines to the status of a normal human being.

But if Great Britain ruled the waves by example, she faced old and new rivals that led her statesmen in the age of Queen Victoria (who reigned from 1837 to 1901) to promote a balance of the great powers in Europe and abroad. The Concert of Europe first seemed to preclude any fears of a continental aggressor, but continental naval rivals arose first in France from the 1830s and then in the newly unified Germany from the 1890s. Abroad, however, persistent concerns were aroused from two rather new powers on other continents, Imperial Russia and the United States. Both nations were appendages of Western Europe, and the navies of both were outgrowths of the British fleet of the late eighteenth century. Russia under Catherine the Great had drawn upon her Baltic and Black sea populations to take to the blue waters, and the New England-centered American republic had created a merchant marine by 1815 second only to Britain's. But in the course of the nineteenth century the energies of both these nations turned toward overland expansion, Russia eastward across Asia and the United States westward across North America, where they posed threats to British imperial hegemony in the Middle East and India on the one hand and in Canada and the Caribbean on the other. Furthermore, by the 1860s both powers reached the Pacific and were moving steadily into the virgin markets of the untapped Orient. As Russia and the United States fought their respective frontier wars with native inhabitants and suppressed rebellions of Poles and Confederates respectively, their political and defensive orientations became largely continental. Their armies remained the senior services, which reflected pro-French attitudes from Peter the Great through Thomas Jefferson and deeply admired the achievements of Napoleon. In this sense, neither country was thalassocratic, nor did their respective cultures especially reflect a maritime-oriented vitality. To be sure, an obscure Russian naval officer named Nikolai Andreyevich Rimski-Korsakov could write the first important symphony of a Russian composer in the 1860s, and an equally unknown American ordinary seaman named Herman Melville could produce two highly acclaimed novels in the 1840s. But such men typified isolated elements of emerging societies that could hardly compare with the cultural greatness of Victorian Britain, a dynamic thalassocracy which produced such geniuses as the likes of Charles Dickens, John Stuart Mill and Charles Darwin.

Only toward the end of this period when the industrial and social revolutions and the imperial urge engulfed all Western civilization, including Russia and the United States, did the political power and intellectual greatness dominated by Britain come to be challenged, then shared, especially by Germany and France. When this happened, not perhaps coincidentally, *Pax Britannica* came to an end.

10
Oceanic Policeman, 1815–1860

The circumstance peculiar to us which determines all others is that for us not land, but sea, is the connecting link of the nation; it is for a most important part of the nation their home, and it is for all of us the great factor of our wealth, of our danger, of our advantage, and of our security.

— MAJOR-GENERAL FREDERICK MAURICE,
British Army, 1897

THE STRATEGY OF EMPIRE

The postwar urge to demobilize and return to the old order initially dominated Metternich's Concert of Europe, fashioned in 1815 by the victor powers Britain, Austria, Russia and Prussia. Even imperial Britain directed by Viscount Castlereagh, prime minister from 1812 to 1822, shunned the prospect of becoming policeman of the world's oceans. Just as the former monarchies were restored on the continent of Europe, so too did the British government and Admiralty reembrace the old system of economic monopoly. Castlereagh even went so far as to encourage the new Netherlands government (politically united with Belgium) to rebuild its Asia-centered empire on the basis of mercantilistic principles. But within two or three years Dutch enterprise in the Indian Ocean, Russian diplomacy in the Mediterranean and growing American maritime strength seemingly everywhere convinced the British government to take active measures to assert its commercial prestige. Internally, the rise of a new merchant-industrial class also led to rejection of the old values. A generation ahead of potential competitors on the continent, these entrepreneurs in coal, iron, cotton and steam-powered machinery wanted open competition so that they could be free to tap sources of cheap raw materials throughout the world and to undersell continental rivals. By the time of Castlereagh's passing, economic reform was inevitable.

British society embraced the principle of free trade in the early nineteenth century as readily as it had supported trade barriers one hundred years before, and with no appreciable change in its national institutions. Part of the reason was no doubt due to the vitality and flexibility of a thalassocratically influenced liberal tradition, but even this was made possible by the singular fact that Britain had remained geographically isolated and thus emerged largely unscathed by the murderous bloodshed of the world wars. Shielded by her navy, Britain had begun her industrial revolution in the 1780s which had barely paused in its phenomenal growth to take notice of Napoleon's demise. The only change was the brushing aside of the timeworn economic traditions as part of the evolving profit-system of the merchant class. Unlike the great changes on the continent, continuity prevailed in British society and culture into the new century. The same king, George III, head of state since 1760(!), even lingered on as titular leader till his death in 1820. By now, however, the crown had long since surrendered its active direction of national affairs, first to the ministries of both Pitts and then to the men who had helped defeat the French dictator before going on to direct British policy in the new age: Castlereagh, George Canning in the 1820s, and finally Viscount Palmerston, foreign secretary for most of the years 1830 to 1851 and usually prime minister from 1855 to 1865.

Economic reform then joined domestic and legal reforms to transform Britain's role but not her goal—which was, as always, prosperity. The old notion of *Mare Clausum* thus faded, to be replaced by new catchphrases: freedom of the seas (a greatly enlarged view of *Mare Liberum),* *laissez faire* (no governmental interference in trade practices), and free trade of imports and exports. Smuggling within the British Isles declined as these practices were adopted, although the new Coastguard's role to blockade smugglers in 1831 had great effect. Tariffs and obsolete customs acts were steadily repealed, the major one being the 410-year-old so-called Corn Laws regulating wheat, struck down in 1846. Three years later the trade barriers that had launched England into mercantilistic conflict in 1651, the Navigation acts, were abolished. And in 1854 foreign vessels were even allowed to participate in the coastal trade of Britain. Smuggling, save for such few taxed luxury items as whisky, tobacco and silk, practically disappeared, and Britain prospered. Her carrying trade dominated Europe and much of the world, although the United States crowded her for half a century. But Britain also interpreted her new free sea policy to include enforced orderly and legal commerce upon the global sea lanes, so that the Royal Navy had to insure that no second-rate naval power dared to create a *Mare Clausum* in any sea and that pirates and slave traders be utterly suppressed.

The navy, now in peacetime, was hardly up to these tasks due to the global requirements for many ships. Traditionally, Britain had policed the Atlantic and much of the Mediterranean, and its fleet was able to help maintain the European balance of power by its continued role in these waters. But beyond the periphery of Europe, heavy demands were made upon the Admiralty. The fear of power plays by the Dutch in Southeast Asia, the United States in Latin America, the Russians in the Middle East and even the French in North Africa meant that appearances of British naval supremacy in these waters had to be maintained. Worse, however, were the non-Western peoples of Asia, Africa and South America who had little use for the legalism of the West and to whom piracy (occasionally still disguised as privateering) and slave trading remained accepted ways of life.

From 1815 to about 1850 the British navy was able to police most troubled waters by means of its wooden sail navy. Steam engines were considered unreliable for large warships, while the paddle wheels were exposed to enemy fire, so the old triple-deckers remained the backbone of the fleet until the 1850s. Lesser vessels adopted steam, however, and after the Swede John Ericsson and the American Robert F. Stockton introduced the underwater screw propeller to replace the paddle wheel, in 1845 the British began converting and building capital ships to steam power. Similar reluctance attended the use of iron for warships, but the work of the Frenchman Stanislas C. H. L. Dupuy de Lôme in the 1840s became the harbinger for dramatic changes in the rise of iron in steam vessels late in the 1850s. Line-of-battle ships, however, best served the role of deterrence in the balance of the great powers. For the demanding work of policing distant and inshore waters, the British and other navies relied on lesser vessels. Frigates remained important work-horses, first as the large wooden sailers, then in the 1840s as paddle-wheel steam-frigates, and finally as screw-frigates thereafter. The development of sailing corvettes, sloops and hermaphrodite brigs (brigantines) and then steam-sloops followed the same general evolution. The same is true of the gunboats, although the Russians and Danes were still building excellent rowing-sail gunboats and gun sloops in the early 1850s when steam-powered gun-vessels appeared. The advent of the Paixhans explosive shell gun by 1839 raised major questions about the use of iron for armor, but iron plate was not introduced until the mid-1850s. It must be realized that when steam engines were first developed, they were for auxiliary power only. With coal difficult to obtain and store, not to mention its great expense, and often with the early engines unreliable, steam warships through the 1850s actually depended primarily upon sail power for cruising; the steam was for maneuverability in battle or in contrary tides and weather.

General peace prevailed in Europe and most of the world during the early *Pax Britannica* from 1815 to the early 1850s, so that the most convenient way of examining Britain's role as oceanic policeman is by tracing the presence of its navy in each major region of the globe and in this order: the Baltic, the North Sea, the Mediterranean and North Africa, the Middle East, the African sea route to India, the Orient and, considered separately, the Western Hemisphere.

The Baltic Sea had so thoroughly become a Russian lake that the Scandinavian nations (including an independent Norway, but until 1905 ruled with Sweden by the same king) were reduced to the status of minor naval powers. By the 1840s Russia had over two dozen line-of-battle ships, Sweden but ten and Denmark barely a half-dozen. The British navy was ready to intervene against any aggressive move by Russia, but Russian interests were more oriented toward the Middle East. Prussia, however, growing ever stronger in the nineteenth century, instigated a revolt of the Schleswig-Holstein duchies from Denmark in March of 1848, and Britain and Russia immediately threatened to intervene on the side of the Danes. A shaky truce was signed in August before any real naval operations took place, although the following April a large Danish ship of the line was so badly damaged by shellfire from a shore battery during a landing at Eckernförde near Kiel that it had to be scuttled upon capture—the first practical demonstration of the effectiveness of the Paixhans-type exploding shell. In 1850 a treaty restored the duchies to Denmark, whose only real source of maritime power—beyond her small fishing fleet, carrying trade and a few islands in the West Indies—was control of the vital Sound, for which she had so often fought over the centuries. But even that was compromised by the naval power of Britain and Russia, who could control the Sound with impunity. Finally, in 1855, the United States refused to pay the ancient Sound dues, whereupon an international agreement in 1857 simply had them abolished.

In the North Sea the continuing rise of Prussia and the relative decline of the Netherlands enabled Britain to control these crucial waters with little effort. Prussia had no navy worthy of the name though her army was growing importantly through the new general staff system, the writings of Karl von Clausewitz, and the new network of military railroads that would later bear on British sea power. The Dutch had always been formidable rivals upon the sea, and even without a battle fleet they still successfully competed with British trade in the Far East. Internally, the Netherlands were vulnerable, however, for in 1830 the fifteen-year-old union between Holland and Belgium was shattered by the latter's secession, a move condoned by a subsequent meeting of the great powers in London. As a result, the Protestant Dutch invaded Belgium in August 1831, attempting to coerce it back into the union. The British fleet sailed into the Scheldt to blockade the Dutch garrison at the fortress of Antwerp, while the British government declared an embargo of Dutch shipping throughout the world. A French army plus naval units also intervened in Belgium to repulse the Dutch attack. By the end of 1832 Anglo-French land and naval forces had taken Antwerp, leading to an armistice and the eventual (in 1839) Dutch recognition of Belgian independence. Throughout the century, however, Britain never had to worry seriously about the occupation of the Low Countries—the pistol aimed at England—by an aggressor.

MEDITERRANEAN BATTLEGROUND

The traditional continental powers of Central and Southern Europe provided no threat to the peace of Metternich, although all suffered internally from the difficulties of the Restoration; liberals at home and in various colonies resisted the return of the despotic monarchs. Britain's prime concerns over these difficulties were insuring that neighboring nations did not intervene in such civil strife to upset the European balance of power and that the restored governments not be usurped. These goals were not easy to achieve, given the growing spirits of liberalism and nationalism exemplified by the Belgian struggle for independence. In the 1820s these forces erupted in wars within the three peninsulas of the Mediterranean—the Iberian, Italian and Greek. As this sea lane had become vital to European political stability and to the British land-sea route to India via the Suez Isthmus and the Red Sea, the British were obliged to intervene. In so doing, Britain aroused the monarchies of France, Austria and Russia, thus undermining the Quadruple Alliance that had been built upon the defeat of Napoleon. Small wars resulted, and the liberal spirit spread in revolt to several of the great powers, especially in 1848. The result was the growth of the liberal democratic influence in all the Western governments. Yet, Britain's role upon the seas did not diminish.

The westernmost Mediterranean peninsula of the three torn by strife in these years involved Spain and Portugal. Civil wars in both countries required the Quadruple Alliance to send the French army into Spain in 1823, while the British navy landed an expeditionary force in Portugal in 1827 to maintain political order. The latter force proved inadequate, for the pretender to the Portuguese throne, Miguel, raised a fleet against the ruling constitutional government and drove out Queen Maria in 1828.

The Portuguese crown had divided its political rule between the home-land and Brazil since the Restoration, however, so that it now drew on its South American resources as well as Anglo-French volunteers first to retake the Azores. When Miguel's fleet attempted to recover the islands, it was defeated in August at Praia Bay. As the Miguelite Wars dragged on, Britain sold a naval squadron to Maria, and in July 1831 the French seized Miguel's fleet in the Tagus. One year later the crown's expedition from England landed in Portugal. Its naval commander, Sir Charles Napier of the British navy, in July 1833 defeated a Miguelite naval force off Cape St. Vincent and moved on to take Lisbon. The Quadruple Alliance then isolated Miguel, bringing about his defeat and surrender the next spring. These civil wars, which continued to wrack Spain through the 1830s and the early 1840s, were all related to the final demise of her American-centered empire. Both Spain and Portugal had degenerated into minor naval nations.

Austria, by the terms of the 1815 agreements, dominated the Italian peninsula and occupied new territory which included the Adriatic Coast from Venice to Dalmatia. This vast coastline thus encouraged Austria again to entertain maritime aspirations. Trade was increased with the Levant from the 1820s, and the small Austrian navy checked Barbary attacks by bombarding the Atlantic coast of Morocco in 1829. The fleet, based at Venice and manned largely by Italians, grew in size and operated with the great powers in the Middle East until, by the end of the 1830s, it had become a major force in the Eastern Mediterranean. It reached its greatest peak under the command of its young but veteran commander, Archduke Frederick, from his appointment in 1844 till his untimely death three years later. Austria, however, was torn by revolts in Italy from 1820, culminating in the general European strike of 1848. In March of that year, Sardinia declared war on Austria, and Venice proclaimed its independence, both states joining their small naval forces to confront the Austrian vessels before Pola and Trieste. The tiny fleets avoided an engagement, however, and Austrian arms gradually tri-umphed on land, aided by a French intervention in 1849. Simultane-ously, the Hungarians revolted against Austria, only to be put down with the help of the Russian army. That year the strengthened Austrian navy was placed under the command of a ruthless Danish admiral who resigned after two years. In 1852 the fleet of fourteen ships now largely manned by Germans cruised the Mediterranean under the new twenty-year-old Archduke Ferdinand Max, an excellent admiral who became commander-in-chief in 1854. But Austrian dominance over the Italian states, and British support of this situation, could never last, thanks to the incessant nationalistic activities of such Italian patriots as Garibaldi and Cavour.

The peninsula of Greece, long a Turkish preserve, erupted in revolt in 1821 and gradually involved the powers. Britain and France at first avoided intervening, but the early successes of the Greeks made the war a democratic *cause célèbre* in Europe, and the fear of Russian intervention added larger strategic dimensions to the struggle. Russia, excluded by Napoleon from the Mediterranean, had allowed Greek vessels to register under the Russian flag, and the Russians were eager to weaken Ottoman Turkey and gain a warm-water outlet from the Black Sea. About the only great power to act early in the war was Austria, which based its fleet at Smyrna for the duration, but as a neutral.

The Greeks quickly drove Turkish forces from most of the Morea and raised a formidable collection of armed vessels; in so doing, they crippled the Turkish fleet, which had relied heavily on Greek seamen. But many of the so-called patriots outfitted their ships as privateers only to degenerate quickly into pirates. The indiscriminate attacks of such vessels upon Western merchantmen increased great power apprehension over the conflict, accounting for the Austrian naval presence at Smyrna. Nevertheless, the Greek revolutionary government established two regular war fleets in the summer of 1821 which skirmished indecisively with Turkish warships, often using the old technique of fire ship attack. In March 1822 the belligerent fleets fought a long indecisive gunnery duel off Missolonghi; in April a Turk landing force massacred much of the population of Chios; and in June a Greek fire ship attack off Chios destroyed the Turk flagship, killing its admiral. The leader of the latter exploit, Konstantin Kanaris, repeated his feat in November at Tenedos, destroying another flagship with its admiral. Sharp skirmishing at sea and coastal raids by both sides continued throughout 1823, and divisiveness within the Greek movement led to a stalemate.

The War of Greek Independence assumed new dimensions in 1824 when the Sultan of Turkey called upon his powerful vassal, Mohammed Ali of Egypt, to suppress the Greeks. This ruthless despot had modernized his army and navy to the point of superiority over the main Ottoman armed forces; his expansionist policies in North Africa had led the Sultan to award him Crete in return for help in the Morea. In June, 45 Egyptian sail and a landing force made a devastating hit-and-run raid on the Greek base at Kaxos near Crete, a Turkish force of 82 craft doing the same at the base of Psara near Chios in July. The Moslem fleets attacked other islands, but were often obliged to draw away upon the approach of the Greek fleet, largely because of their fear of Kanaris and his relentless fire ships, which sank a 54-gun Ottoman frigate in a skirmish off Samos in August. The Turko-Egyptian fleet of some 130 warships covered the crossing of Mohammed Ali's army in 150 transports and skirmished with the Greek fleet of 75 war vessels, but again never really closing out of respect for the fire ships. The latter thereby repeatedly frustrated Moslem attempts to cross the Aegean to the mainland of Greece. The Egyptian commander and son of Mohammed Ali, Ibrahim Pasha, embarked part of his army in warships and made the crossing while the Greek fleet had retired for the winter. More Egyptian troops from Crete landed in Greece early in 1825, and Ibrahim established a loose blockade, though at the sufferance of the intrepid Kanaris with his fire ships. The land-sea blockade of the Greeks at Missolonghi was lifted late in July when the fire ship-led Greek fleet drove off the Moslem ships. But the Egyptians under Ibrahim were overrunning the Morea, and though the Greek navy was keeping supplies running through the Ottoman blockade to Missolonghi, Ibrahim finally assaulted and took the fortress in April 1826. Now the Turkish fleet under Khosrev Pasha attempted to take Samos, but was attacked at its main base of Mitylene by the Greek fleet under Admiral Andreas Miaoulis, September 10–11. The hard-fought action was a draw, but by now the general situation of the Greeks was dire, while Ibrahim was generally triumphant. Against these reverses, public opinion in the Western world clamored for Greek independence.

The great powers decided to act. In 1826–27 Great Britain, Russia and France agreed to isolate Ibrahim in Greece, while British officers took command of the Greek forces, with Admiral Lord Cochrane leading the navy. The Austrians remained neutral, though their ships acted as mediators and chastised Greek pirates. Greek republican fortunes continued to wane, however, and Ibrahim sent another large expeditionary force under Tahir Pasha from Alexandria to Navarino late in the summer of 1827, hoping ultimately to capture the key Greek island naval base of Hydra. But now an Anglo-French fleet under Admirals Sir Edward Codrington and Henri G. de Rigny had arrived to blockade Tahir Pasha's fleet at Navarino, while Cochrane's reinforced Greek fleet moved into the area. Early in October the allies were also joined by a Russian squadron. Tensions mounted until finally, on October 20, the allied force of 20 men-of-war, each mounting 28 to 84 guns, sailed into the Bay of Navarino and were given battle by the similar-sized Ottoman force; many smaller vessels took part on both sides. The allied guns crushed their foe, who burned what damaged ships were not sunk in the fight. The shore batteries were also silenced. The Turkish fleet had been virtually destroyed in one stroke, the remnants being allowed to return to Constantinople and Alexandria, while the British and Russian vessels retired to Malta, the French to Smyrna. While the powers then pondered their next moves, the British and French wiped out a Greek pirate base on the west end of Crete early in 1828 and tightened a blockade around the Egyptian-held ports of Navarino and Modon.

The independence of Greece was now assured, despite the fact that Turkey lashed back by initiating open war with Russia in April 1828. In May Admiral Codrington declared a general blockade against all Moslem forces in Greece and initiated direct negotiations with Mohammed Ali for the evacuation of his forces, which occurred between August and October. The French landed an expeditionary force in Greece which overran several Ottoman positions in October, while the Russian squadron in these waters remained in a nonbelligerent status. Then the Greek navy joined in the seizure of Lepanto and Missolonghi in May 1829. Meanwhile, the Russo-Turkish War had focused on the Black Sea, where the Russian Rowing Fleet supported the army's advance across the Danube to take Varna in the west and the thrust eastward which captured Anapa during 1828. Later that year, a second Russian squadron arrived at British Malta from the Baltic, then moved up the Aegean to Tenedos to blockade Constantinople from the south. In 1829, the Russian army and navy pressed south from Varna, the fleet taking Sizeboli for raids on the north coast of Turkey. A makeshift Ottoman fleet failed to check these operations, and in August the Russian ships bombarded, assaulted and took Midia, only fifty miles from Constantinople, while the army took Adrianople. In September, the Turks sued for peace, giving up to Russia the delta of the Danube and the eastern shore of the Black Sea from Anapa southward, also granting Russian merchant ships passage through the Bosporus. The Ottoman Empire also lost Greece, which was declared an independent kingdom by treaty in 1832.

The events of the 1820s had reaffirmed the status of the Mediterranean as the prime area of strategic importance in Europe, a predominance dating from the post-Trafalgar warfare against Napoleon. The great powers, Britain, Russia, France and Austria, all had economic and thus political interests there and supported maritime stability in the face of incessant depredations of the Barbary corsairs of Morocco, Algeria and Tunis. Even the young United States continued its naval presence in the region after forcing Algeria to terms during a brief war in 1815. The American squadron began using Port Mahon in Spanish Minorca as a makeshift base that year, until Mahon became a permanent base facility supporting the seven-ship squadron in 1825. These ships paid annual visits to each Barbary port from 1816, with special pressure on Algiers again in 1822, protecting American commerce which pressed eastward into the middle sea until, in 1830, the United States signed a formal trade agreement with Ottoman Turkey. The American squadron continued its presence, save for its absence during the Mexican War, after which it based at Spezia in the Gulf of Genoa. The British, however, held the Mediterranean balance of power, and from their bases of Gibraltar, Malta and the Ionian Islands they policed the Mediterranean. In 1816 an Anglo-Dutch force bombarded Algiers, a British blockade and threat of bombardment again brought Algeria to terms in 1824, and a blockade of Tangier four years later achieved the same result from Tunis. The lesser powers of Spain, the Two Sicilies and Sardinia relied largely on British protection, but France with its own southern ports and the island of Corsica began to use its own initiative, blockading Algiers from 1827 to 1829.

The French naval recovery from the defeat of 1815 became evident gradually with the French naval actions in Holland and Greece, culminating in 1830 with a French overseas expedition which easily conquered Algeria. The French fleet had only slowly begun to be rebuilt by June and July when this event occurred, simultaneous with a revolution which placed Louis Philippe on the throne of France. For Europe, the French conquest of Algeria meant the end of the main source of Barbary piracy; the French heralded their military colonization of this North African state as the beginning of *la Paix Française*. For Britain, however, the event marked the beginning of a new French overseas empire which now stood athwart British communications to India. Furthermore, the pacification of Algeria with large troop reinforcements was accompanied by French pressure throughout the Mediterranean littoral, leading directly to Anglo-French antagonism.

The advent of steam in the English Channel eventually became the leading source of British fears regarding France, though the real geographic confrontation of these two powers occurred in the Mediterranean. The concentration of the new French fleet at Toulon and the annexation of Algiers in the 1830s disturbed Palmerston and the British because of what the French might ultimately do—which was to make a power play in the Moslem world. In fact, the French lost no time in supporting Mohammed Ali in his revolt against Ottoman Turkey; should he overthrow his master, France might then block British trade across Suez and the Red Sea to India or develop an alternate route overland to the East via the Euphrates River and the Persian Gulf. Britain intervened in 1840 to halt the Egyptian revolt, however, and the French enterprise in the Middle East did not materialize. In the Western Mediterranean, Britain suspected French designs on Spain and downright resented a French incursion into Morocco and naval bombardments of Tangier and Mogador in 1844 as part of the pacification of Algeria. The same year, the commander of French naval operations in Morocco and son of the king, Admiral the Prince of Joinville, wrote a pamphlet describing how easily the new steam vessels of the French navy could mount a cross-Channel invasion of England. This pamphlet, the Moroccan affair and the French annexation of Tahiti in the South Pacific created an invasion scare in England and brought the two countries to the brink of war during the late summer of 1844. However, the crisis passed, although Joinville led France's naval building program until he and his father were overthrown in the revolution of 1848—a year which witnessed a second naval scare in England. Anglo-French relations remained cordial until yet another invasion panic during the creation of the so-called Second Empire under Louis Napoleon throughout 1851–1853. Such fears proved unrealistic, however, for France's new imperial commitments required that its fleet not be concentrated on the Channel coast but in the Mediterranean.

The Russian naval menace to the British, like that of the French, was supposed to be in the Atlantic, particularly the Baltic, but was really focused in the Mediterranean. During the first half of the nineteenth century, in fact, Russia enjoyed a brief period of maritime activity; for instance, no fewer than thirty-six Russian voyages circumnavigated the globe by 1850. The Russian Baltic Fleet caused Britain anxiety through the 1830s, and the presence of the Russian squadron in Greek waters in the 1820s aroused British suspicions about Russian intentions in the Mediterranean. Simultaneously, 1825–1828, Russia fought a boundary war with Persia which was so successful that it gave Russia naval control over the Caspian Sea and crippled Persia permanently as a Middle Eastern power. The Russian victory over Turkey in 1829 so humbled the already weak Ottoman Empire that the powerful Mohammed Ali of Egypt rose in revolt and threatened to destroy the political power of the sultan. Russia began to strengthen Odessa and Sevastopol as naval arsenals in order to maintain the control she had already won over the Black Sea. Britain therefore feared for the integrity of the Ottoman Empire. Should it collapse, either under the weight of Russian pressure or by the advance of the French-supported forces of Mohammed Ali in Egypt, a rival power could cut British Middle Eastern communications to India. In addition, the Russians were expanding eastward, overland toward the Pacific, arousing British fears (though unsubstantiated) of a potential Russian descent on India itself. Thus the British, led by Palmerston, from the 1830s assumed the role of shoring up a Middle Eastern buffer zone against Russia that centered on the Persian Gulf and included, west to east, Turkey, Persia and Afghanistan.

The Middle East had degenerated apace with the Ottoman Empire, leading to constant warring among Turks, Persians and independent Arab tribes such as the Wahhabis who had established a livelihood from piracy in the Persian Gulf by 1810. The Egyptians of Mohammed Ali and Ibrahim destroyed the Wahhabis in Arabia in 1818, but their fleet of some 250 war dhows continued to create havoc with coastal trade between Basra in the Gulf and Bombay. In 1819–20 the Bombay Marine combined with British regulars and sepoy troops to occupy points along the north "Pirate Coast" of the Gulf, but the piracy continued. A six-vessel East India Company Gulf Squadron began to cruise the Gulf, operating mainly from Basidu, in 1821, but with uneven success, since continuous maritime wars with the various Arab principalities (as between superior Muscat and Bahrain 1829 to 1835) bred indiscriminate raiding. Both Persia and Turkey were powerless as sea powers to stabilize the area when, in 1831–32, Mohammed Ali's Egyptians overran Ottoman Syria and defeated the Ottoman army. The Turkish appeal to Britain was refused, simply because the Royal Navy was overcommitted elsewhere in the world, whereupon the Turks reluctantly signed, early in 1833, a defensive alliance with Russia. A Russian squadron then anchored off Constantinople, but Turkey sued for peace, ceding Syria to the Egyptians. In the 1830s Turkey hired American shipwrights who came to Constantinople to begin rebuilding the Ottoman navy up to rough parity—a dozen ships of the line plus frigates—with the Egyptian fleet and Russian Black Sea Fleet. But without British support this balance of power could only be temporary.

In April 1839 the Turks attacked the Egyptians in an effort to reassert their supremacy in Mesopotamia, but were so shattered in land battle in June that the great powers had to intervene in order to save the Ottoman Empire from utter ruin. In July the entire Ottoman fleet defected to the side of Mohammed Ali, while an Anglo-French fleet of nineteen of the line moved to Cyprus. By now, the British were thoroughly alarmed, for Russia might come to dominate Turkey and the Dardanelles; France might join Egypt to control the Middle East; and Mohammed Ali might occupy the vitally strategic coasts of the Red Sea and the Persian Gulf. To frustrate the latter design, British forces had occupied the strategic island of Kharak (modern Kharg) near Bushire on the northwest coast of the Gulf in the summer of 1838; the following January a Bombay landing force had occupied Aden at the entrance to the Red Sea; and in June 1839 the commander of the East Indies Squadron moved to defend Bahrain Island in the Gulf against Egyptian occupation. Concurrent British naval commitments in China, however, frustrated an attempted warship demonstration in the Gulf for later that year, and as 1840 began, the British feared an Egyptian descent on the Pirate Coast. The French became increasingly bellicose during that winter, contemplating even a bombardment of British Malta, so confident were they of their fleet's superiority. But the prospect of a French presence in the Middle East at the expense of Turkey was unacceptable to Russia, Austria and even Prussia, and all three joined Britain in July 1840 in declaring their intentions to uphold the Ottoman Empire—a stroke of strategic genius by the calculating Palmerston.

Allied naval strength now outnumbered that of the French and Egyptians, enabling the powers to expel Mohammed Ali from his conquered dominions. They moved none too soon, for in June a large naval expedition had left Alexandria to suppress an uprising in Syria. Anglo-Turko-Austrian naval forces under the supreme command of Admiral Sir Robert Stopford now concentrated off Alexandria and Beirut, cutting Mohammed Ali's sea communications to Syria, and in September they bombarded Haifa, Tyre and Sidon, followed by Beirut in October, and a large land-sea assault took Acre early in November. The next month Mohammed Ali ended the war by negotiating his immediate withdrawal from Syria with the local British commanders. Early in 1841 he and Ibrahim withdrew from Syria, Crete and Arabia, thus quieting all British fears of French power in the Middle East and of the possible loss of the Persian Gulf to one overall ruler. The British evacuated Kharak at Russian insistence, but made Aden into a permanent base commanding the Red Sea. The two Egyptian Moslem rulers died before the end of the decade, but not before establishing a dynasty that lasted until 1953. The teetering Ottoman Empire was thus shored up, and the powers agreed in July 1841 to close the vital straits of the Dardanelles and the Bosporus to all foreign warships in time of peace—a happy solution to all the powers (except Russia), a situation which has survived generally intact to the present, with some modifications.

The British also solved their apprehensions over the internal chaos of the Persian Gulf by establishing an ingenious arrangement known as the Trucial System. The six Arab maritime sheikdoms on the south coast of the Gulf had warred indiscriminately against each other for centuries, for piracy and pearling were their major incomes. The maritime power in the region had been the united kingdom of Muscat and Oman, since 1806 ruled by Seyyid Said, who, however, in 1828 established a base in Zanzibar and in 1840 shifted his capital there and his power into East Africa, away from the Gulf. The only other political units of consequence were the non-piratical sheikdoms of Bahrain and Kuwait within the Gulf. The virtual political vacuum was thus being filled, however inadequately, by the East India Company's cruisers (designated the Indian Navy in 1830). After a stunning blow by one of these cruisers over six pirate vessels in April of 1835, however, Captain Samuel Hennell secured a maritime truce among the six piratical sheikdoms. A neutral highway on the Gulf was closed to war dhows, and the tribes abstained from fighting at sea during the summer pearling season, though they still warred on land. The rival tribes so honored this maritime truce that it was made formal in 1843, followed by a "treaty of maritime peace in perpetuity" in 1853. This so-called Trucial System was administered by the East Indies Company, whose vessels, with occasional help from the Royal Navy, policed the Gulf. The System, administered by the Royal Navy after 1859, was so successful that it survived down to 1971. Company flotillas in the 1840s also patrolled the Red Sea and Tigris, Euphrates and Indus rivers and protected Bahrain's independence from Persia and in 1851 from Turkish encroachment.

Shielding the Persian Gulf from outside aggression by sea, Britain also needed to uphold Persian sovereignty as part of its buffer against Russian expansion—a considerable task, as Persia had a long continental frontier. This was similarly the case with the subcontinent of India, a virtual island sealed off from Asia by the Himalaya Mountains, and with the intermediate kingdom of Afghanistan. In addition, the British continued to be occupied with the final pacification of India itself. As the British began to penetrate into Afghanistan, Russia persuaded Persia to invade Afghanistan, an attack repulsed through British aid in the war of 1836–38. These events led to First Afghan War, 1839–42, in which the British East India Company army failed to occupy Afghanistan as a buffer against primarily Russia. The Russians, however, had little real interest in India or Afghanistan, but rather Persia, wresting more territory from that luckless country between 1849 and 1854. The Company fought two Sikh wars to subdue India finally in the 1840s, so that by the early 1850s Britain generally had achieved its strategic goal of creating the buffer zone against Russia from the Bosporus to the Khyber Pass on the northwest frontier of India—although the Russians still persevered in their eastward drive to reach the Pacific.

Behind this continental defense perimeter lay the vital British sea lanes to India. The route from Liverpool to Bombay via the Suez camel road was eventually improved by a rail line from Alexandria to Suez in 1858, but the major commercial and military track remained completely by sea around the Cape. Three major shipping companies operated British troopships gradually converting to steam in the late 1830s to speed up the transit which with the old sailing East Indiamen had taken over four months. By steam, England to India, the time was cut to six weeks via Suez (the steamers having insufficient coal storage capacity for the Cape route) by the 1850s. The speed would be increased even more when the canal, begun in 1859 by a French company, was completed across the isthmus of Suez.

Continued French interest in the Middle and Far East led to continued rivalry with Britain along the Indian Ocean trade route. Having lost the key island of Mauritius to Britain in the Napoleonic wars, France was left with only tiny Réunion Island. The former Portuguese island of Socotra appeared as a possible base for controlling the exit of the Red Sea, but both Britain in 1836 and France in 1845 abandoned it after only brief occupations, poor health conditions being a major reason. So the French focused on Madagascar, on which they had had sporadic settlements since the mid-seventeenth century. Both British and French warships bombarded points on the island in these years, disputing the native government, but in general the French failed to reestablish their former posts on the island. The major importance of Madagascar in the early nineteenth century, however, was as a center of Arab slave trading.

The Western crusade to stop the slave traffic (Britain's decision in 1807) and then the abolition of the institution of slavery altogether (Britain in 1833) corresponded in time with new British and French imperial conquests along the African coasts. This coincidence thus heightened the tension between the Christian settlers, the black chieftains who dealt in slaves, and the Arab merchants who transported such human cargo throughout the world of Islam, a faith which embraced slavery. West Africa provided slaves to the Barbary States, the Sudan to Egypt and Asia Minor, and Abyssinia and East Africa to Arabia and the Persian Gulf. In West Africa, the British drove the Ashanti tribe from the Gold Coast 1824–31; the French occupied the Ivory Coast 1842–43 in addition to their older post at Senegal; and the United States established the independent state of Liberia with freed American slaves between 1822 and 1847. In South Africa, the strategic Cape Colony remained unsettled by continual strife between the British, Dutch Boer farmers and various local tribes such as the Zulus and Kaffirs which erupted in open wars during the 1840s. The Boers protested British annexation of Natal in 1843, but found no interference when they created the neighboring South African Republic and Orange Free State. In East Africa, where the slave traffic was greatest, Seyyid Said of Muscat-Oman gradually extended his political control southward through Mombasa and Zanzibar to border the Portuguese colony of Mozambique across the channel from Madagascar.

With heavy strategic commitments across the globe, the suppression of the slave trade was an added burden on the Royal Navy. All Western maritime nations endorsed the suppression of slaving soon after Britain did so, but vested interests immediately compromised these decisions in every country but Britain. Slave-holding Portugal and the United States were particularly reluctant to enforce their anti-slaving laws. The American Congress outlawed the slave trade in 1808 and twelve years later equated slavery with piracy and made the trade punishable by death, but politicians from the slave-holding Southern states frustrated rigid enforcement and Southern naval commanders were purposely lax during anti-slave cruises. France simply refused to join Britain in any cooperative effort until 1845 when each country agreed to employ cruisers off the coast of West Africa, but France never contributed its full share of the responsibility. The new Latin American republics were also reluctant to accept the abolitionist sentiment of the northern nations, Brazil not closing its slave market till 1853. Two issues remained at the center of unsuccessful British efforts to get cooperation: the right to search was jealously guarded by each nation, so that as late as 1861 British, French and American vessels would never search suspected slaving ships flying one of the other's flags; and the equipment clause, gradually accepted by all after an Anglo-Dutch treaty of 1822, declared that even vessels without slaves but equipped for slaving could be seized. All prizes were dispensed by bilateral admiralty courts, while the British even awarded slave prize money to successful crews. Finally, Seyyid Said of Oman and Zanzibar was downright opposed to abolishing the chief income of his Arab subjects. Instead of being an easy problem to solve, the slave trade expanded to its greatest proportions after it had been declared illegal by most countries in the 1830s. And the Royal Navy, though occasionally assisted as well as hindered by foreign warships, had to be the chief agent of enforcement.

British naval strategists and diplomats thus virtually alone developed the techniques and means that eventually destroyed the illegal slave trade. Even the British were reluctant at first, so that separate attempts with but few warships were made from isolated captures at sea from 1807 (while the Napoleonic wars were far from over) to the first interventions at Mauritius and Mombasa in the 1820s. Then in the 1830s, with abolition as British law, the British launched a massive effort, sending anti-slaving cruisers to their various squadrons around Africa: 26 to North America and the West Indies, 23 in the Mediterranean, 16 off South America, 15 at Lisbon, 14 divided between the Cape and West Africa, and 10 in the East Indies. In the 1840s other nations began to cooperate more fully, with even Ottoman Turkey and Said at Zanzibar outlawing the external slave trade. By 1847 Atlantic anti-slave patrols included 30 British, 7 French, 7 Portuguese and 5 American cruisers usually operating separately to capture a total of 55 slaver vessels in that year alone. In addition, the Royal Navy began the practice of going ashore to make treaties of cooperation with African chiefs and destroying the coastal installations of slave shippers. Slaving was thus virtually stopped from Cuba and severely restricted from West Africa, while diplomacy remained the chief weapon in East Africa. In 1852 Persia agreed to allow the British to search its vessels and Said remained cooperative till his death in 1856, though the Trucial States kept the Arabian side of the Persian Gulf active in slaving. The Brazilian supply of slaves was cut off in the 1850s, but the aggressiveness of pro-slave Americans helped revive the Cuban trade. By 1860, the slave trade had been checked everywhere except in the Caribbean Sea and Indian Ocean, where all depended on internal conditions within the United States and the Arab sheikdoms.

REOPENING THE ORIENT

The suppression of slavery and piracy also went hand in hand with the commercial rivalries and search for political stability in the waters east of India. And, equally typically, Great Britain dominated Western activities in the Far East through its East India Company. From Trincomalee on Ceylon to Calcutta and Chittagong, the Company commanded the Bay of Bengal, with small bases at Penang Island off the Malay coast and Bencoolen on Sumatra; in addition, it utilized the Andaman and Danish Nicobar islands. But when the Dutch began returning to the East Indies in 1816, they threatened to restore their old commercial monopoly, whereupon the East India Company in January 1819 occupied Singapore Island off the tip of Malaya. This brilliant strategic move gave Britain virtual possession of the Malacca Strait which commanded the trade route between the Indian Ocean and Canton, China. The Dutch had no choice but to acquiesce, and in 1824 they ceded their last Indian settlements as well as Malacca and their claims in Malaya to the British in return for Bencoolen. The Dutch, however, from their base at Riau opposite Singapore tried to undercut British trade to China, but were continually frustrated by Royal Navy units of the East Indies Squadron. Still, Dutch trade in the Far East flourished, and Holland continued to enjoy the trade monopoly to Japan, still shut off from the rest of the world. The Portuguese at Goa and the Spanish in the Philippines had long been reduced to impotence, though the latter were able to beat off a French attack on the Sulu Archipelago in 1845. France became only slowly involved in the Far East, its warships beginning to intervene in Vietnam from 1824 to protect Europeans there. But just to check Dutch and French alike, the British occupied coastal points in northern Australia near present-day Darwin between 1824 and 1849, but these enterprises failed.

The search for stability was the prime concern of all Western nations in the waters of the Far East, so that their navies were mostly employed against Asian natives resisting European overlordship on land or acting as pirates at sea. The European powers often cooperated to protect their shipping, while even the United States created an East India Station in 1835. In the colonies, anti-pirate activities were often part of the general pacification, and Indochinese frontier wars occasionally involved the British. The three Oriental areas of active naval combat in the early nineteenth century were the mainland of Southeast Asia (Burma, Siam, Vietnam), the offshore islands and waters (Malaya, East Indies, Philippines) and the Chinese coast.

On the mainland of Southeast Asia, the East India Company soon became involved in the continuing struggle of Burma to dominate the region, particularly at the expense of Siam, although Vietnam, Cambodia and Laos were constantly fighting among themselves. Burmese advances into Indian territory below Chittagong led to open war in March 1824. Basing in the Andamans, a British expeditionary force departed aboard Bombay Marine and Royal Navy vessels to drive up the Irrawaddy River. The fleet included much of the old and new: sailing frigates and brigs, a flotilla of twenty armed rowboats, the first British paddle-wheel steamer to see action, and an arsenal that included Congreve rockets. In opposition were a force of formidable 100-oar Burmese bireme-type praus. Rangoon took most of the remainder of 1824 to be invested, while the winter river drive was slowed by unenlightened army command and tropical disease. Nevertheless, throughout 1825, the British expedition pushed up the Irrawaddy almost to the Burmese capital of Ava destroying the Burmese army in the process. Early in 1826 Burma surrendered much of the coast below Chittagong to Britain, and later in the year Siam agreed to halt its designs on British Malaya. The British needed a buffer for eastern India as in the western part, but the Burmese were uncooperative. Renewed war threatened in 1838–39, then occurred early in 1852 when another Company amphibious force took Rangoon and then required another year to annex South Burma. As on the Afghanistan frontier, sea power proved inadequate, and imperial ground forces were needed to maintain the British defense perimeter on the Asian continent.

The waters of the South China Sea required extensive naval activities for policing. The Spanish fought a centuries-old war against the Moro pirates of the southern Philippines, while in 1816 the Dutch at Batavia created a special Colonial Marine which they soon integrated into the regular Netherlands navy for anti-pirate operations throughout the Indies. Heavily committed to pacification operations in Java and Bali, however, the Dutch required help from the Spanish and British against the pirates, particularly in Borneo. The main source of pirates were the Lanun and Balanini tribes of southern Mindanao and Sulu islets, far out of reach of Spanish authorities. These pirates annually sailed south and west in a fleet of 200 praus before breaking into squadrons of some twenty vessels for operations based on the north-west coast of Borneo. In addition, local Malay tribes plagued British colonial waters, so that regular patrols were instituted in the Malacca Strait in the early 1830s which also helped Siam put down various in-surrections. By such cunning as using disguised merchant vessels as decoys, British commanders later in the decade began the effective suppression of the Malay pirates. By terms of the Anglo-Dutch treaty of 1824, the British could not operate off Borneo, but when in 1841 the local sultan made a British sailor-adventurer named James Brooke rajah of the Sarawak coast of Borneo the situation changed. The British East Indies Squadron destroyed a pirate stronghold at Marudu Bay in North Borneo in 1845, found coal at Sarawak, and helped Brooke establish a naval station at Labuan Island in mid-1846, simul-taneous with the assault and capture of coastal Brunei. But it was Brooke of Sarawak, and not the British fleet, who thereafter waged successful anti-pirate operations henceforth in northern Borneo. The last major anti-pirate offensive was undertaken by the Spanish, who in 1848 assaulted and took after three attempts the main Balanini stronghold in the Sulus. By 1850, Western efforts had effectively checked major pirate operations in the waters of Southeast Asia.

Policing of Chinese waters was undertaken only after the British government ended the East India Company's trade monopoly to China in 1834, and then events quickly led to war. The Manchu dynasty had been so weakened internally that by 1800 many pirates easily ravaged Chinese coastal waters, one fleet numbering over 500 junks. Most of the Western powers let the pirates go unchecked, although the Chinese government in 1806 had wedded its rather ineffective water force to a small Portuguese squadron at Macao for some defense. Piracy tended to abate after 1810, but the English (and some American) smuggling of opium from India into China increased so much that Sino-British relations rapidly deteriorated in the 1830s. Finally, late in 1839, the First Opium War erupted. China's defenses were purely continental: coastal fortifications supported by the Manchu armies and a motley array of war junks. So the British decided to blockade the Chinese coast, neutralize the junk fleets, and take key cities in am-phibious and river operations. After the first naval skirmish near Canton in November 1839 in which several British warships defeated a junk fleet, the British moved against North China. In the summer of 1840, a British expeditionary force landed on Chusan Island and blockaded the mouth of the Peiho River leading to the capital at Peking. When the Chinese agreed to negotiate, the fleet moved south to Canton; then the negotiations broke down. The British resumed hostilities in 1841 by taking Canton in May, Amoy in August, Chusan again and Ningpo in October, and despite stretched logistics and severe living conditions, held on to their gains, utilizing a new base they had occupied early in the year below Canton—Hong Kong. Taking Shanghai in June 1842, the British moved up the Yangtze River toward Nanking, forcing the Chinese to sue for peace. In addition to extensive economic and legal concessions, China formally ceded Hong Kong to Britain.

Suddenly, Britain assumed the role of policeman of the lawless Chinese waters, while the Chinese government reeled helplessly under the impact of Western culture. Another treaty with Britain was followed by similar agreements with France and the United States, 1843–44, while in the latter year the Taiping Rebellion began against the Manchus, growing until it had split all China with the capture of Nanking in 1853. Tradition-bound, the Manchus generally ignored reforming and modernizing their coastal-river navy, which, however, won important victories over the equally old-fashioned rebel vessels on the Yangtze and Poyang Lake in the mid-1850s. The Western powers made little impact on these events, but British Hong Kong and the East Indies Squadron were now faced with the monumental task of eliminating the Chinese pirate menace. The reluctance of the Chinese government—which depended largely on coastal convoys—to accept British naval aid made policing difficult, until 1848 when the regime finally acquiesced. The next year British warships took the offensive, joining the naval forces of Vietnam in destroying one great pirate fleet in three separate battles. But lesser squadrons of pirates persisted, requiring the British in 1854 to lead a joint expedition of Chinese, Portuguese and American warships to seek out and destroy a large number of pirate craft. Until the governments of these nations and that of France as well mounted a major effort, however, the British assumed the full responsibility for combating pirates in China. Hong Kong became a key advanced base, Trincomalee a backwater, and Singapore the pivot as the British extended their *Pax Britannica* into the Pacific.

As an extension of events around the Asia littoral, various Western nations began to penetrate farther eastward to establish formal colonial governments in Pacific islands where only adventurers, outlaws, missionaries and occasional traders had gone before, often at the expense of the natives. The Dutch annexed western New Guinea in 1828, the French the distant Tahiti and the Marquesas Islands in 1842–43, but again it was the British who dominated the white settlement of Oceania, most importantly asserting authority over the entire continent of Australia by 1829 and proclaiming official sovereignty over New Zealand in 1840. Generally, such colonization was loose and peaceful, but the British developed differences with the Maori natives of New Zealand that led to open war, 1843–48. Warships of the Australasian Squadron based at Sydney, Australia, operated along the New Zealand coast, using their guns, Congreve rockets and landing parties to help counter the very effective guerrilla tactics employed by the Maoris. Gradually, by this colonizing thrust eastward, the European maritime powers were filling the vacuum left by the collapse of the old Spanish Empire and would eventually link up with their trade routes in the Americas. But first, they had to settle some lingering differences in Europe.

THE TURBULENT 1850s

The tottering Ottoman Empire suddenly became the object of French and Russian imperial designs in the early 1850s, though the ostensible issue was religious supremacy in the Holy Land. All Europe mobilized in defense of Turkey, but only Britain, France and Sardinia actually rallied armed forces to her side. Hostilities opened in the fall of 1853, with the Russian and Turkish armies clashing on land and their Black Sea naval squadrons concentrating for support and raids on rival seaports. After some indecisive bombardments and isolated skirmishes, on November 30 a Russian squadron of three 120- and 84-gun line-of-battle ships, two frigates and three steamers under Rear Admiral Pavel Stepanovich Nakhimov attacked a Turkish force of seven frigates, three corvettes and two steamers at Sinope on the north coast of Turkey. Using the new shell guns, the Russians in but one hour utterly annihilated the Turk squadron, allowing only one steamer to escape. This crushing victory proclaimed the obsolescence of wooden warships, and the French immediately began to introduce armor on board their warships. Strategically, Western Europe arose against this Russian aggression, and in January 1854 an Anglo-French fleet entered the Black Sea to protect the integrity of Turkey. Early in the spring Britain and France declared war on Russia, which reciprocated—the first war between major powers since the Congress of Vienna.

The Crimean War caught the British and French unprepared, a fact revealed in their makeshift and downright shoddy prosecution of the war. Former rivals, they now joined fleets in the Baltic and Black seas in hopes of destroying the Russian navy, while Austria and Prussia forced Russia to quit its advance into the Danube basin. In addition,

Anglo-French forces occupied Piraeus, frustrating Greek designs to join Russia and thus grab adjacent territory from Turkey. The much-vaunted Russian command of the Baltic proved empty, for the Russian fleet elected not to move against the combined Anglo-French fleet of Vice Admiral Sir Charles Napier. Still, the Russians utilized the latest weapons of the Industrial Revolution to defend their northern coasts: steam vessels easily violated the blockade, while submarine mines protected the Baltic Sea Fleet at Kronstadt and Sveaborg. Needing something to do, Napier's force took the Aland Islands after an eight-day bombardment and siege in August 1854. But, aside from a minor shelling of Sveaborg one year later and some raids, this was the extent of Baltic operations, and the Russians were totally unable to send reinforcements to the Black Sea via the Mediterranean.

Initial Black Sea operations, however, were little more impressive; in April 1854 the British and French landed troops at Varna to help force the Russians from the Black Sea and bombarded Odessa. Then they decided to destroy Russian naval power by taking the base at Sevastopol. The force at Varna was sealifted aboard 300 transports escorted by an Anglo-French fleet under Vice Admiral Sir James Dundas, and finally landed in the Crimea thirty miles up the coast from Sevastopol in September. Russian naval power was then liquidated when the crews and Naval Infantry went ashore to help man the defenses, and the ships, including Nakhimov's veteran vessels of Sinope, were scuttled to block the entrance to the harbor. But the Russian army stalemated the allied expeditionary force, which was then subjected to a harsh winter of siege. In mid-1855 the mismanaged campaign finally led to amphibious-land assaults which took Kerch in May, Sevastopol in September, and Kinburn in October. Ninety allied war steamers, including French ironclad floating batteries, made a dramatic impression at Kinburn, adding to the general Russian decision to end the war. After evacuating their defenses at Ochakov, Russia sued for peace early in 1856.

The settlement of the Crimean trouble did much to eliminate further causes of war and to resume the Concert of Europe and *Pax Britannica,* with Russia making the necessary sacrifices: no new Black Sea fleet for Russia or Turkey, and the neutralization of the Black Sea and Danube basin for the commerce of all nations, including the razing of the defenses and naval installations of Sevastopol. Though warships of all nations were now excluded from this great sea, the naval power of Britain remained available as usual to enforce the terms of the peace. The Russian influence over Ottoman Turkey was thus eliminated, the latter managing to survive politically for several more decades. The legalistic spirit which neutralized the Black Sea also led to the Declaration of Paris during the peace negotiations of 1856, issued by Britain, France, Austria, Russia, Prussia, Turkey and Sardinia. The Declaration abolished privateering, allowed neutral shipping of noncontraband materials to belligerents, and stated explicitly that for a blockade to be legal and binding it had to be effective; that is, blockaded ports had to be patrolled by warships of the blockading nation. But again, such a statement of international law depended upon the adherence of the maritime power which commanded the seas, namely, Great Britain. With such new rules of sea war the European powers turned to converting their navies to steam, armor plate, iron and shell guns.

Post-Crimean Europe was generally stable politically, with the seeds of future conflict in the growing forces of nationalism among subject peoples and the imperialistic and commercial enterprises in the non-Western world. One short war erupted in Europe, as the Italians renewed their attempt to unify and achieve their independence from Austria. Sardinia (Piedmont) concluded a secret treaty with France, gaining her support in the attempt, then mobilized early in 1859. In April war broke out, Sardinia and France against Austria. The very respectable French fleet laid a blockade on the Austrian coast, while the allied armies soundly defeated those of Austria. Peace followed quickly in July, Sardinia gaining new territory but allowing the Austrians to keep Venice. Displeased, the Italians led by Cavour and the king of Sardinia revolted in 1860, Garibaldi leading an army over water from Genoa to liberate Sicily in May, June and July. Obtaining British aid, Garibaldi crossed the Strait of Messina and took Naples in August and September. The French again intervened, stationing a squadron off the Neapolitan coast, and occupied Rome to protect the Pope. But the Italians launched a pincers movement, a Sardinian army advancing from Piedmont in the north into the Papal States and Garibaldi driving from the south against Gaeta in September and October. He besieged Gaeta in November, and after the withdrawal of the French squadron in January 1861 used the Sardinian navy to bombard Gaeta into submission. In March 1861 the united kingdom of Italy was proclaimed, save for French-occupied Rome. Thus a new unified power appeared in the Mediterranean to check the maritime thrust of Austria.

Britain, ever sensitive to its Middle Eastern defense perimeter against Russia, remained embroiled in fighting there in the late-1850s. Expecting a Russian victory in the Crimean War, Persia had broken diplomatic relations with Britain, leading to a British naval demonstration in the Persian Gulf early in 1854. The next year Persian troops occupied Afghan territory, leading the British to intervene. In November 1856 the Indian navy sealifted an expeditionary force into the Gulf from Bombay and other Indian ports. It took Kharak and Halilah Bay early in December, moving up the coast to invest Bushire in January 1857. While the British negotiated a peace settlement to preserve Persia's national integrity, Company steamers supported a drive up the delta of the Tigris River. By spring, the fighting was ended, Britain obtaining the same trade concession enjoyed by Russia with Persia; the border dispute with Afghanistan was not really settled. Peace was concluded none too soon, for in May 1857 the Great Indian Mutiny broke out. The bloody uprising lasted thirteen months before it was crushed, and in September 1858 the British government ended the rule of the East India Company in India. Regular forces would thereafter operate with sepoy troops under direct command of the crown. Britain became understandably anxious about her northwest frontier, for the Russians were moving down the Syr Daria River to conquer the last Mongol tribes, using steamboats in support of the army, while farther north Russia was pushing into Eastern Siberia toward the Pacific, intruding upon China.

The chaotic condition of China, rent by the growing Taiping Rebellion, made the country vulnerable to possible economic or even territorial designs by Great Britain, Russia and the United States. The inability of the enfeebled Manchu government to suppress either the Rebellion or piracy led to the assistance—however unwelcome—of the Western powers, particularly since many of the pirates themselves were Western adventurers. From 1853, United States warships began to work in active concert with those of the Royal Navy against pirates and hostile Chinese ashore. Then, in October 1856 the Chinese seizure of a British vessel at Canton led to a second war with Britain over larger issues centering on treaty revisions. In this, the Arrow War (named for the vessel seized) or Second Opium War, China was feebler than in the First, for the Taiping Rebellion undermined internal unity. Admiral Sir Michael Seymour's ships quickly reduced the forts below Canton, then shelled and briefly occupied the city itself. The next month, November, the Chinese brought on the wrath of the local American squadron when one of their forts fired on ships' boats being led away from Canton by Commander Andrew H. Foote. Foote then under the cover of his guns personally led an assaulting naval brigade that took all four barrier forts below Canton. Sino-American relations were not hampered, although the Americans agreed to assist the British whenever necessary to protect Western lives and property. Also, Chinese butchery of at least one French missionary brought in France as an active enemy. With Russia moving eastward along the Amur River, China faced a coalition of unfriendly Western nations.

Attacked from within and without, China during 1857 and 1858 resisted ineffectively and turned halfheartedly to diplomacy, for the inexorable advance of the Western powers threatened China on all sides.

To check the Russians, in May 1857 China ceded the left bank of the Amur to Russia, which included her Maritime Provinces. Below her southern frontier, in Vietnam, the murder of a Spanish missionary led to a joint Franco-Spanish naval bombardment and occupation of Tourane in August and September of 1858. The force, commanded by Vice Admiral de Genouilly, for logistical reasons transferred to Saigon in 1859, beginning the French conquest of Cochin China. Anglo-French operations against China focused on Canton, where Chinese fire rafts, mines and junks only delayed the ultimate attack which came in December 1857. Canton fell to a naval bombardment and amphibious assault led by Admiral Seymour, who then—the following May—directed a similar seizure of the Taku forts at the entrance to the Peiho River leading to Tientsin and Peking. Turning as a last resort again to diplomacy, China made peace in June 1858—granting additional trade concessions and opening more ports to all the Western powers. These losses were too much to bear, however, and China renewed hostilities.

The Arrow War resumed when, in June 1859, an Anglo-French naval force attempted to retake the Taku forts. These defenses had been strengthened, however, and the attackers were repulsed with heavy losses. The neutral American warships present assisted their withdrawal downriver, thence to Shanghai. The allies now resolved to settle the issue with a massive assault on the Taku forts, using the new Armstrong guns for the first time. Rendezvousing at Hong Kong, the new allied force under General Sir James Hope Grant occupied Chusan Island in March 1860 for a forward staging base, the British going on to Dairen, the French to Chefoo in the Yellow Sea. The combined landings in August were made on the coast above Taku, whose forts were then taken from the rear. Pressing up the Peiho to Tientsin, General Hope Grant divided his force for the advance on Peking—perhaps because of his disdain for the French performance. With the British and French gunboats and service craft in the river, the British army on the north bank, the French on the left, the allied force drove toward Peking which fell early in October. The Chinese had no choice but to submit to the terms of the treaty of 1858 and to cede Kowloon to Britain, leaving them powerless to halt the Russian penetration of the Maritime Provinces and to view with some apprehension the sudden reappearance of ancient Japan.

While Britain was so heavily occupied in China, Russia and the United States both sought to force open Japan, thus ending her centuries-old policy of seclusion and broadening the base of her commercial intercourse from the Dutch monopoly. A Russian naval force left the Baltic in October 1852 with this object in view, but did not arrive before an American naval squadron under Commodore Matthew C. Perry achieved the same feat, arriving at Tokyo Bay in July 1853. After a short visit,

Perry wintered at Macao, returning to Japan the next year to obtain the treaty. Granting the Americans trading rights at three ports, the Japanese were soon obliged to conclude similar agreements with Britain, Russia, France and the Netherlands, 1855–58. Thus committed, Japan soon opened other ports and lost little time in seeking to understand the West. In one respect, naval knowledge, Japan was most interested; the apparent power of Perry's four ships led the Tokugawa regime to seek Dutch advice late in 1854. The next year, the Dutch, losing their long trade monopoly, established a naval training detachment at Nagasaki, teaching the Japanese the art of steam engineering before being asked to leave early in 1859. Unlike wartorn and backward China, Japan was eager to improvise and modernize and began turning also to the British, Americans and French for assistance—although various feudal lords were more progressive than the government, which was criticized by its conservative traditionalists. Somehow, the Japanese seemed to realize the inability or undesirability of the Russians to assist them in naval matters, and aside from a brief association in 1855–56 Japan never again turned to Russia. A wise choice, for the aggressive Russians reached the Pacific coast opposite Japan in 1860.

Russia in the late 1850s had reached something of a strategic crisis. Defeat in the Crimean War had cast doubt on the traditional thrust into the Middle East. Indeed, loss of Black Sea bases necessitated a Russian base at Villefranche on the French-Italian border from 1858 to 1860. Now, however, a new school of strategic thought developed under Commodore Andrei A. Popov which advocated that the prime area of expansion be into the Far East. In the late summer of 1854 a Russian frigate and shore battery had repulsed a landing attempt by five allied vessels at Petropavlovsk on the Kamchatkan peninsula; otherwise, the British fleet in Asia had discouraged any Russian naval movements in the Pacific during the Crimean War. Now, the Russian fleet was being modernized with steam vessels under its new commander-in-chief, Grand Duke Constantine Nikolaevich, whose key administrator for shipbuilding was Popov. Popov wanted his nation to promote overland and maritime expansion and to use the Amur River as a base for a major Russian Pacific fleet for wartime attacks on British colonies and stations in the Orient. Believing the United States could act as a political balance between Britain and Russia in the Pacific, Popov advocated the use of California ports by Russian raiders. Jealous of the British presence in China, the Russians founded the town and port of Vladivostok in 1860–61 and in July 1861 occupied Tsushima Island between Japan and Korea, lest the British grab it. In addition, now Rear Admiral Popov was dispatched on a reconnaissance mission to study the suitability of a Pacific strategy. By now, however, a British squadron had reached

Yokohama, Japan, and threatened to visit Tsushima. Taking the hint, the Russian government ordered the island evacuated late in 1861. From this incident, Russian relations with Japan deteriorated, and Anglo-Japanese rapport grew.

Pax Britannica was a reality by the beginning of the 1860s. In Europe, even the Crimean War had failed to upset the balance of power, with Britain's traditional French antagonist allied. The revolution in steam had been expanded by the advent of armored sail-and-steam seagoing battleships, with Dupuy de Lôme's 5600-ton iron-plated *Gloire* being launched in 1859. Not surprisingly, this vessel and other innovations helped to create another British invasion scare in 1859–60, abated in the latter year by the 9000-ton British iron-built *Warrior*. Across the world, the British had acquired twenty-five bases and posts manned by 45,000 regular troops by the time of the Crimean War. Among the most important naval depots outside Britain were Lisbon, Gibraltar, Capetown, Malta, Aden, Bombay, Trincomalee, Calcutta, Singapore, Hong Kong and Sydney. Obtained during the last days of sail, this system of bases became a ready-made network of coaling stations for steamships, while Britain and her colonies provided sources of cheap coal—advantages the French could never emulate. The chief maritime competitor during the first half of the century, however, had been the United States. And though Britain often differed with its progeny, political stability in the Western Hemisphere required general Anglo-American cooperation. So, the base system was maintained at Halifax, Quebec and Jamaica and extended to British Honduras and the Falkland Islands. With such heavy global responsibilities, the British had good reason to beware of the growing influence of the embryonic American colossus, particularly in the least patrolled regions of the Western Hemisphere and the Eastern Pacific.

11
The Western Hemisphere
and American Empire,
1815–1860

Our confederacy must be viewed as the nest from which all America,
North and South, is to be peopled. . . . My fear is that [Spain is] too
feeble to hold [her colonies] till our population can be sufficiently ad-
vanced to gain them piece by piece.

—THOMAS JEFFERSON, 1795

LATIN AMERICAN INDEPENDENCE

The extension of the *Pax Britannica* into the Western Hemisphere
became particularly necessary, for Britain relied heavily on the imports
from Latin America, required adequate defenses of Canada in North
America, and faced a potential power struggle in the Eastern Pacific,
the solution of which would decide the level of political stability in the
vast waters between the Americas and the Far East. Because of the wide
virgin continents beyond the influence of British sea power, the task
of policing the Americas was particularly difficult, except wherein
the Royal Navy could control seaborne communications between Spain
and Portugal and their American empires and also check the particular
designs of Russia and France to create new colonies in the Americas.
But the position of the United States was quite another matter. Strategically placed between Canada and the British West Indies with aggressive pioneers pushing across North America into territory claimed by
Britain, the American Republic also boasted a dynamic maritime community that exerted a great influence on the affairs of Latin America
and which came to compete successfully with the British merchant carriers everywhere else in the world. The United States thus provided
the key to the Western Hemisphere, and when that burgeoning nation

grew into a sprawling continental empire and was then wracked by a monumental civil war, Britain and the other powers had to treat their diplomatic policies vis-à-vis the United States with great care. The technological and strategic impact of the American Civil War upon Europe was profound and bore significantly upon the future of the *Pax Britannica* and great power relationships in general, not the least result being the emergence of the United States as a major industrial nation.

Anglo-American relations in the years after 1815 first involved the defensive frontiers of both countries. Sensitive to the recent British blockade and bombardments of its Eastern seaboard, the United States returned to a strategy of coast defense. Beginning in 1817, for the first time, the American government began to systematize its permanent fortifications from Maine to Louisiana, but relying upon the navy as the first line of defense. Line-of-battle ships and 44-gun frigates had been laid down during the War of 1812, and these plus new construction could now theoretically deal with British fleets operating out of Halifax, Bermuda and Jamaica. In the postwar demobilization, however, most of these large warships were decommissioned and placed in reserve, so that the navy's real contribution to coast defense remained in floating batteries and harbor gunboats supporting the forts. But such half-measures were not critical, as no foreign invasion ever threatened in these years.

More serious were disagreements over the Canadian-American frontier extending from Maine to the Rockies and pivoting on the Great Lakes, where American war fleets had prospered during the late war. Because the rapids above Montreal closed the Upper St. Lawrence River and Great Lakes to oceangoing warships, Britain still had to construct ships of war on the Lakes to defend the Canadian shores; the Americans as well had no direct river course from the Atlantic coast to the Lakes. Yet, both countries sought to economize by reducing their respective armed forces on the Lakes, so that in 1817 both nations agreed mutually to dismantle these forces, and the next year they (along with agreeing to fishing rights in the Gulf of St. Lawrence) formalized the Canadian-Louisiana territorial boundary to the Rockies at the 49th parallel. Nevertheless, to stabilize the balance of power in North America, both countries maintained their frontier forts, kept their ships in reserve, and began building canals which by mid-century improved direct water communications between the sea and the Lakes (though for gunboats and supply boats rather than men-of-war). The British naval establishment on the Lakes, however, closed down in 1834, by which time the American force had also withered away. A rebellion in Canada three years later and boundary quarrels from Maine to the Louisiana line kept up Anglo-American tensions, until 1842 when a compromise treaty settled these borders and the passions. The balance of power centered on the Lakes thenceforth declined in importance, and rivalries between the two English-speaking peoples shifted elsewhere.

The weakened state of the Spanish Empire had left the British masters of the Caribbean, but renewal of the Latin American uprisings after 1815 brought nearly overt support of the revolutionaries from the United States, which also wished to dislodge Spain from Florida. The United States in the final years of the Napoleonic period had simply taken over the Gulf coast, from Baton Rouge to beyond Mobile Bay (Spanish West Florida), which along with New Orleans made the United States a Caribbean power to rival the British and Spanish. The United States government felt obliged to pass new neutrality laws in 1817 and 1818, but the people favored the liberal revolts, and American warship captains continued to aid rebel governments by carrying their specie. In order to suppress fresh outbreaks in South America, the Spanish authorities weakened their police forces in Texas, East Florida and the Caribbean. The result was Indian raids into Georgia and the establishment of privateer-pirate bases first at Galveston in 1816 and then in 1817 at Amelia Island off northeast Florida to aid the Latin American republics. Privateers were already operating out of Baltimore and New Orleans, but those of Galveston and Amelia were clearly piratic, attacking even American merchantmen. Spanish-American relations worsened, whereupon the British decided to remain aloof. In November 1817 President James Madison ordered the seizure of both Amelia Island and Galveston, and the next month a frigate and five lesser American warships covered an Army landing at Amelia, thus forcing pirates to abandon their enterprise there. Galveston was not yet taken, but early in 1818 General Andrew Jackson undertook the First Seminole War by crossing into Spanish Florida in pursuit of raiding Seminole Indians. He took the capital, Pensacola, and infuriated the British government by executing one of their merchants who had been assisting the Indians. But he pacified the Indians and by his unauthorized actions hastened the cession of all Spanish Florida to the United States by treaty early in 1819.

The actions of Madison and Jackson eased Spanish-American tensions, helped suppress Gulf coast piracy (also with the enforcement of the neutrality laws), and forced the pirates to shift to the Spanish Main. The treaty had left the Gulf coast from the Sabine River to Mexico in Spanish hands, so that the notorious Laffite band of pirates continued to use Galveston as its base, particularly for raids on the delta of the Mississippi. Other pirates were using islands in the Bahamas and off the coasts of Nicaragua and Venezuela. So the United States government launched an intensive anti-pirate campaign in 1819–20 which had the main effect of finally protecting the American coast. Piracy laws in both years were enforced by naval patrols in and around the Mississippi delta which began capturing pirate vessels. Jean Laffite—with some sentiment toward the Americans, with whom he had helped to defend New Orleans against the British in 1815—in the spring of 1820 abandoned Galveston and shifted to the Mexican coast where the revolutionary spirit was reviving. Simultaneously, American courts began ordering the execution of convicted pirates, while naval patrols entered West African waters to deal with slavers. These actions enraged the Spanish colonials, the pirates and the revolutionary privateers, so that the United States had no choice but to increase its naval strength. Much also depended on the ability of the revolutionary governments to control the activities of the privateers using their flags.

Meanwhile, naval power played a key role in the Spanish American revolutions. The Latin American revolt had intensified in 1815 with the end of the Napoleonic wars and the dispatch from Spain of an expedition of 10,000 troops in 42 transports escorted by 18 warships to pacify the colonies bordering on the Caribbean. But the Spanish navy had been so weakened by the long wars that it could not begin to suppress the revolutionary privateers, let alone provide sufficient support for restoring Spain's authority in Latin America. Initially, during the spring of 1815, this squadron assaulted and took the insurgent position at Margarita Island off Venezuela, going on to blockade and retake Cartagena, the capital of Colombia (New Granada), between September and December, including winning a naval skirmish there in November. But thereafter Spanish naval fortunes waned, for the insurgents began to purchase warships and enlist volunteer crews from Britain, the United States, other European countries and throughout Latin America. These activities placed the former two nations in something of a dilemma. For Britain, though committed to restoring the Royalists in Europe, could use her command of the sea to thwart their pacification of colonial America and thus insure her own trade monopoly over Latin America. The United States, officially neutral, ideologically espoused such causes of democratic self-rule, so joined Britain in treating these conflicts as civil in nature and providing aid only unofficially. Anglo-American aloofness deteriorated, however, as the Spanish position in Latin America weakened after 1817. The revolutions, supported by growing naval forces, centered on two fronts: General Simón Bolívar in northern South America (Colombia, Venezuela and Ecuador) and General José de San Martin in the southern regions (Argentina, Chile and Peru).

Bolívar's campaign for the Spanish Main began at sea and evolved into a continental effort. While in exile in Jamaica in 1815, Bolívar received the services of seven privateers under Luis Brión, a Dutch Curaçao Creole who rose to become admiral over Bolívar's navy, the nucleus of which he had provided. Shifting to Haiti, Bolívar in 1816 mounted a seaborne expedition which retook Margarita Island after one initial failure. Brión's squadron then supported the attack on and capture of Angostura at the mouth of the Orinoco River, after which British sailors and troops began to arrive in Bolívar's camp. Throughout 1817 and 1818 Bolívar's warships blockaded the Spanish coastal positions and fought single-ship duels on the high seas as his armies fought inland, and the Spanish navy at home and in the Caribbean deteriorated. It had countered the insurgents by trying to blockade their base at Margarita, but being reduced to four vessels it had to abandon that task early in 1819. From Margarita, Bolívar's forces carried out amphibious raids and captures—the fleet growing to twenty-seven well-armed vessels during 1818. As the fighting wore on in 1819 most of the provinces of Colombia and Venezuela went over to Bolívar, and the next year a revolution in Spain crippled reinforcement plans for the Spanish forces in America. Early in 1820 Bolívar mounted a seaborne offensive along the Spanish Main, and Brión's fifteen-ship squadron defeated the Spanish squadron at Tenerife. Belated Spanish reinforcements could not halt Bolívar, who in 1821 attacked and took Cartagena by land and sea. His navy closed the blockade and two years later defeated the Spanish warships on Lake Maracaibo, leading to the fall of that key Venezuelan city. The Colombian warships drove the last Spanish troops from their new country in November 1823 to assure Bolívar's victory.

San Martin's campaign in the south resembled Bolívar's in its continental character and the sagacious use of naval forces in support. San Martin realized early that the Spanish naval power that defended the rich province of Peru had to be eliminated. He therefore planned a naval expedition at Buenos Aires to round the Horn and attack Spanish shipping on the west coast of South America. In the winter of 1815–16 such a force of three privateers did just that, destroying much shipping, bombarding and briefly blockading Callao itself. One year later, San Martin crossed the Andes Mountains, defeated the Spanish army and occupied Valparaiso in February 1817. He then set about raising a fleet at Buenos Aires to defend Chile and for an eventual advance on Peru. The small Spanish squadron from Callao then blockaded Valparaiso until discouraged by audacious attacks by British-led Chilean vessels in April 1818. More Chilean ships were purchased, such as a 64-gun former East Indiaman, and were captured; more Anglo-American officers were enlisted; and a naval academy was established, so that in the fall of 1818 a five-ship Chilean squadron was able to break up and capture a Spanish convoy from Cádiz.

Late in that year the fiery Lord Cochrane, formerly of the Royal

Navy, was appointed vice admiral in command of the seven-vessel Chilean navy, improving his fleet for engaging the Spanish squadron at Callao which included eight warships and twenty-seven gunboats. After a skirmish off Callao in February 1819, Cochrane declared the Peruvian coast under blockade, while Chilean privateers attacked Spanish shipping in the Pacific. Failing to lure the Spanish squadron to sea for battle with rockets and fire ships in October, the following June his forces bombarded and took the port of Valdivia, thus clearing the Chilean coast entirely of Spanish garrisons. San Martin now determined to invade Peru by sea, and in September 1820 Cochrane's eight warships escorted his sixteen-transport convoy to their successful landing at Pisco. The fleet then blockaded Callao again, with Cochrane personally leading a boarding party to seize a Spanish 44-gun frigate there in November. San Martin's army finally took Lima in July 1821, and Callao—besieged by land and sea—surrendered two months later. South American independence was virtually assured, for Spain had lost the riches of her most valuable colony.

In 1822–23 the British and American governments, seeing both Spain and Portugal convulsed in revolution at home and abroad, recognized the independence of the Latin American republics. To assure noninterference by the continental monarchs, Canning of Britain and President James Monroe and Secretary of State John Quincy Adams of the United States proclaimed that intervention would not be tolerated. Though this famous policy came to be known as the Monroe Doctrine, its strength rested solely on the ability of the Royal Navy to enforce it. The other European powers generally acquiesced in the edict, except in the realm of suppressing piracy. The new Latin republics began to exert controls over their privateers in these years, so that the obvious pirates in the Caribbean moved from Latin islands to ports in the Swedish, Danish and Dutch West Indies, Spanish Cuba and Puerto Rico, and independent Haiti. Beginning in late 1821, the maritime powers moved to counter these outright murderers and pillagers. The United States created squadrons in the Eastern Pacific and West Indies; the Royal Navy reinforced its units in the Caribbean and off Brazil; a small French naval force operated out of Martinique; the Danes at St. Thomas tried to control the pirates there; Haiti did the same; while American warships blockaded Swedish St. Bart's to achieve similar results. When the Spanish appeared unable and unwilling to act against their pirates, and fearing British seizure of Cuba, United States naval forces in March 1822 occupied Key West Island and demonstrated before Puerto Rico. In the winter of 1822–23 the British threatened to land in Cuba to suppress the pirates, while Commodore David Porter was authorized to convoy vessels of all nations from his base at Key West. Despite the intense tropical heat, the usual diseases and not a little mutual suspicion, British and American forces attacked the pirates at sea and in 1823 were finally assisted by the local Spanish authorities in chasing them onto Cuban territory. By the end of the year, when the Monroe Doctrine was formally announced, major Caribbean piracy had been confined to coastal waters.

Meanwhile, Mexico and Brazil revolted from Spanish and Portuguese rule, while the Spanish were trying in vain to reverse the situation in Peru. In September 1821 Mexico proclaimed its independence, generally succeeded in driving out Spanish ground forces, and was visited by Admiral Cochrane's Chilean fleet that attacked Spanish shipping and coastal posts in the Californias early in 1822. In September 1823 Spain ordered its shipping out of Mexican waters, leaving only the fortress of San Juan de Ulua in Vera Cruz harbor in Spanish hands. Bombarding the port, the guns of the castle forced the town's evacuation and the Mexican government's raising of a navy in the manner of the Chileans to reduce the fortress. Meanwhile, in July 1822, San Martin had handed over all his military strength to Bolívar, who took the next three years to clear Peru of Spanish forces. Cochrane felt his work done and left Chilean service late in 1822, but the Chilean-Peruvian fleet had to blockade Callao during the Spanish reoccupation of it in 1824–25 and ended its operations by taking the Chiloé Islands in January 1826.

Brazil broke from Portugal in 1822 and like Chile and Mexico sought outside help in raising a navy, although two Portuguese frigates and a number of other vessels had fallen into Brazilian hands. With 4700 miles of coastline to defend, the new republic eagerly recruited Portuguese, British, American and other officers and in March 1823 appointed Lord Cochrane as First Admiral of the Brazilian navy. In the meantime, the Portuguese garrisons at Montevideo and Bahian Salvador had been isolated, and in April Cochrane blockaded the Portuguese warships on the coast of Bahia and profited from generally inferior Portuguese leadership. In a 74-gun flagship and leading 8 other vessels, Cochrane frustrated a Portuguese sortie of 17 warships escorting over 70 transports from Salvador to the northern port of Maranhão by capturing some of the transports and the port itself in July and chasing the rest of the convoy all the way to Portugal. Simultaneously, a Brazilian frigate took 18 prizes in Portuguese waters. In 1824 Cochrane helped to quell a rebellion in Brazil, and the next year Portugal accepted Brazilian sovereignty.

Spain was less realistic and painfully tried to salvage something from her disintegrating American empire. Helpless to reverse the situation in Peru, the Spanish hoped to center their efforts on the Caribbean—Cuba, Mexico and Colombia, though the latter two would have to be retaken. Even Cuba was a problem, for anti-pirate operations brought Anglo-

American landing forces into Cuban and Puerto Rican territory in 1824 and 1825, although in August of the latter year Britain, France and the United States jointly renounced any designs to take Cuba. Piracy was thus practically extinguished in the Caribbean, and the Spanish could devote their major energies to recovering Mexico and Colombia. But this proved unattainable. Collecting twenty vessels in the Caribbean and others on the west coast at Acapulco and San Blas, the Mexican navy increased the pressure on the garrison at San Juan de Ulua. Seven vessels from the base at Sacrificios Island below Vera Cruz turned away two Spanish relief forces in October 1825, leading to the castle's surrender the next month. Meanwhile, Colombian privateers were attacking Spanish shipping, and plans were discussed for joint Mexican-Colombian naval operations against Spain, to be joined by the Central American republics which had easily thrown off Spanish rule. The scheme was not realized, but the Latin American pressure continued.

Mexico in the summer of 1826 gave command of its growing fleet to David Porter, recently court-martialed by the United States Navy. Since Havana had become the focus of Spain's attempts to recover her lost colonies, Porter with four vessels harassed Spanish shipping off Cuba late in 1826 until he was chased into Key West by a Spanish squadron. The port had been abandoned as a base by the American squadron in favor of newly acquired Pensacola, so Porter decided to base there himself—a clear violation of American neutrality which Spain protested, but in vain. Returning late in 1827 to Vera Cruz, Porter sent out his warships to augment Mexican privateers attacking Spanish shipping and lost his best vessel, a 22-gun brig, in battle against a Spanish 64 early in 1828. The efforts of Spain achieved nothing more than stalemate. An expedition to recover Colombia in 1827 failed, and though Mexico ended its attacks on Spanish shipping in August 1828, Spain's fortunes did not improve. Porter left Mexican service a year later, just as a Spanish expedition from Havana against Tampico was repulsed by the Mexican troops of General Antonio López de Santa Anna. In the political upheavals of Mexico, Santa Anna took over the government and abolished the too-expensive Mexican navy in 1830. But by then Spain's American empire had been reduced to Cuba and Puerto Rico.

Anglo-American support of the Latin American revolutions had isolated the politics of the great powers from the Western Hemisphere, but it otherwise had little effect on the internal situation in Latin America. Even foreign officers such as Cochrane and Porter had been victimized by the unsettled political intrigue of their adopted causes. Indeed, the political upheavals that have continued to plague these Latin American republics to this day have generally led to dictatorships of strong army officers such as Bolívar and Santa Anna whose major concerns have been internal security and frontier defense. Naval forces they have considered extravagant, and with no maritime populations of any consequence these new nations depended initially on former Spanish and Portuguese officers and then on foreign navies altogether. When Uruguay with Argentine help revolted against Brazil in 1825, the fleet formerly led by Cochrane blockaded Buenos Aires, leading to British mediation which—combined with allied victories on land—in turn led to Uruguayan independence by 1828. Similarly, Peru invaded Bolivia in 1827, supported by a naval squadron which took Guayaquil early in 1829; however by March of the latter year the Bolivians had repelled the invader. And small naval forces figured in the Venezuelan revolution of 1848–49.

But as the Latins warred among themselves, they were vulnerable to naval attack. In fact, to improve their position relative to the Americas, in 1833 the British occupied the Falkland Islands off the coast of Argentina. Five years later, in response to pleas from French nationals living in Mexico, a French squadron of three frigates and lesser craft under Admiral Charles Bandin anchored off Sacrificios and bombarded San Juan de Ulua until it was evacuated. The French then occupied Vera Cruz from April 1838 until Mexico satisfied French demands the following March. Similarly, an Argentine intervention in the Uruguayan civil war of 1843–52 was checked partly by an Anglo-French naval blockade of the River Plate and the occupation of some Uruguayan territory in the years 1845–49. Generally, then, the Latin American republics were isolated by the British navy and yet were protected by the Monroe Doctrine. This dependence placed them somewhat at the mercy of the expanding United States.

THE CONTINENTAL UNITED STATES

The United States after 1815 declined as a potential maritime power commensurate with the passing of New England's predominance in the Union. To be sure, the American merchant marine by the 1840s rivaled closely that of Great Britain, but it depended upon that nation's capital ships to command the seas in protection of free trade. The United States in fact compared with France as a continental power, employing a large merchant service and second-rank navy. The American Congress in 1813 and 1816 authorized twelve 74-gun ships of the line, all of which were built, but half of which stayed in reserve for a national emergency. Rather, the United States relied—like France and Russia—upon frigates for commerce protection and *guerre de course* and upon gunboats and fortifications for coastal and river operations. As American overseas trade expanded, along with the need for home defense and anti-slaving operations, the United States established naval squadrons throughout the world: the Mediterranean in 1815, the Eastern Pacific 1818, West Indies and Caribbean 1822, Brazil 1826, East Indies 1835, the Home Station 1841, and Africa 1843.

As the French-style planter aristocracy of the South and the frontier-oriented Western men led by Andrew Jackson dominated the national government, American public opinion less and less appreciated the need for a large and expensive navy. Indeed, so suspicious were the politicians of professional naval officers—conservative and aristocratic by nature—that they kept supreme naval authority in the civilian Secretary of the Navy even during the major administrative reforms of 1815 and 1842, refused to create a rank as high as rear admiral (even commodore was temporary and honorary), and allowed the creation of a naval academy in 1845 only because of the demands for education in steam engineering. No real admiralty existed, nor a senior officer like Britain's First Sea Lord, the Admiral of France, or even the United States Army's General-in-Chief. Though extremely busy, the small United States Navy was reduced to minor proportions during the Presidency of General Jackson in the 1830s. Lacking a long naval tradition, the Americans were fully prepared to accept innovations in propulsion and armament. With no real need for a blue-water navy to command the sea, American naval strategy in the early nineteenth century was subordinated to the needs of the Army.

The continental thrust westward, accompanied by a small frontier and militia army, depended logistically on increasingly improved roads, canals (especially the Erie in 1825), rivers and coastal traffic. Especially important was the river steamboat, which dominated internal transportation in the United States during the 1830s and 1840s until challenged by the railroad in the 1850s. The steamer, in fact, hastened the shift of American society westward, for the Mississippi River came to rival the seaports of the Atlantic and Gulf coasts. Cotton from the South moved down the Tennessee and Cumberland rivers to join the Ohio and Mississippi; manufactured goods from the East and the wheat of the Midwest followed the Ohio to the great river thence to New Orleans. Similarly, coastal shipping rounded Key West to supply the Gulf coast as far as Mexico. The Mississippi, then, became the natural highway for the penetration into Louisiana territory; thus the Army, supplied by its own river transports, moved up the tributaries called the Red, Arkansas, Missouri, Platte and Des Moines to build a line of riverbank frontier forts protecting settlers against hostile Indians. The work of the United States Army was thus peacekeeping by pacification, linked with the East by its own system of riverborne logistics. But when mobility was required along the coasts, especially in Florida, Texas and California, the Navy joined in this task. By this rather crude and expedient military strategy, the United States fashioned its continental empire during the nineteenth century. Small wonder, then, that the American people had minimal interest in an oceanic strategy or fleet.

The United States Navy therefore developed in the nineteenth century (in addition to its adherence to coast defense and *guerre de course*) a strategy and doctrine of inshore warfare. Since this evolution was discontinuous—dating back to colonial and Revolutionary times—it was never actually formalized. This was perhaps due to the unconventional and unglamorous nature of inshore fighting, and to American disinterest in formal military doctrines. Nevertheless, along the coasts, rivers and marshes, the Navy joined the Army in combined operations, some amphibious, some dealing with pacification and counter-guerrilla operations, others in blockade and bombardment, and occasional naval battles with fleets of enemy inshore craft. The principal events of this half-century of inshore naval operations between the 1820s and the 1870s were the rivalries with Britain on the Oregon coast and with Mexico on the Gulf and California coasts, the Second Seminole War, the Mexican War and the Civil War.

Though the Army was largely responsible for carrying out the wanton pacification of the native Indians as part of the inexorable westward expansion, the Navy became involved early in the Second Seminole War. When the Florida Seminoles rejected the general removal of Eastern Indians to the trans-Mississippi West by the Army, a virtual guerrilla war developed across most of Florida. Shortly after hostilities began late in 1835, the West Indies Squadron based at Pensacola began to provide support to the Army's operations around Tampa Bay. Early in 1836 Navy vessels cruised the west coast of the Florida peninsula between Tampa and Key West to blockade and interrupt Seminole movements by water as part of the strategy of the senior Army commander, Major General Winfield Scott. The naval aspects of this campaign proved fruitless, for the Seminoles were largely self-sufficient save for arms which could be spirited in from Spanish Cuba aboard small coasters. As the Seminoles moved southward into the Everglades, naval brigades composed largely of Marines made landings on the coast. In order to force all the Indians southward where they could be isolated, naval forces based at St. Augustine joined the Army for the campaign late in 1837. These combined operations brought on much fighting but no clear result, even after Colonel Zachary Taylor's forces crushed the main Seminole force in pitched battle at Lake Okeechobee on Christmas Day. Taylor succeeded to command in Florida and even employed his own naval forces, which hampered Army-Navy cooperation, but pointed up the need for a separate special inshore force to operate on the coasts, rivers and lakes of the Everglades region. In 1839 such a force was organized: the "Mosquito Fleet" (named for a lagoon), comprised of schooners, barges, flat-bottomed boats and canoes under Lieutenant John T. McLaughlin of the Navy. Beginning in the spring of 1840, this fleet of sailors, soldiers and Marines began offensive water operations into the Everglades, culminating in a major expedition in the autumn of 1841. As the last Seminole defenders retreated, McLaughlin's Mosquito Fleet pursued them relentlessly during the first half of 1842 until major resistance ended. Since all the Indians did not submit, total pacification was not completed until 1858. But the Navy had made a major contribution—however makeshift—toward winning the Indian wars.

Just as American settlers drove the Indians from their native soil, simultaneously they penetrated into northern Mexico and attempted to wrest it from the new Latin American country; in the summer of 1835 these Texans revolted and the following March proclaimed their independence. The active fighting of 1835–36 had important naval aspects, for both Texans and Mexicans depended logistically on the neutral port of New Orleans, and the American West Indies Squadron had to insure its country's neutrality. Under the dictatorial presidency of General Santa Anna, who personally led the invasion of Texas, the Mexican navy had virtually ceased to exist, so that the four schooners purchased in the United States to comprise the Texas navy had little opposition in their operations against Santa Anna's waterborne logistics. Unfortunately, they also captured American and British vessels, raising the charge of piracy. In April 1836 the Texas army defeated and captured Santa Anna in the San Jacinto campaign, followed in the summer by a Texas naval blockade of Matamoros and the mouth of the Rio Grande. One year later, three brigs and two schooners of the revitalized Mexican navy blockaded Galveston, captured one of the Texas schooners, and were soon involved with American vessels. Taking advantage of the American preoccupation with the Seminole War and of political unrest in the Mexican province of Yucatan, in 1837 two Texas warships raided that coast and continued their policy of open *guerre de course* in the Gulf of Mexico before the small squadron was run aground off Texas by the Mexicans late in the summer. Stripped of her small fleet, Texas was about to be blockaded again by Mexico when the French suddenly occupied Vera Cruz in 1838–39. The Texans took advantage of this respite to build six sailing warships at Baltimore and to purchase a paddlewheel steamer, all under a dynamic former American naval officer, Commodore Edwin W. Moore. This force then operated with much success along the Mexican coast and rivers, supported by rebellious Yucatan, from late 1840 to early 1842. During these years, Texas, though bargaining for American statehood, became a sovereign power as the United

States, Britain, France and the Netherlands recognized the Republic.

Mexico steadfastly refused to recognize Texan independence, and in 1842 began to reinforce its navy, quickly hastening a showdown. When it seized several Yucatan warships and purchased two British-manned steamers, the Mexican Navy grew, while an unsympathetic administration under President Sam Houston allowed the naval force of Texas to decline. Nevertheless, Commodore Moore sortied from New Orleans with a 20-gun sloop and 16-gun brig to besieged Campeche, where he joined six Yucatan gunboats late in April 1843. He was seeking an engagement with the Mexican fleet of six vessels, half of which were armed with Paixhans guns, plus auxiliary vessels. Skirmishing with the Mexicans, the Texas squadron entered Campeche, thus raising the siege. The new Mexican squadron commander, Captain Tomás Marín, sent away all but his three Paixhans-armed vessels, filled his depleted crews with soldiers, and daily prepared for battle with Moore's two largest warships. The battle of Campeche finally occurred on May 16, 1843, an erratic gunnery duel in which the Texas sail craft drove off the Mexican steamers, leading eventually to the total abandonment of the siege of Campeche. President Houston, at odds with Moore, branded his cruise an act of piracy and dismissed him from the Navy. The United States then mediated a truce, while Britain and France were committing themselves to the independence of Texas. Fearful of British designs in North America, the American Congress early in 1845 annexed Texas to the Union. Thus another small navy had played its part in the balance of power in the Western Hemisphere, weakening Mexico and contributing to the tension between the continental United States and maritime Great Britain.

Along with the Great Lakes and Texas quarrels, Anglo-American rivalry grew on the Pacific coast of North America from the War of 1812. Other European powers involved initially were Spain and Russia, but neither maintained its claims vigorously. The Russians controlled Alaska and established trading posts as far south as northern California, and in 1821 the tsar tried to exclude foreign vessels from coastal fishing, whaling and sealing to one hundred miles out from the Alaskan shore. Protests from Britain and the United States, plus the proclaimed doctrine of Monroe and Canning, helped induce Russia to make treaties with both countries in 1824–25 granting reciprocal trade and setting Russian territorial claims at the parallel of 54° 40′, the southern tip of Alaska. Meanwhile, Spain in the treaty of 1819 over the Florida question had limited its northern imperial border at the 42nd parallel in Upper California, only to lose all its coastal territory to independent Mexico three years later. Between Russian Alaska and Mexican California lay the Oregon country, jointly claimed by Britain and the United States but who in 1818 had agreed to coexist there. British maritime penetration into the Eastern Pacific paralleled their drive into the Western Pacific and led to the creation of a separate Eastern Pacific station at Valparaiso in 1837, although the major port for all maritime carriers and under British protection had become Honolulu in the Hawaiian (Sandwich) Islands. The gradual settlement of traders and farmers from various nations in Eastern Pacific lands, plus occasional visits by warships, did not reach crisis proportions until the early 1840s when accelerated American expansion westward was accompanied by the French thrust into the South Sea Islands.

The shifting of naval forces in the Eastern Pacific to achieve a re-adjusted balance of power led first to fears of war, then to treaty settlement. In 1840–41 the Canadian boundary dispute, the issue of Texas and disagreements over suppression of the slave traffic combined with the Oregon question to lead to a naval arms buildup in the United States. The United States created (largely from West Indies units) a Home Squadron in 1841 to defend the American coast in event of war and placed its ships in the Pacific on alert. The American commodore there, fearful of a British naval annexation of Mexican Upper California, in 1842 seized the port of Monterey, then withdrew. The next year a British warship captain, apprehensive over the French naval expedition to annex parts of Oceania, proclaimed the British annexation of Hawaii, but was not supported by his government. By that time, American pioneers were pouring into the disputed Oregon country over the Oregon Trail. In 1845 six British warships operated in the coastal waters of Puget Sound and the Columbia River. The Canadian boundary had been settled at the 49th parallel in 1842, and the United States annexed Texas early in 1845, but war appeared imminent over Oregon. Finally, in 1846, the two English-speaking powers agreed to divide the Oregon country, extending the 49th parallel boundary from the Rockies to Puget Sound. Vancouver Island became a British colony in 1849 and was joined to the mainland as British Columbia in 1866, but separate from the provinces of Canada east of the Rockies. Also in 1846 Britain and France made a treaty honoring the independence of Hawaii, thus easing tensions there. Throughout these events, Russia gradually began to roll back its settlements in North America, while Mexico became ever more helpless to administer its distant subjects in Upper California who had revolted successfully early in 1845.

By the beginning of 1846, with Oregon and Texas being brought under the American flag, relations between the United States and Mexico were steadily deteriorating. American settlers had led the Texas revolt and were now claiming the territory beyond the Nueces River as Texan, a claim not recognized by the Mexican government. The

Texans, now as Americans, wanted the vast territory to the Rio Grande, running northwest to tiny El Paso and thence north to Santa Fe, terminus of the overland Santa Fe Trail from Missouri. In addition, American settlers had gained the Oregon lands on the Upper California border and others were playing no small part in the California revolt. More internal discord in Yucatan and along the Gulf of California further weakened the central government at Mexico City. So the Mexican army remained the chief force for internal order and home defense, while the navy consisted of a small force of two steam frigates and three brigs plus light sail craft that had suffered from the attacks of the Texans. The United States, by contrast, was generally unified, save for the slavery issue dividing North and South, its people imperial-minded with a small but seasoned frontier army and growing sail-and-steam frigate and coastal navy clearly superior to that of Mexico. With two great coastlines to defend from the Rio Grande to Yucatan and from above San Francisco to below Acapulco, plus a vast continental territory, Mexico was in no position to wage war on the United States.

THE MEXICAN WAR

Nevertheless, the Mexican War broke out in the spring of 1846 and quickly assumed the proportions of a land war supported by America's inshore fleet. The armies battled around the mouth of the Rio Grande throughout the second half of 1846, while the American Home Squadron under Commodore David Conner instituted a blockade of the Mexican Gulf coast, operating from distant Pensacola to close the major port of Vera Cruz. In order to achieve an effective blockade, the United States Navy needed command of the sea, which it achieved by default at the opening of hostilities. The Mexican government in the spring of 1846 had decided to fight without a navy, allowing its two steam frigates to be repossessed by their British owners. The rest of the fleet was virtually retired: the three brigs and six schooners in the shallow Alvarado River forty miles southeast of Vera Cruz, and three new schooners at Tampico, some 200 miles north of Vera Cruz. Mexico did make a major effort to enlist privateers by issuing letters of marque throughout the world, using the unprecedented scheme of naturalizing the crews of any Mexican privateer. This thin disguise of Mexico's maritime weakness combined with America's maritime prestige and world opinion against privateering and its practical abuses to defeat this scheme. The one privateer that sailed, a felucca from Algeria, made a single capture, only to be hunted down by the Spanish navy early in 1847. Thus Mexico's feeble naval policy embodied coast defense with fortifications and encouraging—with some success—blockade runners to help supply the army in the field.

American naval efforts therefore aimed at blockade and supporting the invasion of Mexico. The only real difficulty experienced lay in natural hazards of the Gulf: intensely hot weather which helped breed tropical diseases, prostration and dysentery and compounded the difficulties of obtaining and keeping adequate food and water. Pensacola lay one month away by round trip, while sudden tropical storms—"northers"—hit ships on blockade station with great ferocity. Lacking forward bases, therefore, the Home Squadron needed to use the anchorage of Anton Lizardo below Vera Cruz and had to seize coastal points in order to provide rest and provisions. The latter stratagem tended to backfire, however, for the shoreline brought the crews into direct contact with yellow fever and malaria. However, the western coasts of Upper and Lower California did not offer such hazards, and the excellent anchorages there not only provided numerous advanced bases but acted as the key to operations in northern Mexico. By contrast, operations on the Gulf coast—save for Yucatan, which elected to stay out of the war—were but the prelude to an overland campaign to capture Mexico City, deep in the interior, and end the war.

North to south, the Gulf ports that the U.S. Navy blockaded were Matamoros, Soto la Marina, Tampico, Tuxpan, Vera Cruz, Alvarado and Tabasco—all of which lay up rivers or behind sandbars that could be negotiated only by shallow-draft steamers. As such steam schooner gunboats were being purchased and/or constructed and deployed, the blockade continued apace. Matamoros, being on the Rio Grande, was easily occupied early in the war by General Taylor's forces, while Soto la Marina was too far from the major objectives to warrant seizure. Tampico resisted a seaborne expedition in June 1846, as did Alvarado in August, Conner trying to destroy the Mexican squadron there, but in vain. The Mexicans hastily strengthened their coastal defenses at Alvarado and placed them with their small squadron under the overall command of Commodore Marín, so that when Conner made a second attempt on the port in October he was again repulsed. Commodore Matthew C. Perry now reported as pending relief for Conner, who immediately sent him to direct the capture of Tabasco with its Mexican shipping. Late in October, Perry's force took Frontera at the mouth of the Tabasco River and then drove upriver to Tabasco where after some stiff resistance the Mexican squadron fell with the town. Perry then withdrew, leaving two vessels on blockade station; of the various craft taken, a steamer and a schooner were converted to gunboats and incorporated into the Home Squadron. Then, early in November, Conner and Perry led an expedition which took Tampico and its three new gunboats, all of which were transferred into the blockading fleet. The Americans raided up the Pánuco River as far as Pánuco, then ferried some of Taylor's troops down the coast from the Rio Grande to garrison Tampico, which became a forward staging base. In December, when Yucatan briefly threatened to enter the war, Perry occupied the tiny port of Carmen and temporarily extended the blockade to include Yucatan. Awaiting more steamers and plagued by erratic weather, the Home Squadron ended 1846 in general control of the Gulf coast and awaiting the assault on Vera Cruz.

The port of Vera Cruz held the strategic key to the Mexican coast and the approaches to Mexico City; thus its investment became the major naval campaign of the war. General Winfield Scott commanded the Army forces, which included Army transports and Army-built special assault boats, and worked in close harmony with the Navy in planning and executing the landing. The expeditionary force of 12,000 men gathered at Tampico, were combat-loaded at nearby Lobos Island early in 1847, and rendezvoused with the Home Squadron at Anton Lizardo. On March 9 the troops transferred from their transports to the men-of-war, then disembarked into their "surf boats" near Sacrificios Island in the afternoon. Bypassing the castle of San Juan de Ulua, which the heavy ships took under fire, the assault forces landed in successive waves on an undefended beach below Vera Cruz late in the day. The fleet gave them close-in fire support while they established a perimeter on the beach. Next day the sturdy surf boats brought artillery ashore and even towed swimming horses so that the land-sea siege of Vera Cruz could begin. Perry now relieved Conner in command of the fleet and sent heavy naval guns ashore. Despite a sudden norther which wrecked twenty-six transports on the beach, the siege held until both the town and the castle surrendered two weeks later. Scott then sent a column overland to take Alvarado, the Navy under Perry supporting from the sea; the town was easily taken early in April, whereupon the Mexicans scuttled the immobile remnant of their navy in the river. In mid-month Perry's steamers towed his gunboats up the Tuxpan River for the successful investment of that port. Taking everything of military value, Perry then withdrew everything but his blockading vessels. Secure with his coastal base around Vera Cruz, General Scott led his army inland to face Santa Anna and the Mexican army defending Mexico City.

Meanwhile, sparse American ground and naval forces had been wresting northern Mexico from their enemies, which included some unsympathetic Californians. Upon the outbreak of war, the Pacific Squadron had in July 1846 occupied San Francisco and Monterey, which they then strengthened. The new squadron commander, Commodore Robert F. Stockton, ferried the pro-American rebel forces under John C. Frémont to San Diego to operate against the Mexicans between that place and Los Angeles. With naval brigades of sailors and marines, Stockton then occupied Santa Barbara and San Pedro, giving the Americans possession of Upper California's five excellent anchorages, and took Los Angeles as well. In September, however, the Californians at Los Angeles revolted and forced the Americans to reembark. Having great mobility to shift his forces by sea, Stockton spent the next several weeks trying to recover Los Angeles, using San Diego as his prime base. Meanwhile, a small Army expedition under Brigadier General Stephen W. Kearny advanced westward from Missouri, took Santa Fe before pressing on to join forces with Stockton at San Diego, doing so in December after a brief skirmish with Mexican forces. Stockton and Kearny then led a combined Army-Navy expedition of some 600 men overland from San Diego to retake Los Angeles. In January 1847 they accomplished their mission by defeating the Mexicans at the battles of San Gabriel and La Mesa and then accepting the surrender of all Upper California. American forces could then redeploy to the Gulf of California, where two sloops-of-war had been operating against Mexican ports and shipping since late August. Especially successful were succeeding blockades of La Paz, Guaymas and Mazatlán by the vessel under Commander Samuel F. Du Pont. Save for the seizure and occupation of La Paz in April, however, the blockade of the Gulf was difficult to enforce, due to the long major supply route around the Horn to the East coast of the United States.

With General Scott's army fighting its way into Mexico City, the war finally swung to American victory during the spring and summer of 1847. On the Gulf coast, Commodore Perry operated eastward along the coast as far as Carmen in May, followed the next month by an expedition upriver from Frontera which used naval gunfire and a naval brigade to fight its way again to Tabasco, only to evacuate it after yellow fever struck. Blockade duty remained difficult because of the weather and disease, while garrisons ashore were plagued by uncoordinated guerrilla attacks. Nevertheless, Perry maintained the blockade for many more months and even managed to supply the neutral Yucatan government with arms to put down a large-scale Indian uprising. Simultaneously, after a hard campaign, in September 1847 Scott's army captured Mexico City, and peace negotiations were begun. On the West coast, the American naval blockade was extended, using La Paz as the forward base. The Pacific Squadron bombarded and attacked several small coastal points, neutralized Guaymas in October, took and occupied Mazatlán in November, and repulsed a Mexican counterattack in Lower California during the winter of 1847–48. Sealed off from the outside, with only Acapulco still open, its capital city and major settlements occupied, its main army defeated and navy destroyed, Mexico had no choice but to agree to American demands. In February 1848 Mexico ceded all her territory north of the Rio Grande and Gila rivers, including Upper California, to the United States.

The American Empire, fashioned on the decay of the maritime empires of Great Britain (1780s), France (1801), Spain (1819—and, indirectly thereafter, Mexico) and to a lesser extent Russia (1824–67), was purely continental in character. The nationalistic expansionism of the young Republic achieved relentless proportions in the early nineteenth century, having no pity on hapless native Indians or helpless Mexico, from which it extracted by barter an additional parcel of territory south of the Gila River in 1853 to fix finally the present borders of the continental United States. The discovery of gold in California in 1848 hastened the thrust of settlers—and the necessary network of Army frontier forts to protect them—across the continent. The Army reverted to a mere peace-keeping function, still utilizing the rivers for logistics and some transporting, but having to break away to trails, desert and mountains where the rivers ended. The coming of the railroad on a large scale in the 1850s and climaxed by the first transcontinental rail line in 1869 hastened the settlement and pacification of the great Western plains. The Navy also declined after the Mexican War until reforms toward steam began in 1853. But it remained essentially an inshore force committed also to police work: hunting slave-traders, punishing unfriendly Chinese during the Arrow War, and even lending some assistance to the Army as in January 1856 when a sloop of war in Puget Sound used its cannon and a landing party to repel an Indian attack on the coastal settlement there. Secure within its vast borders, the United States had little to fear from its neighbor below the Rio Grande which was convulsed in civil war in the late 1850s, although its neighbor above the Great Lakes and 49th parallel remained troublesome.

The balance of power in the Western Hemisphere continued to rest upon the naval supremacy which underpinned the *Pax Britannica* and the Monroe Doctrine. During the Crimean War (1854–56), an Anglo-French squadron operated against the Russians occasionally from San Francisco as well as Hawaii and Vancouver, and another Anglo-American boundary dispute—over the San Juan Islands in Puget Sound—in 1859 led to the establishment of a British naval base at Esquimalt on the Sound. The Royal Navy, which also had to help pacify British Columbia where gold was discovered during the 1850s, had good reason to fear American expansionism. But British naval supremacy in the Pacific was growing, for in 1859 the Australasian Station was officially established, and in 1862 Pacific squadron headquarters was moved from Valparaiso to Esquimalt. The British were also interested, naturally enough, in constructing a canal across Central America either at Nicaragua or Panama, thus linking up their merchant fleets and naval forces. The United States had similar ideas, and in the late 1840s both countries infiltrated the isthmian regions, the British obtaining rights to the east coast Nicaraguan port of Greytown. As tension mounted, the diplomats sought a compromise and agreed finally in 1850 to share in the eventual construction of—but never to fortify—an isthmian canal. It should be noted that in these tense years 1848 to 1851 the British commander-in-chief in North America and the West Indies Station was none other than Admiral Lord Cochrane, veteran of the Aix Roads operation (1809) and former celebrated leader of the Chilean, Brazilian and Greek navies who certainly inherited the mantle of Nelson in the era of *Pax Britannica*. Yet, apparent American intentions of annexing portions of the Caribbean seemed thinly disguised when a "filibustering" expedition mounted in the United States failed to "liberate" Cuba in 1849–51; an American warship bombarded restive Greytown in 1854; a Spanish-American crisis arose over Cuba the same year; and unsuccessful American filibusterers attempted to conquer Nicaragua in 1856–57 and then Honduras in 1860. Mutual Anglo-American suspicions continued, although in 1859–60 Britain withdrew formally from her holds on Honduran and Nicaraguan territory, and both countries increased their efforts against the illicit slave trade.

American maritime and naval policies in the 1850s generally avoided identification with those of Britain and therefore followed a different course. The gold rush to California stimulated the American fast clipper ship trade from 1848 and helped the American merchant marine to reach its greatest peak—5,151,000 tons to Britain's 5,251,000—in 1855. But then, quite suddenly, the American foreign carrying trade fell off mostly for reasons directly attributable to the British competition. The British government, unlike the American, heavily subsidized private shipbuilders who now began converting to steam propulsion —a change their Yankee counterparts could ill afford. Furthermore, Lloyd's insurance practices discriminated in favor of British shippers, while the railroad began to take some of the American internal trade from coastal vessels. Save for a brief flurry during the Crimean War, then, American maritime trade began a steady decline, crippled severely by a major financial panic in 1857. Regarding merchant craft in time of war, the United States had long depended on privateers as a naval weapon in place of a standing fleet, and thus played no part in the 1856 Declaration of Paris which outlawed privateers. When British warships began searching American-flag slavers in 1858, Southern Congressmen demanded more steam gunboats to defend the Gulf coast against Britain; the unusual interest of the agricultural South in the Navy was due to the desire to protect slavers and was led by Florida Senator Stephen R. Mallory, Chairman of the Senate Naval Affairs Committee. The South thus reflected the attitude of the other sections of the country for a small, defensive inshore navy. The Navy continued to reject any blue-water pretensions and was still slow to adopt steam power fully. Thus when the Home Squadron concentrated off Sacrificios and Vera Cruz to press certain demands on Mexico in the autumn of 1860, it was a hodgepodge of the old and new: one steam and one sail frigate, two steam and three sailing sloops, and four steamers. Then, to further weaken the American position at sea, the Union began to disintegrate politically, and in January 1861 the Home Squadron itself dissolved. America's brief attempt to challenge Britain's maritime superiority in the 1850s thus deteriorated.

12
The American Civil War, 1861–1870

*Nor must Uncle Sam's web feet be forgotten. At all the watery margins
they have been present. Not only on the deep sea, the broad bay, the
rapid river, but also up the narrow muddy bayou, and wherever the
ground was a little damp, they have been and made their tracks.*

—ABRAHAM LINCOLN, 1863

NAVAL STRATEGY, NORTH AND SOUTH

The American Civil War proved to be a watershed event in the history of navies and of warfare, not to mention its sweeping impact on industrialization, human rights and internal American politics. The secession of eleven Southern states from the Union between December 1860 and June 1861 and their formation into a new nation, the Confederate States of America, reflected the deep divisions between the sections that were not only political and cultural but also economic and imperial. The United States—now including the North, West, and Pacific coast—had aggressively extended both American empire across the continent and economic wealth across the oceans of the world. Northern capital, reinforced by industrial manufacture, maritime shipping, and now the railroads, had arisen to exert control over Southern cotton. As this wealth grew, the South became ever more isolated and conservative, dependent upon the will of Northern financiers who by 1860 threatened absolutely to dominate American politics. Northern men compromised with the South by allowing Negro slavery to survive and to expand into some newly acquired territories, but by 1860 Northern sentiment had so swung against that antiquated institution that Kansas territory, especially, was embroiled in war over it and the largely Northern-officered Navy was finally enforcing the ban on Southern slave imports. In order to preserve its institutions, of which slavery was the heart and symbol, the South chose to form its own country even to the point of war. The remaining states of the Union adhered to their federal government and under the leadership of President Abraham Lincoln acted to restore the seceded states to the Union. The obvious result was war, at first a fairly limited one, but as the fighting continued Lincoln's government realized that success required the utter destruction of the Southern socioeconomic system. This conflict, then, heralded the coming of industrialized total war—the complete and unconditional defeat of an enemy with the first new weapons capable of waging such a fight upon the entire enemy citizenry.

From the beginning, the Union took the offensive, the Confederacy the defensive, the latter seeking only to gain foreign recognition of its independence with the resulting foreign aid necessary for victory. Believing that Great Britain and to a lesser extent France were utterly dependent upon its cotton, the South realistically counted upon British support and possible intervention. Certainly, the Palmerston government would welcome this opportunity to weaken further the already-hurting American carrying trade, while France under Napoleon III stood eager to overturn the Monroe Doctrine and reassert the French imperial presence in the Western Hemisphere. Thus Southern armies had only to protect their frontiers and coasts from Northern invasion and prove the political stability of the Confederate government so that the powers would rally to their side. Northern strategy was consequently placed in the difficult position of defeating the Southern armies, blockading the Southern coast and cotton exports and thus discrediting the rebellious states—all the while observing international law and not antagonizing Britain and France. The difficulty of this task became evident in the first year of the war when the North raised tariffs that hurt Britain, tried to establish a blockade, and so flagrantly violated international law that Britain came to the brink of joining the war against the United States—a distinct possibility, since the British government and textile manufacturers clearly sympathized with the South.

A curious similarity between the Union and Confederacy lay in their common naval tradition, though the North had a clear superiority from the beginning because of its large industrial and maritime complex and existing fleet. In both nations, the army predominated, especially in the South with its planter-aristocracy, while the navies drew upon the same inshore-coast defense-*guerre de course* mentality that dated from the Revolution. Both governments continued the strong civilian control over the navies, and were fortunate enough to have experienced Secretaries, in Connecticut politician Gideon Welles who had administered the clothing and feeding of the Navy during the Mexican War and former Senator Mallory of Florida whose association with naval matters included not only Congressional committee work but inshore service in the Second Seminole War. Neither side had admirals at first, preferring instead the old rank of commodore and the higher but more obscure title of "flag officer." So there was no senior naval officer in either the United States or Confederate States navies and no formal naval staffs to advise each Secretary on naval strategy and policy. Indeed, in both navies, though many officers had wide experience, their initial employment depended largely on enlightened generals with some experience in combined operations; Confederates Robert E. Lee and P. G. T. Beauregard had served on General Scott's staff during the landings at Vera Cruz, where the Northerner George B. McClellan began a career which later included observing the Anglo-French attacks on Sevastopol.

Where the Union and Confederacy differed was in attitudes toward maritime warfare. The North had a thalassocratic tradition and physical plant—forty-two commissioned warships, eight naval shipyards and most of the officers and skilled ratings upon which to mobilize a bluewater navy. The South had no such heritage or plant: two shipyards, seventeen small state vessels and some 200 experienced officers. It also had vital raw materials like wood, iron and coal and skilled carpenters and mechanics, but the Army indiscriminately conscripted the latter and commandeered the South's small rail network which was needed to concentrate building materials at the shipyards. Therein lay the major strategic difference between the belligerents. Effective industrial and manpower mobilization would be key elements in modern total war, and for this the North was eminently more suited. Further, such strategic mobilization and then direction depended upon centralized control, which under Lincoln's firm hand the Federal Union enjoyed, whereas the Confederacy remained true to its name: a number of sovereign states reluctant to centralize. The Confederate government was headed by former U. S. Army officer and Secretary of War Jefferson Davis, who had virtually no experience or interest in naval matters. The Southern naval effort was therefore doomed to makeshift expedients and reliance upon whatever Britain and France might provide.

The rival strategies became apparent from the month that hostilities began, April 1861. The Union would have to command the seas; the Confederacy would have to defend its coastlines. That month General Beauregard bombarded into submission Fort Sumter in Charleston harbor, while seceding Virginia seized the great naval arsenal at Norfolk. This prize plus others gave the South vast numbers of new Dahlgren guns and older-style cannon so vital for coast defense. Simultaneously, Lincoln declared a blockade of the Southern coast, and Navy vessels brought volunteer troops to Washington via Annapolis when Maryland threatened to secede, while a flotilla gathered in the Potomac River to protect the appproaches to the capital. In May and throughout the summer of 1861 both sides fumbled toward their respective objectives. For the North, a temporary strategy board headed by Captain Samuel F. Du Pont of the Navy and General-in-Chief of the Army Winfield Scott independently concluded that the blockade should be implemented by a cordon of advanced bases along the coast (as during the Mexican War) for the coaling of steamers and logistical support in general; the board advocated the seizure of New Orleans to cut off traffic down the Mississippi, while Scott would make that river into a third coast, to be occupied by Union garrisons. Secretary Welles opposed this scheme, which gained the popular label of the Anaconda, since he envisioned the struggle as a mere insurgency and not a total war aimed at strangling the South. By the same token, public opinion in the South favored the total defense of the long 2700-mile coastline from Hampton Roads to the Rio Grande, but Secretary Mallory could only turn to local commanders and state resources for this impossible task. The Confederate government issued letters of marque, and a number of privateers put to sea to claim seventeen Yankee merchantmen before withdrawing in the face of the Union navy by the autumn. Privateering had been so discredited as semi-piracy that Lincoln refused to utilize it, and by 1863 it passed out of existence as a tool of the world's navies. Mallory did, however, launch two ambitious projects: the construction of fast steam frigates in foreign shipyards for commerce raiding, and the conversion of inshore and other craft into ironclad armored gunboats—both projects eventually gaining considerable results. But time was on the side of the North.

Following the repulse of a Union army at the melee known as the first battle of Bull Run in northern Virginia in July 1861, both sides resigned themselves to a long war and started implementing their strategies. Despite Welles's reluctance, the Northern blockade as envisioned by Scott was gradually implemented, though Scott himself at the advanced age of seventy-five (and a general officer since 1814!) retired. As the Union navy took time to construct and convert warships for blockade duty, it received unexpected help from the Confederate government, which placed an embargo on its own cotton exports. Hoping to force British recognition, this diplomatic device instead nearly crippled the Southern economy. Welles's unwillingness to mobilize naval forces on the Western rivers led the Army, under the authorization of General McClellan, to raise its own Western fleet of ironclad and wooden gunboats for later offensive operations. In the East, however, Welles was persuaded by favorable circumstances to begin the cordon encirclement of Confederate seaports. Despite the loss of Norfolk, the Union held nearby Fortress Monroe, easily recaptured Newport

News, and from Monroe launched combined amphibious operations which captured Hatteras Inlet, North Carolina, and Port Royal, South Carolina, in August and November, thereby completely disrupting Confederate coastal traffic as far south as Savannah and giving the Union two key blockading bases. These captures suddenly exposed the weakness of Confederate coast defense and led Secretary Mallory to initiate the outright construction of wooden gunboats for harbor defenses, including 100 small Jeffersonian-type gunboats advocated by Commander Matthew F. Maury.

Such losses also hastened a new overall coast defense strategy being implemented by General Robert E. Lee, commanding in South Carolina, Georgia and East Florida. Lee decided to draw back Confederate troops away from the range of Union naval guns, to abandon indefensible positions along the coast such as islands, and to concentrate available forces inland for employment only at crucial areas wherever the enemy actually landed. Although this stratagem could not stop Union landings, Lee hoped to draw his adversary inland away from naval fire support and there to defeat such expeditionary forces. Though this was a more realistic policy than total coast defense, Lee missed the strategic point that Union coastal operations were not designed—indeed, were not strong enough—to invade the South from the coast, but were merely intended to establish advanced base enclaves for the blockading fleet. So additional places fell to Union forces along the North Carolina and Florida coasts in February, March and April 1862, and in the latter month a major amphibious attack took Fort Pulaski, Georgia, commanding the seaward approaches to Savannah. Thus, unwittingly, Confederate strategic decisions immensely aided the Union blockading effort early in the war.

The success or failure of the blockade depended upon the reactions of Britain, traditional arbiter in international maritime law. The British government, though quick to declare its neutrality, soon found that such a statement did not solve all the legal implications of Lincoln's blockade. To be legal, a blockade had to be effective, and investigating British warships often found Southern ports to be clear of Yankee blockaders. Nevertheless, the British carefully avoided setting any precedents by rashly challenging the blockade, much to the continued displeasure of Confederate diplomats. Then, in November 1861, Captain Charles Wilkes on blockade duty halted the British mail packet *Trent* off Cuba and forced two rebel diplomats on board to surrender. This blatant, unauthorized violation of British neutrality enraged Britain, and although Lincoln wisely repudiated the act and released his prisoners before the end of the year, the Royal Navy prepared for war. Troop reinforcements were hastened to Canada,

Bermuda and the British West Indies, while thirteen warships crossed the Pacific from the China station; these forces were in position for fighting by the spring of 1862. The British were also angry with Mexico, whose recent civil war had so ruined its financial situation that it refused to repay its European creditors. As a result, a joint Anglo-French-Spanish expeditionary force occupied Vera Cruz in December 1861—a violation of the Monroe Doctrine, though the United States was too busy elsewhere to act. Britain and Spain withdrew the following April, but Napoleon III—anxious to add Mexico to the French Empire—decided to remain, against the advice of his expeditionary commander, Admiral J. P. E. Jurien de la Gravière. France declared war on Mexico, blockaded her Gulf coast, increased the expeditionary force to 40,000 men, and began a rugged overland campaign to conquer the country. Hurt by the Confederate cotton embargo and dependent ultimately upon British sea power, France elected not to antagonize the United States beyond this breach of the Monroe Doctrine. But American relations with Britain and France remained strained throughout 1862.

British actions at sea during the Civil War carefully avoided the taking of sides, but did aid both Union and Confederacy considerably. For the North, and with Lincoln's full cooperation, the British moved to destroy the Atlantic slave trade once and for all. In 1862 an Anglo-American treaty allowed each nation to let warships search slavers flying the other's flag, and since the American African squadron withdrew to fight in the war the British could act alone to stop the slave trade. It did so with great dispatch, also choking off slaving to Cuba by 1865. But the North was uncooperative regarding neutral waters, which the warships of its North and South Atlantic and East and West Gulf Blockading squadrons continued to violate. Not only did the British build and outfit Confederate cruisers, especially the very successful *Alabama* commissioned under Captain Raphael Semmes off the Azores in August 1862, but British merchant steamers ran the blockade to and from British Bermuda and the Bahamas, the Danish West Indies (Virgin Islands) and Spanish Cuba; at least five captains of blockade runners were Royal Navy officers on leave. Their sleek sail-steamers could easily outrun the slower, fuel-conscious blockaders by making the short dash between Southern ports and neutral islands. In this manner, British ships aided the Confederacy, and British arms and goods supplied the Southern war effort. Northern warships therefore violated neutral waters to try to frustrate these practices; the West Gulf Squadron even blockaded the neutral Rio Grande River delta to discourage trade between Matamoros and Brownsville, Texas, while in the autumn of 1862 Commodore Wilkes led a "flying squadron" that virtually blockaded Bermuda and anchored at Nassau, contrary to the orders of local British authorities. Wilkes and other officers continued to seize British merchantmen, and one American warship in May 1863 fired onto the beach at British Eleuthera while engaging a blockade runner. Such illegal acts led to tangled legal cases, but the North got away with them because the Union navy commanded North American waters and because the British were ever sensitive about a possible future war in Europe in which the maritime United States would be the neutral. Thus pro-American precedents were being set by the British recognition of the Union blockade.

Also sensitive to protecting its own commerce, the industrial North insured the security of its trade lanes to Europe. In this respect, the Union was most successful. Realizing that the Confederacy could never have more than two or three commerce raiders active simultaneously around the world, the United States believed convoys to be unnecessary since scattered merchantmen would spread thin Confederate cruiser depredations. This doctrine proved correct, as the five major and several lesser cruisers sank but 261 merchant vessels totaling a mere 110,000 tons during the war. Only one convoy was regularly maintained: the Panama-to-East-coast run of California gold, and it was never attacked. Rebel attempts to outfit privateers in the Pacific never matured, and a Confederate army thrust toward California was repulsed by Union forces in New Mexico in the spring of 1862. Most neutral nations allowed vessels of both navies to use their ports, although Ottoman Turkey returned American favors by closing its ports to the few cruisers of the South. But while Northern wartime shipping remained generally protected, the American merchant marine was nearly destroyed. Its decline since 1855 was accelerated by the war. Lloyd's insurance rates for Yankee vessels soared because of the increased risk, while fear of rebel cruisers discouraged many New England shipowners from even putting to sea. The greatest loss was incurred, however, when these shippers transferred no less than 800,000 tons of Yankee bottoms to neutral foreign registry, including the English which afforded protection by naval power and low insurance. A slow recovery of Northern shipbuilding began as the panic subsided late in 1862, but the merchant marine would never regain its former strength. Still, the war effort continued to be maintained by shipping of all registries, and the Northern naval effort on the high seas concentrated almost totally on blockading the South.

INSHORE WARFARE, COASTS AND RIVERS

As the two nations mobilized their armies and strategies in the winter of 1861–62, the subtle influence of naval power appeared. Henceforth, all major Union armies in the field were named after rivers, while garrison forces in the Gulf of Mexico were titled the Army of the Gulf. The main force, the Army of the Potomac under General McClellan, would attempt to capture the Confederate capital at Richmond, Virginia, while the armies of the Mississippi, the Ohio, the Cumberland and the Tennessee under various commanders delineated the major areas of Union operations in the West. Whenever these armies won control of their namesake rivers, the South would be seriously humbled. In the East, McClellan planned to utilize his naval superiority by moving down the Chesapeake from the defenses of Washington, basing upon the sea at Fortress Monroe and driving up the James River and the so-called Virginia Peninsula to take Richmond. In the West, General U. S. Grant would depart by land and river from his base at Cairo, Illinois, to attack the forts controlling the Tennessee and Cumberland rivers below their northern junction with the Ohio and Mississippi rivers. A second force in the West would push south from Cairo toward Memphis, beginning to clear the Mississippi. The fact that the North early in the war could mount three separate offensives, plus coastal forays, demonstrates the advantages of attacking from the exterior position with superior numbers of men and amounts of equipment. The Confederacy, which named its main armies after territory, operated from the interior position but with insufficient manpower to meet each thrust, and was further hindered by a vast territory broken by the Appalachian Mountains and served by an inadequate rail network. Furthermore, the rivers in the Confederacy—the defense of which the Navy assumed absolutely no responsibility—favored not internal traffic but invasion from the North. So the simple charge of the Army of Northern Virginia under General Joseph E. Johnston and the Army of Mississippi under General A. S. Johnston was to defend the Tennessee-Virginia frontier from a Union advance by land and river.

McClellan's offensive, known as the Peninsular Campaign, was foiled by the caution and respect for Confederate coast defenses of McClellan himself. Having witnessed the first real ironclad operations in the Crimean War, he had a healthy respect for one of Mallory's new coastal ironclads, this one converted from the captured hull of the former Norfolk-based steam frigate *Merrimac* (now renamed *Virginia*). Late in February 1862 this vessel and five gunboats formed the James River Squadron under Captain Franklin Buchanan and then moved against the Union defenses of Newport News. Though the popularly known *Merrimac* was unsuited for operations beyond the sheltered Hampton Roads, McClellan and his naval commanders believed that the vessel threatened the entire Union blockade, let alone their planned advance on Richmond. McClellan preferred to await the arrival from New York of one of three experimental Union ironclads, the *Monitor,* before attempting to drive up the James. Then, on March 8, Buchanan sallied forth with the *Merrimac* to sink two wooden Union frigates in Hampton Roads. McClellan prepared to evacuate Newport News, but next day the *Monitor* arrived and engaged the *Merrimac.* This monumental first duel between ironclad warships ended in something of a draw, though the *Monitor's* performance saved the other wooden vessels present. But *Merrimac,* refusing entreaties to renew the action, still blocked the James. Thus, strategically, this greatly over-rated coast defense vessel by its very existence forced the Union army to make far-reaching changes. McClellan now moved his army by transport to Fortress Monroe, but had to abandon the James in favor of the York River on the north side of the peninsula, at best a swampy and thus inferior approach. Furthermore, the Union navy was so concerned about the *Merrimac* that it refused to transfer ships away from Hampton Roads to support and transport McClellan's army up the York. Without the swift mobility of water transport, McClellan's army bogged down in the mud before a small Confederate force at Yorktown, to which he then stupidly laid siege.

Confederate coast defense policies produced results. Early in March 1862, General Lee was relieved of command of the South Atlantic coast and ordered to Richmond to be President Davis' military adviser. His defense-in-depth strategy on the coast also enabled him to transfer many of those troops to reinforce Richmond. By April Lee had realized the line of McClellan's advance and ordered Johnston's army to shift from northern Virginia to the peninsula. He also sent a force under General T. J. "Stonewall" Jackson to demonstrate in the Shenandoah Valley, whereupon Lincoln withheld part of McClellan's army to defend Washington. In May, Johnston and the rebel army evacuated Yorktown and Norfolk in order to better defend Richmond, leaving the Confederate navy no choice but to blow up the deep-draft *Merrimac* which could not move up the shallow river. The lighter-draft *Monitor* and other Union gunboats then pressed up the James, only to be severely repulsed by shore batteries at Drewry's Bluff. By then, McClellan's army had gone up the York and was scattered in its adjacent swamplands when Johnston struck late in May. McClellan held his position, and Johnston himself was wounded and replaced by General Lee. The Navy ferried reinforcements from Fredericksburg via the Rappahannock River, Chesapeake and York to McClellan, while Jackson marched overland from the valley to reinforce Lee before Richmond. With the Army of Northern Virginia endangering his position on the York, McClellan decided to shift his base south to the James, where the Navy could now support him. Lee stood in

his way, so he had to fight—in the Seven Days' Battles—across the
peninsula in late June. He succeeded, but got no closer to Richmond.
The campaign then ended, a brilliant strategic scheme partially frustrated by one warship.

In the West, the Union army and naval forces enjoyed dramatic
successes over the thinly distributed Confederate forces. In February
1862 Grant and the gunboats of Flag Officer A. H. Foote bombarded
and captured Forts Henry on the Tennessee and Donelson on the
Cumberland, enabling the warships to raid as far south on the Tennessee as northern Alabama and also to press up the Cumberland to
capture Nashville, the key to Tennessee. General A. S. Johnston now
took advantage of the Confederate coast-defense-in-depth strategy to
call up the major garrison forces from Mobile, Pensacola and Galveston
on the Gulf for one massive counterattack on Grant's army. He struck
Grant by surprise at Shiloh on the west bank of the Tennessee early
in April only to be finally repulsed by Union reinforcements and gunboats; the Battle of Shiloh also cost Johnston his life. Simultaneously,
a combined Union Army-Navy force captured Island No. 10 on the
Mississippi in western Tennessee. These events severely weakened the
Confederate coast defenses of New Orleans, now dependent upon
coastal forts and a makeshift force of gunboats. Union forces had
occupied Ship Island off the delta of the Mississippi the previous December, and now, in April, the West Gulf Blockading Squadron under
Flag Officer David G. Farragut easily brushed aside rebel defenses
and took New Orleans. The remnant of the Confederate River Defense
Force then hastened north to inflict a surprise defeat on Union gunboats at Fort Pillow below Island No. 10 early in May. The Union
army rushed its own new Ram Fleet to augment the gunboats on the
Upper Mississippi; between them they destroyed the rebel squadron
at the naval battle of Memphis early in June before steaming down
river as far as Vicksburg, Mississippi. Farragut from New Orleans also
briefly reached that point, but retired below Port Hudson when the
Army could not support him. Without question, the capture of New
Orleans was the most important Union conquest of the war—strangling
Southern commerce on the river and along the Gulf coast.

These stunning Union victories on the Western rivers in mid-1862
had serious repercussions everywhere for the South. Encouraged by
the performance of the *Merrimac,* the Confederate Congress scrapped
its plans for Maury's wooden gunboats and voted funds for ironclads
and batteries for coastal and river defenses. Warship construction
within the Confederacy thus accelerated, some 150 new and converted craft being projected, with 22 armored and 5 wooden vessels
eventually being completed, along with a few conversions. That more

were not was due largely to the dispersal of makeshift shipbuilding facilities well inland on the rivers; also, the yards at New Orleans and Norfolk were lost, and in May Pensacola was abandoned to the blockading forces too. Secretary Mallory and local generals also began experiments with floating (mines) and spar torpedoes and submersibles (submarines, except that they never totally submerged). On its three coastlines, the South had yielded important points within the first eighteen months of the war. On the Atlantic coast, in addition to the Hatteras operations, Flag Officer Du Pont's fleet sank stone-laden hulks off Charleston and Savannah late in 1861, then went on in March 1862 to take the northern Florida ports (Jacksonville, St. Augustine, Amelia Island and Fernandina) and in April Fort Pulaski, Georgia. On the Gulf coast, New Orleans and Pensacola were taken in the spring, Galveston in October, and Farragut was only prevented by inactive superiors from seizing the coastal forts below Mobile. On the Mississippi, Grant was similarly frustrated by his superiors but by July had narrowed rebel control to the narrow strip of river between Vicksburg and Port Hudson. The Confederates could not even mount guerrilla attacks near occupied inland waters without facing strong Union countermeasures: the Army employed its own Ram Fleet and elite Mississippi Marine Brigade with specialized landing craft and floating logistics to help the Navy police the upper Mississippi, while gunboats and transports ferried Union forces on the Tennessee and Cumberland rivers to engage guerrillas. Losing so much territory, the South lost prestige abroad.

The Confederacy could hope for British recognition and intervention only if Lee could crush the Union armies in the East. By his experiences facing the Union navy on the Atlantic coast and in the James River, Lee realized he could not hope to win as long as he operated near the Chesapeake shore. As it was, water transport gave the Northern armies exceptional mobility not only between Washington on the Potomac and Fortress Monroe on the James but on other rivers such as the Susquehanna in Pennsylvania and Maryland and the Rappahannock in Virginia. So he strengthened the shore batteries and fortifications at Drewry's Bluff and around Richmond and Petersburg and moved inland. A new Union army marched southward from Washington while McClellan remained on the peninsula, and Lee with Jackson thoroughly defeated it at the second battle of Bull Run late in August 1862. Lee now resolved to invade the North but being careful to march well inland from Union gunboats, which would navigate up the Potomac to the falls only ten miles above Washington. Lee led the Army of Northern Virginia up the Shenandoah Valley, crossing the Potomac into Maryland early in September. McClellan, by his transports and overland marching, covered the national capital and stopped Lee's army at the Battle of Antietam at mid-month. Lacking reinforcements, Lee could do nothing but retire back into Virginia. When McClellan failed to pursue Lee vigorously, Lincoln relieved his naval-minded general from command. Coinciding with Southern military reverses elsewhere, the Antietam campaign sobered European interventionists. In addition, Lincoln used the occasion to emancipate the slaves, with which the British generally sympathized. The war thus became a moral crusade which the North would conclude only by annihilating the Confederate political and socioeconomic system.

From this time forward, the possibility of British intervention waned, along with any real hope of Confederate victory. Though affected by the blockade, Britain received enough cotton from surpluses, blockade runners, and new sources in Egypt and India to avoid recognizing the South. To be sure, English shipwrights continued to outfit rebel cruisers, but the British government became increasingly sensitive to these practices as Union victories mounted. Palmerston also realized that the Yankee privateering of 1812 could be repeated in a future war, or American-built cruisers outfitted for enemies of Britain. Even in 1863, during an Anglo-Russian crisis, the Russian Baltic Fleet visited New York and its Pacific Fleet went to San Francisco, moves which encouraged Britain to remain neutral and thus not tempt the Americans into seeking a combination with any of Britain's European rivals, now or in the future.

The Confederacy, however, taking advantage of the sluggish Union high command, tried to retrieve its fortunes during late 1862 and the first half of 1863. In the East, Lee soundly defeated two overland thrusts by the Army of the Potomac in northern Virginia—at Fredericksburg in December and Chancellorsville in May. He then retraced his 1862 steps up the Shenandoah Valley across the Potomac well inland from Union gunboats, heading apparently for Harrisburg, Pennsylvania. The Potomac River Flotilla moved up the Chesapeake Bay to the mouth of the Susquehanna; beyond lay the Schuylkill River and the Reading-to-Philadelphia rail line, both of which brought the blockading squadrons their weekly supply of 3000 tons of anthracite coal. However, the excellent Northern rail network was rushing troops from the North into southern Pennsylvania, while the Army of the Potomac also hastened there, intercepting and defeating Lee's army at the Battle of Gettysburg the first three days of July 1863. In the West, the Union slowly tried to cut off the trans-Mississippi states. The United States Navy finally created the rank of rear admiral and gave it to Farragut, who pressed on Port Hudson from New Orleans. Acting Rear Admiral David D. Porter (son of the former American-Mexican commodore) took command of the vessels on the upper river; cooperating with General Grant, Porter besieged Vicksburg by land and water. In July, both Vicksburg and Port Hudson fell, giving the Union absolute control of the Mississippi. On the coasts, the South sent its first admiral, Buchanan, to build up the naval defenses of Mobile and reassigned General Beauregard to command at Charleston. The Union, especially Secretary Welles, had a fetish about capturing Charleston, but when Rear Admiral Du Pont's monitors tried to reduce its defenses in April 1863, Beauregard's guns drove them off. Du Pont's relief, Admiral Dahlgren, fared no better during the summer, the defense of Charleston being the single triumph of Confederate coast defense. But the combined Union victories at Gettysburg and Vicksburg dashed the hopes of the South, and the British government used the occasion to seize two large Laird rams then under construction for the Confederacy in England.

The fact that the South survived for two more years is remarkable and was due to continued Union mismanagement and several inferior generals and to Confederate ingenuity. The blockade got tighter in 1863–64, but some four-fifths of the runners that tried to break through during the war actually succeeded, so difficult was it to maintain a close blockade in the age of steam, even with advanced bases. Worse, Yankee merchants either collaborated with corrupt Union commanders to trade munitions and other goods directly with the South, especially in the Chesapeake Bay-North Carolina Sound area, or traded indirectly by shipping goods to neutral Bermuda, Halifax, Nassau and Havana for passage by blockade runner. The New York-to-Matamoros trade, virtually nonexistent before the war, also thrived and materially aided the South. Irresolute Union generalship led to inaction in Virginia, coupled with a serious Union defeat at Chickamauga in the West in September, a disastrous campaign up the Red River in Louisiana during the spring of 1864, and persistently successful rebel cavalry forays seemingly everywhere. Beauregard's defenses at Charleston included two attacks by Confederate submersibles which sank one and badly damaged another Union warship. The one bright figure for the North throughout these difficulties was General Grant, who drove the Confederate Army of Tennessee from the environs of Chattanooga in November 1863 and to whom Lincoln then gave supreme command of the Union armies the following March.

As Lee's army in Virginia became the prime objective for Union military and naval efforts, the Far West became isolated. The Confederate Trans-Mississippi army command had been virtually independent since the beginning of the war anyway, having its own Texas Marine Department. Texas troops had been drawn back in the defense-in-depth scheme away from the range of naval guns, but they had succeeded in recapturing Galveston early in 1863. The fall of Vicksburg severed the Trans-Mississippi completely from the Richmond government, enabling the district to reap the full benefits of the Matamoros trade. In November 1863 Union forces occupied Brazos Santiago Island near Brownsville and fanned out along the coast to Corpus Christi and Matagorda Bay. This movement failed to affect the repulse of the Red River expedition and proved logistically difficult for any new thrust at Galveston. So the troops were all concentrated at Brazos Santiago during the summer of 1864 where they might at least influence the blockade of the mouth of the Rio Grande.

The Union concern for this region after Vicksburg's fall had less to do with the South than with the apprehension about the French presence in Mexico. In 1863 the French blockaded the Mexican Gulf coast and launched an overland offensive which captured Mexico City in June. Placing the Austrian Archduke Maximilian—formerly Admiral Ferdinand Max of the Austrian navy—on the Mexican throne, the French waged an anti-guerrilla war against the patriots and established a naval blockade of the Mexican Pacific coast in 1864. French warships had bombarded Acapulco early in 1863, then occupied it with landing parties in June 1864. British, French and Russian warships visited San Francisco in 1863–64; the Russians also went to Hawaii, while Anglo-American vessels patrolled from Esquimalt to Valparaiso. A Spanish squadron visited these coasts in 1862–63 and in 1864 occupied the Chincha Islands over a dispute with Peru. Chile and Peru mobilized their small fleets for war with Spain, but British, American and French warships successfully averted any hostilities by the beginning of 1865. These busy activities of the European powers in the Western Hemisphere clearly violated the Monroe Doctrine, so that United States military and naval vigilance over the Western territories and Pacific coasts was maintained even in the midst of the Civil War.

THE GRAND CAMPAIGN OF 1864–65

At the beginning of 1864, the Union turned to proved practitioners of modern total war, replacing those leaders who had failed to act decisively. By placing Grant in supreme command, Lincoln could now expect a grand strategy for the first time in the war. Grant made his headquarters with the Army of the Potomac and appointed Western veterans to his chief commands. The grand campaign aimed at destroying Lee's army and thus taking the capital city that it was defending. It was a strategy of concentration, Grant's Army of the

Potomac holding down the Army of Northern Virginia while the other army and naval forces swept through the Confederacy destroying Lee's logistics and communications. This meant finally closing the last four major seaports east of the Mississippi—Wilmington, Charleston, Savannah and Mobile; destroying the great granary of central Georgia and its key railhead of Atlanta; and doing the same to the Shenandoah Valley. Not all existing commanders were successful, but as the campaign progressed throughout 1864 competent leaders emerged. Farragut remained in the Gulf and moved against Mobile, defended by forts and a force of coastal ironclads and gunboats under Admiral Buchanan, while Dahlgren tightened the blockades of Charleston and Savannah. General William T. Sherman took supreme command of the Western armies, and while Porter pacified the Mississippi marshes Sherman's forces pressed south from Chattanooga to Atlanta. Opposing him was the greatly weakened Army of Tennessee under Johnston. Grant himself would send his own forces headlong into Lee's army, while other Federal units operated in the Shenandoah and another force moved up the James River peninsula from Fortress Monroe against Richmond. Along with the Army of Northern Virginia, Richmond was defended by General Beauregard's fortifications and the James River Squadron of three new ironclads and several gunboats. This grand campaign went into motion in the spring of 1864.

In Virginia, Grant and Lee displayed their continued respect for naval power as the Wilderness Campaign unfolded. Grant crossed the Rapidan River above Fredericksburg in May and repeatedly attacked Lee's army, but always keeping his rear on the coastal rivers for his logistics. When Lee's army withstood these bloody attacks, Grant merely extended the lines of his much larger army toward the coast, forcing Lee to retreat lest his position be flanked or he be forced to operate near the coast and the Union navy. By this stratagem, which cost him heavily in men (which the Northern draft easily replaced), Grant pressed toward Richmond, hurting Lee who could no longer draw upon the exhausted Confederate manpower supply. Simultaneously, the Army of the James under the incompetent political-general B. F. Butler moved up the James by boat only to be pinned down by Beauregard against a bend in the river called Bermuda Hundred. But Grant pushed around the east side of Richmond, crossed the James to free Butler, and by late June had thrown siege lines around the east and south of Richmond and Petersburg. He established a base at City Point on the James where the Navy could supply and support him. Meanwhile, the feeble Union drive into the Shenandoah had been repulsed, and Lee decided to launch a counterthrust up the Valley for a direct descent on Washington. With two thirds of his army, he faced

Grant at Richmond and sent the other third up the Valley under General Jubal A. Early. Early kept well inland as Lee had done twice before, crossed the Potomac early in July and approached the exposed Northern capital from the northwest. Lee had again successfully threatened Union strategy.

But Union sea power frustrated Lee's last offensive. Grant refused to abandon his lines and dispatched one army corps by water from the James, up the Chesapeake and the Potomac to disembark at the Washington docks the very day that Early attacked the forts on the northwest side of the city. Union gunboats again concentrated in the Potomac and at the mouth of the Susquehanna, while Grant ordered another army corps by sea all the way from New Orleans to Washington via Hampton Roads. Early, outnumbered, had no choice but to fall back though not before raiding into southern Pennsylvania late in July. Grant now created the Army of the Shenandoah from the troops gathered around Washington and ordered General Philip H. Sheridan to use it to crush Early's force and then to burn the Valley crops to the ground. Sheridan fulfilled these orders in the early autumn of 1864, thus destroying a part of Lee's army and its nearest source of food. Rejoining Grant before Richmond and Petersburg, Sheridan's force gave Grant overwhelming superiority. Still, Lee held on during the winter, supported by his active James River Squadron, which, however, was badly battered by Union batteries during a sortie late in January. By then, however, the operations of Sherman, Farragut and Porter had combined with those of Sheridan to begin the progressive starvation of Lee's once fine army.

In the West, Sherman began the Atlanta Campaign in May and by a series of outflanking maneuvers pushed Johnston's army back on Atlanta. Reaching the outskirts of the city, Sherman was attacked boldly by a new rebel commander, General John B. Hood, but in July and August defeated him and took the city. Simultaneously, in August, Farragut's squadron braved floating mine fields to defeat the Confederate flotilla at the battle of Mobile Bay and to bombard the coastal forts there into submission; although the city was not invested, it was now closed to commerce. General Hood, following Lee's example, now thrust northward into Tennessee toward the main Union supply base and rail head at Nashville, while his cavalry actually captured and briefly manned one Union gunboat and five transports on the Tennessee. But Sherman, like Grant, refused to be diverted from Atlanta. Instead, he sent General George B. Thomas to Nashville, which Hood besieged, while Union troops in the North hastened by river and rail to reinforce Thomas. Sherman then burned Atlanta, cut his communications with the North altogether and set off across Georgia, living off the land and applying the torch to whatever supplies his army did not need. Sherman's "march to the sea" in November and December 1864, virtually unopposed, eliminated the last major supply area for Lee's army, while Sherman reestablished his own communications by taking Savannah from the land side and linking up with Dahlgren's offshore fleet. Simultaneously, Thomas sallied forth from his defenses at Nashville and virtually annihilated Hood's army in mid-December. The year finished with the Union victorious nearly everywhere.

The ending of Lee's resistance focused on the closing of the last two ports which supplied him, Charleston and Wilmington. The latter port was especially difficult to close, its defenses being dominated by Fort Fisher at the mouth of the Cape Fear River. The last stronghold for blockade runners, Wilmington was also the base for the runner-turned-cruiser *Tallahassee* which sortied in August 1864 to destroy thirty-three Yankee merchantmen off New York and New England, refueling at Halifax, and then again in November taking six vessels off Delaware. Grant therefore gave Admiral Porter command of the North Atlantic Blockading Squadron and ordered him to take Fort Fisher and thus to close the port. Porter undertook the task in December, but the operation was bungled by his inept Army commander, the troublesome Butler, whom Grant finally removed. Trying again in mid-January 1865, Porter used forty-eight ships and five ironclads to expend 22 tons of ammunition on Fort Fisher preparatory to the successful assault by 10,000 Army, Navy and Marine Corps troops. The Confederacy was falling, its navy virtually finished too. The raider *Alabama* under Raphael Semmes, after sixty-nine captures, was sunk by the steam frigate *Kearsarge* off Cherbourg in June 1864 in the last sailing-ship gunnery duel in history, and by year's end only the new cruiser *Shenandoah* remained at large, operating against Yankee shipping in the North Pacific. In February 1865 General Lee was belatedly given supreme command of Confederate military fortunes, with Rear Admiral Semmes commanding his James River Squadron. But that same month Sherman moved inland into South Carolina, flanking Charleston and forcing its evacuation, while Grant ordered part of Thomas' army by water from Nashville to Cincinnati, thence by rail to Baltimore and again by sea to Fort Fisher. This force captured Wilmington late in February and linked up with Sherman marching into North Carolina. After final battles in North Carolina and Virginia, Grant trapped Lee west of Richmond early in April 1865, forcing his surrender. At the same time a final amphibious assault took the port of Mobile. The Confederacy then collapsed, and all the other Southern military and naval forces soon capitulated.

Union naval policy during the Civil War continued the American inshore tradition though based throughout on undisputed command of the sea. A battle fleet had been unnecessary, though several squadrons and flotillas had been formed to counter the few makeshift Confederate inshore naval units. The blockade initially proposed by Scott and opposed by Welles had taken nearly the entire war to become fully effective, although the last blockade runner entered Galveston over a month after Lee's surrender. Eventually, the four blockading squadrons had employed about 300 naval vessels to capture five times that number of blockade runners. But the blockade was run successfully perhaps 8000 times, or roughly over 80 percent effectiveness if one includes the illicit Yankee trade across the Rio Grande and through Union lines. Still, the blockade was a success, because its very existence discouraged normal trade: untold numbers of merchantmen refused to run the risk of capture, while those which did usually charged disastrous prices and brought in unnecessary luxury items, neither of which helped the Confederate war effort. Furthermore, the so-called Anaconda used many of the same blockaders to harass and help assault Southern coastal and river towns, thereby requiring a major effort at coast defense which the Confederacy could not afford.

Union mobility by water thus provided strategic and tactical back-up for the Northern armies, while Southern naval efforts were isolated and makeshift and rarely utilized in conjunction with land forces. To be sure, the Confederate policy of *guerre de course* indirectly chased nearly half the Union merchant tonnage to foreign registry, but the North prospered from goods carried in these same newly-neutral vessels. The major naval innovations by both sides were technological—in ordnance, armor and steam propulsion, but especially in the revival of attack beneath the waterline. Of the mines, torpedoes, submersibles and rams, the latter made the greatest impression and helped to revive a tactic obsolete since the days of the great galleys. In reality, however, ramming attacks had been largely unsuccessful, and the long-term impact of Civil War naval operations would be in submarine warfare. Amphibious and other inshore activities were significant, but overshadowed by the impressive achievements of the many armies in the field. In sum, Union command of the sea helped to reunify the nation and to reestablish its global naval prestige.

The United States had also asserted sufficient military and naval power to reinterpret international law to suit its own needs—the common attitude of nations commanding the sea during wartime. The Lincoln government had generally adhered to the principles of the 1856

Declaration of Paris which the United States had not signed, leading to the final collapse of privateering as a device of naval warfare and increasing the rule of the effective blockade—though stretching the definition of "effective." The North had firmly adhered to freedom of the seas in principle but had elected to violate neutral shipping whenever contraband was suspected of being carried. Thus the *Trent* affair had symbolized the many Union infringements on free shipping while one cruiser had actually entered the harbor of Bahia, Brazil, in October 1864 to seize the successful rebel raider *Florida*. Such instances, usually repudiated officially, all pointed to a growing reality of total war, namely, that all goods enabled a nation to make war and that therefore the old distinction for contraband items was becoming obsolete. And neutrality itself might even be a fiction in total war, and with it the notion of free trade in wartime. Thus the Civil War signaled the end of more than wooden sailing warships.

ENFORCING THE MONROE DOCTRINE

The War ended, the United States also asserted firmly, for the first time, its lawful prerogatives in the Monroe Doctrine. To discourage the French project in Mexico, General Grant immediately sent Sheridan with an army to the Rio Grande, and the Navy dispatched a four-ship squadron around the Horn in a show of force. Napoleon III finally yielded to this pressure and to the great expense of the inconclusive guerrilla war, and in 1867 he withdrew from Mexico, forever ending the French pressure on Latin America. Similar American legalism by force was impressed upon the Spanish.

Spain made its last attempt to restore its prestige in Latin America during the 1860s, trying in vain to take advantage of the many quarrels in the Western Hemisphere. From their last toeholds at Cuba and Puerto Rico, the Spanish in 1861 accepted an invitation of the people of Santo Domingo to return, only to be then faced by a bloody insurrection and American protests. Then came the altercation with Peru and Chile in 1864 which suddenly flared up again in September 1865. Spain decided to quit Santo Domingo that year but ignored American protests by blockading Valparaiso and hastening Chilean and Peruvian declarations of war (which were supported by Bolivia and Ecuador). The warring nations fought a number of skirmishes at sea, including an indecisive squadron battle off the Chiloé Islands in February 1866. The American squadron rounding the Horn joined a British force at Valparaiso but neither admiral could persuade the Spanish squadron there to halt its plans to bombard the port. The weak Chilean defenses and privateer-oriented navy were no match for the squadron of Admiral

Méndez Nuñez which destroyed Valparaiso by shelling on the last day of March. With nine warships Nuñez then blockaded Callao, but when he moved in for a bombardment early in May the Peruvians drove him off with severe losses from their English-built artillery and mines, two ironclads and three gunboats. The Spanish ships limped away, five years later using American offices to negotiate a formal peace and thereby thus ending their brief imperial plans.

The years 1864 to 1870 also witnessed a bitter war between aggressive Paraguay and the "triple alliance" of Brazil, Argentina and Uruguay, involving considerable inshore and river fleets. To support its invasion southward, the Paraguayan river steam flotilla with troops on board in June 1865 attacked its Brazilian counterpart at Corrientes, Argentina, on the Parana River, deep in the interior, only to be defeated with heavy losses. From then through October the allied armies and flotillas on the Parana and Uruguay rivers drove the Paraguayans from Corrientes province, after which Brazil reinforced its fleet of thirteen gunboats at Corrientes with four ironclads. Following skirmishing on the rivers early in 1866, in April the allies mounted an invasion of Paraguay by way of the Parana, their armies embarked on Argentine and Brazilian vessels. The army landed and worked overland while the river craft brushed aside mines and fire rafts to lend logistical, sealift and fire support, but the ground forces met a repulse late in September.

Gradually, however, the allied river campaign broke through Paraguay's defenses. In the summer of 1867 ten Brazilian ironclads and the allied army could not press farther upriver due to Paraguayan fortifications and a falling river, so Brazil hastily built shallow-draft monitors which helped the allies to resume their upriver offensive during the winter of 1867–68. In February they captured Asunción, the capital of Paraguay, and while Paraguayan raiders in camouflaged canoes failed to take several Brazilian ironclads the allies cleared the river banks of enemy outposts. By December 1868, when the allies took Angostura, the desperate Paraguayans had to strip their naval crews for home defense ashore, giving the allies absolute command of the rivers. Paraguay scuttled its remaining vessels in June 1869; guerrilla fighting continued; and the next year the United States negotiated a peace settlement.

Spurning offers to annex Santo Domingo and the Danish Virgin Islands in 1867–69, the United States increasingly used the Monroe Doctrine to exert increasing authority over the Americas. Even Britain and Russia were yielding to the reunited American colossus in its obvious sphere of influence. Russia, preoccupied with consolidating her own continental empire in Central and Eastern Asia, abandoned North America altogether in 1867 by selling Alaska and the Aleutian Islands to the United States. This event only increased the British tension over possible American annexation of Canada and British Columbia, anxieties which had been heightened in 1864–66 by Confederate and patriotic Irish Fenian activities along the Canadian-American border. By 1867, up to sixteen British warships had based annually at Pacific squadron headquarters at Esquimalt, and that year Britain gave Canada dominion status within the Empire, thus strengthening its ties with the mother country. Continuing Fenian challenges to Canadian unity and the festering border dispute over the San Juan Islands were then over-shadowed by postwar American demands for British reparations pay-ments to cover damages made by Confederate cruisers built in England, especially those of the *Alabama*. Anglo-American relations again be-came strained, but Britain had no desire to antagonize the United States. Already, power changes in Europe and other events had led to the reduction of imperial forces in North America, so that Britain pre-ferred settlements of lingering problems with the United States. So in 1870–72, by a number of agreements, Britain paid a compromise sum for the *Alabama* claims, ceded by arbitration the San Juan Islands to the United States, put down the Fenian agitation, and joined British Columbia to a finally unified Dominion of Canada. The *Pax Britannica* thus continued in North America, partly because of British respect for American power.

The United States by the 1870s had fashioned its general conti-nental empire and had taken advantage of its own Civil War to emerge as a major industrial power in the world. But it had neither military nor maritime aspirations beyond those of the prewar era. The Grand Army was immediately demobilized and the regular forces returned to the frontier where they supervised the settlement of the continental in-terior and completed the destruction of Indian resistance. Financial investment centered on industrial production and railroad expansion, not on maritime trade. Such oceanic trade flourished, to be sure, but most of it in foreign, particularly British, bottoms. The American merchant vessels that had transferred to foreign flags during the war were refused repatriation by Congress in 1866; financial and labor re-sources shifted away from shipbuilding to the new industrial corpora-tions; progressively higher protective tariffs were instituted; and the government still refused to subsidize American shipowners at a time when Britain was helping her own convert to steam and iron. So the blow to the merchant marine by the Confederate navy combined with these and other factors to accelerate the decline begun after 1855. American merchantmen were therefore inferior to newer British com-petitors and came to be manned increasingly by foreign sailors. Yet this trend was only natural, for the American political center in the 1860s definitely shifted westward as new states entered the Union from West of the Mississippi. New England shipping interests became a political and economic minority, and though the coastal schooner trade grew the American overseas carrying trade steadily decayed.

With no overseas imperial, military or mercantilistic aspirations, not surprisingly the American Congress laid up its fine wartime Navy. By December 1864, when the United States Navy had numbered some 700 vessels mounting nearly 5000 guns, it was—in terms of sheer numbers— the most powerful navy in the world and that very month elevated its most exalted naval officer, Farragut, to the unprecedented American rank of vice admiral. Farragut went on two years later to reach the full rank of admiral, followed by Porter in both ranks in 1866 and 1870. But these were virtually honorary appointments for wartime services rendered, for no other rear admirals achieved these distinctions. And in the autumn of 1867 the demobilization of the Navy began, stripping the force to but 52 vessels in commission and mounting under 500 of the same old guns by 1871. This had been generally an inshore navy anyway, useless outside North American waters, and four major seagoing monitors under construction had been scrapped late in 1865.

Strategically, this naval policy was realistically attuned to American political goals after the war. As usual, cruisers were sent abroad to protect commerce or maintained at home for coast defense, and the old naval stations were reestablished under new names: European (from Mediterranean and African), North Atlantic (Home), South Atlantic (Brazil) and Asiatic (East Indies), while the standing Pacific Squadron was twice divided into North and South squadrons (1866–69, 1872–78). These decisions were all realistic and provided a small but almost adequate-sized navy. Unfortunately, Congress neglected to modernize the old vessels or to authorize new ones, so that sail returned, coal for steam was severely restricted, wood continued over armor, and the old smoothbore cannon were retained. With the usual postwar letdown and desire to economize, the United States thus handicapped its navy.

From 1815 to the beginning of 1870s, the United States grew geographically into a sprawling continental empire, enjoying also until the mid-1850s a superior merchant marine. Its navy had never needed nor had it entertained blue-water aspirations, but had engaged instead in inshore operations in which command of the sea had been virtually automatic. Adequate as this navy was, however, it would never meet future needs if the United States was ever to assume the full dimensions of a modern major power. Isolationistic by habit and temperament, preferring freedom from the global quarrels of the older powers, the United States would never be able to resist the consequences of a shrinking world without a battle fleet. For in 1866 the Atlantic submarine telegraphic cable was laid, and three years later the American continent was joined by a coast-to-coast railroad. On the other side of the world also in 1869 European and Asian sea lanes were shortened by the opening of the Suez Canal. The days of America's splendid isolation were henceforth numbered.

13

The Golden Age of Naval Thought, 1867–1914

*. . . limited war is only permanently possible to island Powers or be-
tween Powers which are separated by sea, and then only when the
Power desiring limited war is able to command the sea to such a degree as to be able not only to isolate the distant object, but also to
render impossible the invasion of his home territory. Here, then, we
reach the true meaning and highest military value of what we call the
command of the sea. . . .*

—CORBETT

THE NEW TECHNOLOGY AND
MATERIAL STRATEGY

Without discernible interruptions, the *Pax Britannica* continued into
the half-century following the American Civil War but with two new
paradoxical features: a global cosmopolitanism that promoted unity,
and neo-imperialism that bred disunity and the seeds of World War I.
The civilization of this half-century, intellectually and culturally perhaps
the most dynamic period of Western history since the Renaissance, drew
much of its energy from the industrial and democratic revolutions en-
gulfing all peoples. Industry and technology spread from Western Europe
to transform Russia, the United States and Japan, though the principles
of democracy and socialism—as alternatives to the time-worn monarchies—could only progress whenever the old order collapsed. That lay
in the new era and century, but the ideas did spread—as the former era
closed—carried by new and rapid forms of communication: steamships,
railroads, automobiles, the telephone, telegraph and wireless and primitive aircraft. Global distances shrank accordingly, most dramatically at
sea between the respective openings of the Suez and Panama canals in
1869 and 1914. A continuing if naive faith in the Victorian peace en-

forced by British naval superiority encouraged the free flow of ideas of philosophers, scientists, artists and social thinkers across national boundaries. Insular Britain could thus no longer monopolize the thalasso-cratic preconditions for cultural vitality, but shared them across the Western world. Witness a cross section of such "global" thought: Freud, Marx, Nietzsche, Darwin, Spencer, Hugo, Mill, Ranke, Einstein, Helm-holtz, Proust, Tolstoy, Dostoyevsky, the Curies, the Jameses, Wagner, Tchaikovsky, Rachmaninoff, Stravinsky, van Gogh, Gauguin, Cézanne, Ibsen and Picasso.

But just as advancing technology seemed to bring the peoples of the West closer together, so too did it create the elements of renewed con-flict. Increased wealth promoted intense nationalism not only in such newly unified nations as Germany and Italy but in the non-Western peoples exploited by the old and newer powers; indeed, new knowledge in medicine and dietetics conquered the last tropical diseases and stimu-lated a population explosion on a global scale. The desire for national greatness through economic strength led the powers to reject the doctrine of free trade in favor of closed imperial systems of neo-mercantilism, preferred tariffs and colonial privilege. International competition intensi-fied throughout this era, creating tensions that steadily undermined the edifice of the balance of the European powers. The days of the *Pax Britannica* came to be numbered as rival powers—no longer content to adhere willingly to British rule upon the seas—imitated Britain with their own merchant fleets, colonies and navies. These powers made feeble attempts to perpetuate the old international legalism of the Enlighten-ment with disarmament conferences at The Hague in the Netherlands in 1899 and 1907 and with the Declaration of London in 1909 which aimed at protecting neutral shippers in time of war. But opposition within Britain itself and elsewhere left the Declaration unratified by any nation, a harbinger of the coming ineffectiveness of international law in total war. New technological weapons would be the final deterrence—or arbi-ter in war. And the new forces of unrest in the colonies unleashed by the new technology and ideas could never be contained by mere gun-boats and imperial police forces, making this half-century the last of undisputed European hegemony in the world.

In no nation did the new technology make a more dramatic impact than Germany, which arose as the major challenge to Britain—despite the fact that Britain perpetuated the delusion that France was still the main threat on the continent until 1900. Germany raced against time and the growth of potentially superior Russia and the United States to become a leading power. Drawing upon a peculiarly rigid class system ruled by feudalistic *Junkers* military aristocrats and *Kaiser* (emperor), Germany mobilized its manpower, raw coal, iron, steel and other metals into a well-organized military-industrial system and borrowed from the British model to fashion an overseas empire and fleet. So impressive did German society become that it soon provided the model for other industrial states. Specifically admired, before 1890, were the peerless political skills of Otto von Bismarck, the industrial success of the Krupp family, the strategic theories of the late Karl von Clausewitz, the general staff organization and military genius of Helmuth von Moltke, the war academies and higher education in general, the military history of Hans Delbrück and the broader framework of German historiography, and the creation of the Imperial German Navy under Albrecht von Stosch and its dynamic growth under Alfred von Tirpitz. Only after 1890 and the new aggressive policies of Kaiser Wilhelm II did Germany begin to appear as a threat to European stability. The new technology enabled Germany and other basically non-maritime-oriented nations to build modern technologically superior navies, but like them Germany remained first and always a continental power with its army as the senior service in matters of policy and strategy.

This technological capacity led to the domination of the material school of strategy over the years 1867 to 1914 in all countries: superior technologically advanced weapons on land and sea would determine victory in diplomacy and war, with the lessons of history to play only a complementary role. The idea of super-warships with improved naval guns, projectiles and armor deciding command of the sea with only perfunctory notice of principles of naval strategy grounded in historical experience appeared as anathema to a number of historian-theorists, notably Captain Alfred Thayer Mahan of the United States Navy and Sir Julian Corbett of Great Britain. Between the publication of Mahan's key work, *The Influence of Sea Power upon History, 1660–1783* in 1890 and of Corbett's excellent *Some Principles of Maritime Strategy* in 1911, these and other men stated and restated the strategic constants of command of the sea. But with their evidence drawn from the age of sail and more recent limited wars, these arguments found subordination by naval planners to the superweapons of the day. Thus, this period is best understood as one continuous arms race of new and better weapons being introduced to control the sea. But, in the realm of naval theory, the debates between material and historical strategists created a golden age of naval thought. The arenas for debate lay in professional associations and journals, academies and war colleges.

The exchange of ideas began to be formalized with the creation of private professional officer societies and the publication of naval and army journals. Britain had pioneered with the Royal United Service Institute in 1831 which started publishing its *Journal* in 1859. The Russians, however, had led the way in naval magazines with the fine *Morskoi*

Sbornik in 1848, followed in 1861 by France's *Revue Maritime* (*et Coloniale* till 1892). The best of all the naval journals, after an inauspicious beginning, came to be Italy's *Rivista Marittima;* another minor but eventually improved periodical was Germany's *Marine Rundschau*. The United States Navy combined the interests of its small officer corps in professional, scientific and literary naval matters by establishing the private United States Naval Institute in 1873 which thenceforth published its members' views in its *Proceedings*. These quarterly and monthly journals were augmented late in the century by various naval annuals, especially those edited in England by Thomas Brassey (from 1886) and Frederick T. Jane (from 1897).

All navies had academies for elementary officer education, but the plethora of advanced naval analysis found its highest institutional form in the naval war college. The model for all such advanced schools for senior officers below flag rank, the Prussian War Academy founded in 1810, led eventually to similar army schools in Britain and France during the 1870s. But the major catalyst for advanced strategic thinking, particularly naval, in such institutions was a veteran reformer in naval education, Commodore Stephen B. Luce, who founded the United States Naval War College in 1884. Luce appointed Mahan to the faculty first as lecturer and then as Luce's successor as College president. Mahan's lectures led to his pivotal book in 1890 which enhanced the reputation of the place as the center of America's broad theoretical studies in naval strategy. Building upon British, German and Italian examples, the Naval War College also introduced naval war gaming to its curriculum in order to analyze and test American naval doctrine and plans. Between Luce's College and Mahan's historical theories, naval studies rapidly became an intellectual focus in other navies, although the American Naval War College after 1900 studied less strategy and more narrowly professional subjects. The Russians adopted a similar curriculum for captains and senior lieutenants at their Nikolayev naval academy in 1895, while the British did the same at theirs at Greenwich in 1900, elevating it to an enlarged Royal Naval War College at Portsmouth in 1907. The same year Italy established its School of Naval Warfare, and in 1910 the Germans, who had a small Naval War College at Kiel but combined their higher military studies at the army-dominated War Academy, began to game naval problems. The French, a major naval power deeply concerned with naval theory, established a school of naval war in 1895, but it had only uneven success.

Because rapid technological change fascinated younger officers and confounded conservative and anti-intellectual admiralties and navy departments, these official institutions and organs of expression were regarded as inadequate by some officers. Consequently, they established various national navy leagues to propagandize naval developments, quit the service to expound their views, or awaited retirement to become full-fledged military pundits. Some "young Turks" in the Royal Navy tried to avoid these extremes; led by Captain Herbert Richmond, in 1912 they founded the private *Naval Review* in order to publish and circulate unsigned critical essays. Lesser navies such as those of Austria, Japan and China simply followed or imitated the theories and techniques expounded by the major naval powers.

The analysts of these institutions and privately published works focused strategic arguments around the capabilities of the new weapons. Guilty of technological determinism, the material strategists centered their discussions around the new steam-and-steel warships, specifically the technical questions of armored battleships versus the big guns of other battleships and the underwater torpedoes of smaller vessels. They either ignored the historical arguments or twisted them to serve their own ends. By the same token, the historians like Mahan and Corbett weakened their own cases for relevance by misunderstanding or playing down modern technology. Ironically, since the big-fleet theories of both schools were rarely tested in battle before 1914, the real fighting developed in the colonial areas and was done by gunboats. Still, the battleship symbolized the era.

The tactics of the 1860s, especially confused because of the sweeping technological changes from wood to iron and sail to steam, felt the impact of the American Civil War. For coast defense, the European powers developed their own turreted "breastwork monitors," while on the high seas ironclad-armored battleships ("armored frigates") mounted underwater rams and new rifled ordnance to replace the wooden ship of the line altogether. Instead of a totally armored and thus very expensive vessel, the British and French from 1865 used only a nine-inch belt of armor around the waterline or plates protecting the batteries ("barbettes" or "casemates"). Technological problems postponed the improvement of submersible craft and slowed the universal adoption of breech- over muzzle-loading. In propulsion, special engineering officers appeared, and the simple expansion steam reciprocating engine (17 knots) gradually made way for the horizontal compound engine (18½ knots) of the next decade. In communications, the searchlight complemented signal flags and pennants and evolved into the venetian-blind blinker. Tactically, "squadrons of evolution" rejected the old line-ahead in favor of grouped ironclads in square or oblique attack formations. The reappearance of the underwater ram, gone since galley days, dictated line-abreast tactics for the ram followed by a ship-to-ship gunnery melee at 2000–3000 yards with the turreted guns firing forward throughout the action instead of in broadside.

By contrast, the strategic alignments of the 1860s did not change markedly. Britain and France matched each other's new ironclad squadrons, while Russia—having angered Britain and France by ruthlessly suppressing the Polish uprising—avoided having its Baltic and Pacific fleets trapped in port in the event of war by dispatching them on timely visits to American ports in 1863. Ottoman Turkey crushed a Greek-inspired revolt on Crete in 1866–68, and Austria abolished its naval ministry after its Admiral Max had gone to Mexico as Maximilian. But Austria had greater concerns with the rise of Italy and Germany, when in 1864 Bismarck called for Austrian naval assistance in Germany's attempt to annex the province of Schleswig-Holstein at the expense of Denmark. The small Danish Baltic squadron blockaded the Elbe and Weser rivers, but the Austrians dispatched Commodore Wilhelm von Tegetthoff with a squadron from the Mediterranean to the North Sea. Assisted by three small German craft, Tegetthoff used his two steam frigates to engage three Danish vessels in May 1864 off the British-owned island of Heligoland in the last wooden-sail naval battle in history (plus the *Alabama-Kearsarge* duel in June). Though a draw, the battle was followed by Austrian naval reinforcements which broke the blockade and helped force Denmark to surrender the disputed province. The Germans now began to construct armored coast defense ships, but under army control.

Bismarck's wars of German unification then engaged Austria and France. In 1866 Moltke's Prussian army crushed the Austrian army at Sadowa in the so-called Seven Weeks War, while allied Italy attacked the Austrians in the Adriatic. When an Italian expeditionary force moved against the Austrian island of Lissa, Rear Admiral Tegetthoff used his ironclad rams to sink one Italian ironclad and drive away the other eight on July 20. This ninety-minute battle of Lissa, the first fleet action between ironclads in history, confirmed line-abreast ramming tactics for the ensuing generation of naval tacticians. Tegetthoff at Pola and a gunboat squadron on Lake Garda supported the Austrian army in Italy, but Austria ended the war in October by ceding Venice to Italy. Seriously weakened, Austria gave Hungary its independence under the new dual monarchy of Austria-Hungary in 1867 and allowed the navy of Lissa to deteriorate—despite the dynamic leadership of Tegetthoff from 1868 till his untimely death in 1871 at the age of forty-four. Bismarck then moved to weaken France, initiating the Franco-Prussian War in 1870. The French Navy began the war in July by blockading the German Baltic coast, but Moltke's ground offensive defeated the French Army at Sedan, causing the fall of the French monarchy and the new Republican regime to strip warship crews for the unsuccessful defense of Paris. Such measures frustrated the French blockade and plans for an amphibious expedition in the Baltic. Paris fell in January 1871, France admitted defeat in May, and the new German Empire emerged from the conflict.

European territorial alignments continued basically unchanged over the next four decades, but technological change made the 1870s a period of transition. The armored battleship remained supreme, with the Italians leading in construction under their superb naval designer Benedetto Brin who also served off and on as Minister of Marine, 1876–1898. Italy in 1876 introduced 12,000-ton, 18-knot battleships with unwieldy 17.7" guns protected by British armor: 14 inches of wrought iron (or two 12" plates for 24") and later of homogeneous steel. British and French warships used compound iron and steel armor. These heavy Italian battleships introduced cellular compartmentation with watertight bulkheads, fearing attack below the waterline—not only by rams but by the new 6-knot automotive torpedo developed by the Englishman Robert Whitehead in Austrian service. These torpedos and the defensive compartmentation soon became standard in all major navies. Replacing the sailing-steam frigate, "cruising vessels" (unarmored) and "protected cruisers" (partly armored) began to appear, but as nearly useless compromises of economic and naval needs, especially in France and the United States. Unable to keep pace with the more affluent nations, such minor naval states as Austria, Argentina and the Scandinavians developed small coast defense torpedo boats, forcing Britain and France to imitate them. Naval communications improved with the introduction of the electric arc light for Morse code signals (and spotting torpedoes and mines).

Two widely separated small wars influenced the growing naval arms race late in the 1870s. With German support, Russia in 1871 began to refortify Sevastopol and reopen the Black Sea, leading to the Russo-Turkish War of 1877–78. The Russian navy continued to flourish under the dynamic leadership and reforms of Grand Duke Constantine, with Admiral Popov leading the construction of new ironclads, monitors and torpedo boats for service on the Black Sea and Danube River. The Turks tried to keep pace, but it was the Russians who triumphed, as the Ottoman Empire ever more declined. Using spar torpedoes and mines, the Russian navy supported the army's drive across the Danube and capture of Plevna. More dramatic, in the eastern Black Sea, Lieutenant Commander Stepan Osipovich Makarov used spar and towed torpedoes before the port of Batum, then employed Whitehead torpedoes to sink a 6500-ton Turkish warship. The Ottomans surrendered Batum to Russia at the end of the war and granted independence to Balkan Rumania, Bulgaria, Serbia and Montenegro. In the War of the Pacific, 1879 to 1881, Chile used a formidable small navy with two British-built armored battleships to gain commercial and territorial concessions from Peru and Bolivia. Capturing the Bolivian port of Antofagasta early in the fighting, Chile clamped a naval blockade on the enemy coasts. When the British-built Peruvian ironclad battleship *Huascar* under Rear Admiral Don Miguel Grau attempted to break the blockade throughout 1879, Commodore Galvarino Riveros concentrated the Chilean fleet to pound *Huascar* into submission and kill Grau off Point Angamos, Bolivia, in October. With command of the waters, Chile invaded Bolivia by sea, overran the coast, blockaded Peruvian Callao and in 1880 captured Arica and Pisco by land-sea attack. The major fighting ended in January 1881 when the Chilean army captured Lima; in 1883–84 Bolivia ceded its entire coastline to Chile. Whereas underwater weapons had been decisive in the former war, they were absent in the latter.

Such events helped to define the two major schools of naval thought crystallizing during the 1880s. The "blue-water" philosophy in the Royal Navy used historical arguments and improved guns and armor to advocate command of the sea with battleships. Homogeneous steel (with 5 percent nickel) increased the armor belt from 18" to 20" and covered two thirds of the 14,000-ton battleship. Improved 13.5" guns with longer muzzles mounted in open barbettes gave a better rate of fire and muzzle velocity, aided by steel-encased shells with new powders (eventually smokeless cordite). And new vertical triple-expansion reciprocating engines gave an optimum speed of 18 knots for evading torpedoes. Rejecting the ram altogether, the British countered torpedo boats with 6" quick-firing guns on the battleships, an escorting flotilla of "cruisers" (formerly armored and protected cruisers, belted steam frigates and corvettes) and "torpedo gunboats."

Opposing this view, the younger, material-oriented officers of the French Navy's *jeune école* (or new school) claimed that this concept of command of the sea had been voided by the torpedo boat, which had made the battleship vulnerable and thus obsolete. Plagued by potential enemies in maritime Britain, continental Germany and Mediterranean Italy, the French Navy suffered a doctrinal crisis during the 1880s exemplified by no fewer than thirty-one different ministers of marine between 1871 and 1902. In general, however, the *jeune école* argument prevailed under the leadership of its spokesmen, Baron Richard Grivel, Gabriel Charmes and Admiral Théophile Aube. Using the first theory of strategic naval bombardment in modern warfare, Aube (naval minister, 1886–87) planned to use his torpedo boats at Cherbourg to attack British seaports, anchored shipping and dockyard installations and his cruisers from Brest to wage *guerre de course* on the high seas, causing economic panic and forcing Britain to terms. Aube went so far as to suspend battleship construction in 1886 and to argue that his torpedo boats would have to ignore international law in their attack on merchant shipping—a harbinger of future underwater total war. But France's torpedo craft proved unreliable and vulnerable in daylight and blind at night during fleet maneuvers in 1887, undermining the entire edifice of *jeune école* reasoning.

In fact, battleships remained the yardstick of international power relations in the Mediterranean during the 1880s. In 1881–82 Germany, Austria and Italy created the Triple Alliance on the continent, but unilateral Italian actions in the middle sea alarmed the French. Following its leading naval strategist, Domenico Bonamico, Italy pivoted its defenses around a new naval base on the island of Maddalena off the north coast of Sardinia, established other new bases at Taranto and Gaeta (near Naples), and heavily fortified the older base at Genoa. When the Italian battleships concentrated at Maddalena with a German squadron for a total of ten capital ships in 1889, France retaliated. Already, Admiral Aube had concentrated five French battleships at Toulon to face Italy and had begun to strengthen the new base at Bizerte, Tunisia, occupied in 1881 largely for reasons of prestige. Now, however, at the end of the decade, France initiated its first major building program since 1872 of new battleships much superior to Italy's untried "central citadel" ships and undertook such an effective economic offensive against Italy that it caused a depression in Italy and related drain on the Italian navy. By the mid-1890s Italy had little choice but to court the friendship of France and to abandon any ambitions in the Western Mediterranean.

Beyond torpedo boats to check Britain and battleships to counter Italy, France strengthened its army to deter Germany and Austria and even embarked upon a new imperial program. Admiral Aube and the *jeune école* advocated a global network of bases linked by a French-built canal across the Isthmus of Panama, and since the Navy had always administered the colonies the government let it continue in this role until a new colonial office was established in 1892 to assist. Defense of the new far-flung colonies, however, remained the Navy's responsibility, so that the Naval Infantry and Marine Artillery had to be posted abroad. All these expenses proved so great that in the midst of continuing doctrinal battles from 1886 to 1905 the Navy lost interest in colonial defense, and the *jeune école* so dissociated itself from imperial concerns as to advocate the sacrifice of both foreign trade and the merchant marine in time of war—an eventuality that would nearly cripple France after 1914. Without a single dominant doctrine, the French Navy was engulfed in the same chaos that wracked French politics from the Boulanger crisis through the Dreyfus affair.

Nevertheless, Britain reacted strenuously in the face of French preparations. The prospect of a swift steam-powered cross-Channel attack caused repeated "invasion scares" in Britain from 1888, especially as most analysts assumed any modern war would be a short one. French torpedo boats neutralized any thought of a close blockade in such a war, and colonies and merchantmen seemed undefendable in the face of the new machine weapons. Or so reasoned British Army analysts of the "brick and mortar" and "bolt from the blue" schools, which reasoned that the fleet should be kept in home waters for coast defense, backed up by fortifications. They accepted the *jeune école* position that blue-water command of the sea had become obsolete. Unmoved by such views, however, the "blue-water" school prevailed. The Naval Defense Act of 1889 authorized the two-power standard—a minimum battleship strength equal to the combined battleship tonnage (but preferably a 5 to 3 superiority) of its two largest rivals, France and Russia, whose growing mutual friendship was solidified by a defensive alliance in 1894. Then the publication of Mahan's book in 1890 gave historical support to the blue-water school. In truth, Britain's policy was based on quantitative material logic, not on strategic realities. The British had no clear idea during the 1890s for utilizing their battle fleet against France, except for maintaining an open blockade in the Western Approaches and concentrating off Gibraltar—à la Nelson—to keep the French fleet divided. The invasion scares of 1893, 1898 and 1900 were based on ignorance, for the French Navy had no real amphibious plans, policy or tactical doctrine.

But the technological improvements of the 1890s gave cause for alarm. The new 14,000-ton battleships incorporated 12 to 14 inches of face-hardened "harveyed" steel armor and breech-loading 13.5" guns with steel-capped, explosive armor- and semi-armor-piercing shells; henceforth, one inch of gun caliber had to equal one inch of armor. The broadside returned as one pair of guns in enclosed barbette turrets and just turrets near the center line replaced open barbettes. Quick-firing light guns remained, but intermediate caliber guns began to disappear as long-range (2000–6000 yards) gunnery duels became standard practice. Accuracy of the guns improved materially when Captain Percy Scott of the Royal Navy introduced the doctrine of "continuous aim"—guns locking on enemy targets by means of a gyroscope despite the roll of the ship. With battle speeds of 15 knots, the battleships could now form in column or line-ahead, as in sailing times, replacing the ram, line-abreast, circular and oblique tactical formations altogether. Center-line turreted battleships with broad arcs of fire could now deliver broadside salvos in the tradition of de Ruyter, Suffren and Nelson. The flotilla now included new "armored" or heavy cruisers—which provided the multitudinous duties of its sailing predecessor, the frigate—and the "torpedo boat destroyer" or destroyer to attack torpedo boats or act as such a vessel itself.

Late in the decade, these small craft began to receive the first steam turbine engines in place of reciprocating engines, giving them battle speeds
of 30 knots and maximum speeds of 36.5 knots!

Such a battleship-centered fleet mix in Britain aroused outright imitation by other "new" navies, all potential enemies of the Royal Navy,
except that most of these also used *jeune école* arguments to give greater
attention to cruisers and torpedo boats in the continental manner. Austria-Hungary, Italy, Russia and the United States remained preoccupied
with coast defense, with their battleships and torpedo boats in that role.
Russia also embraced the strategy of *guerre de course* by creating a
"Volunteer Merchant Fleet" of armed merchantmen in 1885. The
United States began to break away from coastal forts, monitors and protected cruisers to build new "seagoing coastline battleships" in the 1890s.
And as the teachings of its own philosopher Mahan began to have effect,
the United States in the 1890s initiated construction of new long-range
battleships.

Like America, Germany represented a potential if unrealistic threat to
Britain during these years. Indeed, the U. S. Navy was considered conservative and removed from the mainstream of American life, whereas
the Imperial German Navy was middle-class and liberal in its origins.
Both navies were thus alienated from their armies: the American army
in wartime remained largely a militia, nonprofessional force, while the
Junkers-led German standing army was thoroughly aristocratic, even reactionary. As navies, however, their divorce from the popular government—their individualism—was typical, and both professional officer
cadres were drawn largely from national cross-sections of their respective populations and were in reality therefore middle-class, God-fearing
and intensely loyal to the point of being apolitical (relative to their
politics-oriented sister services). Both the American and German navies
were subordinated in military matters to strong civilian control and army
seniority. The Americans steadfastly refused to create a senior admiral
or admiralty board (like the Army's general-in-chief), with the civilian
Secretary of the Navy giving orders. In Germany, a Chief of Admiralty
reported to the Kaiser, but the first two chiefs were army generals with
army uses for the navy: Albrecht von Stosch from 1871 to 1883 concentrated on coast defense, and Leo von Caprivi from 1883 to 1888
followed the French *jeune école* in promoting cruisers and torpedo boats.
With the accession of Wilhelm II in 1888, the navy command was
reorganized into three separate offices which further weakened and de-
centralized it under the vague direction of a Naval Cabinet. Under Bismarck's regime, therefore, the navy had been typically continental,
tolerated but rarely promoted by the army.

Suddenly, however, Britain faced a major threat, for in the 1890s

Kaiser Wilhelm II changed everything, and the German army and navy alike became aggressive and expansionistic. Bismarck's cautious diplomacy had come to an end with his dismissal as chancellor in 1890. Continental expansion was advocated by the army with pronouncements of *Drang nach Osten,* and Wilhelm II followed the advice of his pro-Mahan Atlantic-oriented "Fleet professors" for colonies and maritime power in order to rival Britain's achievements, if only for reasons of prestige. Krupp's industries retooled for modern steel warship construction, while home naval defenses were strengthened by the purchase of Heligoland from Britain in 1890 and the completion five years later of the Kiel Canal across the base of the Jutland peninsula. The canal gave German warships easy transit between the North and Baltic seas, thus bypassing the easily blockaded Sound of Denmark. Although the major force behind naval armament was the kaiser himself, his chief agent was the dynamic Admiral Alfred von Tirpitz, a career officer and torpedo specialist whose big-navy attitude combined with his own political machinations to lead to his appointment in 1897 as State Secretary of the Imperial Naval Office.

Utilizing internal political troubles to advantage, Tirpitz promoted anti-British bias to fashion his "risk theory" *(Risikogedanke)* whereby Germany would build such a formidable battle fleet at home that Britain —with her navy scattered to protect her vast global imperial commitments—would never dare risk a naval war with Germany. The German Naval Bill of 1898 called for nineteen battleships in commission, which alarmed the British, who feared such a fleet in alliance with another armada like the French or Russian. Two years later, however, Tirpitz secured a second naval bill which called forth enough battleships to create a fleet that could by itself threaten Britain. The mistake Tirpitz made was the same other material strategists were making, however; with no firm political or strategic goals, the battleships became ends in themselves, prestigious, to be sure, but not integrated into any coherent naval policy that took into consideration the strategic evidence of history. The senior service, the army, under the successors of Moltke continued its Eastern Europe-oriented anti-navy biases and refused to coordinate army-navy planning, despite the warnings of the historian Delbrück and the eminent General Kolmar von der Goltz. Nevertheless, Tirpitz charged ahead to make the Imperial German Navy the second largest in the world.

Britain had no choice but to accept Germany's challenge, with the new Anglo-German naval arms race based on material considerations. Between 1900 and 1905 Britain's battleship inventory increased to some forty 16,000-ton, 18-knot ships mounting four 12" guns with ranges up to 4000 yards, vessels which Germany now imitated. But new technological developments quickly antiquated even the newest of these ships. Better guns, aimed "continuously" with excellent optics, increased their effective range up to 15,000 yards. The lighter steel armor could now cover the entire vessel, and new turbine engines could give it greater speed. Shipboard electricity and telephones enabled gun directors on the bridge to directly coordinate the turrets for salvo fire. And of major importance, British Captain Henry Jackson and Italian inventor Guglielmo Marconi pooled their work on the wireless to introduce maritime radio into the Royal Navy after successful tests in the fleet maneuvers of 1899. This achievement, promoted also in the Russian navy by physicist Alexander Popov and Admiral S. O. Makarov, not only improved fleet coordination but, of broader import, now enabled all oceangoing ships to maintain contact with the shore—a revolutionary advance in seafaring.

Combining these advances and those of naval architecture especially in Italy and the United States, Britain's new First Sea Lord, Admiral Sir John Fisher, designed and in 1904 laid down the *Dreadnought.* As the prototype for Britain's—and subsequently all nations'—battleships, this all-new battleship type of 18,000 tons had total armoring; mounted only big guns—ten 12" guns in twin turrets, with most along the center line; eliminated secondary armament, save for an anti-torpedo battery of twenty-seven 12-pounder, 4" quick-firers; had five 18" underwater torpedo tubes; and was propelled by steam turbines for a sustained high speed of 21 knots. From its commissioning in 1906, the *Dreadnought* added an entire new dimension to the arms race. Germany, with a new navy, had fewer changes to make and thus quickly conformed to the new weaponry.

Such new proof of material superiority practically killed the threat of the torpedo boat, but simultaneously the *jeune école* embraced the submarine as its new anti-battleship panacea. The submersible had not survived the American Civil War for lack of good engines and underwater stability. Experimention went on, however, in continental France and the United States, both seeking to neutralize British surface superiority. In 1888 the electric storage battery and hydroplanes solved the two basic shortcomings for a true workable underwater boat, and ten years later gyroscopic steering overcame another hurdle. Then, in 1899, France launched the submarine *Narval,* cigar-shaped for better stability and propelled by a triple expansion engine for surface cruising and for recharging batteries for submerged cruising. The cumbersome smokestack in the conning tower was then replaced by the battery-charging internal combustion engine and later the oil-driven diesel engine. Imperfections led to serious mishaps, such as escaping battery gases that could asphyxiate crews while submerged. But suddenly here appeared a warship that could range 500 miles on the surface at 10 knots and cruise submerged at 6½ knots to attack with underwater torpedoes that could move at 30 knots toward targets 800 yards away. Imperfect torpedoes continued to plague torpedo boats and submarines alike, but all navies henceforth pressed sub construction, especially the lesser powers—France, Russia and the United States. Admiral Fisher thus followed suit, as did Tirpitz. But the Germans preferred Mahan's teachings over those of the *jeune école,* simply because the naval high command under Tirpitz was too conservative to accept the revolutionary claims surrounding a new and untried weapon, and as long as no real tactical use could be found for the submarine the Germans gave it lowly status as a defensive torpedo boat. So the *jeune école* failed to convince the Germans, and its prestige even in France waned as the *Dreadnought* mesmerized naval and public opinion throughout the world.

By 1906, the weapons for total war existed, the last important one being the airplane, invented in 1903 by the Wright brothers in the United States. But neither sub nor plane could compete in their primitive states against the technologically perfected battleship. And yet, the arms races of Europe and now also the Pacific would not be resolved until the larger imperial rivalries were somehow settled and the elements of historical strategy fully appreciated.

THE NEW IMPERIALISM AND HISTORICAL STRATEGY

Strategic thought surrounding the questions of empire fell within the province of the historical school, especially after the publication of Mahan's book in 1890. To be sure, the material school had its effect, but in a more negative sense. Preoccupied with the technological aspects of the arms race, naval analysts gave prime attention to them and either minimized or neglected the doctrinal and tactical aspects of overseas operations. Worse, British superiority in battleships encouraged a smug complacency regarding amphibious and limited warfare, so that it was conducted on an *ad hoc* basis. Lack of staff organization in Britain negated formal interservice coordination; British imperial successes from the previous half-century encouraged conservatism; and general anti-intellectual attitudes stifled an open dialogue. Nevertheless, several officers defied rigid officialdom to join civilian scholars and analysts in considering at least the larger strategic questions raised by historical evidence. Britain as the first and only fully developed maritime empire of the period from 1867 to 1914 set the strategic example for aspiring new empires and sought to enforce the increasingly tenuous *Pax Britannica.*

The naval historians of these years produced the first critical naval histories in modern times and advanced new theories of imperial defense. The British naturally pioneered in this field, by opening up documentary archives and by popularizing naval history in their books, articles and lectures. Most instrumental in initiating the whole subject of naval history was Sir John Knox Laughton, from his first published article on Admiral Suffren in 1867 to the founding of the Naval Records Society in 1893 which began publishing documents from British naval history. The Colomb brothers simultaneously utilized historical data to advance theories on imperial defense: Captain Sir John Colomb of the Royal Marines Artillery in 1867 first pronounced Britain's need for a global network of bases, while Vice Admiral Philip H. Colomb elaborated on the same subject to the point of distorting the evidence in a series of articles in the 1880s published as a book in 1891. Amphibious strategy and tactics received significant if uneven attention from Army officers Major General Sir John Frederick Maurice and Colonels G. F. R. Henderson and Charles E. Callwell and from Major General Sir George G. Ashton of the Royal Marines.

But from 1890—and the subsequent writings of the American Captain Mahan—several brilliant histories of the great age of sail and the more recent applications of sea power received international prominence. Mahan led in the United States, Sir Julian Corbett and Herbert Richmond in Great Britain, and Gabriel Darrieus, René Daveluy and Raoul Castex in France—all naval officers or civilians closely associated with their own national navies. Other nations produced writers who imitated or borrowed heavily from these historians. In general, however, the historical school (*école historique* in France) centered in Britain, where the Society for Nautical Research began publishing its own historical journal, *The Mariner's Mirror,* in 1911.

Mahan was the advocate of imperialism and big navies of the era, though his theories were too often accepted uncritically. By focusing on the British Empire between 1660 and 1815, Mahan resurrected the old beliefs in monopolistic mercantilism and the concurrent need for overseas trade, colonies and navies to protect it all. His analysis of eighteenth-century Britain was essentially correct, but his analogy between that nation of old and the United States of the 1890s was not, for the Industrial Revolution could simply not be compared with the preceding age of agriculture and closed trade. By advancing his belief that "sea power"— trade, colonies and maritime and naval shipping—held the key to national greatness, Mahan convinced his own country and unwittingly induced France, Russia, Italy and Japan to do the same. He offered no alternatives to his formula, so that non-maritime powers eagerly accepted his ideas, while Britain took advantage of his teachings to reaffirm its own imperial strategy. That Mahan was a racist cannot be doubted, for the undeveloped, non-Western regions of the world were the helpless targets of his blatant imperial message. By asserting that battle fleets had determined command of the sea in the past, he provided an additional stimulus for battleship construction at the turn of the century, though his followers failed to note that only *superior* sea power guaranteed imperial greatness. And he ignored modern technology and the larger historical strategic questions of trade protection, amphibious operations, blockade, economic power, international law, and the whole area of limited warfare and colonial pacification.

Where Mahan—and his many popularizers—erred, Corbett generally succeeded, though his major 1911 book on principles of maritime strategy appeared too late to affect the imperial rivalries. Utilizing the critical techniques of a professional historian, Sir Julian clearly codified the major lessons of naval strategy not only from the age of sail but from the few small wars between 1854 and 1905. Like most of his contemporaries, Corbett was unconvinced about the potential effectiveness of commerce raiding cruisers, torpedo boats and crude submarines, and thus like them he minimized the importance of protecting trade. He also criticized the big battleship-big battle determinism and spoke to the more subtle applications of naval power, such as blockade, amphibious operations and the whole relationship of the navy to army objectives.

Most importantly for the imperial question, Corbett expanded upon the incomplete theories of Karl von Clausewitz to formulate guidelines for conducting limited war with naval forces. Clausewitz, wrote Corbett, mistakenly regarded the question of limited war and possible escalation to unlimited or total proportions only in vague continental terms, whereas Corbett believed that true limited war could be waged only by maritime empires. The key to waging limited warfare overseas, Corbett concluded from historical evidence, lay in two factors: deterrence and geographic isolation. With overwhelming strategic forces such as the British home fleets, the prospect of an unlimited counterstroke would deter other powers from threatening the island homeland. This achieved command of the sea, which, extended across the waters to threatened territories such as those on the Asian periphery, would lead to absolute isolation of the disputed area from outside interference by enemy navies. Once an area such as Malaya, Korea, Madagascar or New Zealand was isolated by naval forces, the area's outside routes for supply and reinforcement would be completely severed, and the area could be expeditiously conquered and pacified by ground forces. Britain as an island nation had generally understood these things, as dramatically shown in the isolation and conquest of Canada in the Seven Years War, though her ignorance of it in the American Revolution had cost her the thirteen American colonies (a fact at which Mahan also hinted). In varying degrees, the imperial powers of the late nineteenth century learned the sagacity of these principles, but through trial and error rather than by doctrinal foresight and planning.

The imperial policies behind the *Pax Britannica* before and after 1861 were reflected in the writings of Corbett, Mahan and others, with Britain always the leader and later imperial powers the imitators. The Western powers in general utilized naval units to suppress the last vestiges of piracy, slavery and smuggling throughout the undeveloped regions of the world, but also used their naval and imperial ground forces to occupy and colonize most of these same areas. The capital ship for policing remote waters remained the inshore steam gunboat, an outgrowth of the Crimean War and the importance of which peaked with the 1000-ton (and smaller) river and coastal sloops, monitors and gunboats of the 1890s. As the maritime colonial powers began to clash in these distant waters, however, cruisers and finally battleships were dispatched abroad —to protect colonies, sea lanes, bases and trade in general and to deter possible attack on any of these imperial vitals. When this happened, at the turn of the century, such disputed territories and their adjacent waters—Africa, Asia, Latin America and the Pacific—became part of a general global balance of power.

British imperial policy in these years underwent dramatic changes induced largely by the invasion scares resulting from the new technology. The fear of steam warships crossing the Channel to invade Britain led the British Army to focus defenses at home and thus to weaken the British naval presence abroad. Consequently, from 1861 a coast defense mania swept the country, leading to the construction of fortifications on the British coasts, the reduction of overseas garrisons, and the increasing reliance upon the larger colonies such as Canada and Australia to defend themselves. The arguments of the Colombs for an overseas network of garrisoned coaling stations went unheeded until the late 1880s when the new imperial rivalries and the larger warships required more substantial naval bases abroad, especially in the Mediterranean. Nevertheless, continuing hysteria over a possible cross-Channel invasion kept major British fleet units concentrated at home, placing an unusually heavy burden upon the gunboats and understrength naval and colonial commands abroad. These demands were particularly acute as Britain under prime ministers William E. Gladstone and Benjamin Disraeli extended the British Empire with new colonial acquisitions. The rise of new imperial powers finally forced Britain to relinquish its absolute maritime supremacy and to seek allies abroad to help continue the *Pax Britannica*. Throughout the last four decades of the century, therefore, Britain struggled, area by area, to preserve the imperial order against growing rivals.

In the Mediterranean, Britain tried to balance the growing imperial strength of France and Italy and to maintain the political integrity of the shaky Ottoman Empire against these powers and Russia. When Turkey proved unable to control its vassal khedive (viceroy) of Egypt, Ismail, whose army and navy (with several former American Confederate naval officers) pushed down the Red Sea into the Sudan in the late 1860s, Britain took over control of the new Suez Canal in 1875 and seven years later bombarded Alexandria from the sea and created a virtual protectorate over Egypt. When the subject Greeks challenged Ottoman authority in 1886, Britain helped blockade Greece; the Turks alone suppressed another Greek uprising in 1896–97. France led by premier Jules Ferry in 1881 used its navy to bombard and occupy Bizerte and Sfax in Tunisia, followed by outright French annexation of the country under the guise of a protectorate alongside French Algeria. Italy in 1882 pushed down the Red Sea to annex Eritrea and parts of Somaliland and Ethiopia and was driven out of Ethiopia by its army in 1896. Spain and France both applied pressure on Morocco, but by 1900 Britain enjoyed firm control over Mediterranean sea lanes from its naval bases at Gibraltar, Malta and Alexandria.

In North America, Britain faced a growing "new navy" of the United States in the 1880s which began to shift from a coast defense to an offensive stance. In 1890 Captain Mahan could envision a possible war with Britain to be decided by an American fleet concentration off New York and an amphibious assault on Nova Scotia as part of an invasion of Canada. But the U. S. Navy experimental "squadron of evolution" of 1889 grew into the seagoing North Atlantic Squadron in 1897 to pose as a potential threat to British transatlantic communications. The economic thrust of the United States and Russia into the Pacific had caused British anxieties for Canada's western defenses, especially during Russia's war with Turkey in 1877–78 and with the establishment of an American coaling station at Pearl Harbor, Hawaii, in 1887 and of the Puget Sound Naval Base at Bremerton, Washington, opposite the British base at Esquimalt, British Columbia. Such fears proved unrealistic, however, especially as the focus of Anglo-American tensions remained in Latin America.

The Caribbean Sea continued to be a British lake, patrolled by warships from Bermuda and Jamaica, but the U. S. Navy—counter to public opinion—from the late 1860s actively sought a base of its own in this "American middle sea." Britain and the United States cooperated to eradicate slavery from Spanish Cuba in 1869, where a war scare erupted between Spain and the United States in 1873–74 before a British warship arrived to stabilize the situation. In the 1880s the French failed to build a canal across the Colombian Isthmus of Panama, and threatening

American warships angered Santo Domingo and supported an unsuccessful scheme for a canal across Nicaragua. In the 1890s, however, the Spanish suppression of Cuban rebels and two German warships forcing concessions from Haiti combined with Mahan's writings to stimulate American imperial designs in the Caribbean. The U. S. Navy's weakness had been dramatized by the victory of the Chilean fleet over Peru in 1879–81, by the Chilean navy's suppression of a dictatorial takeover attempt in 1891 and by the subsequent diplomatic break between Chile and the United States over an incident involving American sailors on liberty in Valparaiso—finally settled in 1892. A similar navy-led revolt in Brazil in 1893–94 failed, with an American naval force standing by for possible intervention at Rio de Janeiro. Immediately thereafter, Britain and the United States nearly ruptured their relations over a boundary dispute between Venezuela and British Guiana, until diplomatic maneuvering ended the war scare early in 1897. By then, the imperial fever had aroused the American people, not against mighty Britain but against poor old Spain.

The Spanish-American War of 1898 developed from American desires to free Cuba from Spanish rule and from the big-navy expansionism of Captain Mahan and Assistant Secretary of the Navy Theodore Roosevelt. When the American battleship *Maine* arrived off riot-torn Havana to protect American lives there early in the year, it and 260 of its crew were blown up by a mysterious submarine mine. The incident and others led to an American declaration of war in April. The U. S. Navy implemented long-standing strategic war plans and turned over strategic direction to a Naval War Board that included Mahan. Neither side contemplated attacking the other's homeland, though the hysterical American public caused substantial naval forces to be tied down to coast defense. The American offensive, relatively swift, clumsy and almost comical, quickly destroyed Spanish naval power. On May 1 Commodore George Dewey—with four cruisers basing at British Hong Kong —easily destroyed the seven old Spanish warships at Manila Bay in the Philippines, despite notoriously poor gunnery. Meanwhile Admiral Pascual Cervera with four armored cruisers and three destroyers slipped into Santiago Harbor on Cuba's south coast, only to be blockaded there by the American squadron of Commodore W. S. Schley. The main American fleet of four new battleships under Rear Admiral W. T. Sampson then arrived and seized the fine harbor of Guantánamo Bay forty miles to the east as an advanced base. Late in June the fleet supported a ragged amphibious assault on Daiquiri and Siboney, twenty miles above Santiago. When these troops gained the high ground over Santiago, Cervera had no choice but to attempt a breakout. On July 3 the Spanish ships cleared the harbor and ran westward, only to be destroyed or beached by Sampson's ships in pursuit. Expeditionary forces then took Puerto Rico late in July and Manila in August. Spain capitulated and ceded its remaining empire to the United States: Puerto Rico, the Philippines and Guam in the Marianas. Cuba became a virtual American protectorate, as Britain saw its strategic dominance over the Caribbean challenged.

In sub-Saharan Africa, the British had few European rivals between the mid-1860s and mid-1880s as they extended their empire over several primitive peoples and used gunboats to police coasts and rivers against slavers and to protect British lives and property. In West Africa, Palmerston's anti-slave strategy led to the annexation of Lagos in 1861, followed by the seizure of Elmina from the Dutch ten years later, war against the Ashanti tribes in 1873–74 and concurrent policing of the Gold Coast alongside the French in Senegal and the Germans in the Cameroons. In South Africa, where diamonds were discovered in 1867, the British fought native wars against the Kaffirs, Basutos and Zulus and battled the Dutch-descended Boer farmers in open war, 1880–81. In East Africa, in addition to a brief punitive expedition into Ethiopia (Abyssinia) in 1867–68, the British between 1862 and 1883 crushed Arab slave trading from Zanzibar and used cruiser sweeps and a naval blockade to stop it along the entire coast. Isolated slaving continued and required naval patrols by the European powers and British military intervention in Nyasaland, but after fifteen nations in 1890 agreed to suppress slavery in concert it was gradually eradicated (Brazil gradually abolished the practice between 1871 and 1885, the last large nation to do so).

The most intense new imperial rivalries erupted in the mid-1880s and focused on Africa for the next two decades, but the British navy still controlled its peripheral waters from the bases at Gibraltar, the Falkland Islands, Simonstown in South Africa, Aden and India. British colonial forces suppressed the Ashantis and annexed Nigeria in the west in the 1890s, tightened controls over South Africa after the discovery of gold there in 1886, and sent gunboats up the Nile to help suppress a fanatical Arab uprising and capture Khartoum in 1884–85 and then assist General Sir Horatio Kitchener to conquer the Sudan, 1896–98, especially at the decisive Battle of Omdurman. The pacification of Uganda followed. Belgium signaled the coming of new rivals in 1877 by initiating the conquest of the Congo. Germany burst upon the imperial scene in 1883–85 by colonizing Tanganyika in East Africa, Southwest Africa and the Cameroons and Togoland in West Africa; marines and warships kept the natives pacified. Later light cruisers were used to help put down a last fanatical uprising in German East and Southwest Africa in 1904–08. France made Madagascar into a protectorate in 1882, used naval bombardments and landings against rebellious natives in 1885 and 1894–95 before turning the island into a colony in 1896 and using the army to pacify it over the next ten years. France and Britain offset Italy's foray into the Red Sea with tiny protectorates there, while Spain moved into West African Guinea and Rio de Oro in 1902 and 1907.

The European balance of power embraced Africa, though all frontier clashes were resolved by diplomacy and strong British shows of force. In East Africa, the British occupied the coast of Kenya in 1887 to thwart further German expansion, and three years later a great power compromise endorsed the French reign in Madagascar, transferred North Sea Heligoland Island from Britain to Germany, and allowed Britain to establish a protectorate over Zanzibar. Between 1896 and 1899 Britain used its navy to subdue the natives there and destroy the last vestiges of East African slavery. In 1898 Kitchener's army forced the French withdrawal from Fashoda on the Nile, but the next year the two Dutch republics of South Africa tried to throw off British suzerainty and courted German assistance. This Boer War (1899–1902) caught Britain unprepared for a major limited war, but its command of the sea enabled a rapid sealift of troops and supplies from England to Durban and the blockade of German contraband at Delagoa Bay in neighboring Portuguese Mozambique from 1900. The Boers initially drove British ground forces back on Ladysmith, where they were besieged before being relieved by reinforcements and three naval brigades supported by naval gun carriages fashioned by Captain Percy Scott. The British counterattack and Kitchener's scorched-earth policy and civilian concentration camps finally defeated the Boer armies, but such excesses of imperialism forced Britain to give South Africa dominion status. With the increasing liberalization of colonial rule throughout most of Africa, the balance of African colonial spheres stabilized. In the last analysis, however, only Britain really profited from the great wealth of its holdings in Africa; the other countries used theirs largely for purposes of national prestige.

British domination of the Indian Ocean littoral continued to act as a strategic buffer against possible Russian expansion. Imperial forces kept the northern Indian frontier pacified, between an expedition into Bhutan in 1865 and a 1903–04 drive into Tibet. British control over the Persian Gulf continued with the Trucial System, treaties with Persia and increased intervention in Muscat and Bahrain to suppress the Arab slave trade. Ottoman Turkey used the fleet of Kuwait to bombard and take Qatif and to help Turkey annex Hasa and Yemen in 1871. To offset Turkish pressure and protect the growing British steam-driven trade in the Gulf, Britain in the 1880s established a protectorate over Bahrain and instituted regular Navy patrols and in the 1890s extended the Trucial System to include Muscat, Qatar and Kuwait. Britain thus brought maritime order to the Persian Gulf, frustrated large-scale gun running and slaving and countered real or imagined Turkish, French and Russian threats there before 1905. By then, the Gulf had become but another arena of the European power balance, and the British profited politically and commercially from their administration of the Trucial System.

The Southeast Asian flank of this Indian Ocean defensive network required British intervention against slavery, piracy and general lawlessness which grew into outright occupation. From Singapore and south Burma, the British responded to French interference in Burma in 1885–86 with a riverborne expedition up the Irrawaddy and the annexation of Burma. Malay piracy in the 1870s brought British naval intervention and eventual control over the entire Malay peninsula, while British and American colonists in nearby Sarawak and North Borneo asked for British annexation, obtained in 1888. The Dutch controlled the adjacent East Indies and western New Guinea (Papua), finally pacifying the last native uprisings throughout the islands by 1908. Moro pirates from the southern Philippines faced Spanish gunboats in a prolonged anti-pirate campaign from the 1860s, but it was U. S. Navy gunboats and Army forces that generally pacified the Moros during the first decade of the new century. Farther south, the British Australasian Squadron and colonial naval brigades put down the last Maori native uprising in New Zealand in the 1860s, and the establishment of British protectorates over the south coast of New Guinea and the southern Solomon Islands in the 1880s and 1890s provided a strategic shield for the growing colony of Australia.

The imperial surge of the late nineteenth century also led to a scramble for relatively worthless islands in Pacific Oceania. In the South Pacific, the British occupied the Fijis (1874), Gilberts and Ellices (1892) and Tonga Islands (1900), while the French made Tahiti and the Society Islands a colony (1880). Britain and France jointly administered the New Hebrides. In 1884–85 Germany claimed the Marshall Islands and part of New Guinea. Germany, United States and Britain claimed Samoa, but after a savage hurricane which ravaged the warships of all three nations in Apia Harbor in 1889 they agreed to neutralize Samoa as an independent country. Over the next decade, however, the agreement was abrogated, Britain withdrew, and the other two powers divided Samoa between them. In 1898–99, with the American victory over Spain, the United States obtained Guam in the Marianas, occupied uninhabited Wake Island, and annexed the Hawaiian Islands at the invitation of the native government. Possession of the Hawaiian and Aleutian groups gave America predominance in the North Pacific. Simultaneously, Spain sold the Carolines and other Marianas islands to Germany. By 1900, the Pacific spheres of influence had been stabilized, with each policed by occasional warships and small colonial and native garrisons.

Major imperial rivalries in the Orient involved Britain, France, China and Indochina (Vietnam, Laos and Cambodia). Manchu China, still resisting Westernization, did not end the bloody Taiping Rebellion until 1864 and then only under the leadership of American and British soldiers of fortune. Neither could China control its own pirates without the naval forces of seven Western nations led by British Admiral Sir Henry Keppel in 1867–69. Anti-Western riots required the presence of Western warships, especially off Tientsin in 1870, so that China during the 1870s began to purchase the obsolete vessels of Western nations and to set up coastal arms factories at Shanghai, Foochow and Tientsin, largely with French assistance. But the weak Manchu leadership kept the Chinese Navy divided between northern and southern commissioners who drew from a Sea Defense Fund (established in 1875) to purchase ships and guns. The dynamic northern commissioner from 1870 to 1895, Li Hung-chang, built up his own Peiyang fleet, created a naval academy, and fortified Port Arthur to offset Japan. The several southern commissioners over these years tried to use their Nanyang fleet to protect the coast from the Yangtze River to the Gulf of Tonkin thus running afoul of the French. The French naval conquests in Indochina in 1858–61 increased their involvement there, leading to a French naval expedition up the Red River to capture Hanoi and face the Chinese "Black Flag" pirates behind Hué in 1873. China then helped the natives of northern Vietnam to close trade on the Red, leading to another French naval expedition to take Hanoi in 1883. When it was severely punished by the Black Flags, the force of three ironclads and two gunboats under Admiral A. A. P. Courbet bombarded Hué in July and forced new concessions, including a Chinese agreement to withdraw its forces in 1884. But resulting fears for her southern frontier led China into war with France.

The Sino-French War of 1884–85 failed to arrest French incursions into Indochina and seriously weakened China. Chinese arms on land initially defeated the French; their wooden vessels and fire rafts could not begin to challenge French armorclad and torpedo launches, nor would Li Hung-chang send any of his warships from the north to assist the Nanyang fleet. On August 23, 1884, Admiral Courbet with eight vessels in twelve minutes virtually annihilated the Chinese squadron of eleven wooden craft at the Ma-wei anchorage of Foochow, then destroyed the dockyard. In October Courbet blockaded and bombarded the coast of Formosa and in February 1885 destroyed a five-ship Nanyang fleet relief expedition. British pressure failed to discourage the French, who captured Langson in northern Vietnam, Keelung and the Pescadores Islands, though their army was crushed outside Langson. The imperialistic Ferry government in France fell, and the peace treaty reestablished the prewar *status quo,* but in 1887 France created the colony of French Indochina from Vietnam and Cambodia. Independent Siam intervened in Laos against French and Chinese alike, whereupon French warships anchored off Siamese Bangkok to force the cession of Laos and western Cambodia into French Indochina in 1893. With mobility by sea, the French Navy controlled this colony in the same manner as Navy and Army colonial leaders kept North Africa and Madagascar pacified. The presence of British naval forces at Singapore and Hong Kong guaranteed Chinese integrity from further French pressure, but the rise of Japan created more complex difficulties.

Japanese anti-Western attitudes and internal rivalries exposed serious weaknesses, but Japan moved decisively to correct its deficiencies. Civil war between the ruling Tokugawa shogunate and the rival Satsuma and Choshu clans in the 1860s brought on a Franco-American naval bombardment of Choshu Shimonoseki and a British shelling of Satsuman Kagoshima in 1863. The next year British Admiral A. L. Kuper in one of the Royal Navy's last active 101-gun first-rate ships of the line led nine British, three French, one American and four Dutch ships—some with rifled cannon—in the reduction of the forts of Shimonoseki and the occupation of Yokohama. The Satsuma and Tokugawa both yielded to these actions to grant more concessions to the West. The civil war did not end, however, until 1868 when the rebel clans defeated government forces led by Dutch-trained Kamajiro Enomoto at the naval battle of Hakodate. Admired by the victors, Enomoto was appointed as the first vice admiral of the new Imperial Japanese Navy, separated from direct army control in 1872. Throughout these wars and after, the Japanese obtained Western warships, naval engineers and professional instruction at home and abroad in a concerted effort to adopt Western technology. Britain dominated Japanese naval development with a naval mission in Japan during the 1870s, during which the new government of the "Meiji restoration" subdued the last Satsuma revolt. So unified, Japan could now join in the imperial expansion of the West.

Though resentful of her strong dependence on Britain, Japan borrowed whatever naval techniques and advisers were necessary to counter neighboring Russia and China. A gradual strategy of defensive expansion led to a punitive though temporary expedition against Chinese Formosa in 1874, the occupation of the Bonin Islands with American concurrence the next year, and the seizure of the Ryukyu Islands (principally Okinawa) in 1879, giving Japan a favorable strategic position opposite Chinese Shanghai. Russia's establishment of a naval base at Vladivostok in 1874 led Japan the next year to occupy the Kurile Islands in the

north, agreeing to Russia's possession of the large adjacent island of
Sakhalin. From this island defense perimeter, Japan turned toward its
ancient target, Korea, whose internal political chaos had led to French
and American naval bombardments and landings at Kanghwa forts
guarding the entrance of the Han River in 1866 and 1871. With
covetous eyes on Chinese Korea, Japan expanded its Army and Navy.
In the 1880s the Army became pro-German, and the Navy replaced its
British advisers with French and German officers; French naval designer Emile Bertin convinced Japan to adopt the *jeune école* scheme
of building cruisers and torpedo boats. The Army dominated strategy,
however, while the Navy expanded the defensive perimeter by occupying
the Volcano Islands (notably Iwo Jima) in 1891. Japanese pressure
against Korea mounted as Japan grew ever more anxious about China
and Russia.

Russian eastward expansion across Asia helped to turn the Orient
into a major area of imperial conflict. Ever worried, Britain made war
on Afghanistan in 1878–80 when that country dared to court Russia.
The new pro-British Afghan government failed to discourage the Russians from conquering adjacent Merv in 1884, after which, however,
Russia looked to the Pacific. When in the 1880s Russian forces tried
to obtain exclusive rights over Wonsan Harbor in northeast Korea, the
British occupied Port Hamilton in southern Korea until the Russians
withdrew. China, beset by the French war in Indochina, simultaneously
submitted to Russian demands around the Amur River and both countries agreed to withdraw their forces from Korea. China remained too
hopelessly divided to resist foreign pressures, its navy separated in four
parts. Only the Peiyang fleet of Li Hung-chang remained strong, reorganized in 1888 with two powerful 7400-ton battleships from Germany, making nine modern vessels concentrated at the new Port
Arthur base under Admiral Ting Ju-ch'ang. Anglo-American advisers
had only limited successes in teaching the stubborn Chinese, whose
naval strategy consisted only of traditional coast defense with strong
fortifications and inshore warships. Japan, recognizing Chinese weaknesses, decided to settle the question of which Eastern power would
dictate the future of Korea and act as a bulwark against further Western imperialism.

The Sino-Japanese War of 1894–95 followed amphibious landings
by both armies near Seoul and a naval skirmish in which the Japanese
sank a Chinese gunboat and drove off a cruiser at Inchon (Chemulpo).
Both sides then ferried troops on transports to Korea, the Chinese via
the Yalu River, the Japanese via Inchon and Pusan. Admiral Ting used
the Peiyang fleet to protect the coast near his bases of Port Arthur and
Weihaiwei on the Liaotung and Shantung peninsulas, while Admiral

Sukenori Ito's Japanese fleet roamed the Yellow Sea and bombarded both bases in August 1894. When Ting escorted a convoy of reinforcements for the Chinese army retreating from Pyongyang toward the Yalu, Ito attacked him in the battle of the Yalu River on September 17— two Chinese battleships and ten cruisers against a dozen better-armed Japanese cruisers. Steaming in line-ahead, Ito's fleet bludgeoned Ting's ships in ragged line-abreast, then maneuvered into two divisions to split the Chinese units and send some of them into panic flight. Losing five cruisers, the Chinese fled to Port Arthur just before the Japanese army crossed the Yalu into Manchuria and landed on the Liaotung peninsula for an overland descent on Arthur. Ting broke through Ito's blockade to reach Weihaiwei before Arthur fell in November, only to be blockaded at Weihaiwei by Ito and an army expeditionary force. In February 1895 Japanese torpedo boats sank a Chinese cruiser, while the larger ships bombarded Weihaiwei and its trapped fleet. Admiral Ting committed suicide, his own torpedo boats failed in a last breakout attempt, and Weihaiwei surrendered on the 12th. When the Japanese overran Manchuria and threatened Peking, China submitted.

The postwar settlement directly involved the Western powers who could accept the cession of Chinese Formosa and the Pescadores Islands to Japan but not mainland Port Arthur. Russia led France and Germany in preventing that from happening and so gave Russia more time to complete the Trans-Siberian Railroad to Vladivostok. In 1896–98 Russia even obtained from China the right to route the track across Manchuria and the outright cession of Port Arthur for the Russian Pacific Fleet. The helpless Manchu dynasty still had nine German-built cruisers, but these were insufficient to challenge Russia, which now threatened Korea. Japan responded however by incorporating the seventeen captured Chinese vessels into its own navy and ordering 12"-gunned 12,000 to 15,000-ton battleships from Britain and armored cruisers, destroyers and torpedo boats from Britain, Germany, France and Italy. Modeling its admiralty, tactics and training closely on the British, Japan determined to create a first-class navy to prevent another diplomatic humiliation at the hands of the Russian-led Western powers.

In 1897–1900 the Western Pacific emerged as an area of strategic rivalries equal to that of Europe, with the *Pax Britannica* succumbing to six naval nations acting unilaterally. The general victim was China: Russia extended its control from Arthur to Dairen and the Liaotung peninsula and pressed into north Korea. Germany occupied Tsingtao and leased Kiaochow Bay. France moved into Kwangchow Bay. Britain secured Weihaiwei and extended Kowloon, near Hong Kong. The United States conquered and annexed the Philippine Islands, but feared for the integrity of China and its own trade position there. So in 1899 the

United States initiated its "Open Door policy" to prevent the economic dismemberment of China, a noble-sounding appeal that the other powers had to accept in principle. The policy gained time for the *Pax Britannica* and for Britain's economic penetration into the fertile Yangtze basin and provided stability in China while America fought the Philippine insurrection (1899–1902) and began the pacification of the Moro tribes. Where the Manchus could do nothing against the West, the fanatical Boxer Rebellion tried by besieging the Western legations in Peking in 1899–1900. For the last time in the Orient the Western powers followed British leadership by accepting the command of Vice Admiral Sir Edward H. Seymour over some thirty warships from Great Britain, Germany, Russia, France, Japan, the United States, Italy and Austria. Repulsed from a landing attempt at the Taku forts at the mouth of the Peiho River, Seymour's fleet bombarded them into submission early in 1900. Then in July and August 18,000 troops assaulted and took Tientsin, drove up the Peiho and fought their way into Peking. The Boxers crushed, Russia immediately occupied all of Manchuria and collected a huge indemnity payment from crippled China. Anxious over Russian expansion, Japan moved to fill the strategic vacuum now developing with the collapse of the British *pax*.

By 1900 the imperial and limited wars of four decades had been absorbed into the larger strategic struggle now developing not only in Europe but on a global scale. Whatever lessons were to be gleaned from these many activities would now be submerged by the naval arms race dominated by the *Dreadnought*. If general war was to be avoided, a new balance of power would have to be constructed, the object of a new system of naval alliances.

NAVAL ALLIANCE SYSTEMS

The Anglo-German confrontation over battleship construction from 1900 required general British strategic realignments that affected power relations everywhere in the world, but these could not prevent the steady plunge of the powers into the catastrophe of World War I. In the first three years of the twentieth century Britain finally perceived Germany to be the real threat to European and thus global stability and the *Pax Britannica*. The two-power fleet standard originally aimed at France and Russia was therefore replaced with a battleship construction program to counter Tirpitz's "risk theory" of building two thirds (38) of British battleship strength. Tirpitz believed Britain would not risk war against such a fleet because of heavy British fleet commitments abroad, enabling Germany to dictate policy on the continent and in the colonial sphere. But Tirpitz underestimated Britain's adaptability to such a threat.

Under the dynamic leadership of Admiral Sir John Fisher, Second Sea Lord from mid-1902 and First Sea Lord from Trafalgar Day (October 21), 1904, the Royal Navy began to replace its old battleships with dreadnoughts and instituted important reforms in administration, personnel and gunnery. And with the conclusion of active imperial pacification operations, gunboat construction ended in favor of the battleship and its flotilla. Most importantly, however, the British initiated a diplomatic policy aimed at reducing tension abroad, ending Britain's virtual political isolation, and thus enabling major fleet units to be reconcentrated at home against Germany. Especially from the fleet redistribution scheme of December 1904, the British naval legions began to return to the strategic center of the Empire.

In the Western Hemisphere, Britain accepted the assertiveness of the United States and henceforth fostered friendly relations. Under the dynamic leadership of naval-minded President Theodore Roosevelt (1901–09), the U. S. Navy became a blue-water battleship fleet dedicated to eliminating all European navies from the Caribbean and protecting both seaboards. Virtually his own Secretary of the Navy, Roosevelt promoted battleship authorizations from Congress, utilized an advisory General Board of senior admirals under Dewey, modernized gunnery and used submarines to complement coastal fortifications, created the Atlantic and Pacific fleets in 1906 and 1907, and in the latter year concentrated all sixteen battleships in the Atlantic Fleet, making it the largest single battle force in the world at the time. Cruisers led the Pacific Fleet and the smaller Asiatic Fleet created in 1910.

With shared suspicions over Germany in the Caribbean, Britain gradually turned over its policing to the United States, including in 1900–01 the right to build and fortify a canal across Panama. When Colombia stalled this American plan, in 1903 Roosevelt engineered and supported a quick and successful revolution in Panama. To guard the Canal, built over the years 1904 to 1914, Roosevelt established fleet bases at Culebra off Puerto Rico and (by lease from Cuba) at Guantánamo Bay in 1903, the same year that German warships bombarded the coast of Venezuela over fiscal difficulties. Needing economic order in Latin America to keep out the Germans and promote American profits, Roosevelt instituted his own corollary to the Monroe Doctrine by declaring the exclusive American right of intervention there. Between 1905 and 1916 therefore the Navy landed Marines and Army troops in several chaotic Caribbean nations to restore economic and political order. Roosevelt consciously courted British favor, as anti-German feeling mounted in the United States. As a result, Britain between 1904 and 1906 (officially by 1911) withdrew its North American squadron from Bermuda, closed the base at Jamaica, abandoned St. Lucia altogether, and downgraded and turned over the major fleet installations at Halifax and Esquimalt to the Canadian government. Henceforth, Britain would depend upon the U. S. Navy—by 1905 the third largest navy in the world—to protect its dominions in the Western Hemisphere and to insure maritime stability there.

But American naval expansion, becoming global, would soon rival the Royal Navy in overall strength. Both the U. S. Navy and Army began—ever so haltingly, devoid of realistic institutional changes— to reform along European lines, while the Navy became the tool of impressing the other powers of American independence of the British naval strength that had so long protected North America. But American fears of primarily Germany led to numerous unilateral shows of naval force: the entire Atlantic battle ("Great White") fleet circumnavigated the globe via Japan in 1907–09, visited British and French ports in 1910–11 and the Mediterranean in 1913, while one division of battle-ships called at ports in Germany, Sweden and Baltic Russia in 1911. Such anxieties, as over a potential German landing in strife-torn Mexico, helped cause American interventions there between 1914 and 1917. An incident involving an American naval shore party at Tampico in April 1914 prompted President Woodrow Wilson to order the occupa-tion of Vera Cruz taken by force by naval and Marine landing parties. After the dispute was settled, the Mexican civil war spilled over onto American soil in 1916, followed by an American overland expedition into Mexico. After the outbreak of war in Europe in 1914, many Ameri-can admirals presumed that Germany would defeat Britain and then cross the Atlantic to stake out an empire in the Western Hemisphere, a fear fed by German diplomatic moves. So the United States planned to fight Germany alone, and in 1915 new naval authorizations provided for new battleships and battle cruisers to command local American waters against the German High Seas Fleet. Without advanced bases along its Eastern seaboard like Canadian Halifax and British Bermuda, the Americans maintained a strong unilateral and independent strategic naval stance for deterring Germany or for fighting its fleet on the open sea.

The sudden rise of Japan as the fourth ranking naval power in the world alarmed both Britain and the United States, but both preferred Japanese to Russian supremacy in the Far East and devised their diplomacy accordingly. In 1902 Britain allied formally with Japan and agreed to intervene in any Russo-Japanese conflict only if a third party —France and/or Germany—joined Japan's enemy. Both powers en-dorsed the American "open door" in China, Manchuria and Korea, a further anti-Russian statement which the United States informally sup-ported by basing its own warships at British Hong Kong and Japanese ports. The Americans used such Chinese ports as Chefoo near British Weihaiwei on the Shantung peninsula, established the Yangtze River Patrol of three former Spanish gunboats at Shanghai, and—much to Russian displeasure—stationed a gunboat at the port of Newchang on the Manchurian Liaotung peninsula. The Anglo-Japanese alliance enabled Britain to recall its heavy fleet units from Asia, leaving Japan to Russia's vigorous reaction. Reneging on an agreement with China in 1902 to evacuate Manchuria, Russia the next year challenged the "open door" and threatened to intervene in Korea. American Admiral Robley D. Evans then concentrated three battleships, two monitors and several cruisers at Chefoo, but Russia strengthened its naval defenses in Asia to thwart Japan. Hastening seven of its twenty-seven battleships to Port Arthur and cruisers and destroyers to there and Vladivostok, with prefabricated submarines going across the Trans-Sib Railway to the latter place, Russia prepared for war with Japan—a smaller and weaker power in the eyes of the Western world.

The Russo-Japanese War of 1904–05 assumed maritime proportions from the outset, with Japan having the distinct strategic advantage. Geographically, athwart Russian communications between its two Asiatic ports, Japan had merely to control these waters and support the Army's transfer to Manchuria. As in antiquity, Japanese naval policy remained subordinate to the Army, but command of the Yellow Sea served this strategy perfectly. Furthermore, the main Russian fleet lay in the distant Baltic, with another element in the Black Sea, whose outlets—the Skaggerak and Dardanelles—were controlled by the British navy. The only possible shortcut between Kronstadt and the Far East, the Northeast Passage, had been closed in 1902 when the tsarist government had stupidly stopped Admiral Makarov's new icebreaking efforts there as unwanted competition to the Trans-Sib Railway.

So before Russia could dispatch more reinforcements to Asia, Japan launched a sneak torpedo boat attack against Port Arthur on February 8, 1904, and one of its cruiser squadrons destroyed two Russian cruisers off Inchon (Chemulpo). Then Japan declared war officially. The main Japanese fleet of six new battleships with escorts led by Admiral Heihachiro Togo mined and blockaded the entrance to Port Arthur, enabling the Army to land at Inchon and drive toward the Yalu. Admiral Makarov took command at Arthur, only to be lost when his flagship struck a mine and sank with all hands in April. In May the first Japanese army crossed the Yalu and a second landed above Port Arthur on the Liaotung peninsula, but Togo's supporting fleet lost two of its six battleships to Russian mines. Then, in July, the inept Russian viceroy for the East, Admiral Evgeni Alexiev, ordered Admiral Wilhelm Vitgeft and his six old battleships to break out of Togo's blockade. Togo intercepted Vitgeft in the battle of the Yellow Sea on August 10 and completely routed him, killing Vitgeft with a lucky hit on the bridge of his flagship. Japanese warships sank one Russian cruiser in this action and another out of Vladivostok, the others escaping back into their own or neutral ports. The latter refuge meant internment for the duration, a rule of international law strictly enforced by the American battleships and monitors at Chinese Chefoo and Shanghai. Russian warships far away in the Red Sea began to seize neutral vessels, mostly British, prompting the British and Americans to apply diplomatic pressure and the British to close the Suez Canal, Dardanelles and all their own ports to Russian shipping. Russia had no choice but to transfer its naval crews ashore to help in the defense of Port Arthur against the Japanese Army, while a relief army hastened thence from Eastern Europe via the Trans-Sib.

To save Port Arthur, Russia then made the desperate decision to dispatch its main fleet from the Baltic on an 18,000 mile voyage as a relief force. Lacking its own merchant marine and raw coal, the Imperial Russian Navy contracted with a private German steamship company to provide fuel en route and arranged to round Africa while another part of the fleet obtained permission to pass through the Suez Canal. Admiral Zinovi Petrovich Rozshestvensky led the "Second Pacific Squadron"—a hodgepodge of aging and new inferior battleships and escorts—out of the Baltic in October 1904, only to succumb to totally unreasonable fears of Japanese torpedo boats in the North Sea by bombarding a group of helpless British fishing trawlers at Dogger Bank. British diplomats thereafter harassed Russian coaling efforts along the way, assisted by the tropical heat of Africa and coal dust which lowered morale already plagued by political malcontents within the fleet. The two Russian squadrons rendezvoused off French Madagascar, only to be threatened by unsuccessful mutinies on two ships early in 1905. Rozhestvensky passed Singapore in April and was joined at Camranh Bay, French Indochina, by another squadron from the Baltic. By then, however, Port Arthur had fallen, and Rozhestvensky had to reshape his course for Vladivostok via the Tsushima Strait, where Togo lay waiting for him.

On May 27, 1905, Togo's compact, well-disciplined and well-gunned four battleships, eight cruisers, twenty-one destroyers and sixty torpedo boats ensnared the dispirited and exhausted Russian fleet at the Battle of Tsushima. Twice crossing Rozhestvensky's line—"capping the T"—Togo's gunners sank three Russian battleships and during the night and following day sank five more and captured the remaining two (one with the wounded Rozhestvensky on board). In addition, the Japanese sank one and captured two coastal ironclads, captured and sank seven cruisers, and sank five destroyers and two torpedo boats. Japan thus sent 146,900 tons of Russian naval shipping to the bottom and captured some 40,000 tons more. Of the surviving four Russian cruisers, three escaped to Manila, only to be interned by the Americans, and the other managed to reach Vladivostok. The Japanese lost but three torpedo boats in probably the most stunning naval victory of modern times. A new Russian army had gathered at Harbin to check a northward Japanese offensive into Manchuria, and Vladivostok held on, sending out patrols of thirteen American-built submarines. But Tsushima had shaken Russian society and the Navy, where mutinies now erupted, most dramatically aboard the Black Sea battleship *Potemkin;* its successful mutineers surrendered the vessel to the Rumanian government and went into exile. Mutually exhausted, Russia and Japan concluded peace in September 1905 at the American naval base at Portsmouth, New Hampshire, with Theodore Roosevelt mediating.

Postwar great power arrangements in the Pacific left Japan generally supreme as a buffer between a retrenching Russia and an active United States. Satisfied that Russian pressure on India had been checked by British special status in Persia, Afghanistan and Tibet and that the seventh-ranked Russian navy had been neutralized, Britain concluded a more permanent alliance with Japan late in 1905 and withdrew its last major fleet units from the Far East. Russia surrendered Port Arthur and southern Sakhalin Island to Japan, along with all claims to Korea, control over which Britain and the United States handed to Japan. All the powers in 1905–07 ceased their imperialistic ventures in China and accepted the "open door," while the enfeebled Manchu dynasty went through its final death throes, 1908–12. Taking advantage of American President William Howard Taft's "dollar diplomacy," the Manchus in 1911 involved American shipbuilders in a Chinese naval revival, but this collapsed the next year with the creation of the new Republic of China. The United States and Japan accepted their mutual spheres of influence in the Pacific, but antagonisms mounted after 1905 over American immigration policies and the naval arms race. Japan sought naval self-sufficiency, commissioning its last battleship in a British shipyard in 1910 and hoping to build a battleship fleet 70 percent that of America's. The United States Navy stopped admitting Japanese midshipmen to its Naval Academy in 1906, made an impressive "good will" visit to Japan with the Atlantic-based "Great White Fleet" in 1908, and evolved a strategic "Orange Plan" for eventually fighting Japan. The fleet would base at Bremerton, San Francisco and Pearl Harbor for any campaign westward, although its forward bases at Guam in the Marianas and at Subic Bay and Manila in the Philippines remained woefully inadequate for such a war. American fears of Germany, however, kept the battleships concentrated in the Atlantic and required that conflict with Japan be carefully avoided.

With the Japanese fleet allied (by renewed treaty in 1911), the American fleet basically friendly and the Russian fleet neutralized, Britain also reduced its strategic requirements in the Mediterranean by accommodating the fifth- and sixth-ranked naval powers, France and Italy. The new French battleships in 1902 suddenly lost importance with the return of the *jeune école* to control, now championing submarines. More significant, Britain and France finally realized their mutual strategic needs for countering the Triple Alliance of Germany, Austria-Hungary and Italy and in April 1904 concluded the *Entente Cordiale*. They initiated military conversations and agreed that Britain should have absolute control over Egypt and that France be allowed to expand from Tunisia and Algeria over Morocco. This antagonized imperialistic Germany, as did American pro-Anglo-French naval shows of force during several diplomatic crises over Morocco in 1904–05. An American squadron of six battleships and eight cruisers demonstrated in the middle sea in May 1904, and the following year another American battleship squadron visited British Gibraltar while President Roosevelt arbitrated a Franco-German dispute over Morocco in favor of France. Italy proved to be no real threat at sea, for despite its alliance with Germany, it had lost the naval race with France, concluded new understandings with that nation in 1902, and begun to counter the small navy of its reluctant Austro-Hungarian ally. But the appearance of German naval units in the middle sea from 1905 converted the region into but one more theater of general European balance of power.

By the end of 1905, British naval diplomacy had succeeded in reconcentrating the major fleet units at home and for the next four years focused on anti-German aims, especially in the Mediterranean. Spain in 1907–08 sided with the *Entente Cordiale* over Morocco and contracted for three new British-built battleships. Simultaneously, the *Entente Cordiale* and Franco-Russian alliance grew into a Triple Entente against the Triple Alliance, with Britain settling its differences with Russia over the Persian Gulf. More difficult was Britain's desire to shore up Ottoman Turkey, "the sick man of Europe," against covetous neighbors Austria, Russia, Italy and especially Greece. When a local naval race between Turkey and Greece commenced in 1908, Britain provided an admiral to direct the Ottoman fleet. But Britain's most strategic change involved the abandonment of the two-power standard. Because the U. S. Navy had become so powerful, Britain could not hope to build a battleship fleet the equal of the next two, Germany's and America's. So in April 1909, thanks largely to the work of Rear Admiral J. R. Jellicoe, the Admiralty decided to build a battle fleet 60 percent larger in dreadnoughts than Germany's. From this time forward, any British thought of war against the United States was simply rejected, naval conversations with the French were accelerated, and all plans for naval war were made with Germany generally in mind.

Between 1909 and 1912 tensions mounted as the alliances grew ever more firm. Russia, intervening with Britain in a Persian revolution, initiated a new dreadnought, cruiser and destroyer construction program, which included the world's first minelaying submarine, and streamlined its admiralty under a dynamic new Minister of Marine, Vice Admiral Ivan K. Grigorovich. France planned to concentrate its six new dreadnoughts at Brest against Germany, but instead based them at Toulon to deter the growing fleets of Italy and Austria. In 1911 France finally landed an expeditionary force at Fez to conquer anarchy-ridden Morocco, and Britain countered the dispatch of a German gunboat thence by diplomatic pressure, while France agreed to cede part of the French Congo to Germany. In Britain, an administrative upheaval led to the resignation of Admiral Fisher as First Sea Lord and the appointment of Winston Churchill as First Lord of the Admiralty. The British, anxious over the Balkan question, dispatched a naval mission to Greece, awkwardly matched by the British advisers in the Ottoman navy. Then Italy determined to grab Libya, the last surviving North African state under nominal Ottoman control, and use it as a buffer against further French expansion. The Italo-Turkish War of 1911–12 demonstrated the effectiveness of the Italian navy led by the reform-minded naval minister Rear Admiral P. L. Cattolica. Calling up its naval reserves, the Italian fleet bombarded the Adriatic coast at Preveza and shelled and captured the Libyan port cities of Tripoli, Tobruk and Benghazi. Moslem Arab guerrilla tactics led to an Italian naval blockade of the Libyan coast, angering France and Britain. The British-led Ottoman fleet retreated behind the Dardanelles, and in the spring of 1912 the Italian navy captured Rhodes and the Dodecanese Islands. When the Italian army overran Libya, Turkey submitted and ceded Libya, Rhodes and the Dodecanese to Italy.

Virtually defenseless, the Ottoman Empire now received Franco-Russian guarantees for the integrity of the Dardanelles and Black Sea against Italy and Austria, but this did not affect the Balkan enemies of Turkey. In the First Balkan War, 1912–13, the armies of Greece, Bulgaria, Serbia and Montenegro overran European Turkey while the Greek navy controlled the Aegean. The imposed great power settlement carved up these lands to the victors, created the new nation of Albania and ceded Crete to Greece. Bulgaria unsuccessfully waged the Second Balkan War in 1913 against her former allies for more territory. Possession of the Aegean islands, taken by the Greek navy in the First war, remained in dispute. So Turkey and Greece vied to purchase battleships in Britain and America, succumbing to the same battleship hysteria that had already engulfed other such unlikely naval powers as Brazil, Chile and Argentina. Turks and Greeks alike ignored their British advisers who insisted such deep-draft vessels would be next to useless in the shallow inlets of the Aegean. Nevertheless, the strategic realignments in the Mediterranean bore importantly on the general European power balance.

Ultimately, in fact, the Mediterranean and Balkan problems drew the powers into war. Germany promoted Triple Alliance advances into the middle sea and even began to replace British advisers in Turkey with its own. The Alliance had Italy's six fast dreadnoughts (promoted by naval writer Giovanni Sechi) and the four of Austria-Hungary, whose Imperial Navy improved with many torpedo boats and submarines under the reform-minded Admirals Count Rudolf Montecuccoli and Francis Ferdinand. In mid-1913, at German insistence, Austrian and Italian naval leaders held joint contingency discussions for war, and two large German warships were placed at their disposal. The Triple Entente moved to check increased German penetration into the Mediterranean in 1912 and 1913. The British and French navies reformed under Fisher's successors and Churchill on the one hand and naval minister Théophile Delcasse and Augustin Boué de Papeyrère on the other. The French fleet and part of the British definitely redeployed to the middle sea, although the Russian navy remained plagued by mutinies and uncompleted construction. But the real arms race involved only Britain and Germany, whose time ran out in June 1914 when a Serbian terrorist in Balkan Bosnia assassinated the Austrian Archduke Francis Ferdinand. Austria demanded redress from Serbia and upset the delicate balance of power in Europe, setting in train the rapid diplomatic deterioration that began World War I.

Between 1906—the *Dreadnought* and the fleet's recall—and 1914, Britain had exploited the naval alliance system to achieve her traditional strategic aims. At the end of 1906, strategic concentration had been achieved: sixteen battleships in the Channel fleet at Dover, twelve in the Atlantic fleet at Gibraltar and eight in the Mediterranean—a system still intact eight years later. Tirpitz's risk theory had therefore failed; the High Seas Fleet was outnumbered by Britain's home forces. In doctrine, therefore, the British "blue-water" school had triumphed over the "bolt from the blue" and *jeune école* schools; the offensive battleship would command the seas, whereas coastal defenses and torpedo-laden vessels could not. And to augment the battle line Admiral Fisher had introduced the battle cruiser, a heavy vessel strong in guns like the battleship but fast and weak in armor like the cruiser. Unfortunately, as events were to prove, the "capital ship" alone could not exert command of the sea without applying the strategic lessons of history. And all historical evidence was either ignored or twisted to fit material arguments, while the nagging questions regarding tactics would only be solved in the crucible of battle. By 1914 and the end of the *Pax Britannica* the dreadnought had become the supreme superweapon and strategic panacea of the technological age—a false distinction that only two world wars would expose.

BOOK SIX

Era of the Total Wars

By maritime strategy we mean principles which govern a war in which the sea is a substantial factor. Naval strategy is but that part of it which determines the movements of the fleet when maritime strategy has determined what part the fleet must play in relation to action of the land forces; for it scarcely needs saying that it is almost impossible that a war can be decided by naval action alone.

—Corbett

World Wars I and II, the result and manifestation of the last surge of great-power nationalism mixed with the new imperialism and uncontrolled arms race, seriously interrupted but did not stifle the growing spirit of global cosmopolitanism of the late nineteenth and early twentieth centuries. The powers that went to war in 1914, then regrouped in 1918–1922 and finally resumed the conflict on an even greater scale from 1939, were playing out the last contradictions of the old European-directed political order. Failing to reckon with the full implications of industrialized total war, the European powers—and Japan in the early 1940s—turned to the traditional forms of armed conflict to achieve the traditional goals of national greatness—imperial territorial gain, economic wealth and self-sufficiency, and military prestige. Rampant nationalism in these years was perhaps not unusual in such relatively new great powers as Germany and Japan, but it was equally rife in France, Britain, Russia, America and the lesser states.

What such tradition-bound powers, old and new, failed to accept
was that the new cosmopolitanism found fresh expression among emer-
gent countries, classes and philosophies which resented the old European
hegemony and which took advantage of the holocaust to undermine the
old order. The leading revolutionary figures of this new thrust were
V. I. Lenin in Russia and Woodrow Wilson in the United States, while
in India the Hindu Mahatma, M. K. Gandhi, was scarcely less important. All sought to replace the antiquated imperialism and nationalistic global hegemony of the European great powers by appealing to
universal human needs for freedom and equality. Though generally unsuccessful in these years because of the stubborn refusal of the old order
to submit, these appeals were sufficiently strong to fill the vacuum left
when Europe finally exhausted itself—after 1945. The era of the total
wars, of uncontrolled nationalism and weapons technology carried to
the extreme, acted as a tragic transition period from the stabilized tensions of the *Pax Britannica* to those of the *Pax Americana*.

The United States occupied a unique role in this transition, for as
war engulfed the Western powers only the North American colossus was
left unscathed by the terrible violence. Geographic insularity combined
with the long American democratic tradition and America's brief experience in thalassocratic expansion to make the United States the
refuge of Western culture and hope in the years between 1914 and 1945.
The Americans entertained the naive belief that a great power could
remain neutral and indeed isolated in the century of total and global
war and cosmopolitanism, but twice, in 1917 and 1941, they reluctantly
and belatedly accepted their responsibilities as a great power and came
to the rescue of Europe. In this way, the United States somewhat resembled the position of Britain in the wars of the French Revolution
and Napoleonic periods; not only was American prosperity and soil not
violated by the two world wars, but scientific, technological and industrial progress continued on an even greater scale.

Despite the American thrust into the Pacific, however, United States
foreign policy had always been isolationistic—save for geographic and
economic expansion within the Western Hemisphere—so that the Americans intervened in Europe only after allied Anglo-French survival was
actually threatened. American reluctance to intervene militarily on behalf
of China kept the United States free of active involvement there as long
as Japan did not jeopardize the balance of the powers in the Pacific.
So the attempt of the new empires, Germany, Italy and Japan, to
assert their hegemony over Europe and Asia respectively, had to be
met by Britain and France—and the uncertain assistance of internally
shaky Russia—but without the concerted involvement of the United
States. The tragedy lay in the fact that the European powers believed

they could continue their nationalistic and imperialistic rivalries with the same relative ease as they had in the nineteenth century. The industrial age did not oblige them, leading to massive total war for which they were unprepared. Not learning from the bloodbath of 1914–18, Europe committed virtual suicide by renewing the struggle in 1939. The world had changed, the level of violence having been magnified to unprecedented and unanticipated proportions by weapons of incredible destructiveness.

Total war in the industrial age demanded rigid centralized controls in order to mobilize entire national populations and economies for breaking the will of the enemy citizenry. Recognition of the need for such centralization came only slowly after 1900 and without any firm direction in any of the powers. Alarmed by its relative unpreparedness for the Boer War, Britain in 1902 had created its Committee of Imperial Defense, but interservice rivalry soon compromised much of its effectiveness as a centralized controlling body; Admiral Fisher viewed Britain's defensive needs in global, imperial terms and distrusted the Army General Staff whose major concern remained home defense and the possibility of sending a wartime cross-Channel expeditionary force to France. Fisher went further and refused to develop a similar modern staff organization for the Navy. The Committee by 1911 had decided on defensive plans for the Empire, with considerable naval autonomy for Australia, New Zealand and Canada, but it did not succeed in unifying Army-Navy planning. Neither did the prime minister and his cabinet. In Germany, the Army General Staff, model of all staff organizations, had developed viable war plans, but only for a land war in Europe. Both German diplomatic and naval leaders remained ignorant of Army plans, with the kaiser and the prime minister unable to unify defense planning. In the United States, the Army's General Staff was very loose, while the Navy had to battle political and traditional service conservatism just to get a Chief of Naval Operations by 1915; otherwise, unity of command and planning rested only with the President. The same was generally true of the other powers.

What total war demanded, from 1914 on, was civil-military-economic command and control at the very top, and so after war came, expert management executives from industry had to be employed to mobilize strategic raw and industrial materials for total war. Jealous of their established constitutional authority—during the two wars and in the long interval between them—statesmen, generals and admirals resisted the creation of permanent military-industrial complexes for directing national policy. As a result, centralized control in the years 1914 to 1945 remained temporary and makeshift, while real unity of command depended upon dictatorial chiefs of state and their powerful industrial managers as aides: in Germany Walter Rathenau, Erich Ludendorff, Adolf Hitler and Albert Speer; in Britain David Lloyd George and Winston Churchill; in the United States Woodrow Wilson, Bernard Baruch and Franklin D. Roosevelt; in France Georges Clemenceau; and in Russia Joseph Stalin.

The pre-World War I ascendancy of the material school of strategy, with its advocacy of super machine weapons as the final arbiter in war, logically pointed to new realities that would develop in an industrialized total war, but such hints of the future devastation were met only by traditional legalistic rationales. Clausewitz had argued from the experience of the Napoleonic wars that total war required that the whole enemy country be overwhelmed, and in 1899 a Polish-Russian economist-military pundit named Ivan S. Bloch in a six-volume study of war predicted that the new superweapons—machine guns, heavy artillery, military railroads—would lead to a stalemate. If each side had them, he reasoned, neither would be able to overwhelm the other, and both would therefore bludgeon each other into impotence. The traditional reaction of the political statesmen to such prophecies was to convene peace conferences at The Hague, but these did not succeed in stopping the mounting arms races. The traditional response of the military men was to seek overwhelming victory by a swift overland offensive at the beginning of the war, the Germans with their Schlieffen Plan, the French with their Plan XVII. As for war at sea, Fisher borrowed the arguments of Mahan and Corbett to claim that his dreadnoughts would crush the German fleet in a pitched battle early in the war, a view Tirpitz had followed in his risk theory when he assumed the British home fleets would be understrength. All of these strategic assumptions rested largely on conjecture, and even the brief experience of the Russo-Japanese War proved little that was conclusive. What no one could know was that Bloch's contention was indeed correct, that is until new superweapons, notably the submarine and airplane, would enlarge the battlefields and undermine the old faith in international law among nations. Equally important, the materialists erred seriously in minimizing the tried and true principles of strategy to be gleaned from history. There were to be no shortcuts in modern total war.

SHIPS AND SEAFARING

The naval weapons for total war, imposing as they appeared, did not fundamentally change through the contemporary era of the world wars. Save for the aircraft carrier, the warships that comprised the major navies in 1914 did not change markedly by 1945, when the long hostilities finally came to an end. In fact, not only did warship categories remain standardized among battleships, cruisers, destroyers and submarines, but each individual vessel belonged to a specific class of its warship type. With such standardized classes of ships, the major navies introduced the practice of painting numbers on each hull, along with the ship's name. In addition, in some navies, each type vessel was given an abbreviation.

The battleship (or superdreadnought) of the world wars remained the index of naval power throughout most of the era, from the five ships of British 30,000-ton *Queen Elizabeth*-class of 1913 to the two 64,000-ton *Yamato*-class battlewagons of Japan and four 45,000-ton American battleships of the *Iowa* (BB-61)-class by 1944. The tactical aspects of battleship war did not change: the range of the gun remained the major factor in naval warfare, balanced by defensive armament and speed. The battleship gun of first 13.5" and 14" and then 15" in the *Queen Elizabeth*s, 16" in the *Iowa*s and 18.1" in the *Yamato*s naturally had varying maximum effective ranges, but the larger calibers could reach 35,000 yards or about twenty miles. Defensive armor—inches of steel thickness—roughly paralleled the gun calibers (13" in the armor belt of the *Queen Elizabeth*), but the Americans set the "all or nothing" trend of again placing heavy armor only over the vital parts of the ship. The concentrated salvos of eight to twelve large-caliber naval guns in double, triple, and/or quadruple turrets thus gave these battleships their punch—not only in relatively flat broadsides but in high-trajectory plunging fire. Speed also became a crucial factor for maneuvering into line-ahead or column battle formation. Geared and electric steam turbine engines had become standard, but the need for higher-pressure steam and high super heat to achieve battleship speeds in excess of 21 knots could not be provided by boilers fired by coal. So oil was introduced with the *Queen Elizabeth,* giving her 25 knots, and soon replaced coal altogether. Improvements in marine engines over these years led to a technological ceiling of about 32 knots in the *Iowa.* Hence, the speedier superdreadnoughts came to be known as "fast battleships."

Naval weaponry thus centered around the need to support and enhance the firepower of these heavy-gunned "capital ships." To give the battle line additional firepower and better armed reconnaissance, Admiral Fisher had introduced a new ship-type, the battle cruiser, in 1907. Armed like a battleship Fisher's *Invincible*-class battle cruiser displaced 17,400 tons and mounted eight 12" guns, but the side armor was thinned to 7" or that of a cruiser to give the battle cruiser speeds up to 26.5 knots. Speed, Fisher reasoned, was the armor of the battle cruiser; it could run away from the killing salvos of the battleships. The Germans quickly designed their own battle cruisers, but with complete 12" armor belts and 11" guns. The battle cruiser proved vulnerable and uneconomical in World War I, however, and was replaced after the war by the aircraft carrier, whose longer-range scout planes provided better "eyes" for the fleet. The brief presence of the battle cruiser, however, led to the removal of the last intermediate-caliber guns from the battleships and the regular assignment of 27- to 45-knot destroyers to the battle fleet to launch torpedo attacks against approaching battle cruisers. The World War I British destroyer of 1500 tons and World War II American destroyer of 2050 tons carried respectively six and ten 21″ torpedo tubes plus four 4.7″ and five 5″ quick-firing guns. The demise of the battle cruiser had no effect on the need for the well-named multi-purpose destroyer, whose torpedoes, guns and depth charges could be used against surface ships, aircraft and submarines. The other ship type for escorting battleships, and for multitudinous independent work, was the standard cruiser. With speeds, armament and duties comparable to those of the destroyer, the heavy cruiser grew in these years from 7100 tons with 6″ guns in World War I to the World War II vessel of 14,000 tons with 8″ guns; in this category also was the interwar German "pocket battleship" of 12,000 tons with 11″ guns and a speed of 26 knots. The light cruiser, scaled down from these dimensions, eventually evolved into an antiaircraft gun platform. The submarine, also considered a fleet auxiliary for scouting as well as attacking, led to anti-submarine tactical countermeasures, anti-torpedo bulkheads and bulges in battleships, and new weapons such as the depth charge. Throughout the world wars, therefore, at least until 1942, the battleship reigned supreme on the seas, supported by its flotilla or escort of battle cruisers (then aircraft carriers), heavy and light cruisers, destroyers and submarines.

But the range of the battleship gun did not increase markedly over these years, whereas the radius of action of the fleet submarine and of shipborne aircraft did. As a result, sub and carrier as new weapons systems promised to replace the naval gun—a future denied as long as possible by tradition-bound battleship admirals. The trials with seaplanes, balloons and submarines between 1903 and 1913 had naturally been unimpressive because of technical limitations. But during World War I, defensive coastal submarines were augmented by those of long-range, oceangoing capability, and at war's end turret-mounted scout planes on battleships and cruisers and water-launched seaplanes were augmented, then superseded, by aircraft carriers. In carriers, Britain's 20,000-ton *Furious* of 1916 incorporated the same basic features of all subsequent carriers to the American 27,000-ton *Essex* (CV-9)-class of 1943. The aircraft complement grew from ten planes on the *Furious* to over ninety on the latter, their round trip ranges increasing from only a few miles to over 500. Plane types were initially divided between scouts and torpedo-droppers, but in the 1920s the scouts started to carry bombs, while fighters were added for defensive purposes. In World War II, carriers with their improved aircraft, aerial bombs, torpedoes and rockets finally replaced the naval gun and battleship in the naval arsenal.

What the carrier did to battle fleets, the submarine did to merchant warfare. The basic design of the sub or U-boat (the German name being *Unterseeboot,*) did not change, though the size did over these years: 400 to 2800 tons, making 17.5 to 20 knots on the surface under diesel power, 7 to 9 knots submerged under electric power, though the Germans in 1944 introduced the air-intake-exhaust schnorkel (invented five years before by the Dutch navy) which allowed diesel power underwater for over 17 knots. Torpedoes vastly improved from a maximum range of 1000 yards at 18 knots in 1914 to 5000 yards at 46 knots by 1945. Carriers and submarines alike flirted with multi-missions but with uneven results: the carrier *Furious* mounted torpedo tubes, the American *Lexington* (CV-2)-class carried 8″ guns, and in World War II some aerial mines were laid by carrier planes; the French submarine *Surcouf* mounted twin 8″ guns and carried a seaplane, as did the Japanese I-class subs; and submarines proved very useful at laying mines. The question of whether the carrier and submarine could completely drive the battleship and its escort surface ships from the seas lay with surface fleet's countermeasures that could be developed against each. The latter effort consequently characterized whole new aspects of naval tactics over this period.

The heavy technical demands made by these new weapons, like those on land (and land-based aircraft), helped to strengthen the material school of strategy. Yardsticks of naval power in strategic decisions, international agreements and war gaming reflected a capital-ship mentality, in which gun ranges and technical considerations predominated in the search for the Mahanian "big battle" to decide command of the sea. Admiral Fisher with his dreadnought and battle cruiser inventions reflected this predilection, as did proponents of the new carrier and submarine.

To understand the technical intricacies of the new weaponry, experts were needed. This led to ever-increasing specialization in naval training and personnel assignments. In officer classes, the new improved technology began to appear after senior flag officers had risen to the highest commands through the older battleship hierarchical channels; their conservatism thus often accounted for much of the early ineffective utilization of the new weaponry. Junior officers had to decide on careers in the older capital ships or in air or subs at the risk of choosing unsuccessful specialties, like those who went into rigid airships. The common enlisted rating generally profited from the new technology, which required well-trained (and well-treated) skilled technicians, while the advent of oil over messy coal made life at sea more bearable. The quality of officers and ratings thus improved with the level of naval education, and the naval profession became ever more attractive. Discipline remained rigid, but the old abuses at last disappeared.

The last vestiges of the older navies faded away as war at sea shifted from daylight battles to round-the-clock, all-weather operations. Radio electronics improved to the point where in World War II surface ships, aircraft and subs could be detected by radar and sonar, their movements recorded and transmitted over vast distances of water by radio. Radio messages could be similarly intercepted and decoded by new cryptography machines. Coastal operations called forth new overseas mobile logistical vessels, the last large monitors and coast artillery, specialized amphibious transports and assault craft, minelayers and minesweepers, and a new swift motor patrol-torpedo (PT) boat.

As technician specialists concentrated on mastering both the old and new machines, their faith in them grew, to the minimization of studying the strategic constants of the past. In many respects, given the awesomeness of the industrial-technical-scientific revolution, this preoccupation is understandable. But, when the strategic realities manifested themselves in wartime, the old problems of achieving command of the sea reappeared: trade protection, amphibious warfare, defense against invasion, and the need for powerful continental allies among the major contenders, Britain and Germany. Like Pitt before him, Winston Churchill more than any other person would reapply historical strategy and techniques. Only then did absolute command over the Atlantic and Pacific oceans become possible.

14
World War I, 1914–1918

The idea that the weapon should determine the strategy to be used is based on the implied assumption that strategy and destruction are synonymous. This simply is not true. Naturally, strategy will be influenced by the availability of weapons, but strategy should use destruction only when there is no other way of gaining or exercising control.

—HENRY E. ECCLES, 1968

BRITISH AND GERMAN STRATEGY

For one hundred years, Europe had not been plagued by a general war, so that the powers plunged into this fray in July and August of 1914 on the assumption that it would be a short war. After Austria-Hungary's declaration of war on tiny Serbia, the opposing alliances followed suit, save for Italy. France, Russia and Britain cemented their entente as a formal Alliance arrayed against the German and Austrian coalition which came to be known as the Central Powers. Italy, despite her recent joint plans to cooperate with Austria, had been arming against that nation and now declared her neutrality rather than face the growing Anglo-French fleet in the Mediterranean. Ottoman Turkey, correctly suspicious of Russian designs to take the Dardanelles and even Constantinople, signed a secret alliance with Germany. Abroad, Japan honored her alliance with Britain and declared war on the Central Powers. The isolation-minded United States remained neutral and called upon the belligerents to respect the rights of neutral shippers as enunciated in the 1909 Declaration of London. But such matters as neutrality and international law were luxuries of a bygone era, as neutral Belgium discovered when Germany opened the war by executing its Schlieffen Plan—overrunning Belgium in order to invade and defeat France. The standing armies and navies were similarly inadequate to meet the demands of total war, so that the mobilizations required the calling up of all reserves (the best naval reserve systems were the Royal Naval Volunteer Reserve, created in 1903, and the U. S. Naval Reserve, formalized in 1915) and eventually mass conscriptions of men and industries. As the armies clashed on the Western front, Ivan Bloch's predictions of stalemate came true, and the powers showed little imagination in seeking alternate strategies to win. Victory upon the sea soon became crucial, and World War I spread into a furious naval struggle primarily between Britain and Germany.

German naval strategy at the beginning of World War I was based on so many miscalculations as to virtually nullify the striking power of the High Seas Fleet throughout the war. Defensively, Tirpitz's fleet lay in the strongest of positions; from the Heligoland Bight, minefields, coastal submarines and cruiser patrols protected the naval bases at Wilhelmshaven and Cuxhaven, the ports of Bremen up the Weser River and Hamburg up the Elbe, and the North Sea entrance to the Kiel Canal, while the naval base at Kiel commanded the Baltic coast of Germany. By 1912, when Admiral Prince Heinrich, the kaiser's brother, was fleet commander, the Germans had simply assumed the British would follow their ancient historical practice of instituting a close blockade of their continental enemy's coast, which would enable the Germans to use their inshore weapons to the full. But when the war broke, the British did no such thing. Whereas the French ports of Cherbourg, Brest and Toulon had always threatened vital British imperial sea lanes, the German North Sea ports lay too far from these to enjoy any such strategic distinction, so that the British Admiralty in 1912 had decided to institute an open blockade not of German ports but of the North Sea itself, from the distant bases of Scapa Flow in the Orkney Islands and Cromarty and Rosyth in Scotland.

A healthy British respect for Germany's inshore defenses of mines and torpedoes also contributed to the British decision to neutralize the German fleet passively rather than by seeking the decisive battle preached by Mahan (who, incidentally, died late in 1914). Totally committed to Mahan's battleship mentality, the German naval staff had no alternate strategic plan to the decisive battle, and—despite Tirpitz's frantic urgings for a decisive fleet sortie—the kaiser and naval staff refused to pit their 15 dreadnoughts and 5 battle cruisers against the 24 British dreadnoughts and 6 battle cruisers. And time worked against Germany, with only 8 capital ships building to Britain's 17 more. The British fleet concentration in the North Sea had handily frustrated Tirpitz's risk theory, and now—in August 1914—the Germans quickly discovered that they had greatly overestimated the importance of their battle fleet and had underestimated the shrewd strategic flexibility of their maritime foe.

The Imperial German Navy was further inhibited by the predominance of the Army in policy and strategic decision-making. Opposed to the war because of unpreparedness, the Navy remained oriented Westward toward the Atlantic and the British enemy, unlike the Army which sought expansion into Eastern Europe—a divergency of war aims that never changed. The Army had not informed the Navy of the Schlieffen Plan, so the fleet had no prepared plans to support the Army's drive through Belgium. That thrust gave Germany the use of occupied Antwerp and the naval bases of Ostend and Zeebrugge, but Tirpitz and the Navy had never seriously considered mounting an overseas invasion of England so had no contingency plans, joint Army-Navy or just naval, for utilizing these new gains. Confident that it would crush the British Expeditionary Force crossing the Channel to reinforce the French Army, the German Army even rejected using the fleet to attack the British Army's transports. But even had the Navy more influence in grand strategy, its own doctrinal rigidity discouraged innovative strategic thinking. It was committed to battleships, around which its disjointed administrative and operational structure had evolved. Superior vessels with superb gunnery, optics, armor, and day and night tactics had led to no other alternative but a blue-water fleet, so that the possibility of a continental naval policy along *jeune école* lines had never been contemplated. Rapid improvements in submarines for long-range operations did not lead to any new commitment to a sub-centered navy; Germany went to war with only twenty-five U-boats—and these for coast defense and fleet reconnaissance—and had made no provisions for major new construction. Consequently, the battle fleet would languish, and morale would deteriorate, complicated by a widening breach between the new Prussianized officer caste and the poorly treated enlisted men.

As the German admirals were realizing their strategic plight, Vice Admiral David Beatty led five British battle cruisers with destroyers and cruisers in a lightning naval raid on the German cruiser patrol in Heligoland Bight on August 28. The British force overwhelmed the German, sinking three German light cruisers and a torpedo boat before running back out to sea. Before the first month of the war ended, then, the basic character of blue-water fleet operations by both navies in the North Sea had been determined: passive naval patrols and lightning raids.

British naval strategy, traditionally predominant over Army thinking, for the first time since Marlborough's day was subordinated to continental objectives. The reason was not fear of invasion, though that possibility continued to bother a great many British generals after 1905, when the "bolt from the blue" group had been thoroughly overridden by the "blue-water" Navy men who guaranteed that Britain's command of the sea would protect British shores. Even should a small German raiding force attempt to land, Admiral Fisher believed that coastal submarines would frustrate its success. Although steam had bridged the Channel, Corbett and others had pointed out that a surprise invasion would be virtually impossible with the advent of the wireless; enemy fleet movements could be announced by radio. Finally, as the Spanish and French had learned in the age of sail, command of the sea was an absolute prerequisite to amphibious invasion. If Germany meant to invade England, reasoned the British Admiralty, it would have to seek battle with the British fleet, which is precisely what the British wanted. For this very reason, in fact, Germany never contemplated invasion, thus eliminating any real possibility of a decisive battle. But to deter any possible German invasion schemes, the British fleet stood ready, along with a home army.

From 1904 to 1911 Admirals Fisher and Arthur K. Wilson, his successor as First Sea Lord, had advocated a traditional maritime strategy in event of war, placing the British Expeditionary Force ashore on the German coast, probably in the Baltic, to divert substantial German forces fighting along the French frontier. But the generals refused to consider this possibility, having no amphibious doctrine for landing against a defended beach. Instead, the Army's planners advocated the transfer of the entire Army to France to tip the balance against the massed German army. In 1911 the issue had come to a head in the Committee of Imperial Defense, with the result that the continental strategy prevailed and the Fisher-Wilson admirals were replaced by others more congenial to the new strategy, notably the new civilian First Lord of the Admiralty, Winston Churchill. Fisher's uncompromising attitudes and refusal to develop an adequate naval staff system left the Navy at the mercy of the newly strengthened and pro-Army committee—led by the energetic Maurice Hankey, formerly of the Royal Marines—and also left both Army and Navy devoid of any joint plans for possible amphibious operations in the future. When war came, the Navy ferried the British Expeditionary Force across the Channel and then protected its vital seaborne lines of communication.

Beyond supporting this continental strategy, the prime strategic mission of the Royal Navy became commerce warfare—protecting incoming merchant shipping and strangling that of Germany. For the first time in British history, shipping became absolutely essential to Britain's survival; two thirds of the food needed for feeding the population was imported, and British industry depended upon raw materials from the outside. Mahan and Corbett had concluded from the days of sail that *guerre de course* had always failed to counter Britain's blue-water command, arguing that the tremendous volume of merchant trade would make an effective comprehensive attack on it by surface raiders well nigh impossible. Furthermore, with the development of the wireless, enemy cruisers could not long survive undetected, and they depended also on fueling bases, whereas in past wars wind had given raiders unrestricted freedom. Privateering had been abolished in 1856 (save for a few Confederate raiders in the 1860s), and modern raiders had not the time to warn victims and take off their crews because of the latter's radio distress calls summoning fleet units. The commerce raider seemed doomed in modern war.

Defense of commerce could best be achieved, reasoned the Mahan-Corbett school, by strong naval concentrations at terminal points of trade routes, where enemy raiders might be expected to lie in wait for their prey. The Admiralty ruled out convoy as too slow and easily detected both by enemy agents prior to sailing and by enemy cruisers seeing the collective smoke at sea. Though both Mahan and Corbett had doubts about their conclusions on convoy, they agreed that dispersed shipping would enable enough merchantmen to get through to support the war effort; in any case, absolute protection had never been possible anyway. The British Admiralty adopted these attitudes and in 1913 had decided to arm merchantmen as a final precaution. What the British failed to realize, however, was that in total war the old legalism of the eighteenth and nineteenth centuries would not deter a modern power like Germany from adopting a policy of unrestricted *guerre de course,* ignoring the old rules of warning victims and rescuing their crews and even sinking neutral shipping bound for Britain. Some fears existed over the possibility of armed German merchantmen disguised as neutrals acting as raiders, but only Admiral Fisher seems to have anticipated in 1912–14 the future use of long-ranging submarines as commerce raiders. By the outbreak of war, the British had totally underestimated the naval threat to their oceanic trade.

British plans for offensive trade war also rested upon apparent historical evidence drawn from Mahan and Corbett. Germany, not being a true maritime power and thus probably not dependent upon overseas imports, would suffer no more than had France of old. Blockade, to be sure, would be instituted, but with the primary purpose of forcing the German High Seas Fleet to seek battle in order to break it. But in 1912, because of the inshore torpedo craft and shore-based scout planes and Zeppelin airships, along with the extreme difficulty of capturing an advanced island base along the North Sea coast, the Admiralty had decided on a distant blockade of the North Sea rather than the traditional close blockade. Not only did this eliminate any real possibility of a decisive battle, but it raised difficult legal questions about neutral shipping to the Central Powers. Most overseas trade reached Germany by way of the neutral ports of Dutch Amsterdam and Rotterdam, thence by the Rhine and Maas rivers to the industrial Ruhr basin.

In World War I, the major neutral shipper to Central Powers and Allies was the United States, so that neither coalition wanted to offend this important supplier of industrial and raw materials and foodstuffs. For Britain, the problem was most acute, having in 1856 and 1909 accepted in principle the freedom of neutral trade whether to a belligerent nation directly or via another neutral port. But Britain's strategic antecedents long predated the tranquil *Pax Britannica,* and by 1914 the Admiralty had no serious reservations about its exercising its ancient rights of searching and seizing neutral vessels trading with the enemy. As the old notion of neutrality in total war died, so too did the trappings of neutral rights. The trade of Scandinavian neutrals to Germany proved virtually impossible to stop in the distant Baltic and at best difficult along the inshore waters of the North Sea, save by alert cruiser patrols. Abroad, the old practices of running down enemy raiders and squadrons and capturing enemy colonies would be easier. But Germany, hardly a maritime colonial empire, could be defeated only by economic victory in the North Sea. Mahan and Corbett agreed with the British Admiralty on the matter of somehow preventing enemy commerce at all costs.

In addition to such difficulties, the Royal Navy's general strategic superiority was threatened by tactical sterility reflected in the key naval leaders, Churchill and Fisher, who returned to his former post as First Sea Lord late in 1914. Fisher's great naval reforms and capital ship creations had included telling warnings about the future of aircraft in war, submarines as commerce raiders, and the need for amphibious craft and training. But Fisher had no use for staff, including the Naval War Staff created by Churchill in 1912, and was violently intemperate with those who disagreed with his point of view, including the much younger Churchill. Worse, though he admired the work of Corbett and Richmond, Fisher had no use for history as an analytical tool, and therefore virtually ignored tactical studies, depending instead on the technical awesomeness of the floating behemoths he had created. Anti-intellectual, like most naval officers of his time, Fisher personified the material school which worshiped the intrinsic value of super machine weapons. By contrast, Churchill astutely read history and was chagrined to discover upon taking office in 1911 that he was virtually alone in the naval service in this respect; Corbett's epic book published that year was largely ignored by professional officers. Nevertheless, Churchill also overlooked much historical evidence by accepting a continental rather than a maritime strategy and by rejecting the efficacy of convoy in wartime. And he flew in the face of modern technology to press for close blockade and to deny the submarine threat.

In fleet tactics, embodied in the Grand Fleet Fighting Instructions and Battle Orders, both Fisher's and Churchill's conservatism stood out; all cruising and fighting had to be done in rigid line-ahead formations, the commanding admiral asserting absolute control over the fleet in an effort to "cap the T" of the enemy line: the concentration of broadside fire on the vulnerable head of the enemy's column. No flexibility or personal initiative could be allowed subordinate admirals, nor exposure of the line to enemy destroyer torpedo attacks, nor pursuit of a retreating enemy fleet which might use torpedoes and mines, especially near its bases. The old formalism had returned; Nelson's spirit but not his teachings survived. And this rigid caution passed down from Churchill and Fisher to fleet commanders Jellicoe and Beatty. In the matter of aircraft the British high command gave only belated attention—in 1912–14—to building airships and seaplanes. Instead, the big gun battle would determine command of the sea. But even such an engagement had its ominous side. Tactical training had been minimized before the war, night tactics all but ignored, and no coordination of gunnery and tactics pressed. And the longer the German High Seas Fleet refused battle, the more entrenched would this tactical sterility become within the British Grand Fleet.

The first months of the war in the North Sea developed into the same general stalemate that characterized land operations on the Western front. In August 1914 the Germans swept through Belgium into France, and the British Expeditionary Force crossed the Channel to help stop the thrust. A hasty British attempt to relieve Antwerp failed, but neither was the British Army pinned down against the sea—as Fisher had feared (and which would occur in 1940). The Allies stopped the German offensive at the Battle of the Marne early in September, whereupon both sides tried to outflank the other, appearing as a "race to the sea" throughout the autumn. The carnage finally ended with the armies in two parallel systems of trenches by the end of 1914, with the British ground forces on the French left and next to the sea. The professional core of the British Army had been slaughtered, so that Britain mobilized its manpower at home and throughout the Empire to reinforce its Army on the Western front. While merchant ships were not convoyed, troop transports were: the two-hour crossing from Dover and Folkestone to Calais and Boulogne, covered by a new destroyer patrol at Dover which offset German destroyers raiding from Belgian Ostend and Zeebrugge; the longer night run from Portsmouth to Le Havre screened by anti-submarine craft; and the first Canadian army units being escorted across the Atlantic by a capital-ship screen.

The British Grand Fleet at Scapa Flow and Rosyth stood ready to thwart any sortie by the High Seas Fleet, but was suddenly threatened by bold German U-boats. In September and October subs sank two cruisers off Scotland and three old cruisers patrolling off the Dutch coast. A German minelayer used mines to sink a British cruiser off Harwich in August, and two months later other German mines sent a dreadnought to the bottom off northern Ireland. Admiral Jellicoe in October moved the Grand Fleet to the west side of Scotland while anti-submarine defenses were developed at Scapa. Admiral Fisher wanted to mine Heligoland Bight to similarly harass the Germans, but prewar backwardness in undersea tactics found the Royal Navy with inadequate numbers of minelayers and notoriously unreliable mines. Instead, the Germans stepped up their harassing operations by initiating battle cruiser raids to bombard the east coast of England, at Yarmouth in November and Scarborough in December, both to cover minelaying vessels and the latter to lure British fleet units in the minefield. Off Scarborough, in fact, the two main fleets narrowly missed a general engagement, frustrating the British Admiralty (which had broken the German codes), as did nuisance reconnaissance raids by high-flying German Zeppelins based in Belgium. Primitive British naval aircraft could not attain those altitudes, but did destroy three of the airships by air raids on their bases.

But the fleets heightened their efforts to trap advance scouting units, Admirals Sir John Jellicoe and Friedrich von Ingenohl using their respective battle cruiser squadrons under Admirals Sir David Beatty and Franz von Hipper to accomplish the feat. On January 24, 1915, the two battle cruiser forces engaged at Dogger Bank, Beatty's five against Hipper's four plus cruisers and destroyers. Confused signals, the rigid tactics and Beatty's fear of imagined German mines and submarines prevented a general rout, but his guns sank one and badly damaged another of Hipper's battle cruisers. The kaiser, alarmed by his losses, relieved Ingenohl from command and forbade further sorties that would unnecessarily risk his capital ships.

From the Battle of Dogger Bank for over a year the main fleets remained stalemated while both sides endeavored to decide the issue on land. The German fleet, now commanded by Admiral Hugo von Pohl, remained at anchor behind the Heligoland defenses as a fleet-in-being. Sowing mines—from U-boats and new minelayers after mid-1915—the Germans hoped to whittle down the Grand Fleet so that a decisive battle between equal fleets would eventually be possible. Also, the kaiser wanted to save his precious capital ships for possible bargaining strength at the peace table. Meanwhile, German submarines and minecraft (sweepers and layers) attempted to break the blockade, while the German Army hammered away on the Western front. The British fleet stood watch over the North Sea—the battleships from Scapa Flow, the battle cruisers from Rosyth—while rejecting any risky foray into the dangerous inshore waters of Germany (including Admiral Wilson's plan to take and hold the island of Heligoland). The daily cross-Channel flow of men and material was guarded, sustaining the futile and bloody offensives of the Allies trying to break the entrenched German Army on the Western front.

With such a stalemate on land and sea, the Royal Navy initiated proposals to revert from the new continental strategy to the tried and true maritime strategy of assailing the enemy's periphery by amphibious assault. Fisher had always advocated such a program, and in the frustrating latter days of 1914 Churchill followed history to adopt the same position. With the main German army held down in Flanders, the logical move was to transform the Eastern front into a powerful offensive. The chief vehicle would naturally be the Russian army, the catalyst an Allied assault on the Central Powers either in the Baltic or the Eastern Mediterranean-Black Sea region.

The Baltic Sea, long dominated by the Russians, provided the most direct route by sea into Germany but was offset by diplomatic and geographic difficulties. Diplomatically, the Allies wanted to keep Sweden, Denmark and Norway neutral for economic and strategic reasons. Scandinavian trade was vital to the Allies, even though Germany was obtaining iron ore from the pro-German Swedish government. Strategically, Denmark as always dominated the entrance to the Baltic and when war broke out her navy mined the Belts (as did the Germans) and the western side of the Sound, making the passage hazardous for ships of war. The Germans could, in addition, pass their warships through the Kiel Canal into the Baltic, although they had long since decided to make this front a passive one until victory was achieved in the West. The Allies were equally unprepared to mount significant operations in Baltic waters, but in August the Russian army swept into East Prussia, only to be stopped cold in the Tannenberg campaign late in the month by Generals Paul von Hindenburg and Erich Ludendorff. The Russian navy also began the war energetically in these parts, due largely to its vigorous Baltic commander, Vice Admiral Nicolai von Essen, who sowed 2200 mines at the entrance to the Gulf of Finland to protect the approaches to Kronstadt and Petrograd (St. Petersburg) and who planned both to deliver an ultimatum to the Swedish fleet at Karlskrona and to use his predreadnoughts to lure the German fleet into his minefields. The Russian tsar vetoed these schemes as too risky, even though von Essen's excellent mines put out of action four of Admiral Prince Heinrich's eight cruisers supporting the German army in Latvia by January.

In addition, Russian minelayers and submarines were joined in October by two British subs under the aggressive Lieutenant Commander Max Horton, basing at Reval on the Gulf of Finland.

With the prospect of this well-led Russian Baltic Fleet being supported by the British, Admiral Fisher moved to introduce a scheme for a British naval offensive into the Baltic. Already, between August and December, Churchill had wanted to provoke a German fleet sortie and battle by seizing a German island—if not Heligoland as Admiral Wilson wanted, then Borkum or Sylt at either terminus of the short German coast, or even, as others suggested, at Zeebrugge. When these proposals were rejected as too risky in January 1915, Fisher resurrected a prewar scheme to place an Anglo-Russian amphibious force on the Pomeranian coast only ninety miles from Berlin, ignoring Churchill's objection that a close blockade of Heligoland Bight—from an advanced captured island base—was a prerequisite. With the help of the historian Corbett, Fisher in January proposed that the entire Grand Fleet enter the Baltic to support a Russian assault, closing the Heligoland Bight and Wilhelmshaven fleet anchorage with (admittedly inferior) British mines. The government rejected the plan, however, largely because of the uncertainties of trying to negotiate the narrow and tricky Sound, along with the unfeasibility of closing the Bight to a possible German fleet sortie while the British fleet was away in the Baltic. Had the plan carried, the Germans may well have sent heavy units into the Baltic to engage the Grand Fleet, and Russian inshore operations would have probably been effective. But the Russian army, ever active, remained an unknown factor, hardly worth the risk of Britain uncovering her command of the North Sea for the project.

The Baltic now became a strategic backwater, attended by the death of von Essen in the spring, and Anglo-Russian sub and mine forces fell back on the Gulf of Riga to help contest the German advance on land. During the summer and autumn of 1915, Commander Horton led Anglo-Russian subs in a Baltic offensive that sank a German cruiser and sixteen merchant ships and damaged a battle cruiser. But then the theater bogged down into a stalemate on land and sea, with political revolutionary discontent spreading through the Russian armed forces.

THE MEDITERRANEAN AND COMMERCE WARFARE

If Russia could not be converted into a major front through the Baltic, then the only alternative was through the Mediterranean, a theater which grew into a major avenue both for Allied strategy on the Eastern front and for Allied merchant shipping. Only by maintaining command over the middle sea could the Allies contain the Central Powers and thus inhibit their naval operations beyond—in the South Atlantic, South Pacific and Indian oceans. Italy had declared its neutrality, and Turkey secretly allied with the Central Powers and in November 1914 declared war on the Allies. So Anglo-French naval forces in the Mediterranean focused on containing Austria-Hungary and Turkey and their limited fleets and in remaining mobile enough to concentrate outside this sea, especially in the Atlantic, to protect Allied commerce.

In late 1914 and early 1915, the Allies exerted their command over the Mediterranean though not without some difficulty. The two German heavy ships at Austrian Pola eluded Allied naval forces in August to shell the French Algerian coast and escape to Turkey, where they aided materially in closing Allied communications with Russia via the Black Sea. The French fleet under Admiral Boué de Lapeyère sealifted important Algerian ground forces to the continent and bottled up the Austrian battleships of Admiral Anton Haus at Pola, lifting Haus's blockade of Allied Montenegro. But when the French tried to support the Montenegrans by sea over the winter and spring, Austrian U-boats damaged a French battleship and sank a heavy cruiser near the Strait of Otranto and caused the French to retire to Pylos for a distant blockade of the Adriatic. The Austrian army retreated from its thrust into Serbia and Russian Poland, covered by three Danube River monitors, but was saved by German reinforcements.

With the German and Austrian fleets generally contained, however, the British in late 1914 could implement traditional maritime strategic prerogatives: control of global trade routes and seizure of German colonies. British imperial forces easily captured defenseless Pacific Samoa, African Togoland, the Cameroons and Southwest Africa, but inadequate amphibious doctrine led to their repulse at Tanga, German East Africa. British and Russian cruisers and a Japanese battle cruiser escorted Indian and "Anzac" (Australia and New Zealand) troop convoys across the Indian Ocean to the Middle East, while the three German raiding cruisers operating in these waters enjoyed only brief success before being sunk or blockaded in East Africa. In this way, along with war risk insurance policies, the British frustrated German surface *guerre de course* strategy early in the war.

The one major enemy overseas threat, the German China Squadron of Vice Admiral Count Maximilian von Spee, required fleet action. Training at Ponape in the German Carolines at the outbreak of war, this fleet of two heavy and three light cruisers found itself cut off from its base at Tsingtao by the Japanese navy. The Japanese besieged and took Tsingtao in November 1914 and easily overran the German Palau, Marianas, Caroline and Marshall island groups, obliging Spee to operate in South American waters. Avoiding Anglo-Japanese forces hastening across the Pacific, the German squadron sank two British heavy cruisers at the battle of Coronel off the coast of Chile on November 1 and then rounded the Horn into the South Atlantic. The British Admiralty hastened Vice Admiral Sir Doveton Sturdee with two battle cruisers and seven cruisers from Britain to defend the Falkland Islands, where they met and destroyed Spee's squadron on December 8. The battle of the Falkland Islands, the last pure gunnery action in history fought without fear of torpedoes or aircraft, ended Germany's policy of waging *guerre de course* with surface ships, and in February 1915 Germany turned to the U-boat as its prime merchant raider.

Before Germany could build enough U-boats for this purpose, though, the British attempted to decide the war by a strategic offensive via the Middle East and Eastern Mediterranean. British imperial forces occupied Turkish Basra in the Persian Gulf late in 1914 to protect the now-vital oil interests there and to support an abortive campaign up the Tigris River into Mesopotamia throughout 1915. Failing to take Baghdad, the British even had a new monitor and two gunboats captured by the Turks. Anglo-Russian forces cooperated in Persia, while the Turks pressed on Russian Black Sea ports and the British Suez Canal. German Admiral Wilhelm Souchon used his German battle cruiser and light cruiser and Turkish cruisers and destroyers to bombard Sevastopol and Novorossisk in the autumn of 1914, and the sultan proclaimed a Holy War throughout the Middle East. British forces strengthened the defenses of the Canal—reinforced by French warships from Indochina and Syria—to break up a Turkish overland offensive which tried to cross the Canal on pontoons in February 1915. Britain annexed Cyprus, France controlled the coast of Palestine, and Russia battled Turkey on the Caucasus frontier to keep the Canal secure for the duration. With such activity in this region, First Lord Churchill decided to mount a major offensive in Europe from the East.

Churchill hoped to create a viable second front in the Eastern Mediterranean, just as Fisher had planned to do in the Baltic, and he pushed the enterprise through the British War Cabinet in January. Churchill planned on an Allied naval drive through the Dardanelles, Sea of Marmara and Bosporus to invest Constantinople and open a fresh and much-needed supply route to Russia. Such a feat would also relieve the Caucasus and Mesopotamian fronts, outflank Austria-Hungary, and hopefully encourage the neutral Balkan states of Greece, Rumania and Bulgaria to join the Allies. Unfortunately, the strategic potential of this brilliant design—maritime strategy at its finest—was partly compromised by political factors: it encouraged France to increase its annexation plans for Ottoman Syria and Palestine, Italy to join in the expected spoils of victory by declaring war on Austria (but not Germany) in May 1915, and Russia to demand the outright postwar annexation of the Dardanelles and Constantinople itself. Traditional British support of the Ottoman buffer against Russia in the middle sea now led to British reluctance to ask for Russian naval cooperation from the Black Sea side. Indeed, Russia, which had also proposed such an operation, used its Black Fleet of five battleships, two seaplane carriers and old destroyers under Admiral A. A. Eberhardt to blockade the coast of Anatolia, support the Caucasian front and now bombard the entrance of the Bosporus. But mutual Anglo-Russian suspicions and Russian ground commitments against the Germans and Austrians restricted Russian cooperation during the campaign to a naval demonstration off the Bosporus and a minefield planted there partly by the world's first mine-laying submarine, the *Krab*.

Churchill's enthusiasm over such a Mediterranean strategy, flatly opposed by Admiral Fisher, suffered from tactical weaknesses. Generally unsupported by historical precedents, Churchill assumed that warships alone (with small Marine landing parties) could reduce strong coastal fortifications, in this case those commanding the Dardanelles which had been strengthened following an Anglo-French naval bombardment in November 1914. Churchill also underestimated the effect of the new underwater weapons against battleships, for the Germans had laid sixteen minefields across the Chanak Narrows connecting the Dardanelles with the Sea of Marmara. Basing at Lemnos, the Anglo-French fleet from mid-February to mid-March 1915 shelled both sides of the Dardanelles and was reinforced to include the new *Queen Elizabeth,* twelve other British and four French battleships, a battle cruiser and many cruisers, destroyers and crude, makeshift minesweepers. Led by Vice Admiral John de Robeck, this force attempted to run the Narrows, only to have six predreadnoughts strike mines; three went down quickly, another being disabled by shore artillery. Within grasp of his objective, de Robeck hastily retired. Then Churchill decided to transform the effort into a major amphibious assault against the Gallipoli peninsula on the European side of the Dardanelles. His error now lay in attempting an operation for which no tactical doctrine, specialized weapons or techniques had been developed. These shortcomings, plus the countermeasures of the Central Powers, doomed the operation from the outset.

The Gallipoli campaign, centered on the assault of April 15, 1915, violated every principle of combined operations that might have been gleaned from history. The Allies did not enjoy local command of the sea because of ineffective minesweeping trawlers and the presence of Turkish destroyers and German and Austrian U-boats. The Navy and Army never solved the issue of unity of command, either from London or locally, where ground and naval commanders displayed uneven qualities and lack of aggressiveness. The element of surprise had long been lost, and the diversionary tactics of two feints and one landing on western Cape Hellas did not fool the defenders led by Generals Liman von Sanders of Germany and Mustapha Kemal of Turkey. Logistical mistakes required that the transports from England be unloaded and reloaded at Alexandria, wasting an entire month and preventing a much-needed rehearsal. For covering fire, the naval gunners had no training or experience for close-in pinpoint fire and showed it by their ineffective barrage. Inadequate naval and aerial reconnaissance led to ignorance of the water currents and landing beaches. Admiral Fisher had produced motorized armored landing barges and steam launches for his Baltic venture, but with its cancellation these were not made available for the Gallipoli operation. Instead, 200 large and hundreds of small makeshift assault craft assumed the burden of landing the 80,000 British, French, Anzac and Indian troops in the face of heavy fire from the 30,000 defending troops.

The Gallipoli assault failed from the first. Sloppy and unsteady ship-to-shore movement left the troops pinned down or slaughtered along the water's edge, thus creating serious delays in bringing up supplies and more men. Then the commanders failed to exploit their beachhead aggressively. Instead of systematically probing weaknesses in the Turkish lines to gain the high ground ahead of enemy reinforcements, the troops dug in on the beach, while the floating reserves were not committed. So the Turks rallied behind Kemal and fought desperately and successfully to blunt the assault on the first day. Nothing changed over succeeding days, except that an enemy destroyer sank another old British battleship and enemy U-boats began to arrive. Bitter disputes between Churchill and Fisher led to the recall of the *Queen Elizabeth* and Fisher's resignation in May as First Sea Lord—never to return, despite subsequent efforts by the Navy to gain his reappointment. But Churchill soon followed him into retirement as the scapegoat for the failure at Gallipoli. Late in May the submarine *U-21*, steaming from the North Sea to Austrian Cattaro, sank two more predreadnoughts off Gallipoli before joining in the general Austro-German U-boat assault on Allied Mediterranean shipping. British subs sank two Turkish battleships and lesser vessels in the Sea of Marmara, and a new surprise Anzac landing on the west coast of Gallipoli in August failed to break the stalemate. Then, in October, Bulgaria joined the Central Powers and overran Serbia and Montenegro, creating a new front before Salonika in neutral Greece and requiring French and Italian warships to evacuate the Serbian and Montenegran armies from the mainland to Corfu. The Allies had no choice but to evacuate Gallipoli, which they did in an unusually masterful withdrawal between late November 1915 and early January 1916. The Gallipoli fiasco had discredited amphibious operations in general and done nothing to alter the strategic stalemate in Western Europe.

Indeed, the entrance of new belligerents into the fighting led to much bloodshed but little else in 1915 and 1916. Despite massive battles at Verdun and the Somme, the Western front did not move, while in the East a Russian offensive crippled Austria-Hungary and brought in Rumania as an Ally, but to no avail. In the Middle East, the Russians drove to Trebizond on the Black Sea before being stopped and lost a brand-new dreadnought to an operational mishap, and the British expeditionary force on the Tigris became trapped and had to surrender to the Turks. Italy declared war on Germany in August 1916 but concentrated its efforts against Austria at the Alps and in the Adriatic. The underwater mines and subs of both sides in the Mediterranean forced the battleships to remain in port at Italian Taranto and Brindisi, British Malta, French Algerian Bizerte and Austrian Pola, although the Allies did use theirs for protecting merchant shipping. Austrian saboteurs, mines, light vessels and naval aircraft from Cattaro, Pola and Trieste countered Italian supremacy and coastal raids in the Adriatic by sinking three Italian battleships in 1915–16. But the Adriatic, like the Italian front, remained a strategic backwater of the war, crucial only as the outlet for German and Austrian fleet U-boats operating against Allied sea lanes to Gallipoli, Salonika and Suez.

As for Germany during 1915–16, the U-boat had begun to prove its worth as a commerce raider, although the prewar niceties of international law embodied in the Declaration of London exerted a powerful check on its full destructive capability. The Austro-German sub offensive in the Mediterranean proved to be so effective during 1916—sinking over one million gross tons (average vessel 3000 tons) that year—that the British began to divert much of their Far East merchant shipping from the Suez route to the Cape. Allied countermeasures against the U-boat in the middle sea were so ineffective that the Central Powers boats closely observed prize rules; they warned each merchantman and took off its crew before sinking it—usually with the deck gun in order to conserve torpedoes. In the Atlantic, however, the proximity of British naval bases made such legalities suicidal, so that only unrestricted submarine warfare—without any warning or thought of the crews—would work. The German Naval Staff, already cool toward this new weapon because it diverted strength from the blue-water fleet, rejected such proposals early in 1915 also for fear of diplomatic repercussions from neutral shippers. Predictably, then, the United States protested the sinking of the British passenger liners *Lusitania* and *Arabic* in May and

August, whereupon the German government in September closed down all U-boat operations in the Western Approaches, English Channel and North Sea in favor of the less-sensitive Mediterranean. When the successes there reconvinced the kaiser and his Naval Staff of the efficacy of unrestricted underwater *guerre de course* in March 1916, its resumption brought about the sinking of the cross-Channel steamer *Sussex,* the usual American protest, the same decision of the kaiser to withdraw his best U-boats from British waters, and his discharge of Admiral Tirpitz. President Wilson in fact had unknowingly saved the Allies with his protests, for an all-out U-boat offensive might well have aggravated serious Allied shortages in war materials in mid-1916 sufficiently to win the war for the Central Powers.

The Allied blockade of the Central Powers succeeded more from diplomatic than tactical devices. The British, less sensitive to American protestations than were the Germans, gradually abandoned their lip service to the Declaration of London in favor of enforcing Orders-in-Council to restrict neutral trade to the continent. The Royal Navy thus mined the Strait of Dover to stop, search and detain neutral vessels and confiscate partial or entire cargoes as contraband of war. British antisub countermeasures in 1915–16 were too halfhearted to blockade or stop the U-boats which tried to create their own blockade of the British Isles. The British simply left the initiative with the U-boat, which had relative freedom beyond British coastal waters to attack non-escorted merchant shipping. Instead of adopting convoy on the high seas, the British armed their merchantmen—often a very successful measure, had them fly neutral flags and maneuver in zigzags, while well-gunned decoy merchant "Q-ships" made several sorties with uneven results. The Navy regularly patrolled only inshore waters, using armed trawlers, yachts, torpedo boats, subs and shore-based aircraft in addition to anti-mine nets and towed explosive paravane sweeps.

The Admiralty preferred to deal offensively with the U-boat, however, by sending out sporadic hunt-and-kill patrols of destroyers armed with depth charges, but this seldom worked because of the great expanse of water, the mobility of the subs, the scarcity of destroyers and the difficulty of underwater detection even with primitive hydrophones. Airplanes and airships occasionally bombed U-boat bases, and early in 1916 British fleet units in the North Sea successfully countered several bold forays by German minesweepers and surface raiders. In the Mediterranean, the French and Italians could not cooperate and lacked any antisub expertise, using ineffective defensive nets and cruiser patrols at the Strait of Otranto. But the Royal Navy gave little advice there, preferring to send battleships (some Allied forty by the end of 1915!) with their large and costly retinue of escorts and service ships to the middle sea. Some antisub reforms early in 1916 made a few improvements, but still the U-boats ran through the straits of Gibraltar and Otranto with relative impunity.

On balance, the commerce war between February 1915 and mid-1916 seesawed back and forth. Germany started the offensive with only twenty-one boats in 1915, but its increased construction gradually broadened the effort as Allied antisub tactics failed to keep pace. Throughout 1915, for instance, German subs sank 748,000 tons of British merchant shipping at the cost of only twenty boats. In addition, mines claimed another 77,000 tons and surface raiders 29,000. Only six Central Powers boats sank ninety-two merchantmen during the autumn in the Mediterranean, and *U-35* under Lieutenant Commander Lothar von Arnauld de la Perière alone accounted for most of the many sinkings there throughout 1916. During the first half of 1916, enemy subs and mines claimed nearly half a million tons of Allied merchant shipping plus two old battleships and two cruisers (one with Lord Kitchener on board) at the cost of thirty-four boats. To be sure, both sides suffered, with the civilian populations of the Central Powers starting to hurt far more than those of the Allies. The Royal Navy steadfastly maintained command of the North Sea against the German surface fleet, but missed the key strategic point that the real threat lay underwater. Instead of centering its strategy on the long and unglamorous method of economic strangulation and defeat of the U-boat, the British Admiralty preferred to regard its blockade as an inducement to force the German High Seas Fleet into a decisive battle. That battle came, but it altered very little, for the final victory at sea would be determined by the success or failure of the submarine.

ANGLO-AMERICAN COMMAND OF THE SEA

The stalemate on land and sea by mid-1916 led both the Allied and Central Powers to seek new solutions to break it. On land, fresh assaults on all fronts displayed a remarkable lack of strategic and tactical imagination and led only to mounting devastation and bloodshed. They merely proved the prewar arguments of Bloch that modern machine weapons only tended to neutralize one another. And at sea, the fleet action off Jutland demonstrated the same fact, so that the commerce war finally impressed itself on the conservative admiralties that the stalemate would only be broken in that quarter. The ultimate German decision for all-out unrestricted submarine warfare would force America's entry into the war, giving the Allies just enough manpower to break the deadlock on the continent and additional naval power to enable them to realize the maritime goals of their basically continental strategy. But the lessons and their implementation took over two more years to learn, making 1916–18 an unprecedented period of intensive warfare at sea.

The opposing battle fleets ended their relatively passive roles as each side sought to make active use of them. Admiral Sir John Jellicoe, an able administrator and conservative tactician, used the Grand Fleet to dominate the North Sea, though with standing orders never to risk his precious battleships against German torpedoes or mines. In March 1916 his cruisers bombarded the Sylt Island radio station and the airship drome at Tondern, while the continuous patrols kept the Fleet busy. Jellicoe looked to the day when he could engage the Germans in a traditional line-ahead action, to achieve tactical concentration by capping the enemy T. But his formalist training precluded initiative by his subordinates and any preparations for night action, while he had not remedied the armor weaknesses of his battle cruisers. His counterpart, Vice Admiral Reinhard Scheer, the new commander of the German High Seas Fleet, instituted a vigorous program of tactical training and raids aimed at whittling down British fleet strength. In April his battle cruisers bombarded Lowestoft, England, and early in May he refused to be lured out by Jellicoe whose units again shelled Sylt Island and Tondern. When the heavy spring weather precluded the use of airships for fleet reconnaissance, Scheer decided to attack British shipping to Norway in the Skagerrak. When Scheer sortied on May 30, Jellicoe did the same, with the result that on the next day the two great fleets collided off the Jutland peninsula in the long-awaited battle.

The Battle of Jutland (or Skagerrak) opened late on May 31, 1916, between opposing battle cruiser forces which tried to lure one another into the jaws of their respective dreadnought lines. Vice Admiral David Beatty had 6 battle cruisers, 4 new dreadnoughts, 14 light cruisers, 27 destroyers and 2 seaplane carriers; Vice Admiral Franz von Hipper had 5 battle cruisers, 5 light cruisers and 30 destroyers. Running south, the two lines commenced firing about 3:30 P.M. at 16,500 yards and closed to 13,000 yards. The superior gunnery of the Germans outperformed that of the British, with the flash from several hits igniting the magazines of 2 battle cruisers, sending both to the bottom. Two destroyers on each side were sunk, but as Beatty's dreadnoughts closed he saw Scheer's battle line approaching. Turning about at 4:45, Beatty tried to lure Hipper north into the main force of Jellicoe, but keeping his superior ignorant of developments. The running gunnery duel then merged into a general engagement that involved Jellicoe's 24 dreadnoughts, 3 battle cruisers, 8 armored cruisers, 12 light cruisers, 51 destroyers and one minelayer and Scheer's 16 dreadnoughts, 6 predreadnoughts, 6 light cruisers and 31 destroyers. Poor visibility neutralized the planes from Jellicoe's one seaplane carrier (another had been inadvertently left behind), while fear of German subs (18 of them were in British waters) and torpedoes influenced Jellicoe. Even so, Jellicoe absorbed Beatty's force at 6:00 and slammed into Hipper's van, seriously damaging 3 German light cruisers. Jellicoe then capped the German "T" by swinging eastward to silhouette Scheer's ships against the setting sun and cutting off his possible retreat back to his base in Germany.

But German tactics quickly frustrated Jellicoe's excellent tactical position. The devastating gunnery exchange at 12,000 yards in this "Windy Corner" claimed a British battle cruiser and cruiser and put four German battle cruisers out of action. Then, about 6:35, Scheer executed what the British considered impossible: a battle turn of 180°. Without melee tactics, the British squadron commanders could not pursue, and Jellicoe held his course. When Scheer tried to break through at 7:00 he found his "T" still capped and encountered murderous fire from the British broadsides. The well-drilled German ships executed another brilliant battle turn at 7:20, covered by their torpedo-firing destroyers which caused Jellicoe's light cruisers to turn away. By sunset at 8:19 the two fleets were running southward on parallel tracks, Jellicoe between Scheer and Germany. Scheer now determined to pass through Jellicoe's rear during the night and conveyed his plan by radio to the German Admiralty, which concurred. British intelligence radio listeners intercepted these messages, but failed to inform Jellicoe. At 11:00, as the destroyers continued to trade blows, Scheer began his move, witnessed by British ships in the rear which did not inform Jellicoe. By twilight at 2:00 A.M. on June 1 Scheer had escaped, which Jellicoe did not learn for two more hours, by which time he had no choice but to return to base. Nothing had changed strategically, while the Germans tactically had sunk three battle cruisers, three cruisers and eight destroyers to their own losses of one predreadnought, one battle cruiser (scuttled), four cruisers and five destroyers. The British had lost 6800 out of 60,000 men, the Germans 3100 out of 45,000.

The duel at Jutland had demonstrated the futility of material strategy. No dreadnoughts had been lost by either side, but neither had the torpedo been decisive. Little tactical imagination had been displayed by any senior admiral, save for Scheer's battle turns, while the battle cruiser had displayed fatal weaknesses. More armor protection would only make it into a battleship, whereas its scouting function had achieved few results. The new experimental aircraft carrier seemed to offer more promise for the future as "the eyes of the fleet." The British had won the battle in the strategic sense, since they still held command of the North Sea, but they had suffered a psychological blow to their naval prestige. Scheer made a last important sortie in August for a bombardment of the Sunderland coast, but Jellicoe's approach to within thirty miles caused Scheer to retire. The High Seas Fleet resumed its status as a fleet-in-being and awaited new dreadnoughts under a remarkably misdirected building program that seemed to ignore the outcome of Jutland. The Grand Fleet also received new construction but prepared to move from Scapa Flow to Rosyth and the Firth of Forth in order to better prevent another German fleet sortie. This continued vigil—necessary because of the failure to destroy Scheer at Jutland—required valuable destroyers that could not be diverted to antisubmarine duty. The expensive battle fleets would not fight again.

The performances of the Central Powers navies at Jutland and Gallipoli did have the strategic effect of sealing off Russia from direct outside help, meaning that the Eastern front would hold only as long as the Russian army could continue its exhausting campaigns. Though the Russian summer offensive of 1916 virtually took Austria out of the war, the Mediterranean theater remained stalemated and both the Black and Baltic seas closed to Allied shipping. With the Dardanelles closed, Admiral Alexander Kolchak, the new commander of the Russian Black Sea Fleet, began to plan and rehearse an attack on the Bosporus but it never took place. The German High Seas Fleet kept the Baltic Fleet neutralized at Kronstadt, but in midyear the British opened up a new supply route via the Arctic. Some 600 Allied merchantmen initially reached Kola on the Barents Sea and Archangel on the White Sea, there joined by British antisub cruisers and minesweepers. But inadequate rail facilities led to the stockpiling of these supplies in port, and the Germans increased their U-boat operations during the winter of 1916–17 to continue the isolation of Russia. Then, in March 1917, a revolution swept over Russia and replaced the tsarist regime with a shaky democratic government which tried mightily to stay in the war. But as long as the German army kept hammering away at Russia and German U-boats, mines and heavy ships kept the Baltic and Black seas closed, Britain could never readopt any peripheral strategy to relieve Russia. Knowing this, the Germans realized the best way to insure the blockade and ultimate defeat of Britain, Russia and France lay in the resumption of unrestricted submarine warfare.

Support for unrestricted U-boat operations against Allied and neutral shipping gradually gained strength within German strategy-making circles throughout the remainder of 1916. U-boat operations, reduced during the summer, intensified in September in the Channel, North Sea and Western Approaches and as far away as Iberia, the Russian White Sea, Iceland and North America. Allied and neutral merchant ship losses tripled to a monthly average of 94,000 tons during the last third of the year. Admirals Scheer and Henning von Holtzendorff, the aged

Chief of Naval Staff, argued for unrestricted operations, predicting that the 150 U-boats available by February (82 in the North Sea, of which 36 were at sea simultaneously) could humble Britain within six months. The Army, encouraged by its summer victories and throwing off its fears of Dutch and Danish military intervention on the Western front from such a U-boat offensive, now supported it and fell back on a new Hindenburg line early in 1917 just to make sure. An additional risk involved Scandinavian underwater weapons, namely Dutch coastal torpedo boats and Danish mines in the Sound, soon to become a major U-boat route in place of the mine-infested North Sea. Yet the Navy had more consuming if unstrategic reservations over any increased U-boat activity. The conservative bureaucracy led by Tirpitz's successor as naval minister, Admiral Eduard von Capelle, feared that the organizational and promotional hierarchy based on the battle fleet would be usurped during and after the war by the glut of submarine officers. And since Britain was to be humbled within six months, both Capelle and Holtzendorff refused to authorize a new and massive U-boat construction program. The government used this timetable—and the exaggerated sinking reports of its U-boat commanders—to decide in January 1917 for unrestricted submarine warfare, effective February 1.

British and American naval capabilities figured importantly in the overoptimistic projections of the German leaders. Though British shipping losses mounted and antisub countermeasures remained inadequate, the Royal Navy after Jutland understood clearly that the commerce war held the key to victory. The British people threw out the government of Lord Asquith in the autumn as evidence of their frustration, and Admiral Jellicoe—now convinced the sub had become the final arbiter— was elevated to the post of First Sea Lord in order to prosecute a vigorous antisubmarine policy. Admiral Beatty succeeded to command of the Grand Fleet. Antisub tactics did not improve or even change at once, but at least the Admiralty created a specialized Antisubmarine Division in December. As long as the Germans believed that the British would not change, the former's strategy seemed wise. And indeed the innovations of early 1917 achieved little: special transit zones and "dazzle" painting of merchantmen to confuse U-boat aiming, strengthened coastal patrols whereas most U-boats operated beyond them at 50 to 300 miles out, the arming of all merchantmen to replace the Q-ship and such desperate experiments as the unsuccessful attempts to train sea lions and sea gulls in sub detection! But in April alone the Central Powers sank nearly 870,000 tons of Allied and neutral vessels. As suspected, the United States responded by declaring war that same month. But the German Army could not conceive how the Americans could raise, equip and train an expeditionary force for service in France in 1917. The German Navy doubted whether the Americans would have enough transports to bring an army to Europe—in 1917 or ever—and correctly assumed that the U.S. Navy had been emphasizing capital ship over antisub construction so as to be a negligible factor against the U-boat.

So the decision for victory lay in the ability of the German Navy to strangle Britain with an unrestricted U-boat campaign before Britain overcame its antisub tactical deficiencies and before the United States could sealift a modern army to the Western front. Six months seemed like more than enough time, but the Germans badly miscalculated the ability of both the Royal and United States navies to overcome doctrinal conservatism and achieve the tactical flexibility to check the U-boat and thus prolong the war until an American army could be mobilized and committed to battle.

German smugness and naval conservatism also hurt the new German strategy. A lingering belief in the efficacy of surface *guerre de course* led early in 1917 to the breakout of three merchant cruisers on successful raiding cruises, and destroyers from Zeebrugge continued to plague Allied shipping in the Channel. Organizationally, the high command simply refused to reform its rigid staff system to allow the overall coordination of the U-boat offensive; when the U-boat chief, Commodore Hermann Bauer, recommended in April that a command sub be stationed off the Western Approaches to coordinate U-boat operations by radio (like the later wolf packs of World War II), he was not only turned down but relieved of command. So the boats of the North Sea and Flanders could not be coordinated—a major administrative flaw. In the High Seas Fleet, the austere officer corps mistreated its crews—already plagued by food shortages and the post-Jutland inactivity—so that enlisted morale in the fleet plummeted as the better officers and ratings began to transfer to the U-boat arm. Growing discontent then led to several mutinies in the fleet during the summer of 1917, an inexcusable consequence since the battle force provided the basis of the Navy's manpower as well as minesweeping in support of U-boat operations. At least Holland and Denmark remained neutral, but the German U-boat strategy of counterblockade would never be fully implemented before its own six-month deadline—by which time the British and Americans would be working in concert.

The United States in fact demonstrated remarkable strategic and tactical flexibility in meeting the U-boat onslaught. True, the administration of Woodrow Wilson had followed a unilateral course of heavy-ship construction—embodied in the Naval Act of 1916—generally to deter Germany in the Atlantic and Japan in the Pacific. And certainly the Americans, sensitive to the British Orders-in-Council violating neutral

American rights, remained somewhat aloof from the Alliance by becoming only an "Associated Power." But any lingering Anglophobia went into eclipse as Wilson mounted a great moral crusade for world democracy, beginning with the salvation of Britain and France from the Central Powers. Completing American defenses of the Panama Canal with the purchase of the Danish Virgin Islands early in 1917, Wilson rejected the fears of several admirals who forecast a German victory and who thus wanted a two-power battleship standard against Germany and Japan. Instead, he adhered to the recommendations of Admiral William S. Sims, ranking American naval officer in Europe, and Captain William V. Pratt in the Navy Department to accept the new British emphasis on antisubmarine construction. And since American shipyards could not build both battleships and destroyers, Wilson opted for the latter and postponed capital ship construction for the duration. More immediately, however, the U. S. Navy hastened many of its available lighter warships to British and French ports for employment as subchasers. When properly utilized, these vessels would make a significant contribution to Allied commerce protection.

Simultaneously with the American entry into the fighting in April 1917, the British finally decided to adopt convoy—probably the most fateful decision of the naval war. Prewar and early wartime arguments against convoy had stressed their invitation to attack, their congestion in port, and their illegality in neutral ports. But local convoys from Holland, Norway and France since mid-1916 had had some success, and now statistics revealed that—especially with American destroyers— the Allies had enough warships to escort merchant convoys. Despite anti-convoy conservatism in the Royal and U. S. navies, several key officials now pressed for it: the energetic new prime minister, David Lloyd George, Sir Maurice Hankey of the War Cabinet, Admirals Beatty and Sir Rosslyn Wemyss and Captain Herbert Richmond, leader of the "young Turks" and an adviser to Lloyd George. As the "black fortnight" of April 17–30 witnessed record U-boat successes, Admiral Jellicoe and the Admiralty reluctantly decided to initiate two experimental escorted convoys to Britain. They sailed in May: 17 merchantmen from Gibraltar at 6½ knots, and 12 from Hampton Roads at 9 knots. Both arrived safely, save for one straggler sunk from the latter convoy. Consequently, the Allies gradually and successfully instituted a regular convoy system over all their sea lanes, leading Admiral Sims to champion convoy in the U. S. Navy, whose Atlantic units were now integrated into the British command and doctrinal system.

Britain reformed its war-making machinery to lead the Allies in this new and vigorous antisubmarine strategy. Lloyd George appointed Churchill to be Minister of Munitions and Sir Eric Geddes first to the new post of Navy Controller—to handle logistics and leave the admirals to concentrate on operations—and soon after to be First Lord of the Admiralty. Never very keen on convoy, Jellicoe was relieved as First Sea Lord late in the year by Wemyss. In the Mediterranean, Allied leaders met at Corfu to reform commerce protection and welcomed the arrival in April of a Japanese squadron of one light cruiser and 8 (later 12) destroyers to assist. In the British Isles, British and American naval aircraft operated from coastal stations in reconnaissance and attack roles against U-boats, also attacking their bases in Flanders. Beatty and Captain Murray F. Sueter improved the British naval air arm by pushing torpedo plane development over the unpredictable seaplanes, catapult-plane towed lighters and 2 experimental aircraft carriers. New mines drove many U-boats from the Strait of Dover and Heligoland Bight to transit into the North Sea via the long Kiel Canal-Danish Sound route. But the convoy offered the most effective tactical device. Even one escorting warship forced the U-boat to remain submerged, throwing off its aim at zigzagging or fast merchant ships. British code-breaking and general intelligence kept U-boat movements under surveillance, while the wireless advised convoys accordingly. Finally, ample numbers of Allied destroyers and subchasers combined with mounting merchant ship construction to counter the U-boat. By 1918, 6 to 8 warships escorted each convoy of 15 to 25 merchantmen between New York, Hampton Roads and Nova Scotia and Allied ports in Europe.

The convoys *always* got through, leading to the relatively swift German admission of failure in the commerce war. German U-boat numbers peaked at 139 (55 at sea simultaneously) in September 1917, including new larger 1870-ton "U-cruisers." From 869,000 tons of merchant shipping sunk in April, these losses declined to 600,000 tons in May and then with convoy to under 175,000 tons (68 vessels) in September. With targets difficult to locate or attack, the German Admiralty early in the autumn shifted its U-boats away from the open ocean of the Western Approaches to the coastal English Channel and Irish Sea. Allied sinkings of U-boats never exceeded ten in any month, but the U-boat had been neutralized in the North Atlantic, and the brief U-boat redeployment succeeded only until the Allies shifted more patrol craft, seaplanes, airships and mines into their threatened coastal waters. In addition, improvements in British minesweeping techniques began to neutralize German mining efforts late in the year. The trend continued in 1918. German tonnage warfare avoided Canadian and American troop convoys altogether in order to sink six million tons of Allied and neutral shipping between February 1917 and January 1918, but convoys and escort forces increased to such proportions that the U-boats rarely attacked them. Allied admirals could not believe the deterrent value of the convoy and mistakenly tried to measure their success in numbers of U-boats sunk. But the Germans replaced most U-boats lost with an equal number of new boats (roughly eighty during 1918). What they could not replace were the experienced U-boat captains and crews lost at sea. By the summer of 1918 the convoys—now extended to coastal waters— had beaten the U-boats, and though they switched back to the Western Approaches for surfaced night attacks and as far afield as North America they could not halt the flow of growing Allied shipping.

The battle fleets of both sides tried to augment the commerce war. Admiral Scheer used High Seas Fleet units to sink two Anglo-Scandinavian convoys in the North Sea in October and December 1917 and to sweep British mines. Admiral Beatty merely added a battleship squadron as convoy backup and in January 1918 made the momentous decision not to provoke a fleet action but rather to subordinate all Grand Fleet activities to the antisubmarine campaign. An unpopular decision in both the Royal and U. S. navies—the latter contributed 4 dreadnoughts to the Grand Fleet in December—it nevertheless recognized strategic realities. In April 1918 Beatty shifted his 34 battleships, 9 battle cruisers and their flotillas from Scapa Flow to Rosyth, and though it failed to intercept an uneventful sortie by Scheer's 19 dreadnoughts and 5 battle cruisers later in the month the Grand Fleet continued to command the North Sea. In addition, Allied naval aircraft controlled the air and British mines closed the Heligoland Bight to U-boats in February, forcing all U-boats to transit via the Sound and Skagerrak. Then, in March, the Allies followed an American proposal to begin the laying of a mine barrage across the 240 miles of the North Sea between the Orkney Islands and Norway—evidence of continuing doubts about the efficacy of convoy. By October, when Norway closed its waters to U-boats, 56,000 American and 15,000 British mines had been sowed, but claimed only half a dozen U-boats. To close the English Channel to German destroyers and U-boats, Admiral Sir Roger Keyes in early 1918 strengthened British patrols and minefields, added searchlights to illuminate the Dover Strait at night, and tried—unsuccessfully— to close Zeebrugge and Ostend with sunken ships during blocking expeditions in April and May. By September, however, 24 of the 43 U-boats based in Flanders had been lost, and the survivors quit the Channel altogether.

Though the Allies tightened their command over the North Sea and Channel, German control of the Baltic Sea helped to take Russia out of the war. Allied ground offensives on the Western and Eastern fronts achieved little during 1917, after which a German thrust along the Gulf of Finland took Riga in September, and High Seas Fleet units cleared Russian mines and supported the amphibious capture of Oesel, Moon and Dago islands in October. Then, as the German fleet controlled the approaches to Kronstadt and Petrograd in November, the Bolsheviks and frustrated Kronstadt sailors overthrew the Russian democratic government and moved to conclude an armistice with the Central Powers. The British ordered their Baltic subs scuttled and looked on helplessly as the Communists signed an armistice in December. The High Seas Fleet, having survived Jutland, remained as a fleet-in-being to deter any possible British naval sortie into the Baltic. The Russian collapse relieved pressure on Germany elsewhere, for the Austrians stubbornly resisted Italian attacks, and even the Balkan front changed little with the entrance of Greece into the war as an Ally. The German Army led by Ludendorff wanted to convert the surrendered Russian Black Sea Fleet into a viable force in that quarter following the occupation of Sevastopol in April 1918. But it was frustrated by the scuttling of several vessels by order of Lenin and even more so by the German Navy's refusal to divert its energies away from the North Sea. Even so, Ottoman Turkey now had nothing further to fear from Russia, although its armies and river gunboats lost Jerusalem and Baghdad to fresh land-river British drives in the Middle East.

These events helped to transform the war into a relentless moral crusade during 1918. The original imperialistic motives were submerged in the growing ideological struggle between Wilsonian democracy and Leninist communism and the global popular disgust with the meaningless bloodshed of the European powers. Unsuccessful mutinies erupted in the French Army in the spring of 1917, the Austro-Hungarian Navy in October and the following February, as they did in the German and Russian fleets. Finland threw off Russian domination late in 1917, only to be crushed in April in a civil war ended partly by German amphibious landings in Finland. To destroy the decadent German, Austrian and Ottoman empires, the Allies tightened their blockade of the Central Powers and centralized their leadership into virtual dictatorships to win the war. Under Lloyd George, Wilson and Georges Clemenceau, a Supreme War Council and British-dominated Allied Naval Council directed the final campaigns. Ground forces were unified under the supreme command of French Marshal Ferdinand Foch in April, just as American Army and Marine Corps divisions began to arrive in France. The British combined their army and naval air squadrons in the Royal Air Force that month, supported by the Allied air forces. Only the French and Italian navies—prewar rivals—refused to cooperate in the Mediterranean. Germany consolidated its leadership behind General Ludendorff, and in August Admiral Scheer took over supreme naval command, succeeded as High Seas Fleet commander by Hipper. But Germany could not break the Allied armies—now reinforced by fresh American troops—on the Western front during the spring and summer and had to fall back before the Allied counterattack in July and August.

At sea, the Central Powers tried desperately to hold, but failed everywhere except in the Baltic. In the Mediterranean, convoy triumphed by midsummer, and the Allies spent five months laying a mine barrage across the Strait of Otranto. The new aggressive commander of the Imperial Austrian Navy, Rear Admiral Nikolaus Horthy de Nagybánya, tried to break the barrage in June with his four dreadnoughts, only to lose one and turn back in the face of an Italian torpedo boat attack. In the Aegean, a Turko-German surface force passed out of the Dardanelles in January to sink two British monitors off Imbros before being driven back by mines and air attacks which sank a cruiser. Turko-German ground forces had better success in pushing back the British from Armenia and the Black and Caspian sea coasts, but this front had become a strategic backwater. Admiral Scheer in September relegated the surface fleet to supporting the U-boats in the North Sea and the Army in the Baltic, and the next month obtained the kaiser's approval for a new U-boat construction program. But this desperate measure came much too late as the Central Powers retreated and collapsed everywhere during the autumn. In October, the Austro-Hungarian Empire fell apart into the revolutionary republics of Poland, Czechoslavakia, Hungary and Yugoslavia. The tottering dual monarchy transferred the fleet to Yugoslavia and its Danube flotilla to Hungary, and on November 1 two Italian frogmen sank the flagship dreadnought of the Austro-Yugoslav fleet with a mobile mine at Pola. The Balkan republics signed an armistice, and Allied warships occupied all their Adriatic ports. Simultaneously, British offensives in the Middle East took Turkey out of the war.

Virtually alone, Germany desperately tried to salvage what it could. When the German Army and U-boats evacuated Ostend and Zeebrugge in mid-October, Allied forces occupied these key bases. On the 20th, President Wilson demanded and got—as a prerequisite to armistice— the cessation of the unrestricted submarine campaign. Scheer recalled his U-boats and reassigned them to the High Seas Fleet to help it lure the Grand Fleet into one last battle. On the 26th a liberal government replaced imperial rule, spreading fear throughout the officer class and relief among the enlisted men. Scheer, Hipper and the reactionary naval high command now rebelled against the new regime by preparing their final sortie as a virtual suicide mission to salvage German honor. The 80,000 sailors of the High Seas Fleet rejected such madness by a general mutiny on the 29th as the ships rendezvoused at Wilhelmshaven for the sortie. Four years of mistreatment by arrogant junior officers fed their efforts, forcing Hipper to cancel the operation the next day. The sailors refused to sail anywhere and gradually merged their mutiny with the political revolutionaries that helped to overthrow the kaiser on November 9. The new German democratic republic signed the armistice—or virtual surrender—two days later.

British sea power had finally eliminated its major naval rival and kept it neutralized through internment of the High Seas Fleet at Scapa Flow later in November. The Anglo-American command of the Atlantic had defeated the U-boat and blockaded the German economy with telling effect, indirectly with Fisher's dreadnought fleet and directly by antisub convoys and destroyers. Final victory overlooked the material deficiencies of the battle fleets and tended to minimize the potential power of the submarine and aircraft, while the Gallipoli debacle had thoroughly discredited amphibious tactics and strategy. Happily for the victors, however, British naval conservatism had yielded to expedient innovations to win absolute command of the sea. Germany's naval conservatives by contrast changed little from Tirpitz through Scheer and could never bring themselves to accept the U-boat as the prime naval weapon of a continental power. The High Seas Fleet had preserved the coasts of Germany from invasion and given a creditable performance at Jutland, but it never really evolved beyond the role of a passive fleet-in-being. Even the sinking of over 7,600,000 tons of British and over 3,000,000 tons of other Allied and neutral shipping could not convince the German admirals of their doctrinal errors. And, finally, the Germans simply did not have the experience and confidence in naval matters enjoyed by their enemy.

Aside from the reassertion of British supremacy at sea, however, the "Great War" had settled none of the great power issues that had led to war in 1914. Britain and France were imposing an intolerable victor's peace on Germany, while—equally alarming—the United States and Japan now resumed their naval arms race in the Pacific. The armistice of 1918 therefore would remain just that, unless somehow a system of naval arms controls could eliminate the possibility of the resumption of total war.

15
Naval Armistice and Arms Control, 1919–1940

A state which adopts the policy of constructing a Navy composed primarily of submarines consciously renounces the struggle for sea power. . . .

—ADMIRAL HERMANN BAUER,
German Navy, 1931

THE POSTWAR BALANCE OF POWER

The devices by which the great powers sought to turn the armistice of 1918 into a permanent condition of international stability and peace were unique, yet firmly rooted in the antebellum legalism of the *Pax Britannica*. They were, namely, formal international organization and a system of naval arms controls. That both failed to prevent the resumption of total war in 1940–41 reveals the naiveté of the powers in their underlying political assumptions. International political unity embodied in the League of Nations came about after the revitalization of the prewar global cosmopolitanism in the wartime idealism of Woodrow Wilson. But without the full participation of all the powers, notably the United States, Soviet Russia and Weimar Germany, such a system could only be at best imperfect. Rather, the treaties ending World War I represented the same traditional notions about European global hegemony and power balances, when in fact the national empires of Europe had been mortally wounded by the disaster of 1914–18. The failure of the League's members to enforce their own rules against aggression while vainly attempting to achieve economic self-sufficiency seriously compromised the powers in their postwar reconstruction programs. Furthermore, rising nationalism within European colonial and power preserves undermined imperial order everywhere; the end of the European overseas empires had been hastened by the heavy costs of the war.

473

The new attempt at naval arms control between the great powers did succeed as long as all the signatories were willing to abide by the warship limitations agreed upon. Cloaked in the misnomer of outright "disarmament," the various international naval conferences in the 1920s and 1930s in fact attempted only to reduce international tensions by establishing naval building holidays and ratios. Actual disarmament of modern machine weapons was not possible, for such machinery could not be separated from the totality of industrial civilization, a fact which the powers seemed to realize. Yet the weapons they chose to limit were not those which were revolutionizing warfare, the submarine and airplane, but rather the same prewar index of naval power, the battleship. The submarine would probably have had to have won the war by defeating Britain in order to be accepted fully as a major weapon after the war, while the smaller naval nations clung to it as their only alternative to big surface fleets. The airplane was still too limited technically to warrant controls, but the powers appreciated its potential by limiting aircraft carriers. So the wartime belligerents found not peace in their armistice and postwar treaties, but merely a breathing spell during which to prepare for the final agony of resumed total war.

The armistice of 1918–19 in itself did not resolve the great power struggles of the time, and three more years passed before relative order could be reestablished between the powers. The final disposition of the German fleet by the Allies and the establishment of the League involved many difficulties. The Russian Civil War led to great power interventions around the Russian periphery as the democracies attempted to help overthrow the Bolshevik regime. Rampant nationalism and religious strife turned the Middle East into a bloody arena of internal warring and power rivalries following the collapse of the Ottoman Empire. Finally, in the Pacific, the United States and Japan resumed their naval arms race with capital ship construction that threatened to lead to open war— placing Great Britain in an embarrassing position, since she was allied to both Pacific powers and was too exhausted economically from the war to participate in this new building race. Only the convening of the Washington Naval Conference in 1921–22 halted the Pacific power struggle, leading to a decade of relative quiet throughout the world.

Great Britain and the United States cooperated in the dismemberment of Germany's navy, but remained otherwise antagonistic over the growth of American naval might which challenged British supremacy at sea. Allied disputes over the disposition of the surrendered High Seas Fleet evaporated on July 21, 1919, when the skeleton crews of that fleet simply scuttled their ships while still interned at Scapa Flow: 400,000 tons of war shipping, including fifteen dreadnoughts. But then President Wilson at the peace conference at Versailles demanded that Britain endorse the principle of freedom of neutral shipping in time of war, which the British regarded as an American economic attack on the Empire and thus refused to accept. Wilson also pressed for and got a League of Nations, while his naval advisers urged the creation of an international League navy. But none of the powers could accept the idea of subordinating their fleets to such a force, and the American Congress refused to join the League at all. The Versailles Treaty of October 1919 thus lacked any real element of collective security without American participation, and though the United States cut back many of its grandiose naval building programs so offensive to Britain, the two great maritime victor nations remained at cross-purposes and continued to act unilaterally. France tended to side with Britain as European powers ever fearful of Germany; Britain remained allied with America's rival, Japan; and all the powers simply excluded Bolshevik Russia from any postwar discussions.

The Communist revolution in Russia had not only alarmed the other powers, but provides one of the few instances of political activism in naval history. The Kronstadt sailors, especially of the cruiser *Aurora*—still enshrined at Leningrad (Petrograd), were rewarded for their part in the revolution with the creation of a powerful Naval Commissariat within the unified defense structure and then, early in 1918, with the Socialist Worker-Peasant Red Fleet. But such leftist activity among sailors proved exceptional, stemming more from injustices within the old navy than from political activism—not unlike the German naval mutiny. Counterrevolutionary naval officers were also active. Admiral Horthy threw out a Communist government and a Rumanian army from Hungary in 1919 and then became national regent. Russian Admiral Kolchak of the Black Sea Fleet seized power there late in 1918 to help bring on the Russian Civil War. And, finally, in March 1921 the Kronstadt sailors again mutinied, this time against their rigid Communist masters, and had to be severely crushed. Sensitive to internal dissension, the new Soviet government also had to reckon with the new Baltic republics of Finland, Poland, Lithuania, Estonia and Latvia, especially since the former wartime Allies decided to support these new nations with active military and naval aid.

Despite the strong anti-Communist attitudes of President Wilson, First Lord Geddes and Admirals Wemyss and Beatty, and the imperial territorial designs of the Allies on Russian territory, their warweary peoples refused to allow any systematic or full intervention. Nevertheless, between 1918 and 1921, the Allies made halting attempts to support the anti-Bolshevik forces during the Russian Civil War. In the Far East, Allied ground forces and warships occupied Vladivostok and British naval gunners helped Admiral Kolchak capture Omsk and briefly man his twenty-one-gunboat flotilla on Lake Baikal until he was defeated and executed. Then the Allied forces evacuated Vladivostok, although Japan did not leave northern Sakhalin until 1925. In South Russia, the British supported the White Russians against the Reds on the Black and Caspian seas with landing forces, aircraft and gunboats in order to protect their oil-rich Middle East holdings. After France and Italy failed to police the Black and Caspian seas respectively, the British withdrew and with the French and Americans helped evacuate the Whites as they were driven back on the coast by a Red offensive. In North Russia, Allied warships occupied Murmansk and Archangel in mid-1918 and sent a small flotilla up the Dvina River. One year later fourteen British and American gunboats, shipped by rail from Murmansk, joined twenty-five Finnish patrol boats to seize control of Lake Onega, while British gunboats and monitors supported an offensive up the Dvina. Stranded in this unpopular war by White defections and Red victories, a battalion of Royal Marines refused to fight on the Onega front, and Britain led the general Allied withdrawal. On these three distant fronts, therefore, the Allies achieved little more than to antagonize the Soviet regime.

On the Baltic front, however, the wartime Allies made a determined effort to resist the Bolsheviks because of their threat to the new Baltic nations. In addition, the Allies retained a large force of unsurrendered German troops as a buffer against the Bolsheviks until they began to seek their own territorial objectives. The British committed considerable naval forces to the Baltic, generally commanded by Rear Admiral Walter H. Cowan and reinforced by French warships and a small but spirited new Estonian Navy under Rear Admiral Juhan Pitka. The U. S. Navy generally confined its operations to civilian food relief. Operating out of Copenhagen, Finnish Helsinski (Helsingfors), Estonian Tallinn (Reval), Latvian Liepaja (Libau) and Riga, Lithuanian Memel and Polish Danzig, the Allied navies sought to control the Gulf of Finland and blockade the Russian Baltic Fleet (Soviet Activated Squadron) at Kronstadt under Comrade A. P. Zelenoy. The Red Russian ground and sea forces, personally commanded by Joseph Stalin, defended the Lake Ladoga front and other approaches to Petrograd-Leningrad. While the armies seesawed across Baltic lands, the Allies and Soviet Russia waged an undeclared naval war from November 1918 into 1920.

Allied strategic mobility at sea aided materially in preserving the independence of the Baltic States, but failed utterly—as elsewhere—even to weaken the Soviet regime. In response to a Soviet ground offensive during the winter of 1918–19 which captured Estonian Narva, Latvian Riga and Lithuanian Vilna, Anglo-Estonian units harassed the coast and captured two modern Russian destroyers; Estonia created a squadron on Lake Peipus; the Poles drove the Russians out of Vilna; and German-Latvian forces retook Riga and Liepaja. In mid-1919 Admiral Cowan supported an Estonian counterattack on land by using Allied vessels in the Gulf of Finland to bombard the coast, support landings and sweep mines. In June, Cowan's torpedo boats sank a Russian cruiser, and in August, covered by a diversionary carrier air strike, they charged straight into Kronstadt roadstead to sink the two Russian battleships and a depot ship there, losing three of their eight to a Russian destroyer. In May the Estonians captured the entire Bolshevik gunboat flotilla on Lake Peipus, and in October Anglo-Estonian vessels, including one 7200-ton monitor with twin 15″ guns, supported a successful White Russian offensive toward Petrograd. The Reds held, but lost three destroyers to Allied mines. Late in the year the Germans made a final bid to take over Riga and Liepaja, only to be driven back by Allied fleet units, Latvian troops and a river flotilla, in addition to which the Allies instituted a blockade of German Baltic ports. The coming of winter cold and ice, discontent and isolated mutinies in the British fleet and Allied indecision finally led to a general withdrawal. In 1920 Soviet Russia made peace with Finland, Estonia, Latvia and Lithuania, but carried on the war with Poland until 1921 when Anglo-French naval units rushed supplies to Danzig and enabled the Poles to repulse the Russians and conclude peace.

Postwar national boundaries in continental Europe reflected the Wilsonian self-determinism accepted at Versailles and were partially influenced by naval patrols. The dismemberment of the Austro-Hungarian Empire and territorial annexations of the Dalmatian coast, Zara and Fiume by Italy between 1919 and 1924 required Allied naval patrols in the Adriatic to assure the political integrity of Yugoslavia. Britain also kept gunboats on the Danube River till 1925, keeping normal trade open. This self-determination frustrated several Allied wartime deals to carve up the Ottoman Empire in the form of mandates that eventually led to independent Middle Eastern states. Britain obtained a mandate over Mesopotamia as the state of Iraq, which had to be pacified in 1920, and the Trucial System and Aden protectorate enabled the British to control the waters around Saudi Arabia, although Egypt obtained its virtual independence in 1922. On the Levantine coast, Britain received the mandate over Palestine and Transjordan, and France took over Syria and Lebanon on the same basis.

A Turkish nationalist movement led by Mustapha Kemal resisted further dismemberment of the country, however, resulting in much bloodshed between 1919 and 1922. Moslem Turk-Christian Greek antagonism prompted Anglo-Greek and Italian landings at Smyrna and Adalia respectively, and the arrival of American battleships with escorts in 1919. When the Greeks then mounted an offensive across Anatolia and Greek warships attacked the coast, the Allies kept the Dardanelles open and early in 1920 occupied Constantinople for defensive purposes. The Italians held Adalia, the French tried to take over Cilicia, and in June Admiral de Robeck used five British battleships and some seaplanes to occupy the eastern shore of the Sea of Marmara and drive back Kemal's army. But during the winter of 1920–21 Kemal negotiated French and Italian withdrawals, obtained rapport with Russia by ceding the port of Batum to it, and profited from the strict neutrality enforced by the naval patrols under American diplomat-Admiral Mark L. Bristol. Then, during the summer of 1921, Kemal stopped a new Greek offensive and drove it back on Smyrna where a disastrous fire and reprisals killed tens of thousands of refugees. The offshore Anglo-American naval units, hampered by logistical and diplomatic limitations, could do little to save the victims. The Greek invasion crushed, the diplomats finally concluded peace in 1923, creating the Republic of Turkey which included European Thrace and neutralizing the straits. Allied warships then withdrew from the Black Sea.

British supremacy at sea enabled the Royal Navy to police all European and South Asian waters, especially in containing Russia—however unnecessary this was, due to total Bolshevik preoccupation with internal matters. In addition to the relatively successful neutralization of the Baltic and Black seas, the British still held the Strait of Gibraltar, Suez Canal, Bab el Mandeb and Persian Gulf. In India, torn by warring Moslems and Hindus, British troops and air forces enforced stability to thwart Russia, especially westward to the Persian Gulf. They pacified a restive Afghanistan in 1919, but yielded to a Russian naval demonstration on the Caspian Sea to withdraw from Persia (Iran) in 1920–21. The Russians also withdrew, leaving that region generally stabilized. By the same token, British forces ended their intervention efforts in the Russian Civil War everywhere. The Anglo-Japanese alliance insured the containment of the new Soviet state in the Far East, but it also created serious tensions with Britain's wartime American ally.

Japanese-American rivalry had been postponed during World War I, but Japan continued to press upon the relatively helpless new Republic of China. Japan had not only occupied Germany's Pacific islands and Chinese base at Tsingtao but had violated early American neutrality in the Philippines, operated its naval vessels as far eastward as the Galápagos Islands and Gulf of California, and in early 1915 had issued "Twenty-one Demands" to China for territory and virtual political submission. As long as China had remained neutral, Japan had had to keep its warships out of Chinese waters, while the neutral American Yangtze gunboat patrol could continue and American diplomatic maneuvers enforced the "open door." Then, in 1917, following a warlord and Manchu upheaval, both China and the United States declared war on the Central Powers, and Japanese warships returned. To quiet Japan, the Americans vaguely recognized its "special interests" in China and kept their major warships out of the Pacific altogether. The end of the war and massive Japanese intervention in Russia signaled the renewal of the Japanese-American naval arms race, in addition to which the powers at Versailles mandated Germany's Pacific islands to Japan. Britain could do nothing in the Far East, for postwar naval retrenchment under the "Geddes axe" of First Lord Geddes' special committee recommendation of 1921 reduced Royal Navy strength outside of Europe. Alarmed by these new strategic realities, Britain's Pacific and Indian ocean colonies—Canada, India, Australia and New Zealand—in 1921 demanded that the mother country replace the Japanese alliance with a new settlement involving the United States as a friendly party.

The United States government, equally tired of the arms race and anxious to reduce tensions with Japan, in 1921 convened the Washington Naval Conference of the five largest naval powers. The United States, Britain and Japan—with France and Italy as minor participants—froze the strategic *status quo* in the Pacific, placed a ceiling on capital ship construction, and recognized the political and territorial integrity of China (the latter with four other nations). The powers agreed not to build new fortifications on their island possessions or mandates in the Pacific, except for British Singapore, American Pearl Harbor and the Japanese home islands, and to respect each other's zones of maritime control: Britain in the South Pacific, Japan in the Central Pacific, France in Indochina, and the United States in the Hawaiian, Aleutian and Philippine island groups. In battleships and battle cruisers, virtually all construction was to cease and a ceiling ratio of $5:5:3:1.67:1.67$ was to be established. Specifically, the five naval powers agreed to limit their capital ship tonnage to vessels under 35,000 tons mounting 16″ guns and totaling 500,000 tons each for Britain and the United States; 300,000 tons for Japan; and 167,000 tons each for France and Italy. These agreements, which superseded the Anglo-Japanese alliance, were to last for ten years, at the end of which another conference was to convene to consider renewal.

The Washington settlements, instead of achieving actual disarmament as many people naively believed, represent the first successful attempt at arms control in history. The shortcomings lay in the type of weapons that were not limited and in the eventual failure of all the powers to perpetuate the compromises of the meeting. But since the senior naval policy makers of all the powers regarded the battleship as the index of naval might, the conference indeed succeeded in checking the arms race and thus extending to the Pacific the same general armistice that prevailed in Europe. Unfortunately, however, France refused to consider any limitation to her ground forces as long as her wartime allies Britain and America would not guarantee her frontier against a possibly resurgent Germany. Aviation was in such a primitive state that any curtailment of military aviation would necessarily require the inherent halting of overall developments in commercial aeronautics, a possibility repulsive to all these modern industrial nations. But in the naval sphere, aviation was to be at least controlled by imposing the same 5:5:3 ratio on aircraft carriers if not their planes; in general, carriers were to be limited to 27,000 tons, with tonnage ceilings of 135,000 tons each for Britain and America; 81,000 for Japan; and 60,000 for France and Italy. The other potentially revolutionary naval weapon, the submarine, received no such restriction. Britain, trying to avert the repetition of its near-defeat by Germany's U-boats, worked to outlaw subs altogether. But France, traditionally a continental nation dependent upon such inexpensive coast defense and *guerre de course* vessels, would have none of it and was supported in large measure by the United States, whose naval planners saw similar uses for the sub in any future war with Japan. So no action was taken on the submarine. Battleships naturally required escorts, but the only restrictions placed were to limit cruisers to 10,000 tons and 8″ guns. Carriers were also limited to 8″ guns, but no attention was given the multi-purpose destroyers. Though the admirals of each country bemoaned these reductions to their operating fleets, they now in fact were unknowingly prevented from expending more funds on the questionably effective battleships while gaining valuable time and freedom to develop the weapons that would eventually dominate future total naval warfare—the airplane and submarine.

The arms races and armed conflict of the early twentieth century thus ended everywhere by the close of 1922, and all that remained was to enforce the various agreements. Throughout the 1920s enforcement proved successful in the Pacific and nearly impossible in Europe. The Treaty of Versailles created a Control Commission of British, French, Italian and Japanese officers to insure that Germany in no way attempted to rearm, but the lack of staffing, clever German evasiveness and the American refusal to sign the treaty all combined to undermine the efforts of the Commission, which deluded itself by closing down its naval unit in 1924 with the statement that the German Navy was effectively disarmed. Attempts by the League of Nations to enforce anything similarly proved fruitless, for the American absence added to the British and French retrenchment to encourage covert German violations of the Versailles disarmament dictates throughout the 1920s.

By contrast, in the Pacific the mutual attitudes of the Washington signatory powers precluded any violation of the non-fortification agreements. Despite repeated warnings from the Navy, the American government did nothing significant to improve the naval facilities in the Philippines, Guam or Wake, while the British allowed Hong Kong's defenses to languish. The Japanese, though refusing to allow any inspection by foreign nations, did absolutely nothing to fortify or develop the mandated islands for military uses during the decade. Despite foreign apprehensions to the contrary, Japan enjoyed an era of relative tranquillity under the new Prime Minister Admiral Tomosaburo Kato and the men who succeeded him upon his death in 1923. Kato regarded the Imperial Japanese Navy as a deterrent force and thus kept it at the treaty strength. The British and American governments were simply not disposed to build up to treaty levels, so that Japan during the 1920s never felt threatened by either or even both powers.

The spirit of naval arms control established at Washington continued until and after the scheduled renewal conference held in London in 1930. Between 1925 and 1928 Germany agreed at Locarno to respect neighboring national frontiers; Britain, the United States and Japan met at Geneva, but failed in their intention to limit cruiser, destroyer and submarine strengths; and the major powers agreed at Paris to outlaw war, but without the necessary corollary of enforcing the agreement. Despite the wild idealism of the latter endeavor, the naval powers met again in 1930 to make some hard agreements for extending naval arms controls. Though Japan had built to Washington treaty limits, and had but one ocean to patrol against the two oceans concerning both Britain and America, Japanese pride had been rankled by the inferior ratio assigned the Imperial Navy, and opposition against treaty extension mounted in the person of old Fleet Admiral Togo of Tsushima fame and a rising militant group of Army and Navy officers.

Nevertheless, the first effects of the worldwide Great Depression of 1929–30 were forcing Japan to retrench economically and to enable Admiral Kato's successors to carry on at the London Conference. Capital ship (including carriers) ratios were generally maintained, with a ratio of about 10:10:7 being established for cruisers for Britain, the United States and Japan respectively. (France and Italy again were negligible participants). Most importantly, parity in submarines was granted across-the-board. In the face of a combined Anglo-American effort to abolish subs altogether, each of which had been far outdistanced in sub construction since 1922 by France, Japan and Italy, the latter powers used familiar arguments for coast defenses to achieve parity and substitute limitation with vague statements about submarines observing international law in time of war. In fact, the powers returned to the same ambiguities and loopholes of the 1909–16 period, wanting the restricted use of subs, but lacking necessary controls. The London treaty would expire at the end of 1936, when another conference would again consider renewal.

The attempt at naval arms control ultimately failed for the same reason that the armistice arrangements of 1918–22 collapsed: several of the powers became impatient at such restrictions which ran counter to new policies of national expansion. Ideologically, the ascendance of fascist regimes in Italy (1922), Japan (1931) and Germany (1933) combined to neutralize the League of Nations and all the treaty arrangements so laboriously worked out after World War I. And France and Italy, still in mutual fear of each other, refused to compromise. Neither the League members (including Soviet Russia which joined in 1932) nor the United States had the desire to try to enforce League or treaty stipulations when Japan conquered Manchuria in 1931, Italy invaded Ethiopia in 1935, Germany reoccupied the Rhineland in 1936, and civil war broke out in Spain the same year. In 1933 Japan quit the League and late the next year repudiated the terms of the Washington and London treaties—to be effective two years hence. Germany, a member since 1926, left the League also in 1933 and two years later denounced the Treaty of Versailles. Italy remained a member of the League as late as 1937, but its belligerence had long since made the League into a mockery. Still gripped by global economic depression, the other powers could do little but complain, begin their own belated rearmament, and seek some kind of new alliance system and balance of power. In the end, however, unilateral national security replaced international trust.

The last attempts at naval arms control sought much and gained virtually nothing. A world disarmament conference met at Geneva over 1932–34 seeking to check weapons of land warfare, but the several international crises led to its collapse. Great Britain, understandably alarmed both by the apparent apathy and inability of her former allies to help her check the growing aggressiveness of especially Germany, entered into a separate naval arms agreement with that country and in so doing repudiated the Versailles arrangements. The Anglo-German Naval Treaty of 1935 allowed Germany to build a navy 35 percent the size of the total naval forces of the British Empire in all classes of warships, except subs. Of all things—in view of the near-victory of the U-boats in 1916–17—the British allowed the Germans parity in subs! In December 1935, Britain, the United States, Japan and France convened at London again to arrange a continuation of the 1930 ratios, but Japan demanded parity in all warship classes, an intolerable objective to the Anglo-American delegates which resulted in the Japanese withdrawal from the meeting early in 1936. Nevertheless, Britain, America and

France agreed among themselves to certain "qualitative" (ship characteristics) limitations on new warships, most of which survived till 1938 and some of which remained binding as late as 1942. The last piece of naval arms control, a special protocol which prohibited unrestricted submarine attacks on unarmed shipping in time of war, was agreed upon at London in early November 1936 by Britain, America, Japan, Italy and France, by Germany two weeks later and by Russia the following February. But again, enforcement depended totally upon the signatories to obey it.

In the last week of 1936, Japanese obedience to the limitations of 1922 and 1930 ended, and, despite continuing overtures for international agreement, naval rearmament went forward unabated in Japan and throughout Europe.

THE INTERWAR NAVIES AND EMPIRES

The art of naval warfare and of colonial pacification resumed after 1918 as if no world war had taken place. Machine weapons, embodied in the strategic bomber and superdreadnought, kept the material school of strategy in the forefront, due partly to an imperfect appreciation of how command of the sea had helped to end the war. The massive armies preoccupied the continental nations as always, as these sought panaceas in the defensive Maginot Line or the offensive tank-air-infantry *Blitzkrieg*. Italian General Guilio Douhet, the foremost material strategist, even reasoned that land-based bombing planes would bomb European military, industrial and urban centers into submission, while the armies and navies remained stalemated. In fact, however, strategic bombers were but a long-range extension of continental artillery which could lay down a barrage for advancing armies and apparently sink advancing warships—just as American General Billy Mitchell's planes dramatically did in tests off the American East Coast in 1921. But Douhet had little to say about the Pacific, where the aircraft carrier evolved into the long-range extension of the naval gun to support amphibious operations, sink other warships and develop its own antiaircraft defenses. Yet, neither the carrier nor submarine could dislodge the battleship in these years as the nucleus of blue-water fleets.

The notion of command of the sea did not change, and the same strategic arguments persisted, but on a much lower-keyed intellectual level. One reason lay in the fact that no naval theorists really matched the impressive material arguments of Douhet or the so-called "geopoliticians" who argued that control of the "heartland" of Central Europe would ultimately neutralize the sea powers. Mahan had died in 1914 and Corbett in 1923, leaving Admirals Richmond and Raoul Castex of France to advance their theories and incorporate the newest technology. Conservative battleship admirals thus returned to the old prewar anti-intellectualism, their naval war colleges and fleet maneuvers looking to another Jutland and virtually ignoring the promise of airplane and submarine. Only Castex envisioned the renewed use of the sub as a commerce raider as in World War I, while Admiral William A. Moffett led a group of American naval aviators outside the battleship navy to theorize that the fast carrier had replaced the battleship as the backbone of blue-water navies. The technical limitations of subs and planes were also part of the reason, so that they were both regarded as fleet reconnaissance and secondary attack elements during the 1920s and 1930s. The memory of Gallipoli discredited amphibious operations in Europe, but the U. S. Marine Corps foresaw their utility in any war across the Pacific against Japan. No navy made any real progress in logistics, and most further centralized their command structures. The only real progress occurred in improvements to existing weapons and in several complementary inventions at the tactical level.

The newer technology and naval treaty limitations in fact hastened the decline of the battleship. The weight restrictions imposed by the treaties demanded economy through qualitative improvements to warship hull design: better steel and lighter alloys, arc welding instead of rivets, and fewer but larger boilers. In propulsion, after 1930 high steam pressures and temperatures were produced from geared turbines, although the Germans used high-speed diesel engines and several navies adopted hydraulic machinery for auxiliary power. Armor did not change, whereas fire control got better. Antisub defenses included underwater bulges on the larger surface ships and the introduction of "asdic" ("sonar" from 1943) echo-acoustical sounding devices for sub detection, but virtually nothing was done to extend wartime convoy techniques. Antiair defenses centered on increased warship speeds and semiautomatic 5″ guns and large machine guns ("pom poms"). Radio assisted importantly in sub and aircraft detection and interception, but shipborne radar in the late 1930s was the most revolutionary development of these years. By bouncing pulsed transmissions of radio microwaves off solid objects, the Germans with the 80cm band could detect surface ships at twenty miles, and British, Americans and French used the 10cm band to detect aircraft up to a hundred miles. By 1941, Anglo-American radar sets could detect ships also, range for gunnery purposes, and enable closely coordinated cruising formations even at night. Radio-direction finders and radar-radio fighter plane direction also developed apace. Other isolated naval research initiated aerial bombsight and rocket devices and improved upon the wartime achievements in cryptography.

Surface ships reached their maximum efficient displacements for high-speed operations under the treaty restrictions. The slower battleship and faster battle cruiser merged into the fast battleship, beginning in the mid-1930s with the two 31.5-knot French *Dunkerques,* although the few surviving battle cruisers like Britain's *Hood* retained their old deficiencies. Main turreted batteries generally mounted 14" to 16" guns (or 11" in the two German *Scharnhorsts* to 18.1" in the two Japanese *Yamatos*). Heavy cruisers tended to exceed their 10,000-ton limit, but still had to sacrifice armor to keep down their weight and yet to mount eight to ten power-driven 8" guns and make at least 32 knots. Somewhat smaller light cruisers had less armor but twelve to fifteen 6" guns for speeds (for Italy at least) as high as 41 knots. Equally swift destroyers bristled with 5" guns, antiaircraft and other machine guns and torpedo tubes, while submarines—limited to 2000 tons in 1930—stayed small also because of high-speed diesel engines, arc welding and high tensile steel. Motor torpedo boats of 20 to 35 tons with highest speeds between 35 and 50 knots remained in the French and Italian navies until Britain, Germany and the United States renewed their construction after 1935. These and such lesser vessels as gunboats and mine warfare craft improved fleet capabilities, but only did aviation really alter naval tactics significantly.

The aircraft carrier dominated naval aviation in these years, though the rigid dirigibles competed until several tragic crashes put them out of business. Britain led with experimental carriers in the 1920s, after which the United States and Japan settled on the construction of the 30-knot fast carrier displacing between 20,000 tons (the American *Enterprise,* 1938) and 30,000 tons (the Japanese *Shokaku,* 1941), plus a few larger ones allowed by the 1922 treaty. Gradually, the flush-deck design with lowered smokestacks gave way to the full wooden flight deck with "island" superstructure for bridge and stacks. Later British carriers incorporated the armored flight deck to withstand land-based air attacks, but at the price of additional weight and reduced oil capacity limiting cruising range, and reduced aircraft stowage limiting plane complement. As "the eyes of the fleet," the carriers emphasized scout-planes, which doubled as dive-bombers, and these were largely replaced in the late 1930s by battleship- and cruiser-mounted catapult float planes, multi-engine seaplanes and land-based patrol bombers. The scout-dive-bomber evolved into an attack plane alongside the torpedo-bombing plane, with both escorted by defensive fighter planes. Finally, antisub air operations were left to the multi-engine non-carrier planes and eventually also non-rigid blimps. The tactical relationship between carrier and battleship was not settled during these two decades, beyond the broad agreement that they should be mutually supporting.

In general, only the U. S. Navy and Royal Navy remained blue-water forces aimed at winning command of the sea, with the other navies being continentalist, interested primarily in coast defense and support of armies and land-based air forces—Germany, France and Italy in European waters; Japan, China and Holland along the periphery of Asia; and Russia on her long Eurasian coastlines.

British naval policy at the Admiralty remained very conservative and material-oriented although the "young Turks" led by Admirals Richmond (who retired in 1930) and K. G. B. Dewar promoted new ideas at the war colleges, and some gradual reforms occurred, thanks to such men as Admiral Lord Chatfield, who was Beatty's flag captain at Jutland and rose to be First Sea Lord, 1933–39. Staff centralization and improvement followed bitter wartime weaknesses with a new Naval Staff College founded by Wemyss in 1919, a new interservice Chiefs of Staff Committee led by Hankey four years later, a Tactical School at Portsmouth in 1924 and the Imperial Defense College under Richmond in 1927. But any service unification was frustrated by the Royal Air Force's refusal to return the Fleet Air Arm to the Navy's full control until 1937. Preoccupied with Jutland and the big battle, especially as it might be fought against Japan, the British minimized strategic studies, ignored the unsolved problems of trade defense save for a smug complacency in the abilities of asdic, rejected amphibious maneuvers because of Gallipoli until 1938, and simply did not develop or appreciate naval aviation or submarines. The battle fleet Fighting Instructions remained thoroughly formalist, though some attention was given to night tactics and destroyer action. Admiralty anti-intellectualism repressed the critical *Naval Review* until 1926, but this could not prevent experimentation at sea, as when Admiral Richmond used his Eastern Fleet to try combined operations off Bombay in 1924 and Admiral Chatfield utilized the carriers of his Mediterranean Fleet in the early 1930s for torpedo air strikes, fleet antiair defenses and at-sea refueling. Convoy was finally accepted again in 1937, but the British simply assumed that they would again command the sea in any future war and resume their 1914 continental strategy of sending the Army and strategic air forces to the aid of France.

The British Empire strategically resembled the pre-1914 situation with the important difference that the Pacific possessions could probably not be defended against an aggressive Japan. Politically, also, Ireland obtained its independence after a five-year civil war in 1921; ten years later Britain granted semi-autonomous "Commonwealth" status to Canada, South Africa, Australia and New Zealand; and over these decades Egypt, Palestine, Iraq and India began to enjoy increasingly liberal home rule. Encouraging these dominions to develop their own defenses, Britain drastically reduced its overseas garrisons in order to concentrate on Europe and the Mediterranean. The British agreed that France should control the Western Mediterranean, and Britain should dominate the rest, including the sea routes to India via Gibraltar, Malta, Alexandria, Aden, Simonstown in South Africa, Trincomalee on Ceylon, Singapore and Hong Kong. Britain planned to meet any Japanese attack by holding Singapore with its 15" coastal guns until fleet reinforcements could be dispatched from the home squadrons. This strategy depended upon peace in Europe, a growing unlikelihood as Germany and Japan cemented their alliance in the late 1930s. As the British inability to defend their Far Eastern possessions became evident, the latter could only turn to the United States for possible assistance.

Britain's wartime ally, France, had even less interest in naval reforms or even naval construction, a reluctance which embroiled the French Navy in serious political struggles from 1924. Subordinated to a rather passive Superior Council of National Defense in 1921 and an ever-dominant Army, the Navy even lost its air arm to a new independent Air Ministry for four turbulent years, 1928–32. French postwar naval doctrine followed the prewar arguments, with the traditionalists advocating battleships, especially when Germany and Italy began building them in 1931, and the more material-minded of them like Admiral Daveluy following *jeune école* thinking for coast defense against Germany and Italy. The reform-minded Naval Ministry of Georges Leygues from 1917 to 1933 tried to accommodate these needs and treaty limitations by first confining construction to *jeune école* fast cruisers, torpedo boats, destroyers and subs and then four new battleships. Historical strategist Admiral Castex tried to resolve these doctrinal dilemmas in a five-volume work on strategic theory between 1929 and 1939 and as commandant of the School of Naval Warfare and Center for Higher Naval Studies and founder of the unified College of Higher National Defense Studies. But real rearmament did not begin until 1938 when Admiral J. L. X. François Darlan led the initiation of a general construction program which included two carriers. This would prove to be too little and too late for France to develop a respectable continental fleet against both Germany and Italy.

The French overseas empire compounded many of the problems surrounding French naval doctrine and strategy. Not only did France need to defend its vital possessions along the North African coast, but it had responsibilities for much of tropical Africa, Madagascar, Somaliland, mandated Syria and Lebanon, Indochina and several islands scattered throughout the world. In the Mediterranean, Franco-Spanish forces completed the pacification of Morocco in the Riff War of the early 1920s and later mop-up operations. To counter Italy in North Africa and complement Bizerte, France built the new naval base of Mers-el-Kebir at Algerian Oran and erected the Mareth defense line across southeastern

Tunisia. Adjacent Casablanca and Dakar remained as French African bastions on the Atlantic coast, but the French depended utterly on British naval protection in the Middle East. The far-flung Asian islands and French Indochina created such impossible strategic demands that Admiral Castex recommended the abandonment of North Africa, the Middle East, Indochina and possibly Madagascar in the face of any major attack. However realistic, such a viewpoint offended French honor and prestige, leading the Navy to sacrifice additional material effort from the prime European arena to these strategically unimportant regions. France, the continental power, at her peril resisted the growing independence movements in these areas to persist in her dreams of imperial grandeur.

Italy also returned to its basic prewar strategic stance, save for the fact that the fascist regime of Benito Mussolini—an inlander from Piedmont—had little sympathy for the needs of the Navy and stifled any new construction and much-needed administrative reforms until 1926. Naval Minister Admiral Thaon de Revel and the new Institute of Naval War, founded in 1921, unsuccessfully fought Mussolini's separate air force of 1923 which embraced the Navy's rather considerable air arm. Consequently, the admirals could not get the aircraft carriers, offensive torpedo planes, adequate reconnaissance planes and defensive fighters that they badly needed. The Washington treaty forbade new battleships, but Italy competed with France in fast cruisers, destroyers and torpedo boats and from 1930 in new replacement battleships. The Italians generally outclassed the French in the Mediterranean, but their admirals— very pro-British from the wartime experience—looked only to protecting the sea route to Libya and took no interest in distant operations, trade protection, sealift of war materials, counterblockade techniques, *guerre de course*, night fighting tactics or foreign technological progress in asdic and radar. Trapped within the Mediterranean, Italy's navy did little to prepare for the war toward which Mussolini drifted during the 1930s.

The Italian Empire also remained confined to the middle sea, save for Mussolini's extension of it into East Africa. France held the Western Mediterranean and tried unsuccessfully to build up the Yugoslav Navy to counter Italy in the Adriatic. During a diplomatic incident with Greece in 1923 Italian naval forces bombarded and briefly occupied Corfu, after which Mussolini wrested disputed Fiume from Yugoslavia and gained virtual control over Albania's economy and military, which included the fortification of Valona on the east side of the Otranto Strait. Mussolini used the "Italian Aegean Islands" (Rhodes and the Dodecanese) to seek Middle Eastern oil, brutally pacified restive Libya and in the 1930s decided to conquer Ethiopia as part of a new Roman-type North African Empire. Directly antagonistic to Britain and France, Mussolini's preliminary moves prompted the reinforced British Mediterranean Fleet to shift from exposed Malta to Alexandria and Eastern units to Aden to block both ends of the Red Sea. When Italy invaded Ethiopia in October 1935 and the League of Nations imposed retaliatory economic sanctions on Italy, Britain refused to enforce them or close the Suez Canal without full French support and use of their bases at Bizerte and Toulon. Also, any war with Italy would weaken the Anglo-French navies now needed to check Japan and Germany, especially after the latter denounced the Locarno pact and reoccupied the Rhineland in March 1936. Two months later the Italian Army completed the conquest of militarily backward Ethiopia but at the complete sacrifice of British friendship. Mussolini turned to court Germany and in April 1939 occupied and annexed Albania. But should war come, Mussolini lay in a vulnerable strategic position, for 70 percent of Italy's imported raw materials had to pass through British-held Suez and Gibraltar. He would require the naval help of the Germans, whom his admirals detested.

Germany, which did not turn fascist until Hitler's takeover in 1933, similarly regarded the Navy as outside the mainstream of national life. Save for the abortive Kapp putsch of 1920, the Navy remained apolitical and loyal to the Weimar and Nazi governments, both of which subordinated naval activities to the continental army. Restricted by Versailles to a few old surface ships for coast defense, the Germans used clandestine means to develop U-boats and aircraft through private industry. A naval war college course also developed illegally, but the former Allies had neither the will nor the means to enforce the Versailles dictates. Severely criticized for its blue-water aspirations under Tirpitz, the Navy planned only for mine warfare and coast defense in the Baltic against Poland and France. But with the administrative reform of the Navy in 1928 under its new Commander in Chief, Admiral Erich Raeder (Hipper's chief of staff at Jutland), the Weimar Navy began to follow the writings of Vice Admiral Wolfgang Wegener for a *guerre de course* fleet in the *jeune école* tradition. New torpedo boats, then cruisers and finally three 11,000-plus-ton, 28-knot, 11″-gunned "pocket battleships" preceded new U-boat construction under Hitler. As *Führer,* Hitler controlled all German defenses and followed Mussolini in creating a separate Air Force *(Luftwaffe)* which absorbed and downgraded naval aviation. From 1934 Hitler saw France and Russia as the enemy and so countered French battleship construction with the two *Scharnhorst*s and two 42,000-ton, 31-knot, 15″-gunned *Bismarck*s, all of them driven by fast turbines. Anxious for British neutrality, Hitler concluded the Anglo-German naval pact of 1935 and promised his admirals as late as 1938 that he would avoid a conflict with Britain at all costs.

The empire of the Third Reich remained oriented to the continent of

Europe, and even the likelihood of war with Britain kept the Navy's strategy devoted to a *guerre de course* philosophy. Surface ship construction, culminating in the Z-Plan in the winter of 1938–39, aimed at thirteen battleships, four carriers, thirty-three cruisers and many destroyers by 1944 to raid enemy shipping individually and in small "task forces"—a concept with which the Germans had experimented for several years. U-boat construction—267 subs under the Z-Plan—would be used by their commander, Commodore Karl Doenitz, in massed, radio-coordinated "wolf packs" in a World War I-style "tonnage war" to blockade the British Isles. Unfortunately for Germany, its limited shipbuilding facilities and oil reserves were divided in equal priority between battleships and subs with inadequate quantities of each to eliminate the mass of merchant tonnage. Furthermore, modern technology had already neutralized the surface raider, but Hitler continued to support his prestigious battleships. The Navy manned all coastal fortifications, but did nearly nothing to develop marines, service forces or amphibious tactics, although fleet units did participate in the seizure of Lithuanian Memel in March 1939. Hitler continued to ignore the warnings of Admiral Raeder about the lack of German naval preparedness for a war with Britain, and in April 1939 he abrogated the Anglo-German treaty of 1935. By this time, both nations lay in the grip of another arms race, so that Hitler made another unexpected diplomatic shift by signing a nonaggression pact with Soviet Russia. The unpredictable dictatorships were pushing Europe toward the resumption of total war.

Communist Russia followed continental Germany and Italy in using the Navy for coast defense but also seeking a prestigious small surface fleet, while the Mahan-influenced former tsarist officers yielded to a Red-inspired naval strategy of *guerre de course (molodaia shkola)* based on the submarine. To exploit Russia's vast interior position against the Germans in the Baltic, Anglo-Turkish forces in the Black and the Japanese in the Pacific, the erratic Five-Year plans for economic recovery assisted the completion of the White Sea Canal which in 1933 connected the White, Baltic and Caspian seas via a system of lakes and rivers, and the Northern Sea Route gradually developed to the Far East from 1927. The Baltic Fleet remained as the principal arm of the "Naval Forces of the Red Army" with one battleship, eight cruisers, a light minefield, an eight-boat submarine barrier, seaplanes and coastal fortifications commanding the Gulf of Finland and the approaches to Kronstadt and Leningrad. Light naval forces comprised the Black, Northern and Pacific fleets. In 1933–35 dictator Joseph Stalin, confronted with the menace of Germany, concluded alliances with France and Czechoslovakia, restored traditional naval ranks, and initiated new cruiser, destroyer and submarine construction for a balanced fleet. In 1938 the bloody Stalinist purge of former tsarist officers and his own enemies deprived Russia of its ablest naval officers. Yet, the next year he ordered his new Naval Commissar Admiral Nikolai G. Kuznetsov to lay down a surface fleet of coastal battleships, cruisers and even carriers to be covered by land-based aircraft. Though designed as a deterrent force, such a navy would never have the real prestige of a powerful Red Army. Russia's vacillating interwar naval doctrine thus resembled Hitler's, and both were baptized in the Spanish crisis.

The opposing forces of the Spanish Civil War (1936–39), the pro-Communist "Republican" (or "Loyalist") government and the pro-fascist "Nationalist" forces of General Francisco Franco, received most of their outside assistance by sea. The Spanish Navy, torn internally by the civil issues, nevertheless remained under general Republican control to blockade Franco's main Nationalist Army in Morocco during the summer of 1936. Alarmed by reports of Republican terrorism, the democracies refused aid to the government, whereupon Russia dispatched "volunteers" from the Black Sea to Barcelona and other east coast ports. But Franco used a troop airlift and dissension within the Republican Navy to break the blockade in September and establish himself in southern Spain, with access to the sea at Seville and Cádiz. Germany hastened two pocket battleships and other ships plus air and army "volunteers" to support Franco, who began to develop his own navy which blockaded Republican ports in November. This effort succeeded in hindering Russian merchant ships en route to Spain, a weakness that taught Stalin the efficacy of surface warships. Early in 1937 Britain led France, Germany and Italy in the creation of a four-power naval patrol to thwart intervention in Spain, but the belligerents' aircraft occasionally attacked these vessels, leading to British protests and the bombardment of the Republican port of Almeria by the German pocket battleship *Deutschland* in May. Worse, Italian subs operating out of Naples and Majorca in August began sinking ships bound for Republican ports, leading to Anglo-French antisub measures that finally stopped the practice early in 1938. Germany and Italy then quit the nonintervention patrol and aided Franco so successfully that they could withdraw their major naval units altogether. Early in 1939 Franco's forces took Barcelona and Madrid, ending the war in a victory for fascism. At least Anglo-French warships had acted in concert for the first time since World War I, and the British pressured Portugal to end aid to Franco and renew her traditional alliance with Britain in 1939.

In Asia, China remained at the center of the endless political rivalries of the great powers for fifteen years after the Washington conference guaranteed the "open door." In that treaty year of 1922 a British gun-boat rescued President Sun Yat-sen at Canton in the growing civil strife between Nationalists, Communists and warlords that threatened the life of the young republic. Renewed Chinese piracy between Hong Kong and Shanghai led to British-escorted coastal convoys, and Yangtze bandits brought on gunboat patrols by the British, Americans, Japanese and French. The general vulnerability of Western and Japanese lives, property, enclaves and legations to the political chaos of the country could only be met by interventions of the powers, as early in 1927 when no fewer than twenty-one cruisers plus lesser vessels from seven nations concentrated at Shanghai with a 40,000-man Anglo-Indian landing force to protect their interests. In March British and American warships engaged Nationalist Chinese forces to cover the evacuation of foreigners from beleaguered Nanking, and a year later Japan placed an expeditionary force ashore at Tsingtao. Whereas Britain and America only policed troubled waters in China, Japan and Russia had more grandiose designs. In 1924 Russia annexed Mongolia and five years later began to fight Nationalist forces over the railway in Manchuria; in October 1929 five Soviet gunboats sank three Chinese gunboats on the Amur River. And Japan had even greater interests in Manchuria.

Japan, gradually becoming fascistic and dictatorial between 1931 and the rise to power of General Hideki Tojo in 1941, focused its revived expansionism on China. Dominated by its Army warrior class, Japan planned to create a "Greater East Asia Co-Prosperity Sphere" centered on the Asian mainland, with the Imperial Navy in support. Japanese air forces remained separate and basically tactical; the Army's aviation was trained during the 1920s by the French, the Navy's by a British naval mission. In 1931 Japan suddenly invaded and occupied Manchuria, and the next year Japanese warships and carrier planes covered a landing of troops at Shanghai until an Anglo-American naval force arrived and the United States Fleet concentrated at Hawaii, pressuring the Japanese to withdraw. But the League of Nations could not prevent the establishment of a Japanese puppet state in Manchuria—the consequence of the Great Depression and the general apathy of world opinion toward intervention. Japan then quit the League, abrogated its treaty commitments and in 1936 allied with Nazi Germany against Soviet Russia. The next year Japan invaded China to begin the second Sino-Japanese War. The German-trained Chinese Nationalist Army of Chiang Kai-shek resisted stubbornly, but could not prevent the seizure of Shantung and Peking; Shanghai and Nanking fell after a barrage from naval guns and carrier planes. Despite the shelling of two British gunboats by Japanese artillery and the sinking of the American gunboat *Panay* by naval aircraft on the Yangtze in December 1937, neither nation actively intervened. The next year Japanese river craft, aircraft and troops pressed up the Yangtze to take Hankow in October, the same month that an amphibious assault took Canton. Then, as the ground war stalemated at the foothills of the Himalayas, Russia fought an undeclared war on the Mongolian-Manchurian frontier during 1938–39 that decisively checked the Japanese in that quarter.

Japanese naval policy remained defensive throughout these events. Centralized under an Imperial Headquarters in 1937, the Navy retained its ancient mission of transporting and supporting the Army and protecting its lines of communication to Asia, also the forward bases at Port Arthur, Dairen and Formosa. With Japan's strategy oriented to the continent, the islands of the Pacific became mere appendages and were consequently never fortified during the 1920s and 1930s: the Kuriles, Bonins, Volcanos, Ryukyus, Marianas, Carolines and Marshalls. Should the Western navies, particularly that of the United States, intervene, they would be whittled down in day and night attacks by Japanese subs and destroyers—both with superior torpedoes, by "flying squadrons" of cruisers and carriers with dive- and torpedo-bombers, and by land-based planes and seaplanes from the mandated islands, where airfield construction slowly began in 1934. Once the approaching American battle fleet had been scaled down, the traditional line of battleships would engage the enemy in the Western Pacific in the manner of Tsushima. Despite the arguments of Admiral Isoroku Yamamoto and others against such a conservative reliance on battleships, the Imperial Japanese Navy did not plan for long-range blue-water operations and did not even begin at-sea refueling of major warships until 1941. It developed superior optics and star shells for night actions, but had no radar and remained deficient in tactical, antiaircraft and offensive carrier techniques. Even as a continental navy, it lacked a balanced doctrine: amphibious and river practices were impressive in support of the Army, but no attention was ever given commerce defense or *guerre de course,* with Japan's excellent subs being employed as fleet vessels.

The European powers, becoming increasingly preoccupied with Germany, gradually came to depend on American leadership in balancing Japanese power in the Pacific. Britain's communications between Trincomalee in Ceylon and Hong Kong improved markedly with the opening of Singapore's new base facilities in 1938, but the French in Indochina could do nothing when the Japanese in 1939 took Hainan Island in the Gulf of Tonkin and the French-claimed Spratly Islands in the South China Sea. The only outside communications of Chiang Kai-shek lay from Kunming overland by rail to French Haiphong and by automobile on the British Burma Road, making both potential Japanese targets. The Dutch in the East Indies tried to do more, since the Royal Netherland Navy was usually concentrated in the Far East to police the islands, operating out of Batavia and British Singapore. In response to

Japan's thrust into China in 1937, Holland concentrated three (two brand-new) of its four light cruisers plus destroyers, subs and mine vessels in the Indies and two years later authorized three new 28,000-ton battle cruisers to counter Japan's heavy cruisers. The United States planned to defend the Philippines with the Asiatic Fleet and fixed fortifications around Manila Bay (and at Guam and Wake) until the main fleet units could sortie to their relief from Hawaii—the essence of the "Orange Plan." But both the Asiatic Fleet and coastal guns remained woefully understrength, as the United States attempted to adopt a realistic unilateral strategy throughout these years.

The United States retreated from its European wartime involvement almost as suddenly as it had entered it and concentrated its naval power in the Pacific. The United States Fleet, created in 1922, was comprised of the twelve newest battleships in the Pacific and the six older ones in the Atlantic, but beyond this the Americans remained rigidly isolationistic—despite the warnings of the Navy's General Board and naval publicists like Hector C. Bywater and William Howard Gardiner. The naval economy practiced by both the prosperity and depression Presidential administrations of the 1920s and 1930s kept the U. S. Navy from growing to full treaty strength and from maintaining peak efficiency, but left it strong enough to continue policing the Caribbean and to deter Japan. A "special service squadron" of very old cruisers and gunboats operated out of Panama to support Marine Corps landings and naval shows of force in troubled Mexico, Haiti, the Dominican Republic, Panama, Honduras, Cuba, Nicaragua, Costa Rica and El Salvador, complemented by British units and on two occasions by Canadian warships. No foreign power, however, intervened in the Chaco War between Bolivia and Paraguay in 1932–35. The American government rested its continental defenses and those of Hawaii and the Canal Zone on wartime railway and fixed guns and antiaircraft guns and the warships existing at the time of the Washington treaty. President Franklin D. Roosevelt in 1933 decided to concentrate on domestic affairs, to end the interventions in Latin America and—particularly through the Congressional campaign of Carl Vinson—to provide funds to improve fleet upkeep and to build closer to treaty strength. But he steadfastly refused general naval rearmament until 1938 and the wake of the *Panay* incident, hoping mightily to avoid antagonizing Japan.

American interwar naval policy reflected the U. S. Navy's firm belief that it would eventually fight Japan, even though inadequate funding—until after 1938—prevented the practical application of the new theories for fighting a war across the vast Pacific. If any one officer dominated these years, it was Admiral William V. Pratt, former wartime planner who attended and supported the Washington and 1930 London arms conferences, held the presidency of the Naval War College in 1925–27 and all the major battle fleet commands, and was Chief of Naval Operations, 1931–33. The Jutland-battleship mentality continued to dominate official American naval thought, but Pratt replaced the simple battleship war gaming at the War College with studies of amphibious operations, logistics, war plans and international relations, all fundamental for the war against Japan. These reforms did not survive his tenure at the College, but other elements of the fleet pursued several of them. The U. S. Marines, used as regular infantry during the war, built upon their pre-war base defense mission to fashion a new role of advance base landing assaults from the theories of island-hopping of its Lieutenant Colonel Earl H. Ellis. Amphibious doctrine improved rapidly after the creation of the Fleet Marine Force in 1933, first in maneuvers and tactical manuals, then with close support aircraft, tracked amphibious landing craft and attack transports over 1938–41. The fast aircraft carrier, though ostensibly a reconnaissance vessel, emerged as an offensive strike weapon through the administrative leadership of Admiral William A. Moffet and the operational direction of Admiral Joseph Mason Reeves. The latter, under the direct command of Admiral Pratt, first used carriers with dive- and torpedo-bombers effectively in independent offensive attack operations in the fleet problem of 1929. Thereafter, the naval aviators ignored the Jutland school to develop their own formulae for fast carrier operations to fight the Japanese fleet, and had several new carriers built during the 1930s for such trials. Commerce warfare received little attention, for American cruisers were seriously weakened qualitatively by treaty economy measures, and submarines were earmarked for scouting and attacking surface warships. The large sub of the 1920s yielded to an all-purpose boat of some 1400 tons in the 1930s which could cruise 12,000 miles, dive faster, lay mines, torpedo ships and sink merchantmen or provide shore bombardment with a 5″ deck gun. Nearly nothing took place in the crucial area of logistical doctrine until 1940 when base facilities began to be expanded at Pearl Harbor and battleships began to refuel at sea (carriers in 1939).

The U. S. Navy expected a war with Japan, that it would begin with a sneak attack, and that Hawaii was the mostly likely target—so that several fleet maneuvers took place in the 1930s anticipating such an attack. Indeed, in 1939–40 the Japanese initiated new base construction in the Marshall Islands and moved a new fleet into the mandates to operate from Kwajalein in the Marshalls, Saipan in the Marianas, and the Palaus and especally Truk in the Carolines. Japan continued to fight in China and created a new fleet in the Kurile Islands which could watch Russia, but fleet activities in the Central Pacific were clearly directed against the United States.

From the summer of 1939, however, the attention of the Western world focused on Europe, where the breakdown of the Versailles arrangements and the postwar treaties threatened to result in renewed total war.

ANGLO-GERMAN WAR

Europe's plunge back into war followed the continued aggressiveness of fascist Germany and Italy and the appeasement policies of Britain and France, the virtual isolation of Soviet Russia and the dogged neutrality and noninvolvement of the United States. Hitler's policies led to a new system of alliances throughout Europe from 1935: France and Russia against the "Axis" of Germany, Italy and distant Japan, with Hitler's armed diplomacy annexing Austria and Czechoslovakia in 1938–39. Russia then made its nonaggression pact with Hitler, but France and Britain prepared for war and guaranteed the integrity of Poland after Hitler seized Lithuanian Memel in March 1939. In the Mediterranean, Turkey sided with the Anglo-French camp, having accepted naval parity with Greece in 1930, refortified the Dardanelles from 1936, and in the spring of 1939 annexed Syrian Alexandretta just as Mussolini conquered Albania, an action which brought Anglo-French guarantees of Greek security. Miscalculating that the Allies would not protect Poland any more than they had Czechoslovakia, Hitler invaded Poland in September 1939. Britain and France declared war, though all the other powers proclaimed their neutrality, a luxury that only delayed their inevitable absorption into the totality of this modern war. The delay was made possible by the simple fact that World War II began as a decidedly limited conflict primarily between Britain and Germany.

Both of these powers, despite their recent buildups, had to rely on emergency measures to wage war upon the sea, but the same World War I strategic relationships in the North and Baltic seas resumed. From Scapa Flow—poorly defended and only accepted as the main base over Rosyth one year before—the majority of Britain's 7 battleships, 2 battle cruisers, 4 aircraft carriers, 17 cruisers, 35 destroyers, 16 submarines and many lesser craft in home waters joined the Royal Air Force in dominating the North Sea. The Germans avoided the immediate wartime blockade by sending 2 pocket battleships and 39 U-boats to sea as commerce raiders just prior to the invasion of Poland, leaving one pocket and 2 regular battleships, 8 cruisers and 34 destroyers blockaded along the North Sea coast but equally free to control the Baltic. But, unlike in World War I, the Germans had no intention of developing another blue-water high seas fleet. The British Western Approaches had been weakened by the release of two Royal Navy bases in southern Ireland to the new Irish republic earlier in the year, but the French Navy had a raiding force of 2 new battleships, one carrier, 3 cruisers and 10 destroyers at Brest. Allied maritime communications in the Mediterranean and South Atlantic enjoyed—with Italy's neutrality—absolute security behind a total of 6 battleships, one carrier, 45 cruisers, 72 destroyers and 57 submarines. But such overwhelming superiority at sea could do little to check Hitler's *Blitzkrieg* into Poland.

The German thrust also involved Russia, as the armies of each carved up helpless Poland within one month and then sought to dominate the Baltic. While German fleet units blockaded Polish ports (though several Polish destroyers and submarines escaped from Gdynia to England), German merchant ships operated out of Russian Murmansk and a Russian river flotilla supported the Red Army's drive up the Dnieper River to Pinsk and destroyed the Polish flotilla on the Pripet River. The Russians then virtually annexed Estonia, Latvia and Lithuania and established Baltic Fleet units at their ports. When Finland refused Russia the use of its naval bases at Hango in the Gulf of Finland and Petsamo in the Arctic, in late November Russia invaded Finland. Isolated from outside help by the Germans in this "Winter War," Finland threw up a defense line in the south, concentrated its small navy at Turku (Abo) to protect communications to neutral Sweden, and used mines and subs to attack Russian shipping in the Gulf. The Russians countered with minesweepers and their own subs (supplied by German surface ships) and amphibious assaults that took several Finnish islands in the eastern Gulf. Russia's ground offensives into Finland failed in December, but succeeded two months later. Finland capitulated in March 1940, ceding Viborg and the adjacent territory as far as Lake Ladoga and leasing Hango to Russia. When Russia annexed more lands to the Ukraine three months later and created a new Danube River flotilla to defend them, the two aggressors had settled into a precarious balance of power in Northern Europe. Russia could then accelerate its own military preparations, and Germany could concentrate on the Allies.

Following the fall of Poland, the conflict became a "phony war" as Hitler unrealistically waited for Britain and France to recognize his conquest and make peace. To avoid further antagonizing them, he refrained from attacking the French Maginot Line or the British Expeditionary Force which had arrived to augment it, kept his powerful *Luftwaffe* out of British skies, and even placed severe operating restrictions on his few active commerce raiders. Hoping to placate France, Hitler forbade his warships to attack French shipping for several weeks. And knowing British sensitivity to international law, he ordered his U-boats to observe the strict protocols of the 1936 submarine convention to warn unarmed merchantmen before attacking them. But when the *U-30* mistakenly and without warning sank the British passenger liner *Athenia* on the first day of the war, the Allies naturally assumed that Germany intended to prosecute unrestricted submarine warfare as in 1917–18. And as subsequent victims radioed for help, Hitler progressively lifted the restrictions on his boats. But Hitler's naval strategy of *guerre de course* still had impressive results. The *U-29* sank the British carrier *Courageous* in the Irish Sea in September, and the next month Lieutenant Commander Gunther Prien took his *U-47* inside the harbor defenses of Scapa Flow to sink the battleship *Royal Oak* with nearly 800 of its crew. German ships, subs and planes sowed ground-magnetic and mooredcontact mines off the British coast which claimed 114 merchant ships, 15 minesweepers and 2 destroyers in the first six months of the war. Hitler's surface raiders had less success. In December, after sinking several merchantmen, the pocket battleship *Graf Spee* was mauled by 3 British and New Zealand cruisers in the battle of the River Plate and had to be scuttled off neutral Montevideo, Uruguay, to avoid internment or destruction by more British fleet units converging on the area. Similar fears also caused the termination of a brief sortie into the North Atlantic by the battleships *Scharnhorst* and *Gneisenau*.

Perplexed by Allied adamancy and countermeasures, Hitler interfered with Admiral Raeder by altering his naval program. He cautiously restricted any unnecessary risk to his few heavy surface ships as raiders, cut back the priorities of the prewar Z-Plan to only subs, and thwarted the implementation of new additional authorizations for U-boat construction. Nevertheless, Admiral Doenitz, directing U-boat operations from shore and first experimenting successfully with group "wolf pack" tactics late in 1939, could boast of his boats sinking, between September 1939 and March 1940, a total of 222 merchantmen aggregating 765,000 tons, at the cost of 18 of his original 56 boats. Surface raiders, mines and aircraft claimed another 181 merchant ships totaling nearly 540,000 tons. And Hitler discovered the fallacy of his adherence to international law when in February the British destroyer *Cossack* ignored that law to enter neutral Norwegian waters and liberate some 300 British prisoners from the German supply ship *Altmark*. With each Allied success, Hitler's impatience mounted.

In fact, Britain and France were determined to frustrate Hitler in every possible way, and the "phony war" gained them invaluable time to press new construction and try to overcome serious tactical deficiencies. But neither navy displayed much strategic innovativeness at the outset, neither the French Navy under Admiral Darlan whose government merely assumed that the economic blockade would defeat Germany, nor the Royal Navy under the reappointed First Lord of the Admiralty Winston Churchill and First Sea Lord Admiral Sir A. Dudley P. R. Pound which recommitted old errors. The renewed reluctance to adopt defensive convoys led to the same World War I preference for offensive hunt-and-kill operations. Convoys were adopted, but only in small sizes, dispersed in the open ocean and escorted by vessels poor in asdic, depth charges and antiaircraft guns. The convoys were further confined to the environs of the British Isles with limited escorting from Freetown in West Africa, from Nova Scotia and in the Mediterranean. The British reinstituted mine barrages in the Dover Strait (successful) and between Scotland and Ireland (unsuccessful) and prepared to repeat the North Sea mine barrage (to have equal lack of success as in 1918) and to aerially mine the mouths of Germany's rivers (with some success). The Royal Navy was not prepared to deal with German magnetic mines or surfaced U-boat night attacks, both of which had been employed in 1918 by the Germans. The unproved Q-ships took to the sea with absolutely no effect. Finally, in the crucial areas of amphibious warfare and naval aviation, the British also erred. They actually closed down their tiny training office of combined operations, and the Fleet Air Arm was so deficient in equipment from its interwar subordination to the Royal Air Force that it had to depend on that service for much antisub work. The Navy's air arm did not develop real antisub techniques, and the RAF would not commit enough land-based bombers to attack German anchorages.

Still, the energetic Churchill sought a viable maritime strategy to turn the German flank just as he had sought to do in World War I. The original continental stance had placed the British Army in France in a passive role as part of the "phony war," while Churchill urged the cultivation of continued Italian neutrality to keep the Mediterranean quiet. This meant the Baltic would be the logical place to strike Germany, and Churchill and his admirals envisioned a fleet sortie thence to cut Germany's iron ore trade with Scandinavia, create a new front and perhaps convince Russia to join the Allied cause. But as the plan gained momentum at the Admiralty late in 1939, serious reservations began to surface, especially from Admiral Pound. Without adequate air cover—which the RAF could not provide at such extreme ranges—the fleet would be at the mercy of the *Luftwaffe* as well as of U-boats, mines and coast artillery. As the project was gradually abandoned early in 1940, Churchill and the admirals considered plans to ignore Norwegian neutrality by occupying the sources of Scandinavian ore near Narvik and/or mining Norwegian waters to stop German shipping.

The niceties of international law thus evaporated just like the precarious naval arms controls of the interwar years as the powers again faced the harsh necessities of total war. The British could not respect Norwegian neutrality if Germany was to be blockaded in the Baltic, and since German *guerre de course* required advanced bases for the resupply of its U-boats, German agents were laying the basis for this use of ports in neutral Spain. The Axis powers of course had nothing but contempt for neutrality, as Norway, Denmark, the Netherlands and Belgium were soon to discover in Northern Europe, while Mussolini in the Mediterranean and the Japanese militarists in the Far East grew anxious to reap the benefits of Allied unpreparedness. The United States repealed its neutrality laws in late 1939 in order to supply the Allies, and Soviet Russia could only hope that Hitler would refrain from turning eastward until its rearmament was completed. Total world war finally resumed in the spring of 1940 as Hitler's *Blitzkrieg* overran Western Europe.

16
World War II, 1940–1945

History has conclusively demonstrated the inability of a state with even a single continental frontier to compete in naval development with one that is insular, although of smaller population and resources.

—MAHAN

THE AXIS OFFENSIVE

The total warfare of 1918 resumed from the spring of 1940 as if no long interlude had occurred, but in fact Hitler, Mussolini and Tojo represented the last attempt of authoritarian dictatorships to restore European (and Japanese) political hegemony along traditional imperial lines. The totality of the new democratic and communistic ideologies introduced by Wilson and Lenin found relentless champions in Roosevelt and Stalin, while the old war-horse Churchill in a very real sense superintended over the sacrifice of the old and mighty British Empire as it initially bore the brunt of the Axis onslaught. Modern machine weapons also promised—but only promised—to transform the face of war, though not until the B-29 very-long-range bomber, V-2 interrange rocket and airborne atomic bomb could be produced and utilized in really great quantities. The limitations of the technology of the early 1940s thus denied the use of any such strategic panaceas, so that the antagonists relied on the same continental and maritime strategies of their many predecessors in history. For the Allies, this meant winning command of the sea—but now also its air.

The dictatorships enjoyed the same strengths and weaknesses of every major despotism in history, only they were compounded by the new technology. Isolated egotists sensitive to any criticism, the fascist strong men by their overcentralized control not only thwarted staff work and effective coalition cooperation, but stifled their scientists and

engineers from producing enough new machines of war. All supported
continental objectives and strategies, kept their armies (and new air
forces) as the senior service and failed to appreciate fully their navies.
In Germany, Hitler personally ran everything through the Supreme
Command of the Armed Forces, a weak staff body which included
only a few naval officers, and the Naval War Staff got only whatever
Admiral Raeder could get for it from Hitler. Hitler so hindered his
scientists that he did not press for jet aircraft, the strategic rocket
or submarine schnorkel breathing device until 1943. In Italy, Mussolini and the Army similarly dominated the Supreme Command, under
which an efficient but overcentralized and unimaginative naval department functioned. In Japan, Emperor Hirohito generally followed the
advice of Tojo's Supreme War Council, to which the Naval General
Staff contributed a junior voice. Soviet Russia was run by Stalin
through the Red Army, to which the independent Commissariat of
the Navy (created in 1937) was subordinate, and in 1941 Stalin reassigned only recently removed political commissars to each fleet unit
—so suspect did the Navy remain to him.

The democracies again centralized in wartime but with sufficient
flexibility to encourage Allied cooperation, good staff work and scientific creativity. And both Great Britain and the United States enjoyed sufficiently dynamic and naval-experienced heads of state to
develop an effective maritime strategy in combination with a suspicious
continental Russia and the new strategic air forces. Winston Churchill,
First Lord of the Admiralty in 1911–15 and 1939–40, in April and
May 1940 succeeded to supreme command in Britain as head of the
new War Cabinet, Prime Minister, head of a central committee of
scientists and virtually his own First Lord. Franklin Roosevelt, Assistant Secretary of the American Navy from 1913 to 1920 and President
since 1933, as Commander-in-Chief created the Joint Chiefs of Staff
to direct the war and the Office of Scientific Research and Development to create new weapons. Such strong political leaders occasionally
meddled in strategic and scientific planning, but generally relied on
their generals, admirals and air marshals who cooperated through the
Allied Combined Chiefs of Staff and with an expanded military-
industrial-scientific complex directed by experienced industrial and
scientific managers. This Anglo-American system thus developed long-
range programs which produced a host of new devices, especially for
the war at sea: radars, radios and loran for navigation; high-frequency
radio direction finders, sonar and magnetic airborne detectors to help
locate enemy ships and planes; new aircraft and warships, such as
the tractored amphibious landing craft (notably the Dukw); antiaircraft
guns and the radio-detonated proximity fuse on antiaircraft shells;

antisub, barrage and aircraft rockets; and finally the atomic bomb. Operational research applied mathematics to achieve statistical analyses of field problems. The greatest hindrance to applying these weapons lay in the tactical conservatism of admirals and generals and their interservice rivalries and anti-civilian biases. But since time favored the Allies, adopted they eventually were.

Between April 1940 and June 1941 the old weapons held the line as Germany and Italy tried to conquer all Western Europe, and Japan to conquer China before Russia and America became involved. Initially, Hitler outflanked Britain in the North Sea by brazenly crossing the Skagerrak in the face of the British Home Fleet at Scapa Flow to invade Norway by sea and air in April 1940 using surface fleet units, twenty-five of Doenitz's U-boats and a newly expanded logistical organization. Norwegian coastal guns and torpedoes sank a German heavy cruiser, but Allied warships and expeditionary forces hastening thence could not dislodge the bridgehead. They did, however, make the Germans pay dearly. In addition to damage inflicted on several fleet units, a British sub forced a light cruiser to be scuttled, Norwegian batteries and British dive-bombers sank another light cruiser, and on April 10 and 13 five British destroyers and then the battleship *Warspite* with nine destroyers and a seaplane combined to sink ten German destroyers and one U-boat at Narvik fjord. All Norway was in German hands by the end of May, Denmark had fallen in one day (April 9), and Sweden stood neutral but isolated. U-boats and surface raiders, covered by the *Luftwaffe,* could now virtually avoid the North Sea to prey on Allied and neutral shipping in the North Atlantic. Whereupon British forces occupied Iceland on May 10.

Encouraged by these northern successes, Hitler now thrust his *Blitzkrieg* westward to take France out of the war. Starting on May 10 the German armies and tactical air forces swept across helpless Holland and Belgium, outflanking the Maginot Line and trapping Franco-Belgian troops and the entire British Expeditionary Force against the Channel at Dunkirk. With the German Navy still battered or committed in Scandinavia, it did not participate in this offensive, so that the French Atlantic Fleet units escaped to the Mediterranean and the small Dutch fleet to England. The *Luftwaffe* aerially mined Allied harbors in April and May, but failed completely to defeat the RAF and the beachhead at Dunkirk, from which some 338,000 Allied troops were evacuated by 861 vessels of the Royal and French navies and private owners between May 28 and June 4. German planes, coastal U-boats and torpedo boats did sink 243 craft, the largest 6 British and 3 French destroyers, but without a real surface fleet and air superiority the Germans could not command the Channel. Italy declared war on June 10, and four days later the Germans took Paris. French naval authorities defended their bases from landward attack as long as possible, enabling Allied vessels to evacuate another 192,000 British and Polish troops plus French warships to England and North Africa. In the meantime, the British lost the carrier *Glorious* and 2 destroyers to the battleships *Gneisenau* and *Scharnhorst,* but not before one of the destroyers and a sub inflicted sufficient damage on both vessels to force them back into the yards for extensive repairs. Italian land-based air strikes forced Anglo-French Mediterranean fleet units to pull back out of range to Gibraltar and Alexandria. But France surrendered to Germany on June 24, giving Hitler key U-boat bases on the Biscay coast to outflank the Western Approaches.

To counter the sudden imbalance in the middle sea and to enable strategic concentration in the Western Approaches à la Kempenfelt and Nelson, the British in June redeployed Home Fleet units to Gibraltar as Force H under Admiral Sir James F. Somerville. At Alexandria lay the Mediterranean Fleet of Admiral Sir Andrew B. Cunningham and the voluntarily inactive exiled French force of one battleship, 4 cruisers and 3 destroyers. When the other French fleet units in northwest Africa proved less cooperative, Force H battleships sank or disabled 3 French battleships at Algerian Mers-el-Kebir on July 3–4; one battleship and 5 destroyers escaped to Toulon. Similarly, four days later, a British carrier and lesser vessels damaged the lone French battleship at Dakar. Unimpressed by the 6-battleship, 105-submarine Italian Navy, Admiral Cunningham used 3 battleships and one carrier with escorts to interrupt Italian communications to Libya and drive back Admiral Angelo Campioni's 2-battleship, 18-cruiser force off Punto Stilo on the Italian Calabrian coast in early July. And an Australian cruiser sank an Italian cruiser north of Crete to help maintain Allied maritime communications. The British had offended French honor by their actions, but France had lost the services of its Navy anyway. The Germans occupied Paris and northwest France, and—by the terms of the "armistice"—a collaborationist government controlled southern France from Vichy, including the remaining fleet units under Admiral Darlan. The French survivors of Dunkirk followed the leadership of General Charles de Gaulle as the "Free French" in England, where their few surviving warships came under British control and the direct command of Admiral Émile Muselier, an undistinguished officer whom Darlan had forced into retirement in 1939. Neither Vichy nor "Free" regimes could really control their far-flung vessels which gradually found their way into the Allied war effort.

Britain, virtually alone, now hastened warship construction, especially of destroyers, to counter the U-boat offensive and prepare to withstand a German cross-Channel invasion attempt. In July 1940 Admiral Doenitz from his new headquarters in France initiated his wolf pack tactics with his U-boats operating through the new Norwegian and French ports. Between June and September his boats sank an average of over 450,000 tons of merchant shipping per month, leading Britain to seek material aid from the United States. President Roosevelt responded in September by transferring fifty World War I-vintage destroyers to Britain in return for the use of British Commonwealth naval and air installations in Newfoundland, Bermuda, British Guiana and the British West Indies. The United States also increased its neutrality patrols in the Western Atlantic and interned several French warships in the French West Indies. But the American government and people were neither willing nor able to give direct assistance to Britain as Hitler laid his invasion plans.

Ironically, Hitler perpetuated his delusions for a negotiated peace until mid-July when he finally authorized Operation Sea Lion. None of the German armed services were enthusiastic about a cross-Channel invasion, with the Navy flatly opposing it in favor of maritime blockade. But the Army took on the project as a virtual river-crossing, with the Navy providing the pontoons and the *Luftwaffe* air cover. None of the services had any real amphibious doctrine or experience; no interservice cooperation developed; the Navy did not have full command of the operation; and the *Luftwaffe* even built its own landing prahms. Indeed, so battered had the Navy been in Norway that it could not begin to command the Channel. *Luftwaffe* chief Hermann Goering accepted the multiple tasks of winning command of the air, interdiction of British land and maritime communications, pre-landing barrage and close air support. So the scheme, despite the buildup along the French coast and mounting British anxieties, was impossible from the beginning, and even before July ended Hitler secretly decided to postpone Sea Lion indefinitely and to invade Russia one year hence. Goering's planes could hammer Britain into submission, but even if that failed the defeat of Russia should convince the British of the futility of further resistance. In reality, Hitler surrendered the strategic initiative, for the RAF turned back the *Luftwaffe* in the Battle of Britain over southern England during August and September, and both air forces commenced their strategic bombing campaigns. On September 17 Hitler officially cancelled Sea Lion, ten days later completed his formal "Axis" with Italy and Japan, and lost the great momentum of the summer *Blitz*.

Though Hitler had failed to break Britain by direct means, he turned to his Navy and Italian partners during the autumn of 1940 to strangle the British in the Atlantic and Mediterranean while he planned for the invasion of Russia. Italian subs joined U-boats in the Atlantic, while seven disguised German auxiliary cruisers and the pocket battleship *Admiral Scheer* successfully attacked Allied shipping in the North and South Atlantic and Indian oceans without being sunk. The German Navy pressed for an active front in the Mediterranean, especially to drive the British from Gibraltar and keep them out of Crete, while Mussolini in September and October invaded Egypt from Libya and Ethiopia, and attacked Greece from Albania. But Franco refused the essential Spanish cooperation for attacking Gibraltar, and the Greek and British armies and air forces repulsed Mussolini—effectively destroying Hitler's faith in him and any real possibility of cooperative Axis planning. And the Royal Navy frustrated Italo-German designs in the middle sea and South Atlantic. In the latter quarter, Vichy French naval forces and diplomatic pressure protected West African Dakar from an Anglo-French naval attack in September, but Churchill had the Free French occupy the Cameroons to help protect Freetown and made plans to occupy the Spanish and Portuguese Canary, Madeira and Azores island groups should Gibraltar fall. Franco's stand made that unnecessary, and British sea lanes to India remained protected by warships operating from South African Simonstown, West African Freetown, the Falkland Islands and Gibraltar. And that base plus Malta and Alexandria enabled the British navy to counterattack against the Italians in the Mediterranean and force Hitler to come to their rescue.

During the autumn, winter and spring of 1940–41, therefore, Cunningham's reinforced Mediterranean Fleet and Somerville's Force H commanded the middle sea while Anglo-Greek ground and air forces counterattacked in North Africa and the Balkans. Cunningham occupied Crete and on November 11 sent Swordfish torpedo-bombers from the new carrier *Illustrious* to attack the main Italian fleet anchorage at Taranto. The twenty-one planes caught the Italians by surprise, sank or bottomed three of their six battleships and got away with only two planes lost. This first dramatic demonstration of offensive carrier air power caused the Italians to remove their fleet units from Taranto to Naples. British warships shelled the Italian army retreating through Albania, and small British forces were able to capture the Italian armies in Egypt, Libya and Ethiopia during the first five months of 1941. In January planes from Malta severely damaged an Italian battleship; in February warships bombarded Genoa and other Italian coastal points; and on March 28–29 Admiral Cunningham with three battleships, one carrier, several cruisers and destroyers defeated a smaller Italian force under Admiral Angelo Iachino off Cape Matapan, southern Greece, sinking three cruisers and two destroyers at the cost of one airplane shot down and a cruiser damaged.

The Italian Navy continued to transport and support the Army in the Balkans and North Africa, to lay mines around Malta and along the Italian coast as barriers, to sweep enemy mines, and to operate submarine and light surface forces against Allied war and merchant shipping, but the fleet had been effectively neutralized by the British. Removed to Spezia, the fleet belatedly began to convert a liner into a carrier and to improve its torpedo planes, without both of which it could never effectively challenge British heavy fleet units. Worse, oil shortages nearly immobilized the Navy by midyear. By contrast, the British Mediterranean Fleet had adopted a new standard fleet tactical formation: battleships, carriers, cruisers and destroyers in a single mutually supporting, antiaircraft circular formation. The old line-ahead of Trafalgar, Tsushima and Jutland thus became obsolete in the face of enemy air attack.

Without a surface fleet to command the Mediterranean, the Axis powers could not conquer its periphery, but the German-led land and air offensives begun in early 1941 nearly succeeded. Land-based Italian and German air attacks pounded Malta and the ships passing through it between Gibraltar and Alexandria. They damaged and sank warships and merchantmen alike, but never with sufficient effect to discourage the British from continuing to operate through Malta. German planes based in the Italian Aegean Dodecanese Islands early in the year dropped aerial mines in the Suez Canal, temporarily closing it. But the British convoyed men and material around the Cape of Good Hope to the Red Sea, enabling them in the spring to regain East Africa and, with Free French help, to drive pro-German troops from Iraq, Syria and Lebanon. The Italian Navy convoyed the new German army under General Erwin Rommel to North Africa without much interference, until the night of April 15 when four British destroyers attacked and sank a convoy of three Italian destroyers and three (of five) transports with their German troops near Kerkenah Banks off the Tunisian coast, losing one of their own number. Rommel mounted an offensive in North Africa, but could not dislodge the British troops at Tobruk in eastern Libya, reinforced by sea with an Australian division. Holding in all these places, the British, however, yielded to a new German ground-air offensive which overran Yugoslavia and Greece in April. The Royal Navy evacuated Allied troops from the continent and enabled the small Royal Hellenic Navy to escape to Alexandria. Neither could the Allies hold Crete, which the Germans took by airborne assault in May, although British naval forces prevented German reinforcements from reaching Crete by sea until all Allied troops could be evacuated by the Navy. Both sides suffered heavy losses in the battles for Greece and Crete, heavy German air attacks and Italian subs and motorboats sinking five British cruisers and six destroyers and damaging a great many more warships, including a carrier and three battleships.

The German attack on British communications gradually improved during early 1941, but enemy resistance and Spanish neutrality effectively delayed Hitler as he prepared his major effort against Russia. Goering's aircraft on Crete and Rommel's tanks before Tobruk threatened to close and even capture the Suez Canal, Alexandria and the oil-rich Persian Gulf area. But heavy losses suffered in the airborne assault on Crete persuaded Hitler to abandon a similar plan to take Malta, which stubbornly resisted continuous Axis bombings. After refusing to help attack Gibraltar, Spain also closed the Canary and Cape Verde islands to German raiders, but Franco did allow U-boats to refuel at Spanish ports. From St. Nazaire and other French Atlantic ports, Doenitz waged his "tonnage warfare" against British shipping in what came to be known as the Battle of the Atlantic. He concentrated his wolf packs in the least-protected but most heavily traveled oceanic areas, especially the Northwest Approaches, to sink almost half of the four million tons of Allied merchant shipping lost during 1940. Such attacks were indiscriminate of cargo carried, so that many really essential war materials got through. Furthermore, U-boat commanders found Doenitz's tight shore-based controls from Brest (later Lorient) too restrictive, for they preferred to attack independent, unescorted vessels. Escorted convoys cost the Germans twenty-three boats during 1940 which could not be replaced until the new construction program of mid-1940 yielded new boats.

British antisub countermeasures did not begin to show significant results until major reforms were instituted early in 1941. At that time, the British discontinued their Q-ship efforts and finally shelved their offensive antisub operations in favor of more strongly escorted convoys. In February and March screening destroyers battled back to sink or capture Germany's three leading U-boat skippers, Lieutenant Commanders Guenther Prien, Otto Kretschmer and Joachim Schepke, the leading World War II merchant killer with over 265,000 tons to his credit. Inadequate Allied antisub air patrols left a "black pit" for unfettered U-boat operations in the mid-North Atlantic beyond the range of planes operating from British and Canadian coastal airfields. But in April, the RAF's Coastal Command was turned over to the Navy for coordination of antisub operations, while airfields were established in Iceland. U-boat sinkings of merchantmen, peaking at nearly 700,000 tons in April, dropped to 500,000 tons in May, at the end of which the first convoy was escorted all the way across the Atlantic, and sinkings dropped further in June. Strong escorts and aircraft seemed to be the proper British answer to Doenitz's tonnage strategy, provided that enough ships and planes became available to counter the new U-boats.

Hitler's stubborn refusal to abandon the surface raider helped weaken the underwater campaign, and Allied aircraft and heavy fleet units—coordinated by radio—generally succeeded in neutralizing these ships during the first half of 1941. Shifted from their North Sea ports to Brest, these battleships and cruisers were subjected to an air-sea blockade by the RAF, minelayers and subs. Lacking advanced bases, these raiders could not stay at sea long, as between January and March when the *Scharnhorst* and *Gneisenau* under Admiral Gunther Lütjens sank twenty-two merchantmen in the North Atlantic, only to be chased back into Brest by British aircraft which then seriously damaged them. Then, in May, a Swedish cruiser alerted the British Admiralty to Lütjens' sortie from the Baltic with the sleek new battleship *Bismarck* and heavy cruiser *Prinz Eugen*. Intercepted by the new battleship *Prince of Wales* and the battle cruiser *Hood* on May 24, the *Bismarck* with an opening salvo blew the *Hood* and 1500 men to bits (like her predecessors at Jutland) and then drove away the *Prince of Wales*. But now British fleet units converged on the force in the North Atlantic, so that Lütjens sent the *Prinz Eugen* on to Brest and set *Bismarck*'s course for the same place. On the 27th, Swordfish torpedo planes from the carrier *Ark Royal* of Force H combined torpedo hits with those from shadowing destroyers at night to slow down the *Bismarck*. Next morning the battleships *King George V* from Scapa and *Rodney* from convoy duty arrived and reduced the *Bismarck* to a flaming hulk; she was sent to the bottom with Lütjens and 2300 of her crew by torpedoes from a cruiser. German auxiliary cruisers operated in the Pacific and Indian oceans, until a British cruiser sank one in May. The *Admiral Scheer* returned from a successful cruise there early in the year, but after the loss of the *Bismarck* Hitler kept his precious battleships at Brest, where RAF bombers continued to attack them.

But the overall German successes encouraged Japan to renew its flagging war against China. With the French collapse, Japan pressured Britain to close the vital Burma Road and attacked Vichy French Indochina while establishing airfields there to operate against Chinese communications and bases during the summer of 1940. Later in the year and early in 1941 Churchill reopened the Burma Road; a Chinese Communist offensive weakened the Japanese in North China; a Vichy French cruiser and four sloops defeated the stronger navy of Japan's ally Siam off the Koh Chang archipelago; and in April Japan concluded a nonaggression pact with Russia. The United States, not as obliging, determined to check Japanese ambitions in the Far East. In the summer of 1940 President Roosevelt put a crimp on the

Japanese war machine by halting the export to Japan of strategic chemicals, lubricating oil, aviation fuel and equipment and scrap iron and steel. In the autumn, American Asiatic Fleet vessels left northern Chinese ports for good, and the United States Fleet followed its last war game by concentrating as a deterrent force at Pearl Harbor in Hawaii. American aid increased to China via the Burma Road, leading Japanese planners to accelerate their preparations to fight the Western powers. The primary strategic objective was war materials to defeat China—now the vital oil, gasoline and rubber of Southeast Asia, notably in British Malaya and the Dutch East Indies. The Imperial Navy planned to follow its traditional policy—ferrying and escorting the Army invasion flotillas to conquer these regions, which would include the adjacent naval bases along such new lines of communication: Manila, Hong Kong and Singapore. Seizure of the Philippines would thus bring in the United States alongside Britain and Holland.

Since swiftness and surprise were crucial for any Asian *Blitz,* the Japanese Combined Fleet could not wait passively for the American Battle Fleet to steam into Japanese waters for the decisive battle, although naval and air installations were finally being constructed on the Pacific islands in 1940–41 to thwart any American advance. Also, since large numbers of fleet units and land-based naval air forces were necessary for the advance into Southeast Asia, they could not be spared for a naval battle. Needing a new strategy to deal with the American fleet, Admiral Isoroku Yamamoto, Combined Fleet commander, developed a very bold one indeed. Always a naval air advocate, he planned to use Japan's six fleet carriers to sink the American battleships and carriers in a surprise air raid on their anchorage at Pearl Harbor. To this end, in April 1941 he created an independent carrier force, the First Air Fleet, and charged Commander Minoru Genda with devising suitable carrier tactics. For weapons, Genda led the development of aerial torpedoes for the shallow waters of Pearl Harbor, with the torpedo and bombing planes to be escorted by Japan's new Zero fighter. For operating formations, Genda realized—from his own tests and from British experiences in the Mediterranean and against the *Bismarck*—that carriers had rendered the old battle-line formalism obsolete. So he formulated two carrier cruising formations —a defensive box of carriers together in mutual support, and separate offensive squadrons of two carriers each, these several hundred miles apart to converge their planes over the target fleet. Though both formations suffered from inadequate antiaircraft screens of destroyers only, they represented the first original naval tactics based on the striking power of independent carrier forces. How soon they would be employed against the United States depended largely on developments in Europe.

Responding both to Japanese aggressiveness and to the German U-boat onslaught against Britain, the United States in 1940–41 mobilized its own war-making capability to protect its own national interests and to shore up the holding actions of Great Britain and China. In the summer of 1940, along with the destroyers-for-bases deal which both helped Britain and strengthened America's Atlantic defenses, Congress authorized new naval construction for a "two-ocean navy" and the following February created the administrative machinery for it, the Atlantic and Pacific fleets. During the winter of 1941, Anglo-American joint staff discussions were held, while the fifty destroyers plus ten Coast Guard cutters were turned over to the Royal Navy for antisubmarine warfare. Whenever the United States entered the fight, the planners agreed, Hitler should be stopped and defeated first, then Japan. To this end, during the spring the Roosevelt Administration initiated the "Lend Lease" of war materials to Britain and obtained the use of British shipyards for American warships. American air bases opened in Bermuda, Newfoundland and Greenland (with exiled-Danish permission); the American Defense Zone—agreed upon with the Latin American states earlier—was extended beyond local coastal waters; and patrolling United States warships began to provide information on German U-boat movements to the Royal Navy. Hitler wanted to avoid a confrontation with America, but his frustrated sub commanders proved difficult to control, as on May 21 when one of them sank the American freighter *Robin Moor* in the South Atlantic. Six days later Roosevelt declared an "unlimited national emergency" for his country.

By early June 1941, the United States government—despite considerable opposition from a large segment of the American public—was all but officially committed to the war against Germany, and Hitler would soon bring in Russia. Repercussions of these events in the Far East would hasten the opening of hostilities there. During the latter half of 1941, therefore, World War II would become global.

GLOBAL WAR

From the summer of 1941 till the spring of 1943 the Soviet Union and the United States reeled under the German and Japanese attacks on them, but doggedly held on in alliance with Britain to turn back the Axis offensives in virtually two separate wars. The continent-oriented Axis powers had to be contained by Anglo-American supremacy at sea, and the main German Army blunted by the Red Army. Significantly, joint Allied strategic planning proved far superior to any Axis cooperation. Churchill and Roosevelt generally unified their efforts, supported ultimately by the exiled French, Dutch and Poles, the Commonwealth nations and most of Latin America in both oceans. Stalin viewed the capitalist democracies with grave suspicion, particularly in light of the interventions of 1918–20, and he remained convinced that Anglo-American delays in mounting a second front against Hitler in the West were deliberately designed to weaken the Russian Communist state in the wake of the German onslaught. Nevertheless, the Russians grudgingly cooperated in Europe and remained neutral in Asia, where China became the major continental Ally.

By contrast, the Atlantic and Pacific Axis powers—save for occasional blockade-running merchantmen and subs—cooperated hardly at all and thereby missed at least three golden opportunities. In the Indian Ocean, no major joint effort was ever made against Allied sea lanes (including one quarter of Anglo-American aid to Russia via the Persian Gulf); although German and Japanese subs operated there, the German U-boat captains finally quit cooperating with the Japanese because of atrocities committed by the latter against some of their victims. In the waters of North America, a joint submarine blockade could have paralyzed Allied shipping there and even closed the Panama Canal, as the Americans fully expected, but no such effort was made. Finally, almost half of the Allied Lend Lease aid to Russia went to Vladivostok via the North Pacific from American West Coast ports, but the Japanese so thoroughly honored their nonaggression pact with Russia that they allowed these Russian merchantmen to pass through the Pacific war zones unhindered. Such was the nature of the fascistic dictatorships—strange bedfellows with their own specific, separate and selfish war aims.

Russo-American entry into World War II took place between Hitler's invasion of Russia on June 22, 1941, and the Japanese attack on the American Battle Fleet at Pearl Harbor the following December 7. In July the U. S. Navy landed Marines in Iceland to relieve the British there and began to escort all shipping to and from that strategic island, thus releasing many Anglo-Canadian escort vessels. The same month, the United States, Britain and the Dutch government-in-exile froze Japanese assets, choking off virtually all foreign oil exports to Japan and thus acting as an ultimatum to Japan to back down in Asia from lack of oil or fight the Western maritime powers to get Indonesian oil. In August the Allies formalized their staff agreements to defeat Hitler before Japan, and their navies began to pool information, especially in amphibious and antisubmarine warfare. During the autumn, United

States naval convoy chores reached halfway across the Atlantic to waiting British escorts and even protected a British troop convoy from Halifax around Africa to the Middle East. The United States also extended Lend Lease to Russia and forbade Axis U-boats to operate in the defensive zone of the Western Hemisphere. Beginning to shoot back, Hitler's U-boat commanders missed an American destroyer in September, damaged one and sank another in October, and sank an American tanker early in December. The Americans began to arm their merchantmen so they could enter the war zone, ended their Yangtze Patrol and transferred the last warships in China to the Philippines. Encouraged by German successes and promises of victory, Japan occupied Saigon and Camranh Bay in French Indochina and decided to conquer Southeast Asia, beginning with the attack on Pearl Harbor. The United States thereafter declared war on Japan, whose German and Italian allies honored their treaty commitments by declaring war on the United States.

Axis and Allied strategies then followed conventional continental and maritime practices. The Germans simply tried to conquer Russia and with Italy aimed to isolate Britain in the Atlantic and Mediterranean until Russia surrendered. The Japanese similarly planned to overrun Southeast Asia and finally China and to form a defensive perimeter in the Central Pacific to contain the United States until Hitler brought on the Russian collapse and forced Britain to terms. The Axis navies operated in support of their respective armies' objectives. The Anglo-American Allies adopted a maritime strategy reminiscent of Pitt's system of the 1750s. The Royal, Commonwealth and U. S. navies would keep open the sea lanes, protecting shipping, eliminating enemy fleet units, and blockading both continents to supply major continental armies in both theaters, namely those of Russia and China. When their navies had won general command of the seas and their air forces command of enemy air spaces, by which time their continental allies ought to have broken the Axis armies, the Anglo-American coalition would land their own armies to tip the balance on land. The crucial factor in the strategies of both sides was time. If the Axis could not win in 1941 or 1942, the tremendous output of American industry would be able to recoup the early losses and mobilize totally against the gradually strained Axis economies.

Everything hinged on Russia's ability to stop Hitler, whose attack took Stalin by complete surprise and drove back the Red Army on a wide front from Poland to the Crimea in the summer and autumn of 1941. The navies of both played only minor roles as Hitler tried to *blitz* his way into the key cities of (north to south) Leningrad, Moscow and Kiev before the onset of the terrible Russian winter. Against

Leningrad, German and Finnish torpedo boats, mines and subs helped the armies overrun the Baltic states, damage two Russian cruisers and sink nine destroyers in the Gulf of Finland as the Russian Baltic Fleet joined in the defense of besieged Leningrad. A German force which included the battleships *Tirpitz* and *Admiral Scheer* moved into the Gulf, where the *Luftwaffe* sank a Russian battleship and old cruiser. But the Russians moved their ships up the Neva River to provide artillery support and naval brigades ashore. Leningrad held, as did the Lake Ladoga region, against the German-Finnish attackers. Against Kiev, the Germans overran the Ukraine before being stopped at Rostov on the Don River, at Sevastopol and just beyond Kerch in November. Neutral Turkey kept the Dardanelles closed and Italian ships out, so that the weak and inexperienced Russian Black Sea Fleet could easily attack Axis shipping and the Axis Rumanian port of Constanta, supply Sevastopol (and Odessa before its fall) and support an amphibious assault at Feodosia which retook the Kerch peninsula in December. But the *Luftwaffe* sank five destroyers and many other units of this fleet, partly the result of ineffective Russian naval aviation subordinated to the Army's air arm. Against Moscow, the German drive simply bogged down before a tenacious defense, overstrained German logistics, a counterattack by Siberian reinforcements and then the winter mud, cold and snow. Hitler had been stopped just at the moment the United States officially entered the war.

With one quarter of Allied aid to Russia going by sea to Murmansk and Archangel on the Barents and White seas (half via the North Pacific, the rest through the Persian Gulf), the Battle of the Atlantic gradually shifted to the North Atlantic, though not intensively until early 1942 when Hitler realized the extent of Allied convoys on this route. Doenitz's tonnage campaign for 1941 roughly equaled the previous year's successes: U-boats claimed over two million of the four million-plus tons of Allied merchant shipping sunk by Axis vessels, mines and planes. But between June and December 1941, 27 German and 13 Italian subs were lost, leaving Germany with 91 operational U-boats (but another 158 working up) by the beginning of 1942. Such losses could not be sustained if more merchant tonnage was not sunk; in other words, Allied shipbuilding and uneven defensive measures were maintaining enough of a balance to keep the war effort alive. Also, the surface raiders never recovered from the *Bismarck* episode: British and Australian cruisers sank 2 auxiliary cruisers in November, and the RAF made Brest so unsafe that the German Navy in February dramatically ran the *Scharnhorst, Gneisenau* and *Prinz Eugen* up the Channel under *Luftwaffe* cover to North Sea ports where they could be used against the convoys to North Russia. The *Tirpitz* and *Admiral*

Scheer were consequently shifted to Norway, where they joined *Luft-waffe* and U-boats to increase the *guerre de course* campaign.

Such a redeployment actually gained time for the Allies in the Mediterranean, for the Axis onslaught of late 1941 seriously weakened Allied sea power everywhere. A British ground offensive in North Africa against Rommel in November and December succeeded in re-lieving the landward threat to the Suez Canal, but a simultaneous offen-sive by German and Italian subs led to sinking of the carrier *Ark Royal* and the battleship *Barham* during November, and the serious damaging of the battleships *Queen Elizabeth, Valiant* and *Malaya* in December. The Japanese carrier attack on Pearl Harbor that month sent five American battleships to the bottom, and land-based Japanese air from French Indochina sank the British battleship *Prince of Wales* and battle cruiser *Repulse* off the Malayan coast. With virtually no capital ships in the Mediterranean, only a few carriers available in the Pacific and Indian oceans, and remaining strength concentrated in the North Atlantic, the Allies had to utilize their strained naval forces carefully and judiciously to maintain a creditable defensive on all the fighting fronts during the winter and spring of 1942.

The Japanese offensive succeeded in its original strategic objective of conquering Southeast Asia and establishing a defensive perimeter across the Central Pacific; it even sank seven Anglo-American capital ships in December, but failed to locate and destroy the fast carriers of the American Pacific Fleet. Absent from Pearl Harbor at the time of the air raid by Yamamoto's six carriers, these American carriers became the main Allied striking force of that fleet under Admiral Chester W. Nimitz, while the United States declared unrestricted sub-marine warfare against Japan. But neither carriers nor subs could pre-vent Japanese amphibious forces from overrunning American Guam, Wake and the Philippines, British and Commonwealth Hong Kong, Singapore, the Gilbert and northern Solomon islands, New Britain and Rabaul in the Bismarcks, and most of New Guinea, along with the Dutch East Indies, between December 1941 and May 1942. American PT boats helped delay the Japanese in the Philippines, and between the Japanese landings in Borneo and Celebes in January and the assault on Batavia, Java, in March, an Allied force of American, British, Dutch and Australian warships fought a series of sacrificial actions. The battle of the Java Sea on February 27 culminated this effort, when Admiral Takeo Takagi used four Japanese cruisers and thirteen destroyers to sink two Dutch cruisers (of a five-cruiser Allied force) and five of ten Allied destroyers led by Dutch Admiral Karel Doorman. Yamamoto's carriers returning from Pearl Harbor struck Port Darwin in northern Australia, while the Japanese Army overran

British Burma and Malaya. The Imperial Navy then thrust into the Indian Ocean to take the Andaman Islands, raid the British Ceylonese bases of Trincomalee and Colombo (where they lost many planes to some RAF veterans of the Battle of Britain), sank the British carrier *Hermes,* two cruisers and a destroyer, and caused the British Eastern Fleet to retire to bases in East Africa.

Though the Japanese had generally established their defensive perimeter, they wanted to add a few outposts and there ran afoul of the surviving American carriers. Throughout early 1942 these vessels, usually commanded by Admiral William F. Halsey, Jr., raided Japanese island positions in the Central and South Pacific and even sent sixteen Army bombers to strike Japan itself in April. The Japanese determined to dislodge the last Allied defenders from southern New Guinea and the southern Solomons, whereupon they could cut American-Anzac communications and counter the Allied sub offensive from Australian ports. But the Americans, having broken the Japanese naval codes, concentrated the carriers *Lexington* and *Yorktown* with escorts under Admiral Frank Jack Fletcher in the Coral Sea to stop them. Admiral Takagi's cruisers escorted landing forces which occupied Tulagi in the Solomons on May 3, but on the 7th and 8th Fletcher's task force engaged the Japanese carriers *Shokaku* and *Zuikaku* in the Battle of the Coral Sea—the first all-carrier battle in history. Though inferior to the Japanese Zero fighters, Fletcher's F4F Wildcat fighter pilots inflicted heavy losses on them, while the SBD Dauntless dive-bombers seriously damaged the *Shokaku* and sank an escorting light carrier. Japanese carrier planes hit the *Lexington,* forcing it to be scuttled, but Takagi now abandoned his designs to take Port Moresby, New Guinea. The same month a British amphibious operation took the Vichy French port of Diego Suarez in northern Madagascar. These operations kept vital Allied Eastern sea communications open across the southern Indian and Pacific oceans.

The surviving American carriers led Admiral Yamamoto to seek the neutralization of Pearl Harbor by taking Midway Island, from which his land-based Navy planes could then bomb the American Pacific Fleet base. But again American knowledge of the intercepted Japanese codes enabled Admiral Nimitz to concentrate his three available carriers at Hawaii to give Yamamoto the battle he so earnestly desired; until the American carriers were all eliminated, Japan would not enjoy command of the sea—and the air over Hawaii. Executing a highly complex plan of lure and deception, Yamamoto unwisely split up his great armada in order to accomplish his purpose. Early in June 1942 two Japanese light carriers, supported by 7 cruisers and 12 destroyers, moved into Aleutian waters to bombard the naval base at

Dutch Harbor, and 18 submarines took station north and west of Hawaii in order to attack the American carriers when they sortied north to defend the Aleutians. But Nimitz had already sent his carriers to sea, not to protect the less important Aleutians, but to contest Yamamoto's main thrust toward Midway. Fletcher led the *Yorktown*, Admiral Raymond A. Spruance the *Enterprise* and *Hornet*, with land-based air and subs to cooperate; the last few battleships had been sent back to California. Yamamoto further separated his 7 battleships (plus one light carrier, 4 cruisers and 12 destroyers) from the 4 fast carriers, *Kaga*, *Akagi*, *Soryu* and *Hiryu* (plus 2 battleships, 3 cruisers and 12 destroyers), thus eliminating the possibility of mutual anti-aircraft support. Once these forces defeated the American fleet, the amphibious attack could be made on Midway from 12 transports (supported by yet 2 more battleships, another light carrier, 2 seaplane carriers, 7 cruisers and 29 destroyers). This separation of units and missions—fleet battle and amphibious assault—compromised Japanese tactics and enabled Nimitz to concentrate his available strength against the chief threat, Yamamoto's 4 attack carriers.

The Battle of Midway, one of the most decisive actions in naval history, took place on June 4, 1942. Japan's four fast carriers, guided by the mistaken information that the remaining American naval strength was en route to the Aleutians, went into their standard but poorly escorted defensive square formation for attacking shore installations and began striking Midway as part of the pre-landing barrage. The Japanese carrier planes were thus armed with general bombs rather than torpedoes and the armor-piercing variety of bombs for use against ships. During the early morning, American Army, Navy and Marine Corps land-based planes from Midway located the carriers, but all missed with their bombs and were either shot down or driven off by defensive Japanese fighters. Then Japanese reconnaissance planes located part of the American fleet, whose carrier planes were now searching for Yamamoto's carriers. The Japanese now began to rearm and refuel their planes for a fleet action, though they could not disperse their carriers according to doctrine as long as they had to attack Midway too. At mid-morning, their launch carefully timed by Admiral Spruance and his staff, the American TBD Devastator torpedo-bombers from *Hornet* and *Enterprise* made contact with the enemy, but because they had become separated from their fighter escort were practically all shot down. However, as this was happening, the SBD Dauntless dive-bombers from all three American carriers chanced upon the Japanese carrier force—undetected, no less. Diving out of the sun, these planes hit *Kaga*, *Akagi* and *Soryu* just as their aircraft were being armed and fueled on deck; by noon all were in a sinking condition. Another attack later in the day also finished the *Hiryu,* but since so many planes had been on board all four carriers refueling, most of their valuable pilots merely jumped overboard and were rescued by their escorts. A later American strike sank a heavy cruiser, while a last Japanese flight managed to locate and disable the *Yorktown,* which was then finished off three days later by a Japanese sub. Deprived of his fleet cover, Yamamoto had no choice but to abandon the Midway operation, though his northern forces did occupy desolate Attu and Kiska islands in the Aleutians.

Though Japanese carrier strength had been whittled down to rough parity with the Americans—some five each—the victories of the Coral Sea and Midway could not relieve Axis pressures elsewhere during the spring of 1942. Germany's spring offensives took Sevastopol and the Kerch peninsula in the Black Sea, and in North Africa Rommel captured Tobruk and pressed into Egypt, while Axis and Allied planes traded blows around Malta and its vital convoys. In March British commandos destroyed the big French dry dock at St. Nazaire, but the Allies had less success against Doenitz's U-boats. The simultaneous need for Doenitz to blockade the American East Coast and to cut the heavy Allied use of the "Murmansk run" overtaxed his 125 boats during the first half of the year. To be sure, his subs between January and June claimed no fewer than 585 merchantmen totaling over three million tons, in addition to another 400 vessels of one million tons sunk by aircraft, mines and surface ships. But Germany and Italy lost 21 and 7 subs respectively in the process, and as the Americans ever so gradually developed coastal convoys and antisub forces Doenitz followed his usual practice of shifting his boats to safer areas: from the United States East Coast to the Caribbean in the late spring, then to the mid-Atlantic during the summer. By that time, the first new prewar Allied naval construction had become available, giving the Allies opportunities to make limited counterattacks.

Allied strategic differences reflected their own pressing needs and historical biases. Russia wanted a second front established in the West by an Anglo-American assault on the coast of France to relieve its armies in the East; traditionally continent-oriented American generals agreed on such a direct approach. But the British, steeped in the maritime strategy of the Pitts, Barham and Churchill—now termed the "indirect approach" by the British military pundit B. H. Liddell Hart —preferred to postpone such a project until Hitler's "Fortress Europe" had been isolated by Allied command of the seas around and the air over Europe and reduced by the Red Army. Also, the harsh experience of Dunkirk was accented in August by a disastrous Anglo-Canadian commando raid on the French coast at Dieppe, creating grave doubts about a major amphibious landing until the Anglo-Americans had overwhelming strength. Rommel's North African offensive threatened the Allies in the Middle East, and Doenitz's U-boats caused the Allies to cut back their Murmansk convoys during the summer. And within the Allied Combined Chiefs of Staff was the outspoken Commander-in-Chief of the United States Fleet and Chief of Naval Operations, Admiral Ernest J. King, a superior administrator and strategist who personally directed the American antisub effort in the Atlantic and unrelentingly insisted on a full American effort against Japan. Unlike his British First Sea Lord counterpart, Admirals Pound and (from late 1943) Cunningham, King got relatively little interference from his chief of state, though he upset the British.

All these elements led to several key Allied strategic decisions in mid-1942: postponement of the cross-Channel attack, victory first in the Mediterranean and a separate American war in the Pacific, despite British disbelief that the United States could wage two simultaneous wars. Stalin's second front for the time being came in the form of Lend Lease convoys and Anglo-American strategic air forces which bombed Germany and drew valuable *Luftwaffe* units away from the Eastern front. Anglo-American maritime strategists thus had their way in first seeking command of the sea in 1942 and 1943 before returning in force to the continent.

All Allied operations in the European theater depended on the success of the convoys in the Battle of the Atlantic, but the U-boat *guerre de course* prevailed through the first months of 1943. Doenitz's boats and other Axis weapons claimed over 800,000 tons of merchant shipping in both June and November 1942 and over 600,000 tons in each of the intervening months and in the following March. But Doenitz's tonnage warfare avoided the crucial well-escorted convoys with their most important cargoes in favor of easier targets in increasingly broad operating areas, as from Hitler's decision in June 1942 to attack Brazilian shipping which hastened that nation's declaration of war and cooperation in Allied antisub efforts. Though the Murmansk route had been temporarily closed, foul weather, uncoordinated *Luftwaffe* units and only partly effective surface raiders weakened the commerce war from Norway. And new U-boats, their "milch cow" supply subs, acoustical torpedoes and wolf pack tactics could not offset Allied counterattacks. At last Hitler virtually suspended all German surface ship operations and replaced Raeder with Doenitz as his naval commander early in 1943.

For the Allies, Admiral King championed defensive convoys over offensive hunter-killer operations until enough antisub vessels were available for them and such new weapons as the forward-fired depth charge and escort carrier could be proved. Air operations with convoys had been originally limited to merchant-ship-launched planes and an occasional escort carrier such as the prototype, the British *Audacity,* which was sunk by a U-boat late in 1941. Shore-based patrol bombers and lighter-than-air blimps of the RAF and U. S. Navy and Army Air Forces covered American, Canadian, Icelandic and British waters, but still left the "black pit" air gap south of Greenland empty of aerial cover. The many new escort carriers and destroyers began to close this gap, so that in March 1943 the Americans turned over all convoy escort duty to Britain and Canada in order to shift to offensive hunter-killer operations with the new American Tenth Fleet, created in May under King's direct command. While these forces operated from the United States, Admiral Sir Max Horton sent hunter-killer groups into the Western Approaches, and Allied bombers began an air offensive against U-boats in the Bay of Biscay. So, between June 1942 and May 1943 the Germans lost 165 U-boats—in May alone 41—and the Italians 29 more. And German merchant sinkings could not offset Allied mass-produced Victory and Liberty merchant ships. Admitting defeat in the North Atlantic, Doenitz withdrew his boats from that quarter late in May to reconsider his strategy.

As Allied supplies got through, Soviet Russia initiated its first counterthrust with the Red Army, supported by warships, naval infantry and a slowly recovering naval air force. Russian destroyers, subs and torpedo boats protected Murmansk in the Kola Inlet and attacked German shipping off Norway until met by a concerted German anti-sub effort there in April 1943. Russian naval aircraft and coastal craft frustrated German naval and amphibious attacks in the Gulf of Finland from September 1942, helped lift the siege of Leningrad in January 1943 and then attacked Axis merchantmen in the Baltic until the Germans instituted convoys and defensive patrols which sank ten Russian subs and erected an enlarged mine barrage to close Kronstadt. Following a German summer and autumn drive along the Volga and Don rivers and Black Sea coast which forced the Russian Fleet from Novorossisk to smaller ports like Batum, the Russians launched a brilliant counterattack in November 1942 which captured the entire Axis Army before Stalingrad the following February. German and Russian naval forces parried around Novorossisk during the winter, but remained stalemated throughout the spring. Such Russian successes forced Hitler to divert reinforcements to the Eastern front from the Mediterranean, enabling the Anglo-Americans to implement their peripheral strategy there.

The Atlantic Allies now moved to regain North Africa by a pincers movement closing in from East and West Africa. In the East, a British amphibious assault took Vichy French Madagascar in September and October 1942, while the British Army stalled Rommel's offensive before El Alamein, only sixty miles from Alexandria. Then, late in October, the British Eighth Army under General Bernard L. Montgomery counterattacked at El Alamein and drove Rommel from Egypt. On November 8, an Allied army under American General Dwight D. Eisenhower supported by naval forces under Admiral Cunningham landed in Morocco and Algeria. Craftily eluding U-boats, American troop convoys and escorting fleet units ferried the assault forces from the United States to land at four places for the investment of Casablanca, while British vessels supported an American landing at Oran and an Anglo-American landing at ʻlgiers—both mounted from England. Defending Vichy French naval, air and ground forces resisted unsuccessfully for two days, then, led by Admiral Darlan, surrendered and went over to the Allies. The sudden intrusion of Allied reinforcements into the Mediterranean gave the Allies final command of that sea, enabling Allied expeditions to seize Bougie and Bône in eastern Algeria days later and to establish airfields to contest the air over land and water. Because of the Darlan defection, the Germans dissolved the Vichy government and occupied the rest of France, but not in time to prevent the French from scuttling their surviving fleet units at Toulon. Rommel withdrew before the Allied pincers into Tunisia by the end of the year and managed to counter Allied blows, but Allied air and sea power isolated his army there. The Axis armies in North Africa surrendered in May 1943, thus reopening the supply route to the Persian Gulf and Russia via the Suez Canal—a much more convenient route than around South Africa.

Allied maritime strategy in the Pacific reflected the American control under Admirals King and Nimitz, though not without the opposition of continental strategists who preferred to concentrate the Allied effort against the Japanese in China, Southeast Asia and the Philippines. But neither Allied-Chinese forces in the China-Burma-India theater nor American-Commonwealth forces under American General Douglas MacArthur in Australia and southern New Guinea could be spared adequate forces from the other fronts to adequately contest the major Japanese armies and their air forces. Japan was most vulnerable at sea, because of the long lines of communications to island bases throughout the vast Pacific. So the U. S. Navy mounted a major *guerre de course* sub effort from Hawaii and Australia against Japanese shipping, a tonnage war that was effective since Japan had no adequate policy of commerce protection and never really developed one. Conversely, Japan missed a real opportunity to attack American shipping by continuing to use its subs in fleet and Army support. To further insure Allied sea routes to the Anzac countries, Nimitz collected his still-meager fleet units and one Marine Corps division to take Tulagi and Guadalcanal islands in the southern Solomons on August 7, 1942. Japanese fleet units and naval air forces at Rabaul responded immediately, beginning a six-month battle of attrition over the possession of Guadalcanal. Throughout most of the campaign, American forces held only the airfield and beachhead and commanded the adjacent air and sea in daylight when convoys brought in supplies and men, whereas the Japanese held the rest of the island, reinforcing it during the night under cover of air and surface ship attacks. As time went on, this otherwise unimportant island became the focus of the war in the Pacific for both sides.

The Guadalcanal campaign raged from August 1942 to February 1943, with each side reluctantly exposing its precious heavy surface units and veteran naval aviators piecemeal as necessity dictated. Planes from airstrips on Rabaul and Guadalcanal and from carriers tangled daily, with the cumulative effect of gradually costing Japan her best pilots, who were not rotated home to train new air groups, unlike the Americans who were. The several naval battles similarly wore away fleet strength on both sides, but to Japan's disadvantage, since her industrial base would take at least one year longer than that of the United States to replace ships lost. The three American carriers supporting the initial landings at Guadalcanal were foolishly withdrawn by an overcautious Admiral Fletcher on August 8, whereupon Admiral Gunichi Mikawa came down from Rabaul to penetrate the Guadalcanal roadstead with seven cruisers; shortly after midnight on the 9th his force sank one Australian and four American cruisers and a destroyer in the battle of Savo Island. Two weeks later, three carriers led a Japanese fleet sortie from Truk into the battle of the Eastern Solomons (August 22–25) with American carriers, whose planes sank one Japanese light carrier and destroyed ninety enemy aircraft. The American submarine S-44 sank a Japanese heavy cruiser in August, but Japan's I-26 crippled the carrier Saratoga and in September I-19 sank the carrier Wasp. In the middle of October, American and Japanese cruisers clashed in the battle of Cape Esperance, costing Japan one cruiser lost and two severely damaged, but two Japanese battleships with cruisers and destroyers bombarded the airfield on Guadalcanal. Admiral Yamamoto now determined to launch a massive air-sea attack to take Guadal, but Admiral Nimitz countered by placing the aggressive Admiral Halsey in command in the South Pacific.

The issue came to a head quickly, with the Americans led by Halsey managing to frustrate Yamamoto's scheme. In the battle of the Santa Cruz Islands, October 26–27, 1942, the small carrier forces again traded blows. The Americans shot down 100 more Japanese carrier planes and put the carrier *Shokaku* out of action for nearly a year, while the Japanese forces sank the carrier *Hornet* and seriously damaged the carrier *Enterprise*. In mid-November reinforcement attempts by both sides led to the prolonged and decisive Naval Battle of Guadalcanal from the 12th to the 15th. During the first night, surface forces slugged it out, leaving two of five American cruisers and four destroyers sunk and two Japanese cruisers sunk and the battleship *Hiei* so badly damaged that it was sunk next morning by *Enterprise* planes. On the 14th American planes also sank two more Japanese cruisers and seven transports, so that Yamamoto rushed the battleship *Kirishima* with four cruisers plus destroyers into the fray. In the final night action, the new American battleships *Washington* and *South Dakota* met and sank the *Kirishima,* credit going largely to the radar-directed guns of the *Washington* against a ship without radar. Unbeknownst to the Americans, this victory gave them command of the seas around Guadalcanal by convincing Yamamoto to evacuate Japan's portion of the island. The Japanese retreat was masterfully disguised, with Japanese fleet and air units sinking one American cruiser and badly damaging three others in the battle of Tassafaronga, November 30, and sinking another in the battle of Rennell Island on January 29–30, 1943. The next week the Japanese successfully evacuated Guadalcanal. Halsey's inspired leadership had resulted in the first permanent dent in Japan's defensive perimeter, but more importantly, Japanese fleet and pilot losses compounded the disaster of Midway.

Having placed the Japanese squarely on the defensive in the South Pacific, the Americans with Commonwealth participation strengthened their positions there and in the North Pacific during the spring of 1943. Land-based Army, Navy and Marine Corps bombers and fighters from Guadalcanal and New Guinea whittled down Japanese naval air strength at Rabaul and adjacent installations and shipping. In March, Army bombers sank four Japanese destroyers and seven of eight troop transports in convoy in the battle of the Bismarck Sea; American PT boats sank the last transport. And in April American fighters robbed Japan of its foremost naval commander and strategist by shooting down Admiral Yamamoto on a flight between Rabaul and Bougainville. In the North Pacific, Japan tried to hold on to Attu and Kiska islands while Japanese planes from Paramushiro in the Kuriles and American planes from Dutch Harbor and other bases in the central Aleutians battled to control the air. The foul weather hampered all operations, and the indecisive cruiser battle of the Komandorski Islands in March settled nothing except that it helped convince the Japanese to supply Attu and Kiska only by sub. In May an American amphibious assault took Attu, and two months later the Japanese executed another carefully disguised evacuation, this time from Kiska. Allied North Pacific routes to Russia and South Pacific routes to Australia were now secure.

As the spring of 1943 drew to a close, the limited Allied offensives had succeeded in throwing the Axis back on the defensive. The U-boat had been successfully checked, North Africa taken, the South Pacific and Indian Ocean held, and Russia saved from the German onslaught. These successes, often undramatic battles of attrition, bought invaluable time for American war industry to reach the production levels whereby it could feed, arm and generally supply the Allied nations and provide the huge quantity of superior weapons for the all-out offensives against the Axis powers across the globe.

ALLIED COUNTEROFFENSIVE

Despite Russian frustration over the continuously delayed cross-Channel attack to open a Western front, several Allied strategic conferences during 1943 guaranteed that the assault would come in the spring of 1944. In the meantime, the Anglo-American navies would test their new post-Pearl Harbor weapons by winning command of the Atlantic and Pacific oceans to blockade both Germany and Japan, while their strategic air forces began the reduction of both countries and their armies took Italy out of the war and prepared for the assault on Hitler's "Fortress Europe." Serious differences between Stalin and Churchill continued as both now looked to postwar political arrangements in Europe. Stalin would guarantee his western frontier against a resurgent Germany by establishing Russian hegemony over Eastern and Central Europe. Churchill would frustrate such an eventuality by sending the Anglo-American armies into the Italian and/or Balkan peninsulas via the "soft underbelly" of Europe to liberate Central Europe ahead of the Red Army. But Roosevelt held the bargaining power with superior American arms and industry and compromised American moralistic goals to generally side with Stalin's position. Fascism, after all, was the enemy, not the Russian Ally. The Americans decided to support Churchill in the Mediterranean only, after which the carefully rationed amphibious craft would be redeployed for the cross-Channel attack. Stalin could liberate Eastern Europe, the Murmansk run would be reopened, and the Americans would undertake their own offensive against Japan's defensive perimeter in the Pacific, instead of through Burma as Churchill wanted. And time decidedly favored the Allies, whose industrial output in mid-1943 beat that of the Germans and Japanese by a full year.

To supply Russia and stockpile men and material in England for the cross-Channel attack, the Allies had to win the Battle of the Atlantic. After the German battleships *Tirpitz* and *Gneisenau* and ten destroyers raided the outpost at Spitzbergen in September 1943, the Allies moved up to neutralize the last German surface raiders in Norway. British midget subs damaged the *Tirpitz* at her anchorage later that month, and planes from five carriers immobilized her the following March, while the *Scharnhorst* attacked a convoy in December only to be sunk by the battleship *Duke of York* and torpedoes from escorting cruisers and destroyers. Allied bombers closed U-boat operations in the Bay of Biscay, and the neutral Portuguese government assisted by leasing the Azores Islands for Allied seaplane, land-based patrol bomber and naval operations. British subs turned from the neutralized German surface raiders to attack German merchant shipping and U-boats in the North Atlantic late in 1943 and were joined by British escort carrier groups. The renewed Murmansk convoys were heavily escorted, forcing Doenitz to shift his U-boats into the mid-Atlantic. There they ran afoul of the U. S. Tenth Fleet's new offensive hunter-killer groups of escort carriers and destroyer escorts. These forces under Admiral King's direction mounted new TBF/TBM Avenger torpedo-bombers; sonobuoys, aircraft searchlights and airborne microwave radars for sub detection; and aerial rockets, faster-sinking depth charges and homing torpedoes. The Allies also utilized quantitative analysis techniques (operations research) to institute larger convoys, three-sub wolf packs (for the Pacific) and systematic aerial mining procedures. Doenitz's own innovations—mass-produced prefabricated U-boats, acoustical torpedoes and schnorkel underwater breathing devices to avoid having to surface—would not begin to be ready until mid-1944. Consequently, Allied monthly merchant losses never exceeded 210,000 tons after July 1943, while Doenitz lost 167 U-boats between then and May 1944—faster than Germany could build new ones. Thus did the Allies win command of the Atlantic sea lanes, prerequisite to the cross-Channel attack.

Russia tied down the main German armies by mounting its general counterattack following the great tank battle of Kursk, 300 miles south of Moscow, in July 1943. To keep the Murmansk-Archangel supply routes open, Russian subs attacked German shipping in northern Norway, requiring the Germans to extend their antisub measures thence during the summer, and Russian destroyers and subchasers assisted incoming Allied convoys. The Northern Sea Route also stayed open for occasional reinforcements from the Pacific. Crossing the Dnieper during the latter half of 1943, the Red Army then liberated Smolensk and Kiev and the western Ukraine early in 1944. Throughout these operations, the Black Sea Fleet under Admiral L. A. Vladimirskij added more ships and planes to operate on the left flank. In September 1943 it assaulted and retook Novorossisk, naval infantry going ashore in 120 landing boats behind cutters which cleared the minefield, and under cover of naval air and coastal gunfire linked up with the army behind the city. Covered by the Azov Flotilla of Admiral S. G. Gorshkov, the same force established a bridgehead on the Kerch peninsula in early November, but was checked by stiff German resistance. Taking advantage of the Russian winter offensive, the Fleet bypassed the Crimea to retake Nikolayev and Ochakov in March and Odessa in April 1944, assaulting across the Kerch Strait to regain Sevastopol in the Crimea in May. Light Russian warships, naval aircraft and subs could then blockade and attack the Axis bases at Rumanian Constanta and Bulgarian Varna and Burgas. By June, Russian fleet units were relieving Axis pressure in the Black and Baltic seas, and the army had kept the *Wehrmacht* sufficiently occupied on the Eastern front to enable the Anglo-American allies to regain the Mediterranean.

While Admiral Cunningham's minesweepers battled subs and planes to clear a path for Allied convoys between Gibraltar and Suez in May 1943, General Eisenhower built up his forces in North Africa to take Italy out of the war. Allied bombings and a threat of amphibious assault led to the Italian surrender of Pantelleria Island in June, after which the 2500 invasion craft for Sicily collected from Britain, America, North Africa, Malta and the Middle East. Well-rehearsed and preceded by days of aerial bombing from North African-based aircraft, the assault of July 10 inaugurated such new amphibious craft as the Dukw, LST, LCI, LCT and LCVP. A silent approach did not effect the planned surprise, and the non-naval tactical air support left much to be desired, but general Axis resistance proved to be lighter than expected—partly the result of an Allied ruse. A sub had planted a body with bogus papers off the Spanish coast seen by German agents who then caused the diverting of important minelayers to Greece and a panzer division to Sardinia, expected landing points. The Allied armies raced across Sicily, but could not prevent the escape of Axis troops across the Strait of Messina in August.

Mussolini's government fell late in July, and the successor regime agreed to an armistice early in September which the Germans would not honor and instead set up Mussolini as a puppet in the north. That month the British crossed into Italy while the Americans assaulted Salerno below Naples, the Germans evacuated Corsica and Sardinia, and British forces landed on several Italian Aegean islands. A German air strike sank one Italian battleship before that fleet surrendered to the Allies at Malta, and on October 13 Italy declared war on Germany. The Germans halted the Allied overland advance and retook the Aegean islands, whereupon the Allies in January 1944 landed north of Rome at Anzio only to be trapped there in Gallipoli fashion by the Germans. Allied antiair and antisub measures thwarted Doenitz's and Goering's spring attacks in the middle sea, and in May the Italian stalemate ended with an Allied breakout that liberated Rome on June 4. Anglo-Italian naval patrols in the Adriatic supported Yugoslav partisans, but the major Allied effort was shifted back to the English Channel. The Mediterranean campaign had tested amphibious techniques and troops alike and seriously weakened Germany in the classic maritime strategic manner.

The turn of the tide in the Mediterranean and Atlantic enabled the British to strengthen the Indian Ocean front. Admiral Lord Louis Mountbatten, who had directed the British amphibious recovery early in the war, in 1943 became Commander, Southeast Asia, and pressed for an amphibious assault from the Bay of Bengal to relieve Allied ground forces in Burma. But the requirements for landing craft in the Mediterranean confined his amphibious activities to coastal operations in Burma from December 1943. He did obtain considerable heavy British fleet units after the neutralization of the German battleships and the Italian fleet, along with surface ships of the reunified French National Navy (in June 1943) and American Pacific Fleet units on loan. Consequently, the Eastern Fleet under Admiral Somerville returned from East Africa to Ceylon in 1943 for operations against a U-boat offensive from a new German sub base at Penang in Japanese Sumatra and for attacks on several Japanese islands. Doenitz's shift away from closely guarded sea lanes in his tonnage war brought him some successes in the Indian Ocean before being contained by Allied countermeasures. And during the spring and summer of 1944 Mountbatten directed several carrier-surface bombardments of Sumatra, Java and the Andaman Islands. These were only nuisance raids against a Japan which was losing the air over China to Allied planes and the North China countryside to Mao Tse-tung's Communist forces but holding off Chiang Kai-shek's Nationalist armies in the South. Also, mounting numbers of Allied warships enabled French and Italian cruisers to help patrol the Central Atlantic and Russia to obtain the loan of several older Anglo-American vessels and later some surrendered Italian warships. Yet, the most impressive concentration of Allied war shipping lay in the Pacific, where the United States determined to wrest command of the sea from Japan.

The American offensive in the Pacific during 1943–44 exploited quantitative and qualitative superiority from the strategic exterior position. With their weakened fleet centrally based at Truk in the eastern Carolines, the Japanese could not utilize their normally advantageous interior position to meet the three simultaneous thrusts the Allies now sent against them. Admiral Nimitz controlled all Pacific warships and the offensives from the South Pacific (Third Fleet) under Admiral Halsey and the Central Pacific (Fifth Fleet) under Admiral Spruance, while General Douglas MacArthur attacked from the Southwest Pacific using Nimitz's warships on loan (Seventh Fleet) under Admiral Thomas C. Kinkaid. The awkward command relationship had resulted from interservice distrust and fundamental doctrinal differences of the Navy's maritime strategists Admirals King, Nimitz and Spruance and the Army's continental strategist MacArthur, who had tremendous political influence, though not enough to concentrate the whole offensive in his theater. For assaulting the islands of the South Pacific, the north coastal enclaves of New Guinea and the coral atolls of the Central Pacific, new amphibious techniques had to be worked out during the actual battles, primarily under the direction of Admirals Richmond Kelly Turner and Daniel E. Barbey and Marine General Holland M. Smith. If the Japanese fleet elected to fight, fleet tactics had to be developed around the many new fast battleships and carriers. The naval aviators of Admiral John H. Towers developed fleet doctrine around the new *Essex*-class carriers and their new F6F Hellcat fighters—proved at sea in 1944 under the command of Admiral Marc A. Mitscher. But Admiral Spruance, last of the formalist battleship admirals, resisted adopting the melee-type tactics of the carriers until forced by the circumstances of battle. So inferior had the Japanese fleet become by this time, however, that even faulty tactics could not seriously jeopardize the American advance. Finally, the submarines of Admiral Charles A. Lockwood heightened their *guerre de course* war of attrition against Japanese sea lanes.

During the summer and autumn of 1943 the three-pronged Allied Pacific offensive went into motion. To first neutralize the great Japanese naval and air base at Rabaul, Halsey and MacArthur worked up the Solomon Islands and New Guinea coast respectively between June 1943 and March 1944, beating off all Japanese air and naval attacks. As Halsey's landing forces took the central Solomons in the summer and fall, his covering forces of cruisers, destroyers and PT boats used radar and superior tactics to fight four night actions which sank one Japanese cruiser and several destroyers and troop transports at the cost of a cruiser and destroyer. On November 1 Halsey's troops landed at Bougainville in the northern Solomons, drawing many Japanese cruisers to the target area. On the 2nd his covering forces sank one of four Japanese cruisers at the battle of Empress Augusta Bay, and three days later a few carrier planes from the *Saratoga* dramatically damaged six of seven Japanese cruisers anchored at Rabaul. Halsey's land-based planes frustrated Japanese naval air forces and from Bougainville began regular strikes against Rabaul. Then, on November 20, Spruance used carrier and battleship cover to land the Marines at fanatically defended Tarawa and Makin atolls in the Gilberts which fell after heavy fighting. Mistakes were made in amphibious and carrier tactics, but the lessons were quickly learned and generally corrected. In December MacArthur jumped from the New Guinea coast to take Cape Gloucester at the opposite end of New Britain Island from Rabaul, while Halsey's forces went on to occupy Green and Emirau islands in February and March 1944. Rabaul had been encircled and isolated from outside help, and Japan's outer defenses pierced in three places.

The sudden success of the new mobile American amphibious-carrier force demonstrated the fallacy of Japan's defensive perimeter and created a new strategic option for the Allies in the winter and spring of 1944. Fortified as "unsinkable carriers" to whittle down the advancing American fleet, Japan's Pacific islands had in fact no mobility against the many fast carriers and land-based Army bombers. They thus offered no refuge as fleet bases for Japan's heavy fleet units, which hastily abandoned Rabaul and Truk before the American approach. This being the case, Admiral Nimitz decided to bypass both those bases and lesser ones, keeping them neutralized by land-based planes from the islands his forces did take. Airfields could be rapidly repaired and enlarged by naval Construction Battalion ("Seabees") and Army engineers. Even while Rabaul was being encircled, in January and February 1944 Nimitz sent Spruance's Fifth Fleet into the Marshall Islands. Admiral Turner's amphibious forces landed and took Kwajalein and Eniwetok under the barrage of his older prewar battleships and escort carriers. Admiral Mitscher's Task Force 58 of eleven fast carriers provided strategic cover, the eight new fast battleships—with no other work to do—giving additional antiaircraft protection along with the Hellcat fighters. Breaking away from the beaches and refueling at sea by fast fleet tankers, Task Force 58 in February headed westward to destroy Japanese land-based air at Truk and in the distant Marianas Islands. MacArthur occupied the Admiralty Islands and Hollandia in New Guinea in March and April as Army planes and the fast carriers destroyed Japanese air in New Guinea and the Palau Islands. From new anchorages in the Marshalls and Admiralties, the Pacific Fleet could now look to the capture of the Marianas and MacArthur to northwest New Guinea, after which the three prongs of the offensive could join together.

Japan could do little with an understrength fleet and a virtually useless policy of trade protection against Lockwood's subs from Hawaii and those operating out of Australia. The Americans replaced malfunctioning torpedoes with new electrical ones copied from German designs and even operated in several German-style wolf packs to sink most of the 3,500,000 tons of Japanese merchant shipping lost during 1943 and the first half of 1944. American subs operated as far as Japanese home waters and even sowed mines off the Chinese coast. Japanese merchant ship construction, like that of its warships, could not begin to offset these losses, while the Imperial Japanese Navy—regarding convoy escort as defensive and unglamorous—never developed sophisticated antisub techniques, using only the oldest and least effective destroyers plus some escort carriers and too few new frigates after mid-1943—even after a special escort command was created that November. A Japanese staff proposal for a defensive mine barrier between Japan and Borneo was delayed because the mines were being harbored for possible use against an increasingly worrisome Russia. As time ran out, Japan would have no choice but to commit its still-inferior fleet and undertrained carrier pilots for the protection of its inner defenses.

By June 1944 Japan and Germany stood alone against the combined might of the Allies. Russian manpower with American equipment had turned back the German armies, and now Russian industry was beginning to recover. Chinese manpower, unevenly effective, was now to be augmented by American B-29 strategic bombers and substantial British support on the Burma front. Allied sea power had regained command of Atlantic, Mediterranean and Central and South Pacific waters, with escort and fast carriers and land-based planes neutralizing Doenitz's U-boats and Japanese naval air power. Allied amphibious doctrine, perfected through much experience, had taken Italy out of the war and regained the key areas of the South and Central Pacific. The full weight of American and Allied industry and manpower could now be employed to spearhead the assault on Hitler's Fortress Europe and to begin the air-sea blockade of the Japanese Empire.

ANGLO-AMERICAN COMMAND OF THE SEA

The final Allied offensives of the war, from the summer of 1944 to the summer of 1945, produced a fanaticism on the part of the Axis powers that delayed, but could not prevent, their eventual collapse. Indeed, the presence of the new Anglo-American-Canadian bridgehead in Normandy and the American capture of the Marianas Islands in June and July 1944 were such sufficient recognition of coming Axis defeat that late in July they induced several high-ranking German officers to make an unsuccessful attempt on Hitler's life and the highest Japanese statesmen to overthrow the Tojo regime. But Allied war aims mitigated against any real possibility of a negotiated end to the hostilities, for early in 1943 Roosevelt had promoted the war aim of "unconditional surrender," meaning that the Nazi and Japanese militarist leaders had no alternative but to fight to the finish. Indeed, the Russo-

German conflict had taken on the dimensions of a religious struggle—
between communism and fascism—so that Hitler could expect no quarter
from Stalin. And the American crusade in the Pacific fully aimed at
eliminating the Japanese state and humbling or even destroying its "di-
vine" Emperor, making the Japanese resistance religious, even suicidal.

With their conventional weapons losing the fight, their economies
being strangled by the Allied air-sea blockades, and with American and
British strategic bombers starting to mercilessly pound their industrial
centers, the Germans and Japanese placed their faith in new secret
weapons—guided missiles. In June Germany began launching V-1 buzz
bombs from France at southern England, followed in September by V-2
interrange ballistic missiles from the Low Countries. During the autumn
Japan unleashed its human-guided projectiles, *kamikaze* planes and
kaiten submarine-torpedoes, followed in the spring by *oka* (or *baka)*
piloted bombs, suicide torpedo boats and even swimmers. Fortunately
for the Allies, these weapons came too late or appeared in such a piecemeal fashion that effective countermeasures could be devised. As for
Allied secret weapons, the atomic bomb headed the list of new developments that would reduce the Axis efforts into relative insignificance.

No Axis secret weapon, as with the older dreaded U-boat and *Luft-
waffe* fighter, could stay the Red Army's steady advance into Central
Europe from the east during the summer and fall of 1944. In the south,
Russian ground forces combined with Black Sea Fleet units to take the
German-held Rumanian port of Constanta late in August, the last land-
sea operation on that front, with Rumania and Bulgaria abruptly changing sides by the time the Red Army crossed the Danube early in
September. During the autumn the Germans retreated from Greece into
Yugoslavia. In the north, the Russians took Finland out of the war
with a massive overland offensive throughout the summer and weakened
the German mine barrier in the Gulf of Finland by steady air strikes
and torpedo boat attacks which sank several light German surface ships.
The collapse of Finland jeopardized German Army units along the
southern coast of the Gulf and Lake Peipus, but naval vessels in both
waters helped prolong the defense until Red Army units outflanked them.
Russian forces took most of the Baltic islands and their subs broke
through the German mine barrier to attack enemy shipping. Still, German destroyers and torpedo boats controlled Baltic waters, avoiding or
sweeping British-laid aerial mines and successfully evacuating most
German troops from Estonia and Latvia during the autumn. Anglo-
Russian air strikes finally neutralized the last heavy German surface
units, RAF bombers sinking the *Tirpitz* in northern Norway in November and forcing those in the Baltic to be converted into antiaircraft
platforms. Simultaneous with these drives, the Red Army pushed into

Poland and Hungary, meeting virtually no resistance in the air and reduced resistance on the ground, as Germany shifted many forces away to fight on the newly created Western front.

The Allied landing at Normandy on June 6, 1944 (D-Day), caught the Germans unprepared. Field Marshal Rommel had only begun to lay mines and set up anti-beaching obstacles along the "Atlantic Wall" and was even confused by an Allied feint off Calais, while Doenitz lost 13 of his 36 defending U-boats which succeeded in sinking only 2 frigates, one corvette and an empty transport of the massive 4000-vessel Allied armada that crossed the Channel on that and succeeding days. The well-rehearsed assault—the greatest in modern times—placed over 175,000 men ashore, and was covered by Allied air forces in England and an Anglo-American-French fleet under Admiral Sir Bertram Ramsay which included 6 battleships, 15 cruisers, one monitor and many destroyers and rocket-launching craft for gunfire support. The Allied Expeditionary Force was commanded by General Eisenhower, with actual landing operations being directed from the amphibious command ship (AGC) *Ancon*. Since the assault took place between the heavily defended ports of Cherbourg and Le Havre, depriving the Allies of docking facilities, two artificial roadsteads—called "Mulberry" and largely the idea of Churchill—had to be fashioned from sunken hulks, though one was demolished several days after D-Day by a ferocious late spring storm. Nevertheless, the assault was an unqualified success and enabled the Allies to develop a formidable permanent bridgehead, which engulfed Cherbourg by the end of June, prior to the breakout across Western Europe in late July and August.

In order to further carve up the German Army defenses in France, the supporting gunships entered the Mediterranean where they reinforced Allied units to reach a strength of 5 battleships, some 20 cruisers, 9 escort carriers and a great many destroyers; these craft supported Franco-American landings in southern France on August 15. Both Allied fronts formed a pincers in August and September to recover or isolate all French seaports, thus ending the last U-boat presence near the Western Approaches and the last *Luftwaffe* threats in the Western Mediterranean, liberating Paris and sending the Germans in full retreat—simultaneous with the Allied advances in Italy and on the Eastern front.

The Germans' reaction to these Allied thrusts into their rear was sufficient to slow, but not to reverse the Allies. U-boat sinkings of merchant shipping declined to new wartime lows, around 50,000 tons in each of the autumn months, and Hitler strengthened his missile and ground defenses as his armies fell back on the homeland. The Allied advance had been so swift, however, that the logistical strain was slow-ing down the offensive, and the approach of winter further inhibited continental operations. If, however, Eisenhower could punch through the northern German defenses the Allies would have the Scheldt and Antwerp as forward bases, enabling them to overrun the V-2 missile sites. But the Germans crushed an Anglo-American airborne drop at Arnhem in Holland in late September, and the advancing ground forces did not reach the Scheldt for another month. On November 8 a British amphibious assault took Walcheren Island, though the rest of the month was consumed by Allied minesweepers clearing the Scheldt before Antwerp could become operational. Hitler then turned his V-2s on Antwerp, increased the attacks of his new schnorkel-equipped U-boats on Allied shipping, and in mid-December sent a massive armor spearhead into the American lines in Belgium and Luxembourg aimed at taking Antwerp. In this "Battle of the Bulge," however, the Allies repulsed his drive and in January 1945 renewed their offensive. Simultaneously, the Russians launched a general winter offensive all along the Eastern front, supported by devastating Allied air bombings of German targets, and in February Turkey and other Middle Eastern states finally declared war on Germany.

The end of Hitler's empire then came swiftly, though the U-boats increased their monthly sinkings to around 100,000 tons through April, and the German escort forces successfully controlled the Baltic for the evacuation of German forces from this theater in order to surrender on the Western front rather than to the dreaded Russians. In the east, most of the surviving German heavy surface ships succumbed to aerial bombs, and in the west Eisenhower's armies crossed the Rhine on naval landing craft in March. Hitler committed suicide on April 30, leaving the final task of surrender to his successor, Admiral Doenitz, who took Germany out of the war finally on May 8.

Japan's resistance promised to be longer and even more fanatical given the great distances and the relative strength of the unbeaten Japanese armies in China and the homeland. The "Mobile Fleet" of 450 planes on 9 fast carriers plus 5 battleships with escorts had moved to a new interior position at Tawi Tawi in the secluded Celebes Sea to counter Nimitz's and MacArthur's drives into the Western Pacific. This preoccupation left Admiral Mountbatten relatively free to mount offensives in the Indian Ocean. From Trincomalee and Colombo, Ceylon, the Eastern Fleet's surface ships, subs and aircraft extended Allied control over the Bay of Bengal during the second half of 1944. They drove German and Japanese subs from Penang to new and safer bases at Soerabaja and Batavia, cut vital Japanese seaborne logistics between Singapore and Rangoon, mined enemy waters by air, and supplied a new and steady Sino-American-British ground offensive into Burma.

Without amphibious craft, however, Mountbatten could not undertake a seaborne offensive into Malaya, leaving the Japanese free to use the excellent base facilities at Singapore and to mount an effective offensive against southern China and Allied air bases there during the autumn. With Japan tenaciously contesting its continental imperial possessions, the main Allied thrust had to come from the Pacific.

Fooled by MacArthur's jumps up the New Guinea coast to Wakde and Biak in May and June 1944 as the principal Allied advance, the Japanese committed their land-based air prematurely, losing much of it to Army planes, and were thus surprised when the United States Fifth Fleet descended on the Marianas in mid-June. When American Marines stormed ashore at Saipan on June 15 (the same time that the great Normandy bridgehead was being established on the other side of the world), Japan had little choice but to use its fleet to try to dislodge the invaders. From Pearl Harbor, Admiral Nimitz spread out his huge Pacific Fleet to support this assault and the anticipated naval battle: Lockwood's submarines scouted the waters between Saipan and Tawi Tawi, while Spruance used Turner's amphibious vessels and 125,000 troops to take Saipan, supported by 7 older battleships, 11 cruisers, 8 escort carriers and many destroyers and covered by Mitscher's 15 fast carriers, their almost 1000 planes and screen of 7 fast battleships, 10 cruisers and 60 destroyers—the most powerful purely naval force ever assembled to that time! Admiral Soemu Toyoda, Combined Fleet commander in Tokyo, ordered his mobile force under Admiral Jisaburo Ozawa to take the 9 carriers from Tawi Tawi via the Philippines to a point 500 miles west of Saipan and to shuttle his 450 planes between the carriers and Guam and Tinian near Saipan, attacking the American fleet en route.

Spruance learned of the Japanese fleet sortie from his subs and dispersed his ships accordingly: the transports moved 200 miles to the eastward, the gunfire support ships formed a battle line on the west side of Saipan, and the fast carriers initially went westward in search of Ozawa on June 18. Lockwood's subs lost contact with the Japanese fleet, which Spruance then concluded—from his experience at Midway—would approach in two parts. Tactically trained as a battleship-oriented formalist and obsessed with the false notion that enemy surface ships could actually outflank his fast carriers, whose planes had an operating radius of 250 miles, the nonaviator Spruance rejected the advice of aviator Mitscher to send Task Force 58 westward to find Ozawa and instead recalled the carriers to remain offshore. On June 19, the Battle of the Philippine Sea began with Ozawa's planes shuttling in from their distant carriers, only to be annihilated by Mitscher's Hellcat fighters in the "Marianas Turkey Shoot," while Lockwood's subs caught up with

Ozawa's ships and attacked; *Albacore* mortally damaged the new carrier *Taiho,* and *Cavalla* sank the veteran *Shokaku.* The battle ended late on the 20th when Task Force 58 managed to get close enough to the retiring Ozawa to sink the carrier *Hiyo* with aerial torpedoes. The Japanese thus lost the battle, Saipan Island and three carriers, but not their fleet.

The American victory at the Philippine Sea forced open Japan's defenses. Marines and Army troops completed the conquest of Saipan Island and assaulted and took adjacent Guam and Tinian during July and August. All three islands were then converted into airfields for the new B-29 bombers, which began operating against Tokyo and other Japanese cities in November. MacArthur completed his drive up the north coast of New Guinea by the end of July, at which time the American Joint Chiefs of Staff yielded to his insistence on the liberation of the Philippines—a political promise he had made to the Filipinos upon the evacuation in early 1942. Strategically, this decision was generally sound, for the object of both Pacific drives was to reach the "Luzon bottleneck"—the narrow funnel between Luzon, Formosa and China through which all Japanese shipping had to pass from the oil-rich East Indies to the homeland. As preludes, on September 15 MacArthur's forces easily occupied Morotai in the Celebes area, and the same day Nimitz's Marines assaulted the fiercely contested Peleliu in the Palau group of the western Carolinas.

What was faulty about the American preparations to assault the Philippines—at Leyte Island in mid-October—lay in command relationships. Since the Philippines were in the Southwest Pacific theater, MacArthur commanded the operation, augmenting his Seventh Fleet with more ships from the Central Pacific; his strategic covering forces, however, were the fast carriers of what was now designated the Third Fleet under Admiral Halsey, who took his orders only from Nimitz and not MacArthur. This violation of unity of command symbolized the mutual suspicions between the Army and Navy, the latter fearing with good reason that MacArthur considered its warships expendable. The arrangement was all the more regrettable in light of the elaborate Japanese plans for the defense of the Philippines. Japanese naval construction now yielded three new carriers, but the "Marianas Turkey Shoot" had eliminated the last trained pilots for any of the carriers. Admiral Toyoda therefore planned to lure Halsey's fast carriers away from the beaches with four of Ozawa's nearly planeless carriers from Japan and to hasten two battleship forces from Borneo and Singapore to strike the shipping off Leyte in Halsey's absence. If this defensive strategy failed, the new *kamikaze*s were to be committed.

The Battle for Leyte Gulf, the last traditional sea battle in history, began with fast carrier and land-based air strikes on Japanese defenses early in October and reached its climax with the repulsing of the Japanese fleet sorties near the end of the month. On October 13 Halsey's carrier strikes on Formosa enticed Toyoda to commit his land-based naval air forces prematurely to action. Toyoda lost hundreds of planes (over 650 by the landing date) in savage air battles with the fast carrier fighters. On October 20 the first elements of 200,000 Army troops stormed ashore at Leyte, and the Japanese implemented their elaborate plan. Admiral Ozawa with his "Northern Force" of carriers, two half-battleships and escorts headed south from Kure in Japan, while Admiral Takeo Kurita and the "Center Force" of five battleships, twelve cruisers and several destroyers from Singapore headed for San Bernardino Strait via Palawan and the Sibuyan Sea, and the "Southern Force" of two battleships, one cruiser with destroyers under Admiral Shoji Nishimura (joined by a three-cruiser force from Japan) left Borneo via the Sulu Sea for Surigao Strait.

To bar the Japanese forces' passage through both straits and their concentration off Leyte, the Americans set new defensive positions. Kinkaid's Seventh Fleet old battleships, cruisers, destroyers and PT boats formed a line across Surigao Strait and virtually blew Nishimura's battleships *Yamashiro* and *Fuso* out of the water during the night of October 24–25. After two of Lockwood's subs sank two and disabled a third of Kurita's Center Force cruisers off Palawan, Halsey launched carrier air strikes against this force in the Sibuyan Sea during the 24th, sinking the superbattleship *Musashi* but losing the light fast carrier *Princeton* to a land-based bomber. Still, Kurita pressed on through San Bernardino Strait which he found uncovered, for Halsey had bitten for Ozawa's bait and had headed north after Ozawa's Northern Force without coordinating his movements with the Seventh Fleet at the beaches. After dawn on the 25th Halsey found the Northern Force off Cape Engaño, Luzon, and began sinking *Zuikaku* and the three lighter carriers. But simultaneously the Center Force suddenly appeared off Leyte-Samar and began shooting up American shipping, joined by the first land-based *kamikaze*s. In the melee, the Japanese sank two escort carriers, two destroyers and a destroyer escort before Kurita suddenly headed out to sea to engage what he thought was Halsey's fleet (really more escort carriers) instead of completing his task, which was basically a suicide mission. Kurita then ran back through San Bernardino Strait during the night before the returning Halsey could cut him off, though Halsey's planes did manage to sink one cruiser the next day. The beachhead at Leyte had been saved, despite the shortsightedness of Halsey and the divided command system that had victimized the American operation, and the Japanese surface fleet ceased to be a major strategic factor, even as a fleet-in-being.

Allied military, naval and air power spent the late autumn and winter of 1944–45 hammering away at Japan's Southeast Asian defenses and closing the Luzon bottleneck to begin the blockade of Japan. The intensive operations of late 1944 had forced Japanese merchant shipping into the restricted operating areas of Asian coastal waters from Singapore to the Tsushima Strait, thus providing easy targets for the many Allied submarines. By contrast, the radarless Japanese subs had so failed to support the surface fleet off the Marianas that all had been recalled during the late summer to be equipped with radar, only to fail again at Leyte and to be wasted thereafter supplying Army garrisons on bypassed islands. (The Japanese Army even took a turn at building its own subs.) Japan's convoy escort force, even with planes equipped with radar or magnetic detectors, still failed to stop the Allied submarine attrition of merchant shipping—some 2,000,000 tons lost to all causes, but mostly subs, between July and December. Indeed, American submarines sank four of Japan's five escort carriers between December 1943 and November 1944, in which latter month the *Archerfish* sank the giant 68,000-ton fast carrier *Shinano* out of Tokyo Bay and *Sealion* sank the battleship *Kongo* off China, and in December *Redfish* sank the new carrier *Unryu* in the East China Sea. Since mid-1943, British and Dutch subs had operated from Ceylon, but during the summer of 1944 they began basing at Fremantle, Australia, with the Americans—the shorter-range British boats to deploy in the Gulf of Siam and the southern Java Sea, the Dutch to patrol the waters of the East Indies, thus releasing the long-range American subs to cruise to the Philippines.

Savage *kamikaze* attacks could not prevent MacArthur's army from securing Leyte and taking Mindoro (south of Luzon) in December, then leapfrogging up to Lingayen Gulf on western Luzon with an amphibious assault in January 1945 which pushed inland to liberate Manila in February. Simultaneously, Allied forces pressed deeper into Burma, supported by several flotillas of British landing craft and gunships off Arakan, reopening the Burma Road in late January. That same month Third Fleet fast carriers swept through the South China Sea sinking merchant shipping, while the four fast carriers of the new British Pacific Fleet attacked Japanese oil refineries in Sumatra. Though the fighting continued on the ground in the Philippines for several months, the United States fleets operating out of Leyte-Samar and Subic Bay-Manila were able to close the Luzon bottleneck by the beginning of March, and the Japanese ended their attempts to run oil from Southeast Asia to the homeland. The blockade had begun.

With the Southeast Asian areas cut off from the Japanese homeland, their bypassed garrisons tried valiantly but unsuccessfully to repel Allied mopping-up attacks. On the mainland, a Japanese offensive in southern China began in January 1945 by taking several American airfields before being checked by the Chinese finally in May, while in March the Japanese eliminated the French government of Indochina and totally occupied the colony. The Burma front was defended tenaciously, especially against the British-Indian-African amphibious assaults mounted from Chittagong against several Burmese islands in January and then worked down the coast during the spring. When a British amphibious assault force arrived off Rangoon on May 2, it found the Japanese had evacuated three days before in fear of a British overland advance. The Japanese retreat into Thailand (Siam) now became general. In the outlying islands such as the Bismarcks, the Solomons and New Guinea, Australian ground forces began the mop-up, while Japanese troops throughout Indonesia fell back on Java, Sumatra and Borneo, the latter island being assaulted and occupied in various key places by Australian and American forces between May and July. In the meantime, Allied surface ships and subs swept through Indonesian waters, bombarding coastal positions and sinking all manner of Japanese shipping, including a light cruiser east of Java by an American sub wolf pack in April, one heavy cruiser in the Malacca Strait by British escort carrier planes and destroyers in mid-May and another in the Banda Strait by a British submarine early in June. Allied command of Indonesian waters enabled the British-led surface ships and subs to plunder interisland convoys, sweep mines from anticipated invasion areas (notably Singapore), bombard coastal positions and even send midget subs into Singapore late in July to damage a Japanese heavy cruiser there. So meager had Southeast Asian targets become that Allied submarine headquarters in the Southwest Pacific were moved from Fremantle to Subic Bay in May, where greater pressure could be applied to the main effort against the Japanese home islands.

Air-sea blockade of the island empire became the Allied strategy for finishing Japanese resistance in 1945, although Allied leaders decided to apply three other stratagems to assist, each, however, proving to be relatively superfluous. The need for a continental army had always been a main feature of maritime strategy, and China had not provided that force sufficiently; although the Chinese Communists had virtually neutralized the Japanese Army in North China, the Nationalists were not able to stop the Japanese offensive in South and Central China until May, so that the American landings in January had been at Luzon, bypassing Formosa and the Chinese coast. But now, at the Allied conference at Yalta in February, the Russians promised to redeploy their

Army from Europe (three months after Germany's defeat) to the Far East to fight the considerable Japanese armies in Manchuria. The second stratagem, largely the U. S. Army's, called for a massive Normandy-type amphibious invasion of Japan in the autumn of 1945. Third, if it was ready and tested, the atomic bomb would be used. But these devices were merely added weight to the crushing air-sea blockade of Japan during the spring and summer. Japan's economy and war machine would be absolutely destroyed: by strategic B-29 bombers from the Marianas blanketing Japanese industrial centers with incendiary bombs and mining Japanese coastal waters with aerial mines; by medium bombers and fighters from forward island bases at Iwo Jima and Okinawa, both to be taken by amphibious assault; by submarines encircling Japan; and by fast carrier air strikes and shore bombardments against the remnants of the Japanese fleet and coastal defenses. Japan's only viable defense lay in the *kamikaze,* which though ultimately unsuccessful made the Allies pay dearly for their efforts.

Assaults on Iwo Jima and Okinawa in February and April 1945 respectively proved difficult against the fanatical Japanese resistance from every quarter, but American forces nevertheless overcame it. Command of the sea became absolutely essential, and both beachheads could be isolated from any outside interference save for *kamikaze*s. That isolation was due to the mobility of the fast carriers, again renamed Task Force 58 under Mitscher and which were now totally supplied by at-sea logistical replenishment groups operating out of several of the many distant captured island bases. Again part of Spruance's Fifth Fleet, the carriers ranged along the Asian periphery attacking even Japanese ports and the fleet anchorage at Kure, though constantly plagued and damaged by *kamikaze*s. A welcome addition in March came in the form of 4 fast carriers of the British Pacific Fleet, giving Mitscher some 16 carriers at all times. The *kamikaze*s sank several smaller ships off Iwo, but Admiral Turner still landed and supported the Marines who conquered the island in the severest fighting of the Pacific War. The Okinawa operation was similar, though on a larger scale, with Turner landing 183,000 Army and Marine troops from the amphibious units of Spruance's nearly 1500 vessels during the first week of April. In addition to the usual *kamikaze*s, the Japanese even dispatched their superbattleship *Yamato,* one light cruiser and 8 destroyers on a suicide mission against the invasion beach. Mitscher's carrier bombers and torpedo planes intercepted these ships and sank them all, save 4 of the destroyers. *Kamikaze* attacks from land bases and fierce Japanese Army resistance on Okinawa dragged on till late June. The struggle cost the United States over 750 planes and 36 light vessels plus several hundred others damaged. But American carrier and land-based planes destroyed perhaps 8000 Japanese planes in the air and on the ground, enabling the Fifth Fleet to complete its ring of island bases around Japan.

While the B-29s pounded Japanese cities, their aerial mines and American submarines closed Japanese waters. During March, April and May the B-29s dropped five types of aerial mines—two of them, subsonic and pressure, unsweepable—into the Tsushima Strait between Japan and Korea, in the main shipping routes along Honshu and Kyushu, all major harbors and the Inland Sea. During June and July most of the 12,000 aerial mines of the campaign were sown, virtually halting all Japanese coastal shipping, while Navy planes from Okinawa were helping to mine South Korean waters. The last preserve of enemy shipping, the Sea of Japan, closed in June when a wolf pack of nine American subs entered it via the well-mined Tsushima Straits to sink twenty-seven merchantmen inside of seventeen days before escaping out via the northern La Pérouse Strait, losing one of their number to a patrol boat depth charge attack. More subs operated in the Sea of Japan over the next two months, but found targets exceedingly scarce. The reason was that, by the end of July, the mines and subs had clamped a totally effective blockade of all major Japanese ports. No ship could move in or out of any harbor, and the Japanese were powerless to sweep the mines. Of the 1,600,000 tons of Japanese merchant shipping sunk during 1945, about three quarters of it succumbed to the mine blockade. The strategic bombers between March and August nearly finished what was left of Japanese urban industry, so humbling Japan that starvation would soon face the Japanese civilians and home army girding for the expected invasion. In addition to millions of militia forces, in June and July Japan withdrew its last 3000 kamikazes, 5000 other planes and 3300 suicide boats to meet that attack.

As Japanese officials debated surrendering in accordance with an ultimatum issued by Allied leaders meeting at Potsdam in July new fury descended on the home islands. The American-British fast carrier armada, again redesignated the Third Fleet, under Halsey, began projecting naval power against strategic targets in Japan—the first instance in history of strategic bombardment on a massive scale from the sea. In addition to bombing industrial and transportation targets in Tokyo and other cities, the 1200 carrier planes struck the anchored Imperial fleet at Kure on the Inland Sea on July 24 and 28, sinking three battleships and three cruisers and severely damaging two of Japan's newest but immobilized carriers. Japan had only a few long-distance submarines with which to retaliate, and one of them, the I-58, managed to sink the unescorted American heavy cruiser Indianapolis in the Philippine Sea early in August. Third Fleet battleships and destroyers even shelled coastal industrial targets at point-blank range, and several typhoons ravaged the Japanese coast. Finally, between August 6 and 9, three sudden events convinced the Japanese government to surrender earlier than expected from the air-sea blockade alone: two United States B-29s dropped atomic bombs on Hiroshima and Nagasaki on the 6th and 9th respectively, and Soviet Russia declared war on Japan on the 8th— three months to the day of the German surrender (as agreed at Yalta).

The unexpected Russian attack had a profound impact on Japan, whose major armies in China had not been defeated in the field and thus had resisted all the surrender talk. The Red Army's mechanized thrust changed such obstinance, driving from Outer Mongolia, the Amur River region and Vladivostok through Manchuria and into North Korea in just one week, ferried and supported by the 8 monitors, 11 gunboats and 52 armored cutters of the Amur Flotilla. The Soviet Pacific Fleet of 2 heavy cruisers, 79 destroyer types and subchasers, 78 subs, 204 torpedo boats and over 1500 land-based naval aircraft plus naval infantry operated mostly from Vladivostok but also from Sovetskaya Gavan farther north and Petropavlovsk on Kamchatka to eliminate the northern outposts of the Japanese Empire. Initially, the Russians had determined to assume a defensive stance in their coastal regions, except for the thrust into Korea, but the virtual collapse of Japanese resistance in Manchuria led them to assume a makeshift offensive into southern Sakhalin and the northern Kuriles. Torpedo boats raided North Korean Pacific ports in preparation for several landings, only one of which met any resistance: on August 13, the same day that U. S. Third Fleet carrier planes made a heavy raid on Tokyo, Russian naval infantry assaulted and took the port of Chongjin without opposition, but then absorbed a Japanese counterattack on the ground before major air and sea reinforcements enabled a general advance inland over the next three days.

The Japanese government yielded to the Potsdam ultimatum on August 15, but resistance did not cease in this second Russo-Japanese war until the 19th. As Russian forces pushed overland on Sakhalin Island, amphibious assault forces landed without opposition at several points along the coast. The only major assault in the Kuriles took place on the 18th at Shimushu Island, but defending Japanese guns sank several landing craft and held the attacking forces to a small beachhead perimeter. Then the defenders joined the general Japanese capitulation by surrendering on the 23rd. The next day Paramushiro Island surrendered, and the Russians airlifted troops into Pyongyang, North Korea, whereupon the fighting ceased, and on succeeding days the Russians occupied all of the Kuriles and Sakhalin Island and Korea north of the 38th parallel. An airborne force also occupied the former Russian naval bases at Dairen and Port Arthur. Soviet amphibious operations had been successful if uneven, combining equally with the atomic bomb to hasten Japan's surrender by several weeks.

Japan's official surrender on September 2, 1945, on the deck of the American battleship *Missouri* in Tokyo Bay came primarily as the result of the air-sea blockade of over three years of fighting. American command of the sea and air had made an amphibious invasion unnecessary in this greatest naval war in history. Once Japan's offensive had been blunted at Midway and Guadalcanal in 1942, the Americans had won invaluable time during which to build and train a new fleet to replace the one lost at Pearl Harbor and after. In the meantime, the long-range American attack submarines mounted their growing *guerre de course* campaign against the Japanese merchant fleet, exemplified by such successful subs as the *Flasher* which alone sank 100,000 tons of enemy shipping and the *Tautog* which claimed twenty-six vessels; in all, the subs accounted for more than half of the some 8,500,000 tons of Japanese shipping lost. (Mines and planes sank the rest.) By the summer of 1943, when the new fleet began to arrive in the Pacific, it was an entirely new conception from the battleship-centered one of prewar years. Spearheaded by the Fast Carrier Task Force which seized and held command of the air and sea, the new amphibious forces could land Fleet Marine Forces ashore at various islands with relative impunity. From the newly won islands, the naval blockade and strategic bombardment closed off and defeated Japan in 1945. The naval battles of the Philippine Sea and Leyte Gulf, fought against inferior Japanese fleets, were almost anticlimactic, as were the atomic bombs and the Russian attack. The American logistic establishment, and its careful protection, proved vital to Allied success, in contrast to Japan's feeble efforts in both commerce protection and submarine *guerre de course*. Completely subordinated to a continental strategy in China, the Imperial Japanese Navy had assumed blue-water pretensions in an impossible attempt to maintain command of the vast Pacific waters. Even the more than 2400 *kamikaze* pilots who perished failed to delay the inevitable defeat.

World War II in Europe also witnessed probably the last traditional application of naval power in a massive worldwide war. The Anglo-American navies, with a superior industrial base and favorable geographic insularity, successfully neutralized the Italian and German surface fleets and early prevented any Axis invasion ever being mounted against the British or American homelands. But the U-boats had presented the same strategic problems in this war as in 1914–18, making the Battle of the Atlantic the key to the Allies' turning from the strategic defensive to the offensive, not possible until mid-1943 when Anglo-American industry produced advanced techniques and many new weapons. German and Italian subs claimed over 2800 merchant ships totalling nearly 14,500,000 tons but at the cost of no fewer than 781 German U-boats and a few Italian boats. As the escort carriers and land-based patrol planes neutralized the U-boats, so too did aviation lead in the blockade and bombing of Hitler's Europe, establishing the essential command of the sea and air prerequisite to amphibious assaults in North Africa, Sicily, Italy and France. Still, the principal Allied striking arm remained the Red Army, until 1944 armed and equipped mostly by long-suffering Allied transatlantic convoys and the unmolested North Pacific merchantmen. The Russian Navy, though crippled early in the fighting, recovered sufficiently to assist in the counteroffensives of 1943–45. Churchill's Mediterranean strategy, whatever its motive, did follow the ancient British maritime strategic practice of the indirect approach to whittle down enemy strength on the continental periphery prior to a major landing as at Normandy. From command of the sea followed continental invasion.

The Anglo-American atomic bomb and German V-2 rocket revolutionized warfare, but not to the often-mistaken end that all the naval lessons of World War II were rendered obsolete. True, battleship actions and fleet battles—even with carriers—lay in the past, but any future naval requirements short of atomic warfare would embrace the same techniques and weapons that had been used in this last great sea war.

BOOK SEVEN

Pax Americana

. . . Russian policy is really to push down southward and command what every writer and every thinking man from the most ancient times knows perfectly well is the great thing to possess, namely, "the command of the seas," and Russia, in my opinion, is determined upon possessing the "command of the seas."

—CAPTAIN BEDFORD PIM,
Royal Navy, 1884

As devastating as were the total wars of 1914–45 and the weaponry which they bequeathed to the future, the global cosmopolitanism which they had interrupted now resumed, to fashion a genuinely new era in human affairs which can be labeled—in the strategic realm at least—the *Pax Americana*. A better label or complete definition is not yet possible for lack of historical perspective, but as the second half of the twentieth century has progressed certain features of this new age have become obvious. A technologically based Western-oriented *Weltanschauung* has engulfed the world, awakening common human purpose to minimize if not eradicate the traditional dilemmas caused by political and economic divisiveness. Aerospace technology has led to rapid global communications via the jet-propelled aircraft (1945), commercial television (1948) and the orbital communications satellite (1965), and has propelled man beyond his own planet into space (1961) and

even to the surface of the moon (1969), in addition to sending un-
manned probes to the other planets of the solar system. Equally significant, rampant scientific industrialism led to the initiation in the
1960s of common efforts to check its excesses, both to the natural environment and to human beings. The outstanding example is the sudden
awareness that the unchecked pollution and exploitation of the oceans
and fresh-waterways will destroy them ecologically and thus eventually
also the human race. The overpopulation of the world, made possible by
modern science and medicine, has led to the general awareness of limitations in natural resources, food and energy sources—the traditional
and principal causes of imperialism and war.

The realization—in the wake of the atomic bomb and its successor
weapons—that total war is no longer politically viable or humanly
acceptable further binds together humanity to prevent its repetition. A
new worth of the individual has thus emerged to challenge the older
assumptions of imperial rule, industrial exploitation, economic and
ideological conflict, and even the demands of nationalism. A new human
vitality—not unlike that of the former thalassocracies—is being forged
on a global scale, but only as the older biases and values are gradually
—and ever so painfully—supplanted.

The generations of the *Pax Americana* have therefore witnessed the
demise of the old European global hegemony, the emergence of postwar superpowers in the United States and Soviet Russia, a host of newly
liberated former colonial states and new power centers in Western
Europe, Japan and the People's Republic of China. The excessive
nationalism of the powers gradually passed as their world-wars leaders
left power: Roosevelt in 1945, Stalin in 1953, Churchill in 1955, de
Gaulle in 1969 and Mao Tse-tung in 1976. In spite of the traditional
temptations of exerting armed force, their successors have matured with
an awareness of the new global and strategic realities that limit traditional
forms of imperialism, overt revolution and war. Great power diplomacy
has thus increasingly sought to restrict the exuberant and dangerous
nationalism of the emerging smaller nations, through bilateral cooperation, the forum of the United Nations created formally in 1945 and
through the international policing efforts primarily of the U. S. Navy.
Like its predecessors of Minos, Athens, Rome, Venice, Holland and
Britain, the United States found itself the only surviving maritime
power capable of maintaining order upon the seas, enforcing international law, and leading multilateral efforts to check piracy (especially
hijacking at sea and in the air) and smuggling (arms and drugs) and
in promoting weather reporting and rescue at sea. By its formidable
military strength at sea and in the air, the United States has balanced
the continental powers of Russia and China and policed the oceans of

the world. Strategically, then, the era can be aptly regarded as the *Pax Americana*.

As other nations have come to share American maritime prosperity, the oceans have assumed universal importance as not only avenues but sources of food and minerals. Since 1945 entire new fields of sea science and oceanic technology have arisen: underwater exploration and drilling for oil and gas; aquaculture ("sea farming") and general fishing; oceanography and marine biology; submersible craft, plus scuba and skin diving; underwater archeology and deep-water salvage; the recovery of early American manned spacecraft at sea; and even the possible domestication and military utilization of the pilot whale and especially the dolphin. But water pollution by American oil and chemical companies, overfishing by Russia, Japan and the Scandinavian countries and underwater weapons systems of the Russians and Americans have led to the need for restraints. International law has continued to promote free use of the seas, but the old 3-mile coastal limit of national territorial jurisdiction became woefully inadequate in the new age, as coastal nations disputed the economic uses of their offshore waters. Fishing "wars" involving gunboats have festered periodically, in spite of international agreements. As always, to be effective maritime laws must be enforced, with the United States and secondarily Russia having the only sizable navies to do it. In 1963 both nations banned underwater nuclear testing and seven years later prohibited nuclear and other massive weapons on the ocean floor ("seabed") beyond the 12-mile limit. But agreements by all nations using the oceans are necessary in this global age, initiated at the United Nations Conference on the Law of the Sea in 1958 and continued in long subsequent discussions culminating in the Law of the Sea Treaty of the 1980s which set offshore territorial sovereignty at 12 miles, established an exclusive economic zone extending 200 miles beyond the shore of each coastal nation, and arranged procedures of seabed mining. As in the past, however, international agreements depend upon the willingness of the participants to live up to them and especially upon the acquiescence of the great powers which are capable of commanding the seas.

Unfortunately, the breakdown of the wartime Alliance, the final collapse of the British and other European empires, and the growing ideological rift between the democratic-capitalistic United States of America and the communistic Union of Soviet Socialist Republics resulted in the Cold War which dangerously delayed mutual understanding and cooperation at sea or anywhere else. Both powers had been traditionally strategic continentalists, save for America's reliance upon the British naval shield, which simply evaporated in 1947. United in their anti-fascist crusade, neither superpower could immediately and realistically resolve postwar political boundaries and spheres of political, economic and strategic influence and thus created two armed camps during the late 1940s and 1950s which included Western Europe in the "Free World" camp and "Red" China in the "Communist bloc." This bipolar balance of power, heightened by the nuclear arms race, gradually disintegrated during the late 1950s and 1960s with the postwar recoveries and autonomous policies of Western Europe, China, Japan and the "Third World" developing nations in Africa, Latin America, the Middle East, South and Southeast Asia. Joined by economically and socially oppressed elements within American and Russian societies, these new nations inaugurated a "revolution of rising expectations" to advance the larger global cosmopolitanism and human rights movements. This effort by the "have-not" peoples against the "have" undermined the brief bipolarity of the 1950s and helped expose the strategic fallacy of the Russo-American Cold War, a fact dramatically demonstrated also by the Cuban missile confrontation of 1962. Soviet-American distrust and antagonism thus yielded, haltingly, to the universal desire to control the stockpiling of nuclear weapons.

As in the political sphere, strategic thought has also been reluctant to throw off its assumptions rooted in the era of the total world wars. The material strategists prevailed for over twenty years with their faith in the panacea of super machine weapons, fed by the false notion that strategic bombing had largely decided the outcome of World War II rather than the Herculean efforts of the United States and Royal navies and the Red Army. In fact, however, the nuclear-armed land- and carrier-based bombers, now capable of strategic bombardment, destroyed the last real distinctions between land and sea long-range artillery in the 1950s, at which time the intercontinental ballistic missile (ICBM) appeared, guaranteeing the eventual doom of the manned strategic delivery system. The hardened missile silo and missile-launching submerged submarine of the 1960s, plus the possibility of orbiting satellite weapons, created a "balance of terror" between Russia and America, both having the separate capability of annihilating the human race in a nuclear war many times over ("overkill"). Nevertheless, material strategists—typified by Herman Kahn and Robert S. McNamara in the United States—persisted in the belief of the viability of nuclear war by using computers, electronic war gaming and mathematical and economic analysis and games theory. Hoping for "damage limitation" in such a war, they ignored or minimized the inevitable massive destructiveness of a nuclear exchange to the transportation, communications and electrical power systems, much less social institutions, upon which modern society (and its weapons) depend for survival. They also seemed to forget the basic historical fact that the nations devastated by World Wars I and II had been able to recover only with the full economic aid of a major nation unscathed by the devastation, namely the United States, a refuge that would obviously be absent after any third world war.

The predominance of material strategists in the major powers thus characterized their defensive stances. The *ad hoc* military-industrial-management complexes of the two world wars thus became formalized, the modern superweapons having to be rigidly controlled in the delicate balance of terror. Expensive weapons had to be made "cost effective" by specialized "organization men" with their bureaucratic staffs of experts and advisers, and military men blended into the political decision-making process to guarantee the optimum use of these weapons. Such a hierarchical rigidity has perhaps been a key element in checking the outbreak of a nuclear World War III, but it has also had a stifling effect on the creative energies of the American and Russian people—and on their military and naval officers. Bureaucracy is by nature conservative, lethargic and self-perpetuating merely for its own ends, but survives as long as national public opinion can be convinced to accept and support it. Also, world opinion has been no small factor in reacting to the decisions of the two bureaucratic superpowers. The blind obedience of the American and Russian peoples that sustained the Cold War leaderships of the late 1940s and 1950s began to wane as the new realities became evident in the 1960s, partly the result of the new global cosmopolitanism which is antithetical to rigid authority but also because of the generally narrow and unimaginative strategic thought and policies of the "cold warriors" that led to confusion and loss of public confidence in them.

Historical strategy did indeed initially seem obsolete in the nuclear age, but not to the thinkers who quietly examined and discussed it. Indeed, the vast post-1945 literature on the phenomenon of war was merely a continuation of academic discussions of the 1930s embodied in such relatively new professional fields as military and diplomatic history and international relations. In most cases, the historical strategic analysts had been trained or had written in that decade and tended to be less impressed by nuclear weapons and machine-computed intellectual tools than were the material strategists. Stressing the continuity of historical experience as preached by their teachers Corbett and Mahan, these thinkers harkened back not only to Clausewitz but even to Themistocles in appreciating the traditional uses of maritime and imperial strategy and limited warfare, hence the efficacy of naval power. In this respect they have not been original in their theories, but by keeping active much thought on the importance of command of the sea, blockade, commerce warfare, amphibious operations and naval diplomacy they have provided alternatives for the nuclear determinism once it proved inadequate during the 1960s.

Significantly, few of the historical strategists have been active officers or policy advisers during the course of their writings, which have been counter to the anti-intellectual conservatism of their nuclear-dominated armed forces. But as retired officers, university professors and professional writers they have taught at war colleges, participated in the "think tank" activities of their material strategy colleagues, and generated much service discussion in their several professional journals. Among the leading historical pundits have been, in the United States, Admirals John D. Hayes and Henry E. Eccles, Professors Bernard Brodie, Robert E. Osgood, Oskar Morgenstern, Theodore Ropp and Anthony E. Sokol (formerly Austro-Hungarian Navy), and writers Herbert Rosinski (former German naval war college professor), Hanson W. Baldwin and George E. Lowe (both formerly U. S. Navy); in Russia Admirals V. A. Alafuzov and K. A. Stalbo and writers N. P. V'iunenko and D. I. Kornienko; in Germany, Admiral Friedrich Ruge; and in Britain, Admirals Sir Herbert Richmond (who died in 1953), Sir Anthony Buzzard and Sir Peter Gretton, Captain Stephen W. Roskill, Professor P. M. S. Blackett, Sir James Cable, and writer Sir Basil Liddell Hart. Interestingly, several army general officers have also shown a genuine appreciation for historical strategy, limited war and navies: British Field Marshal Viscount Montgomery of Alamein, American Generals Douglas MacArthur, Maxwell Taylor and James Gavin, and French General André Beaufre. Supporting the analyses of these individuals have been the treatises of many traditional historians, of which the present work is an example.

The historical strategists had little impact on political policies until the inadequacies of material nuclear strategy began to become evident. For Britain, Russia and the United States respectively, the eye-opening events were the Arab-Israeli crisis of 1956, the Cuban blockade of 1962 and the Vietnam War of 1965–73. Gradual buildup of limited war forces followed but without any systematic strategic rationales. National leaders, overawed by nuclear weapons, tended to see only irrelevance in the past and the more-lasting maritime principles expounded by Mahan and Corbett. One glaring example of ignorance was their neglect of Corbett's warning that limited war by a maritime power should be undertaken only when the battlefield can be geographically isolated—in modern parlance, interdicted—from outside supply and reinforcement by command of the sea. This proved possible in the British and American limited wars during the early 1950s in Malaya and Korea, peninsulas bordered mostly by water, but could never be possible in the one-coastline divided country of Vietnam on the continent of Asia; the United States paid dearly for its ignorance of this fact in the protracted Vietnam War. But as nuclear weaponry has become obviously useless in conflicts short of general war, the historical strategic arguments gain in acceptance.

Below the nuclear arena, therefore, the naval weapons of the *Pax Americana* have differed but little in their tactical roles from their predecessors; indeed, many veteran warships of World War II themselves have far outlived their originally expected longevity. Roles and missions of the basic warship types have not changed, save for the complete replacement of the battleship with the carrier and the advent of missilery. Modern nucleonics have made large-scale overseas invasions unlikely, but defense against underwater ballistic missile attack has required ever more sophisticated antisubmarine weapons systems. The ballistic missile sub and to a lesser extent the attack carrier have new missions of strategic bombardment, both being capital ships, the former for general war, the latter for limited war. But the increasing inadvisability of nuclear war has tended to remove missile subs from the equation of normal naval strategy and tactics and into a separate political status, while fear of escalation into such a conflict has acted as a check on the use of tactical nuclear weapons on carrier planes, antisub forces and patrol craft (and ground and air forces). Nevertheless, American and Soviet admirals seem to be thinking in unrealistic terms about another potential sea war, so that fleet tactical attack functions and defensive techniques tend to blend with the missilery of the nuclear realm. The attack carrier is defended by escorting vessels with surface-to-air (SAM) antiaircraft missiles, homing torpedoes and antisub rockets (ASROC). Carrier fighters use air-to-air missiles (AAM), carrier attack planes aerial bombs and air-to-surface missiles (ASM). Antiship surface-to-surface sub and shipborne "cruise" missiles (SSM) have replaced the naval gun except in shore bombardment. Offensive and defensive mine warfare craft and systems have grown in sophistication but unchanged in mission and delivery techniques. Attempts to counter the intercontinental and interrange ballistic missiles (ICBM, IRBM) in flight in the form of antiaircraft guns and missiles, notably the antiballistic missile (ABM) missile, have proved prohibitively expensive and tactically doubtful in effectiveness. Nuclear deterrence has thus depended on offensive missiles, with the rest of the missile inventory being employed in traditional naval missions.

Naval operations have been revolutionized by developments in propulsion and communications. Ship propulsion machinery has progressed into improved diesel engines and steam and gas turbines and the advent of nuclear reactors to replace conventional systems in providing steam power. The latter system, only gradually replacing oil, provides virtually unlimited cruising range at sustained high speeds (over 35 knots). Communication improvements have included more sophisticated radar and sonar, magnetic sub detectors, electronic countermeasures (ECM), navigational devices, radios using fixed antennae and communications satellites for short- and long-range circuits, and computers (dating from the U. S. Navy's IBM Naval Ordnance Research Computer, Norc, in 1954). Jet engines have gradually replaced most piston-engines on carrier fixed-wing aircraft; the multi-engine land-based long-range patrol plane (usually piston-driven) has supplanted the seaplane altogether; and the helicopter has emerged as a workhorse of multitudinous benefits. For warships, larger and heavier missiles, engines, aircraft and electronic equipment have meant increased displacements: the American nuclear carrier *Nimitz* 92,000 tons and the Soviet vertical launch carrier *Kiev* 38,000 tons; the Russian nuclear battle cruiser *Kirov,* 28,000 tons; the helicopter carriers of the *Iwo Jima* and *Moskow* classes 17,000 and 15,000 tons; the American guided missile nuclear-powered cruiser *Long Beach* and frigate *Truxton* 14,000 and 8000 tons respectively; Russian and American ballistic missile subs of 25,000 and 18,700 tons respectively; and destroyers of both nations in excess of 8000 tons, nearly as large as the newer missile cruisers.

Enlarged ship sizes and concurrently greater speeds have led to the development of revolutionary alternative concepts in fundamental ship design which minimize or eliminate altogether both the resistance of the waves to ship's hull and the skin friction due to the movement of the wetted surface. One is the hydrofoil, whereby the hull is lifted out of the water on small submerged wings as it speeds forward to some 50 knots. The Russians produced the first hydrofoil warships—inshore patrol craft and subchasers—in 1965. The other and more exciting invention is the hovercraft (air cushion vehicle; ground effect machine; surface skimmer), in which the vehicle rides on a cushion of air a few feet off the ground or water at speeds of over 80 knots at sea (but up to 300 miles per hour over monorails on land). Largely a British invention, the first experimental naval patrol hovercraft joined the Royal and United States navies in the late 1960s, but the type has endless possibilities especially as an amphibious vessel which can virtually ignore traditional natural obstacles. Experimentation in all facets of seaborne operations promises eventually to liberate the major navies from many traditional technological limitations—in the use of spacecraft for navigation, the increased placing of improved alloys such as aluminum and plastics in ship fittings or entire vessels (like the Royal Navy's all-plastic minehunter launched in 1972), new hull designs like the catamaran, strengthened deep submergence vehicles, vertical takeoff and landing aircraft (VTOL) and maybe even new uses for wind and sails. Given the accelerating pace of modern science and technology, major scientific breakthroughs can be expected henceforth in ship and aircraft design, assigning many old *and* new weapons systems to hasty obsolescence and causing naval planners to weigh ever more carefully their strategic priorities in building new weapons of exceedingly high cost.

Still, new technical weaponry has not significantly changed the functions of navies, a hard fact learned again by all fleets in the tumultuous early years of the *Pax Americana,* during which the much-vaunted super-weapons failed to offer strategic panaceas in a rapidly changing world. Men—as always—and not machines have remained the final arbiters in harnessing the sea for peaceful advantage or defensive purpose. Joined by women naval personnel on board some American warships from the early 1970s, seamen now enjoy the best health, pay, training and general living and working conditions of any sailors in history.

IMPERIAL COLLAPSE AND COLD WAR

The Russo-American Cold War developed as the direct result of the collapse of European hegemony in the world, but especially of the inability of Great Britain to maintain the strategic balance of power on the continent of Europe and to police the global sea lanes. The demise of the empires of Italy, Germany, Japan, Britain, Holland and France between 1943 and 1954 left political and economic vacuums to be filled either by the two new superpowers or the emerging small nations. Though cloaking their diplomatic policies in ideological rhetoric, the United States and the Soviet Union restored balance of power relationships in Europe and the Far East and returned to the historic practices of establishing spheres of influence. Instead of colonies, this type of imperialism assumed economic and ideological dimensions that led to involvement in limited "wars of national liberation" and ultimate ideological failure as the emerging former colonial peoples avoided American democracy and Russian communism in favor of unilateral courses. Under the umbrella of self-neutralizing nuclear weapons, the United States assumed the historical maritime strategic stance of the whale (eagle?) and Russia the historical continental posture of the elephant (bear?).

At first, the naval weapons that had survived World War II helped to demobilize the great armies but also fell victim to the awesomeness of atomic weapons, either in tests or by comparative obsolescence. The Japanese fleet was totally scrapped, while several German and Italian vessels avoided this fate by going into the Russian Navy, especially the newest U-boats which taught the Russians much. Under its nuclear monopoly, the United States further tested two atomic bombs in the Marshall Islands in July 1946 which sank or gutted two American fast carriers, one Japanese and three American battleships, one German and two American cruisers, an American sub and a destroyer. The ubiquitous mines could not be disposed of quite so easily, the Germans not ending their minesweeping operations until 1971 and American mines continuing to sink an occasional Japanese vessel even after that. The United States yielded its atomic monopoly to Russia in 1949, and both countries developed the hydrogen bomb in the early 1950s. But the Red Army defended the "iron curtain" across Central Europe and American land-sea-air power projected conventional power across the oceans of the world. The weapons of World War II thus continued to meet real strategic needs while the powers continued to explore and debate the utility of nuclear weapons.

The United States, despite its rapid postwar demobilization and reluctance to become oceanic policeman, had to look to its maritime posture which seriously deteriorated during the late 1940s. The unification of the armed forces—Army, Navy and a separate Air Force—under Secretary of Defense James V. Forrestal in 1947 led to a fierce interservice rivalry for the retrenched budget which favored nuclear weapons. Fearing obsolescence to new Air Force strategic bombers, the Navy under the leadership of Admiral Forrest P. Sherman (Nimitz's wartime planning officer) nevertheless survived and late in 1949 sent its first nuclear-armed attack planes to sea aboard its newest carriers. Postwar 1947 force levels were set at 15 fast attack carriers and 100 diesel-powered submarines. So the carrier gained a limited role as a nuclear deterrent, joined in the early 1950s by several cruisers and subs mounting Regulus surface-to-surface nuclear-tipped guided missiles. The similarly threatened U. S. Marine Corps turned to dispersed amphibious operations using the newly improved trooplifting helicopter from carrier and assault vessel decks. The American merchant marine, never a serious commercial competitor to the continental railroads, highway trailer trucks, canal-river barges of the Mississippi Valley or intracoastal oil tankers, lost its wartime inventory to the reserve "mothball" fleets, or by sale or gift to needy allied maritime nations in 1946–48. Most remaining American shippers escaped high maritime and longshoreman union wage and employment guarantees by shifting their registries to Panama, Liberia or Honduras, which would provide the necessary trade and profits. But these flag reductions hurt the American strategic posture dependent upon such vessels for sealift and logistical backup for its military forces during times of crisis. And the trained mercantile manpower followed the ships to the foreign registries. The new unified Military Sea Transportation Service of 1949 thus had too few and too old reserve supply ships, and the government refused to provide expensive new ones. Cutbacks in warships and overseas base facilities also reflected the false sense of security offered by nuclear weapons. The United States thus had no systematic preparations for fulfilling its new strategic missions and could respond to emergency situations only as they arose—a dangerous, shortsighted non-policy typical of the isolation-bound American people whose free strategic security behind two ocean barriers had in fact come to an abrupt end.

Soviet Russia had even less interest in maritime enterprises than its new enemy. Stalin reunified his armed forces under Red Army control in 1947 including a larger but still inferior land-based strategic air force. Russia's economic strength lay in the newly conquered "satellite" states of Eastern Europe and the interior regions of Russian Eurasia, all made more accessible to the industrial centers by an ever-growing railroad system and postwar improved inland waterway network of rivers and canals that connect Russia's five seas—the White and Baltic in the north, the Caspian, Sea of Azov and Black in the south—with traffic to and from the Russian Pacific coast going via the Trans-Sib Railway and Arctic Northern Sea Route. With such a strategic interior position, the Red Navy in the immediate postwar years adopted the same prewar stance of an active defense, but incorporated several tactical lessons of World War II. Stalin remained the chief proponent of this policy, even restoring the independent Navy Commissariat in 1950 (abolished again upon his death in 1953), though the major uniformed figure was Admiral Kuznetsov, wartime Navy commander-in-chief till 1947 and again 1950–55. This "fortress fleet" included all the familiar continental naval elements of inshore mines and torpedo craft, land-based naval aircraft, coastal fortifications and naval infantry for coast defense and submarines for commerce warfare. But Stalin sought more balance by building new and larger cruisers and destroyer leaders and by projecting for a few aircraft carriers. In addition to the older coastal regions, new Russian territorial gains from the war required such a buildup. The Baltic Sea returned to absolute Soviet control with the acquisition of the Karelian Isthmus to protect Leningrad, the absorption of Estonia, Latvia, Lithuania and East Prussia and its new ice-free Russian fleet base at Baltiisk (replacing Kronstadt), and the control and use of the ports of occupied Poland and East Germany. The Black Sea also came under Russian control with the absorption of Rumania and Bulgaria—with their ports—into the Soviet bloc. Russian naval defenses there were augmented by the Danube River Flotilla of patrol boats, minelayers and amphibious troops. Russia's Pacific defenses included all of Sakhalin Island, the Kuriles and Port Arthur, jointly operated with China, plus a very large river flotilla on the Amur River. From these coastal regions Russia's small merchant fleet, including several wartime American Lend Lease Liberty ships, operated into the oceans. But the Navy still remained an adjunct to the Army, its geographic outlets dominated by foreign powers at the Danish Sound, Turkish Dardanelles and Japanese Tsushima and La Pérouse straits.

The other European nations became minor naval powers generally dependent on the two superpowers for postwar recovery. The United States by disposing of its wartime merchant fleet over 1946–48 to Scandinavia, France, Holland and Italy restored their economies, and by its Cost-Sharing Ship Construction Program of the early 1950s provided them with light warships. Only Great Britain retained an independent blue-water naval posture, but in 1946–48 the new permanent Ministry of Defence cut back the Royal Navy's ships, planes and bases to give priority to the strategic bombers of the RAF. Without a nuclear role, the Navy in 1949 concentrated in qualitative research for its carrier-centered and antisub fleet, developing the angled deck, steam catapult and mirrored landing system for its carriers—improvements quickly imitated by the U. S. Navy. But in 1951 the British navy accepted the reality that it too had to depend on the American fleet in time of war. The United States and Britain supplied light surface ships and subs to several new or older underdeveloped nations; several of their light anti-sub carriers found their way eventually into the navies of France, Holland, Brazil, India, Argentina, Spain and Canada. By the same token, Russia eventually supplied smaller naval vessels to its satellites and to neutral powers like India and Indonesia.

The immediate Cold War issues focused on Russia's consolidation of its defensive frontiers during 1945–46. In addition to the assimilation of Eastern and parts of Central Europe into the Soviet sphere, the Russians made territorial and maritime demands on Iran and Turkey for control of the Dardanelles, for a Mediterranean base and for more influence in the Persian Gulf. Counteracting these moves, Britain began moving warships and troops into these regions, also to the Adriatic to sweep mines and support the Greeks against Communist guerrillas only to be taken under fire by Albanian shore batteries in May 1946. But Britain, economically prostrate from two world wars, could no longer restore the balance of power in these waters, and had to request first American assistance, then outright American leadership. Following the advice of Secretary Forrestal, President Harry Truman used naval demonstrations to help influence the Russians to stop their demands on Turkey and Iran. The battleship *Missouri* visited Istanbul (formerly Constantinople) and Athens during the spring of 1946, followed by the new carrier *Franklin D. Roosevelt* with its 123 planes during the summer, both relying on their mobile logistics rather than a base network, though the British made theirs available. American naval power redeployed to the Atlantic during 1946, nine attack carriers and three battleships, leaving six carriers and one battleship in the Pacific by the end of the year.

Europe's postwar economic plight became so severe that early in 1947 the British decided to quit both Greece and Turkey, and the new American Secretary of State, General George C. Marshall, advised Truman to go to the aid of all Europe, but especially Britain, Greece and Turkey. The Russians had counted on Western Europe's reliance on Polish coal, Rumanian oil and Hungarian wheat for its economic recovery, but in March 1947 Truman announced his "doctrine" to provide American economic aid and military equipment to Greece and Turkey and any other countries threatened by communism, followed in June by the Marshall Plan of massive American foreign aid to Europe. While Forrestal's warships demonstrated around European waters, Marshall's economic planners took the offensive by mobilizing the American merchant marine to transport vast quantities of grain and coal from the United States and oil from the Middle East to help the European economies recover. When Russia and her new satellites were invited to join this American-directed effort, Russia not only declined, but used Czechoslovakia's acceptance as part of the pretext to crush the few vestiges of independence left in that country early in 1948. America's large maritime effort to provide merchantmen for the economic and military sealift to Western Europe, supported by Anglo-American naval power, began to have immediate success. By 1948, Russian-American animosities had hardened, with Truman following a policy of "containment" of international communism—the work of George F. Kennan, along with Marshall and Forrestal—and Stalin cautiously probing for ways by which to dislodge the Americans from establishing an anti-Russian solidarity in Western Europe. And to reinforce the great success of the Marshall Plan, in June 1948 the U. S. Navy established the Sixth (Task) Fleet in the Mediterranean—a task force of two carriers, two or three cruisers, at least nine destroyers, and an attack transport with 1000 Marines embarked. Simultaneously, an American naval force was also stationed permanently in the Persian Gulf.

The American- and Soviet-led blocs quickly crystallized during 1948–49. When Communist Yugoslavia bolted from the Russian alliance in June 1948, Communist supply lines to the Greek guerrillas were severed, and the Greeks used American arms to crush the guerrillas by late 1949. Also in June 1948 the Russians blockaded "Western" Allied overland traffic through eastern Soviet-occupied Germany to the American, British and French sectors of Berlin. The Allies responded by stopping all trade with East Germany and instituting an airlift of cargo planes which frustrated Soviet designs within a year. Then, in April 1949, these Allies joined formally into the North Atlantic Treaty Organization (NATO): the United States, the United Kingdom, France, Canada, Belgium, the Netherlands, Luxembourg, Denmark, Norway, Iceland (independent since 1943), Italy and Portugal. Two years later Turkey and Greece joined, while neutral Sweden, Finland, Yugoslavia and Spain remained friendly, Spain even leasing naval and air bases to the United States in 1953. The political restoration of Germany also began, but in two separate parts belonging to the opposing camps. The creation of NATO effectively checked Russian expansionism in Europe and the Middle East, the general NATO deterrent based on superiority in the air and at sea rather than on the ground against the formidable Red Army. General Eisenhower, who became Supreme Allied Commander in 1950, simply never had enough troops from the economically strained NATO nations, so he relied on the American strategic air forces for nuclear intimidation and Allied naval forces to contain the Russians on the flanks of the European peninsula. The Supreme Allied Naval Commander—from 1951 always the commander of the U. S. Atlantic Fleet based at Norfolk, Virginia—controlled the Royal Navy-centered fleet units in the North Sea and the augmented U. S. Sixth Fleet in the Mediterranean. For their part, the Russians strengthened their "iron curtain" across Europe and looked elsewhere to test Allied strength.

Beyond Europe, the collapse of the old European empires offered many opportunities for superpower involvement, but these emerging peoples doggedly resisted further great power encroachments. The Latin American nations joined in the Organization of American States in 1947–48 and remained preoccupied with their endless internal turmoils. In the Middle East, Jewish Israel was formed after Britain's withdrawal in 1948 and then had to fight its Arab neighbors during 1948–49 to preserve its political integrity. Arab Egypt became a republic under Gamal Abdel Nasser in 1953–54 and pressed for British withdrawal from the Suez Canal, though the British hold on the Persian Gulf and the Trucial System did not change. North African Libya became independent in 1951 and two years later granted the United States and Britain rights to military bases there. In South Asia, Britain lost the heart of its Empire in 1947 when it granted independence to Hindu India and Moslem Pakistan, and a year later to Burma and Ceylon (Sri Lanka). During all these political dislocations, Anglo-American naval patrols provided a modicum of control. More importantly for the Cold War, Britain wisely promoted the friendship of her former colonies —often in the loose Commonwealth association—and all shared Britain's traditional desire to deter Russian economic and political incursions.

Southeast Asia created special problems due to the collapse of the Japanese Empire, the Chinese civil war and the determination of France and Holland to restore their colonies. The United States and Britain respectively granted independence to the Philippines (1946) and Malaya (1948), but would not withdraw their forces until political order was restored and the native Communist rebels crushed. American aid helped the Filipinos put down the Hukbalahaps by 1954, and between 1948 and 1954 the British and Malays waged a larger war against Communist guerrillas. While the British sealed off the Kra Isthmus from outside reinforcement in the Corbett manner, British ships bombarded enemy coastal positions, their planes provided tactical air support, and helicopters airlifted British, Malayan, African and Gurkha troops to defeat the guerrillas, though terrorist activities continued until 1960. Thailand (Siam) remained independent, while the Indonesian principalities of Sarawak, North Borneo and Brunei became British crown colonies at their own request in 1946. But the other Indonesians under Achmed Sukarno had to fight a five-year war against Dutch and British troops before the Dutch East Indies could become the Republic of Indonesia in 1950. Anglo-French-Chinese Nationalist forces alike battled the nationalist-Communist Vietminh forces of Ho Chi Minh in French Indochina in 1945–46 until the French assumed the burden alone. Laos and Cambodia accepted virtual independence within the new French Union in 1949 but the North Vietnamese fought on. French naval forces helped to pacify the Mekong River delta in the south in 1945–46, then based a new river fleet at Saigon to concentrate on the Red River in the north. As "river assault divisions," these forces used American-built landing craft, former Japanese junks, French river launches and occasional destroyer escorts or converted aviation tenders to battle crude Vietminh mines and ambushes in this largely ground-fought war which dragged on into the 1950s.

The Cold War in East Asia reflected the political vacuum left by the Japanese collapse. The United States filled it in the Western Pacific, establishing General MacArthur as Supreme Allied Commander over Japan, permanent naval bases there, at Okinawa and in the Philippines and a "trusteeship" over the hard-won Pacific islands. Russia could do little to challenge any of these moves, even agreed to evacuate Manchuria and shared Port Arthur and Dairen with the Chinese. But China remained wracked by civil war during the late 1940s between the Nationalists of Chiang Kai-shek and the Communists of Mao Tse-tung. American air and naval forces helped the Nationalists reoccupy the cities and ports of North China in 1945–46, with U. S. Marines guarding the rail lines between the cities as the Communists regained control of the countryside and even frustrated several American landings along the coast. Reluctant to become involved in this war, both the United States and Russia withdrew their forces from China in 1946–47 as Chinese Communist fortunes gradually improved. Early in 1949 Mao's forces captured Peking, then swept across the Yangtze and down the coast, driving Chiang's forces from the continent in December to Formosa, Hainan and several lesser offshore islands. In Korea, the Russians and Americans had occupied the peninsula jointly, divided at the 38th parallel, in 1945 and then had gradually withdrawn their forces. By the beginning of 1950, however, the Russians decided to test America's containment policy in Asia by instigating a North Korean attack on South Korea. In February 1950 Russia allied with Red China, which took Hainan Island in the Gulf of Tonkin in April, but which probably had no influence on Russia's Korean decision. The North Koreans crossed the 38th parallel on June 25, 1950, but the Russians had miscalculated, for two days later President Truman—with United Nations approval (possible because of the timely absence of the Russian delegation)—ordered the Seventh Fleet to support South Korea and to interpose itself in the Formosa Strait both to protect Chiang and to prevent any attempt he might make to return to the mainland. United Nations ground, air and sea forces would then go to Korea. With American forces returning to the continent to thwart another Russian parry, the Chinese Communists had good cause for alarm.

The Korean War (1950–53), the first real limited conflict of the Cold War and initial proving ground for the Russo-American struggle, proved frustrating for all participants, who were unable to practice their respective arts of war perfected during World War II. The United States, traditionally Army-oriented and now oversold on strategic bombing, found the thought of using nuclear weapons both politically risky—out of fear of escalating the struggle into a global World War III—and morally repulsive and therefore had to turn to the traditional weapons of maritime strategy so recently under political attack as obsolete: naval blockade and sealift, amphibious operations and the use of a conventional and relatively small ground army and tactical air forces. The new wrinkle was fighting for limited objectives, namely for only containing Communist aggression and not fighting for total victory, the full implications of which were painfully learned during the tenure of General MacArthur's command in the first year of the fighting. Still, the United States prosecuted its forced maritime strategy only halfheartedly. It pulled many World War II warships and Liberty and Victory merchant ships out of mothballs to meet the emergency. New construction was authorized for amphibious and mine warfare craft and aircraft carriers, but no new merchant fleet was laid down, while the projected new *Forrestal*-class attack carriers were built with a primarily nuclear deterrent capability in mind. Worse, the United States refused to accept its new strategic status as a maritime power by utilizing its belligerent rights under international law to institute a naval blockade. It did so through the United Nations against North Korea in July 1950, but rejected the pleas of MacArthur and Admiral Sherman to do the same against Red China when that country entered the war in November, following the dubious legalistic reasoning that the war was not declared and that it violated the old American belief in freedom of the seas. The United States thus failed to utilize the full extent of its ability to command the sea with a blockade that would have stopped trade to China by sea and taxed Russia's ability to supply China over the Trans-Sib Railway.

The Communists were also frustrated. Although Russian personnel did supervise the mining of Wonsan Harbor with Russian mines in July and August to prolong American minesweeping techniques, the miscalculation that America would not fight meant that the North Koreans could not be allowed to drive the Americans into the sea (as well they might have done in August) for fear that American recovery might be possible only with nuclear weapons. The Russians no doubt had apprehensions about the Chinese intervention early in the war because it ultimately meant that the Chinese would assume the larger direction of the war. Mao's Chinese could not exploit their superior guerrilla tactics in the mountainous, positional terrain of Korea and thus could rely only on their massive manpower. Before long, all three major powers and the United Nations accepted the inevitable realization that the fighting should be as limited as practicable and that the ultimate goal be a return to the *status quo antebellum.*

As the North Koreans drove into South Korea during the summer of 1950, the U. N. forces formed a defensive perimeter around Pusan and exploited the maritime advantages of their peninsular position to counterattack. South Korean, British, Australian and New Zealand naval forces operated on both sides of the peninsula below the 37th parallel and Anglo-American fast carriers shifted between west and east to strike North Korean targets and lines of communications above that parallel. Then, on September 15, the U. S. Seventh Fleet under Admiral C. Turner Joy landed General MacArthur with one Army and one Marine division at Inchon, supported by three fast and two escort carriers, to outflank the North Koreans just as Allied forces broke out from the Pusan perimeter. The pincers drove the Communists back into North Korea, after which U. N. forces landed at Wonsan on the east coast in October, the general offensive driving toward the Yalu River. With the seeming victory and the unification of Korea at hand, Allied fleet units began to withdraw.

But the new and still unsettled Chinese regime of Mao Tse-tung would no more tolerate any alien army on its Yalu River border than would Russia in Central Europe (or, for that matter, would have the United States along the Rio Grande), and at the end of October the Red Chinese began sending troops across the Yalu. The Red Chinese government could ill afford to weaken its effort at internal consolidation by the liquidation of its buffer in North Korea, where an unfriendly government might provide an avenue for the return of Chiang Kai-shek's Nationalists, whose troops both MacArthur and Chiang wanted, but were not allowed to use in the Korean War. The Chinese Communists were sensitive to all their borders, and in October began the rapid conquest of Tibet on the south. At sea, they were generally successful in eradicating the age-old problems of Chinese piracy, and they allowed the British to retain Hong Kong as their entrepôt to the West, but they repeatedly clashed with Japanese fishermen over territorial fishing rights. Red China had no real navy to speak of and was relatively powerless against the limited blockade imposed by Nationalist vessels. But her army and Russian-trained air force drove MacArthur out of North Korea during November, many U. N. units having to be evacuated by sea. Early in 1951 the Allies recovered and re-established the front around the 38th parallel, whereupon MacArthur was relieved of command in April for criticizing his superiors who would not allow him to bomb air and supply bases inside Manchurian China. Mao's government had restored its North Korean buffer and forced the United States to reassess its goals and strategy.

By 1951 both the United States and the Soviet Union had achieved a stalemate everywhere in the world and now sought to strengthen it without seeking further gains. The United States allied with Australia and New Zealand (ANZUS), began to rearm Japan and West Germany as anti-Russian buffers and restrained its military leaders from further offensives into North Korea. Russia organized its satellites in Europe, crushed East German uprisings in 1953 and carefully avoided further involvement in Korea. The Red Chinese worked to isolate that conflict by honoring certain Allied sanctuaries: the bases and air-sea operating areas in Japan, South Korea and even the Sea of Japan. The Allies did the same by staying away from Chinese waters and air space. Exploiting their command of the seas around North Korea, though, Allied naval forces blockaded the coast, used Wonsan Harbor as an advanced base, and swept enemy mines, while the fast carriers of Task Force 77 attacked Communist supply routes in North Korea. American naval jets were so inferior that they required cover from Air Force fighters against Russian-built Mig interceptors, but Navy-Marine close air support clearly excelled along the battle line, and battleship and destroyer fire assisted importantly along the coast. Despite the strategic limitations, Admiral J. J. Clark used his four Seventh Fleet fast carriers from May 1952 to the end of the war in July 1953 to knock out the great Suiho Dam complex on the Korean side of the Yalu, heavily damage industrial targets and pound enemy rear areas with his "Cherokee strikes," all of which helped force the Chinese to accept the armistice. The Seventh Fleet had atomic bombs by 1953, but never even contemplated using them.

The political and military settlements of 1953–54 generally stabilized great power relationships in the Far East and ended the first phase of the Cold War. The new administration of President Eisenhower made Nationalist China on Formosa an Allied bastion against Red China and refused to provide the French with an atomic strike from First Fleet carriers against Vietminh forces besieging the French garrison at Dien Bien Phu, French Indochina, in 1954. When that fortress surrendered in May, France quit Indochina altogether by granting outright independence to Laos, Cambodia and Vietnam, the latter being divided —by international agreement at Geneva—into North and South at the 17th parallel. The U. S. Navy helped the French evacuate North Vietnam and then increased its own support of South Vietnam. The armistices at the 17th and 38th parallels seemed transitory, like the nuclear arms balance, for the ideological struggle between democracy and communism and the anti-colonial revolts against European overlordship were mounting. To meet so many challenges and create a viable *Pax Americana,* American command of the sea remained essential.

NUCLEAR BALANCE AND CONFRONTATION

The decade following the Korean and Vietnam settlements and the first operational deployment of thermonuclear weapons was one of nuclear superpower competition, improved delivery systems and continuing political dislocations—not only in the demise of the old European empires, but in the beginning disintegration of the superficially monolithic "free world" and "Communist" blocs. The "Western" alliance system became the stronger of the two with several improvements: West Germany's admission into NATO in 1954–55; the creation of the European Economic Community (Common Market) in 1958; the founding of the Southeast Asia Treaty Organization (SEATO) of the United States, Britain, France, Australia, New Zealand, Thailand, Pakistan and the Philippines in 1954–55; and the forging of a Central Treaty Organization (CENTO) over 1955–59 among Britain, Turkey, Pakistan and Iran, all of which made unilateral defensive treaties with the United States. Though French intransigence weakened NATO and SEATO and though Cuba went Communist in 1959–61, American Presidents Eisenhower (1953–61) and John F. Kennedy (1961–63) asserted firm if uneven leadership over the Western nations. The "Eastern" bloc had less success following the death of Stalin in 1953 and the rise to power of Nikita Khrushchev in Russia by 1956. The Soviet government organized its European satellites under the Warsaw Pact of 1955—Russia, East Germany, Poland, Czechoslovakia, Hungary, Rumania, Bulgaria and Albania—but had to suppress riots in Poland and a general uprising in Hungary in 1956. This seeming Russian weakness and Khrushchev's apparent desire to peacefully "coexist" with the West led to Chinese Communist separatism from 1957 and a final break in 1960. Russia then recalled its technical advisers from China, which grew increasingly militant toward the United States and neutral India and in 1961 won over Albania to its side. Thus the brief Communist monolith melted away even as the Western alliances appeared to strengthen.

Nevertheless, the Cold War went on, with the United States leading in technological weaponry. Nuclear energy was harnessed for ship power plants under the aegis of Admiral Hyman G. Rickover, first in the submarine *Nautilus* in 1955 and the carrier *Enterprise* in 1961. The Navy tried to share the offensive nuclear attack role of the Air Force with an unsuccessful jet seaplane patrol bomber and the very successful 60,000-ton *Forrestal*-class carriers from 1955 using long-range A3D strike aircraft, the same year that Admiral William F. Raborn, Jr., began to develop the Polaris solid-fuel ballistic missile. With this weapon system, launched underwater and navigated by extremely accurate inertial guidance systems, the Navy fought off Air Force attempts to obtain operational control to fashion this ultimate offensive deterrent of the Cold War—alongside the land-based missile, over which it had the advantage of mobility and the ability to hide. Converting 5 of the first teardrop-shaped high-speed *Skipjack*-class nuclear-powered attack subs into "Polaris" boats, the Navy commissioned and deployed the first in 1960, the 5900-ton *George Washington* (SSBN-598), armed with 16 A-1 Polaris missiles with ranges up to 1400 miles. Five specially designed Polaris subs of the 6900-ton *Ethan Allen*-class followed in 1961–63, each with A-2 Polaris missiles with a range of 1700 miles. Then, between 1963 and 1967, 31 Polaris subs of the 7300-ton *Lafayette*-class joined the fleet, mounting A-2 and 2900-mile-ranged A-3 missiles. With unlimited cruising ranges, these vessels were based at New London, Connecticut; Charleston, South Carolina; Holy Loch, Scotland; Rota, Spain; Pearl Harbor; and Apra Harbor, Guam. American sea-based missiles on 41 boats thus ringed Soviet Russia by the mid-1960s.

The Soviet Union, although superior in numbers of conventional attack subs, responded only slowly to the American missile challenge. The Russians of course pioneered with the missile-launched Sputnik

heavy payload satellite and the hardened ICBM, but had greater difficulty reducing such large payloads to fit their subs. Finally, however,
during the 1960s, the Russians placed 2 to 4 guided or ballistic surface-
launched missiles on several of their conventional boats and inaugurated
nuclear power and the teardrop hulls in some 100 new boats, each
displacing upwards of 3500 tons with up to 8 ballistic missile tubes.
The Russians finally matched the Polaris boat in 1968 with the "Y"
class ("Yankee I"-NATO designation), armed with 16 Sawfly underwater missiles with initial ranges to 1500 miles. Lesser boats carried
the shorter-ranged Sark and Serb missiles, 375 and 1250 miles respectively. Practically a decade behind the United States in the development of ICBM subs, the Russian Navy thus posed its greatest
threat in conventional torpedo-armed attack boats, especially the 150
1000-ton diesel-powered medium-ranged "Whiskey" class boats of the
1950s. But the Russians kept turning out so many new, improved subs
that by the 1970s they had a grand total of some 375 of all types in
commission!

American and NATO naval efforts thus concentrated on antisub
warfare (ASW) and antiaircraft (AAW) protection against land-based
Russian aircraft. The United States between 1953 and 1963 continued
to build *Forrestal* and larger attack carriers with their heavy defensive
jet fighters, converting most of the older *Essex*es to ASW work with
piston-driven S2F Trackers and HSS helicopters, while Britain completed four new attack carriers and France two. Following the last
battleships into retirement, antiaircraft guns yielded to surface-to-air
missiles on all surface ships. Joining ASW carriers and their escorts
were seaplanes, land-based patrol planes and hunter-killer subs, both
diesel and nuclear-powered, in the British and French navies as well as
the American. For amphibious operations, the U. S. Navy led the
other two and lesser Western navies by utilizing the helicopter on
board special assault carriers ("commando," British) to provide vertical
trooplift envelopment complementary to conventional landing craft.
The U. S. Marines officially adopted this new doctrine in 1955 and six
years later centered their air-sea assault on the Fast Amphibious Force
of one helicopter carrier and four LSDs (landing ship, dock—carrying
helicopters, landing craft and Marines). Unable to match such a surface capability, the Russians in 1957–61 turned to a *jeune école*
philosophy—surface-to-surface tactical guided "cruise" missiles (capable of being nuclear-tipped) on board cruisers, destroyers, subs and
patrol boats of the *Komar* and *Osa* classes: the Strela with ranges up to
112 miles, its successor Shaddock to 248 miles, and the 12-18 mile
short-ranged Styx. Phasing out their cumbersome surface-to-surface

Regulus missile, the United States and allied navies had to rely on carrier aircraft until they could develop their own similar tactical missiles.

Not surprisingly, missiles and nuclear weaponry led to highly rigid political-military controls and a preoccupation with this dimension of potential conflict. In the United States, the Defense Department was streamlined in three reorganizations between 1953 and 1965 and overcentralized under Secretary of Defense Robert S. McNamara, 1961–68. As virtual deputy commander-in-chief to the President and with his own staff of "whiz kid" economics and management experts, he bypassed the uniformed Joint Chiefs of Staff to give direct orders to Polaris boat commanders and those of the Air Force's Strategic Air Command, a necessity imposed by the nature of atomic weapons. Internally, the U. S. Navy followed these trends by centralizing authority in the Chief of Naval Operations, electronically simulating its war gaming at the Naval War College from 1957, giving Admiral Rickover virtual dictatorial authority over the nuclear power program, and in 1962 creating its own "think tank" of experts, the Center for Naval Analyses, the logical outgrowth of operations research. Such changes were followed and influenced by the British, whose RAF (Bomber Command) was centralized under defense minister Duncan Sandys (1957–59) and a Unified Ministry of Defence in 1964. Russia did the same, Marshal Grigori Zhukov (1955–57) controlling the Long Range Air Force and Strategic Rocket Forces.

The emphasis on strategic air forces led to attempts in all three nations to downgrade seaborne strategic and tactical forces. That these were unsuccessful was due to the ICBM boats, persistent demands for warships in limited war situations and the dogged leadership of three dynamic navy chiefs—Admiral Arleigh A. Burke, American Chief of Naval Operations from 1955 to 1961; Admiral Sergei G. Gorshkov, Soviet Commander-in-Chief of the Navy from 1955 into the 1980s; and Admiral Earl Mountbatten, British First Sea Lord 1955 to 1959 and thereafter Chief of Defence Staff. The sheer expense of especially aircraft carriers led to the criticism of them: in 1963 the demand for a superior American carrier fighter resulted in McNamara's driving Burke's brilliant successor, Admiral George W. Anderson, out of office; in Britain Sandys' 1957 Defence White Paper ended carrier construction; and in Russia Stalin's successors ended the independent naval ministry and fostered the return to a sub-centered fleet over a balanced fleet which might have included carriers. Especially in the United States, nuclear proponents under Secretary of State John Foster Dulles and then McNamara placed primary faith in nuclear deterrence through such doctrinal slogans as "massive retaliation," "counterforce" and "controlled thermonuclear war." But late in the 1950s military theorists like Bernard Brodie and Henry Kissinger began to recognize the utility of non-nuclear conventional forces, and between 1957 and 1963 American strategists evolved "balanced forces" capable of a "controlled and flexible response" to diplomatic crises. But the strategic material determinism exemplified by McNamara, Sandys and Zhukov resisted real non-nuclear development—until actual political realities demanded it.

The strategic balance focused on Europe during the 1950s, where NATO and the Warsaw Pact alliance remained precariously stalemated. The former controlled the Danish Sound, North Sea and North Atlantic, and the Russians confined their surface navy to the Baltic and even returned Arctic Porkkala to Finland. The West continued to use its nuclear weapons to deter the Red Army on the continent, where the Russians erected the Berlin wall in 1961 after a series of Cold War diplomatic crises. NATO vessels also patrolled the Mediterranean, where the Suez crisis of 1956 involved the Russian-backed Arab world led by Egypt and the Anglo-French-supported Israelis. When Nasser nationalized the Suez Canal, with Israel desiring free access to Eilat on the Red Sea Gulf of Aqaba, England, France and Israel in October launched an attack on Egypt without consulting the former two nations' major NATO ally, the United States. Neutralizing Egyptian naval units in the Eastern Mediterranean and Red seas, the allies mounted an amphibious invasion from Cyprus, Malta and Marseilles to take Port Said and the Canal. Anglo-French carriers, a French battleship and other escort and bombardment ships supported airborne-seaborne landings in the delta of the Nile early in November. World opinion and U.S.-U.N. pressure forced a cease-fire, but the war had intensified the Cold War. Under a new "Eisenhower doctrine," the U. S. Sixth Fleet escorted Israeli merchantmen through the Gulf of Aqaba, demonstrated off Jordan in 1957 and the next year landed Marines at Beirut, Lebanon, to prevent the institution of Communist government there. When Iraq, which quit the Western alliance in 1959, attempted to annex Kuwait in the Persian Gulf in 1961, two British carriers and Marine Commandos intervened. So conventional Anglo-American naval forces prevented Middle Eastern states from actively siding with the Soviet Union—a tactical lesson not lost to the Russians.

Western policy in the Mediterranean did, however, discredit the NATO powers there and hastened the collapse of the French Union in Africa. Tunisia got its independence in 1956, but allowed France to retain its military bases. In 1961 Tunisian forces attacked the French garrisons, whereupon a French carrier-cruiser force fought its way into Bizerte, only to be withdrawn after U.N. mediation the next year, leaving the French in control only of their air bases there. A

French Army mutiny failed to save Algeria, which got its independence in 1962, and Franco-Spanish-American forces withdrew from Morocco between 1955 and 1964. The British joined the French in granting independence to their colonies in tropical Africa, though generally maintaining economic and some military ties: British Ghana and Nigeria in 1957 and 1960, French Madagascar (Malagasy Republic) in 1960, the Belgian Congo in 1960, British Tanganyika and Zanzibar in 1961 and 1963 (combined into Tanzania, 1964) and British Kenya in 1963. These movements were far from bloodless, but the wars were generally internal and not against the European powers or part of the Cold War struggle. Racially torn South Africa left the Commonwealth in 1961 but guaranteed Britain's use of Simonstown in time of war. Otherwise, these nationalistic wars and states successfully resisted the meddling of the Cold War antagonists.

Similarly, the Far East situation reflected wars of national liberation that were only fortuitously connected to the Russo-American confrontation. Russia even gave up Port Arthur in the mid-1950s to Red China, while Britain steadily reduced its naval commitment east of Suez. This left the United States to enforce the Korean and Vietnamese armistices and to contain communism to mainland China and to begin the gradual development in 1954 of "self-defense forces" in Japan. The Seventh Fleet protected the Nationalist Chinese on Formosa and tried to minimize the skirmishing between the two Chinese governments in that region. The Red Chinese Navy, headed by former Army marshal Admiral Hsiao Ching-kuang, began growing into a respectable coast defense force after 1953 with Russian submarines, destroyers, subchasers, minesweepers, torpedo boats and naval advisers who in 1956 helped China begin building "Whiskey" class subs. This fledgling navy, however, could deal only with minor navies and not the American. Early in 1955 American Seventh Fleet units led by no fewer than five carriers effortlessly evacuated Chinese Nationalists from the disputed offshore Tachen Islands, and in the summer of 1958 a Communist attempt to blockade Nationalist Quemoy Island with artillery bombardments was thwarted by American warships escorting troop convoys to Quemoy. By 1960, when the Russians withdrew their aid to Red China, the Seventh Fleet kept three carriers on separate patrols in the Western Pacific as the warring Chinese factions continued to spar with raids and shellings. Admiral Hsiao's navy was sufficiently established, however, to continue its growth through home construction of existing types plus thousands of motorized junks and several hundred land-based naval fighters and torpedo-bombers.

American forces also had to police the sea lanes of South and Southeast Asia as the new nations there flirted with Russian and Chinese communism. India, relying on British naval aid, tried to remain neutral and expelled the colonial Portuguese from Goa and Diu in 1961, but after China attacked the Indian border the next year India began to seek active military assistance from Russia. This move offended the United States, which was allied with Pakistan, India's antagonistic but weak neighbor. In South Vietnam, American advisers replaced the French after 1954, and five years later the United States increased its aid against the growing militancy of Communist North Vietnam under Ho Chi Minh and of the Communist Pathet Lao in Laos. The Kennedy administration used Seventh Fleet units in 1961–62 to help the South Vietnamese Navy patrol its coast against Communist guerrillas, while ground forces assisted Laos and Thailand. In Indonesia, Sukarno in 1957 began harassing the Dutch in their last Asian colony of West New Guinea, leading in 1960 to the dispatch of Holland's one carrier with three destroyers to the region but with no marked success. Sukarno demanded that the Dutch leave New Guinea and in 1962 stepped up his infiltration, though in January Dutch naval vessels sank one of three Indonesian torpedo boats trying to land guerrillas. By August, the retrenching Netherlands agreed to Sukarno's demands and began to withdraw. Emboldened by this success, in December Sukarno turned on Malaya, whose anti-Communist struggle had only finally ended two years before. The emerging Federation of Malaysia, officially proclaimed in 1963 and comprising Malaya, North Borneo, Sarawak, Sabah and Singapore, appealed to Britain, which sent one commando carrier with its Marines to preserve the Malaysian frontier near the last protectorate of Brunei, Borneo. Aside from these minor naval and advisory efforts against insurgents in South Vietnam and Malaysia, by 1963 Southeast Asia was relatively tranquil.

The same was true of Latin America, save for American intervention in Guatemala in 1954, until Fidel Castro turned Cuba into a pro-Russian Communist state and made the Caribbean into a Cold War battle front with the Cuban missile crisis. American and several Latin American warships made anti-guerrilla patrols in 1959–61, culminating in an abortive American-supported anti-Castro amphibious assault at the Bay of Pigs on Cuba's south coast in April 1961 that failed for lack of naval and air support. The next year American reconnaissance planes discovered that the Russians were erecting interrange ballistic missiles in Cuba, leading President Kennedy to meet the challenge of Chairman Khrushchev. Dismissing the advice of his military advisers to invade Cuba or bomb the missile sites and thus possibly trigger a nuclear World War III, he decided to use indirect means, thereby giving the Soviet Union a chance to understand American determination and thus to back down.

After obtaining the support of NATO and the Organization of

American States to "quarantine" Soviet flag and chartered vessels from taking more missiles into Cuba, Kennedy on October 24, 1962, ordered the reinforced Atlantic Fleet of 183 ships, including eight aircraft carriers and over 30,000 embarked Marines, into Caribbean waters, where they were joined by token naval units from Argentina, Venezuela and the Dominican Republic. With absolute command of the sea, the United States thus added a new aspect to international law in the nuclear age, namely, the use of limited coercive force to interdict alien weapons deployment dangerous to American and hemispheric security and to the delicate equilibrium of the global balance of power. No actual force had to be used, although American antisubmarine units forced six Russian submarines to the surface in waters adjacent to the quarantine. Kennedy personally directed the strategic aspects of this blockade, while Secretary McNamara interfered with Admiral Anderson and the established Navy chain of command to deal with the tactical aspects. But, on balance, the operation was an unqualified success. The two superpowers had come to the brink of nuclear war, whence Khrushchev realized his miscalculation and agreed to withdraw Russian missiles and bombers from Cuba, and Kennedy agreed to end the blockade. In mid-November, after American warships observed the withdrawal, the quarantine was lifted, and the crisis ended. Both sides had relearned the efficacy of the traditional uses of naval power in diplomacy and political strategy.

The Cuban confrontation conclusively demonstrated the folly of nuclear saber-rattling as a tool of international rivalry and convinced the superpowers to cooperate in promoting arms control. In April 1963 a telecircuit "hot line" was opened between the Kremlin and the White House, followed in July by the Limited Nuclear Test Ban Treaty that ended testing in the atmosphere, space and underwater (leaving only underground). Antarctica and outer space were denuclearized altogether in 1959 and 1966, and the Geneva Disarmament Conference began to consider overall arms control in 1962. Many of the fears of both sides about a possible "missile gap" evaporated with the advent of highly accurate intelligence-gathering earth satellites that eliminated the guesswork from the arms race, and two new superpower leaders emerged in the mid-1960s to hasten the reduction of Russo-American tensions, Lyndon B. Johnson and Leonid I. Brezhnev. The need became all the greater with the increased quantity and quality of ICBMs. The U. S. Navy began replacing its A-1 and A-2 Polaris missiles with the A-3 and the more accurate C-3 Poseidon, each housing the multiple independently targeted reentry vehicle (MIRV) of some ten to fourteen separate H-bomb warheads. Deployment of the Poseidon began in 1971. Russia, which shifted its primary naval targets from American carriers (with their A3D bombers) to Polaris boats in 1964, kept pace by increasing the range of its Sawfly ICBMs to 3500 miles by the 1970s. Underwater sub detection proved difficult, and the defensive ABM system expensive and doubtfully effective, so that offensive deterrence seemed to be the key to the arms race and any arms controls.

Russia and the United States had additional pressures from new nuclear nations. Great Britain developed its own nuclear weapons in the 1950s and the next decade purchased A-3 Polaris missiles for its five new *Resolution*-class ICBM subs to augment NATO's nuclear deterrent. West Germany and Italy also depended on American technology, all the NATO powers rejected the Multilateral Nuclear (naval) Force in the early 1960s, and in 1960 France bolted from the NATO defensive system. Developing its own nuclear weapons, France laid down four *Redoutable*-class nuclear subs each with sixteen Polaris-type ICBMs ranging to 1250 miles for service in the 1970s. China also exploded its own nuclear devices in the 1960s and considered nuclear-powered missile subs. To check the further spread of nuclear weapons, the United States and Russia with some sixty other countries signed the Nuclear Non-Proliferation Treaty in 1968. China and France avoided all nuclear arms controls, and Japan, West Germany, India and Israel continued to be apprehensive about them. Nevertheless, the two superpowers forged ahead with the Seabed Treaty of 1970 prohibiting nuclear weapons on the ocean floor and with the abolition of chemical-biological weapons the next year.

But the most important step toward nuclear arms control was the Strategic Arms Limitations Talks (SALT) initiated in November 1969 and held at neutral Vienna and Helsinki. These culminated in a Russo-American arms limitation treaty in May 1972 in which the United States sacrificed its lead in nuclear weapons—if "lead" is an appropriate notion after "overkill" has been reached—in favor of parity, although holding superiority in H-bombs within its MIRV missiles. The two-part agreement limited each nation to 100 defensive ABMs around Washington and Moscow and another 100 at another site and froze the number of land-based ICBMs and ICBM-launching subs. This meant 42 Russian and 41 American ballistic missile subs by the mid-1970s (or ultimately no more than 62 and 44 respectively), a majority of American missiles being MIRV-tipped, plus some 1000 land-based American ICBMs and 1600 for Russia, the MIRV giving the United States a lead of 5700 to 2500 H-bomb warheads. All this was exclusive of less-important manned strategic bombers and tactical nuclear weapons. (American B-52 bomber bases became so vulnerable to Soviet missile subs that early in 1972 the B-52s were redeployed throughout the continental United States.)

Strategically, America and Russia had at last officially acknowledged the universal danger of nuclear weapons and their lack of utility in international competition and military rivalry. The possibility of nuclear war was importantly reduced, at least for the five years of this initial pact, with each superpower seeking to impose its policy goals at lower levels, using traditional strategic and tactical tools, not the least of which is conventional naval power.

RUSSO-AMERICAN NAVAL RIVALRY

The revealed unviability of nuclear Cold War, especially between the Suez and Cuban crises of 1956 and 1962, along with American carrier and submarine developments and the defection of Albania, convinced the Soviet Union to undertake blue-water naval construction to challenge the U. S. Navy's supremacy in the *Pax Americana*. The historic role of command of the sea thus remained with conventional naval forces and not ICBM vessels as the Russo-American rivalry reached into the maritime sphere in the 1960s. Nevertheless, the U. S. Navy has remained an offensive maritime force and the Red Navy a continental fleet subordinated to the Army. The United States has enjoyed at-sea logistical mobility, an overseas network of bases, amphibious and general surface superiority and a sophisticated balanced limited war fleet centered around its attack carriers. The Navy has thus become the senior service in the United States, forming the basis of a traditional maritime strategy, with the U. S. Army being reduced to a professional limited war force alongside the smaller Marine Corps and land-based tactical Air Force. The huge Red Army and Chinese People's Army can only be contained by nuclear forces, so that American defensive policy has gradually become ocean-oriented and committed to reducing the risks of escalation into the nuclear sphere. Russia has followed the precedents of many continental forebears in trying to transcend its geographic priorities and limitations by imitating America's blue-water strategy. Much of the Russo-American rivalry in the decades following the Cuban missile crisis can thus be understood as two superpowers trying to appreciate the ramifications of these strategies.

The nuclear balance of terror in the naval sphere has not changed in its essentials. Though the 1970s SALT arms ratios have continued in spirit if not always officially between the two superpowers, both have improved the quality of their sea-based strategic missile systems through replacement programs and both remain ready to increase their submarine inventories quantitatively should SALT fail completely. In conventional naval weapons, the Russians have steadily expanded their capability since the Cuban crisis, fashioning a surface navy generally along American lines, technologically if not strategically. And yet, in spite of this naval arms race—slower in periods of "detente", accelerated during renewed "cold warring"—both nations must exert continuing control over their respective spheres of influence, against the resentment and nationalistic aspirations of their allies and subject peoples and the Third World nations.

The ballistic missile-carrying nuclear-powered submarine deterrent has sharpened with new and ever more sophisticated boats and missiles. For the United States Navy, during the 1980s the new Trident I C-4 MIRVed ICBMs with a range of 4500 miles have replaced the older Polaris missiles, followed a decade later by the Trident II D-5 of 7000 mile ranges. The first Polaris subs were retired in favor of the big new 18,700-ton 24-missile *Ohio*-class Trident subs in the 1980s. The Russian navy began replacing its 16-missile Yankee class ballistic missile subs in the 1970s with 16-missile Delta III boats and in the 1980s the giant, fast (43 knots submerged), deep-diving (to 2000 feet) 25,000-ton, 20-missile Typhoons—the largest submarine ever built. The Russian subs carry SS-N-20 ICBMs, MIRVs with ranges over 4000 miles. By 1983 the Soviet Union had 85 ballistic missile subs to America's 33, the latter's deadlier with more warheads. The gap will narrow with Russia's ultimate aim of 62 modern boats as agreed by SALT.

In the conventional sphere, the Soviet navy has continued to take on blue-water appearances as it assumes ever-increasing balance in ship types during the long tenure of Admiral Gorshkov's leadership. The principal targets of Russian attack submarines and surface ships are still American subs and surface ships, with the Russian ships defending themselves against air, missile and torpedo attacks. The largest element of this navy is the sub force—by 1983 (in addition to the ballistic missile boats) this stood at 220 attack subs, nuclear and diesel-driven, and 70 antiship cruise-missile subs, highlighted by the largest general purpose sub ever built, the 18,000-ton, nuclear-powered 24-missile Oscar type of the 1980s, whose underwater-launched SS-N-19 cruise missiles range over 240 miles. By contrast, the Americans by 1983 had, along with their Polaris-Trident boats, 96 attack subs (all but five nuclear-propelled). Their replacement program is aimed at having 100 nuclear-powered attack subs by the year 2000, almost half of them belonging to the 6900-ton *Los Angeles* class, the first of which appeared in 1976.

To counter the constant Soviet underwater threat and ever-growing surface navy, the United States has since 1962 continued its basic if sometimes erratic maritime strategy. Its four numbered fleets have shifted warships from home ports to forward bases which ring the Eurasian land mass for deployment in patrolling task forces. In the

Pacific Fleet, headquartered at Pearl Harbor, the Third Fleet (First until 1973) is based on the West coast, the Seventh Fleet at the advanced ports of Yokosuka, Japan and Subic Bay, Philippines. The Atlantic Fleet, headquartered at Norfolk, utilizes the Second Fleet along the East and Gulf coasts, the Sixth Fleet in the Mediterranean (using facilities variously in Sicily, Italy, Greece and Spain), and task forces in the North Atlantic, making use of NATO ports. In only one area has the United States exercised virtual control, the Caribbean, where Castro's Communism required intervention in the Dominican Republic in 1965 and active diplomatic and economic aid and military advice to the other eternally-shaky Central American governments since then.

With such a global responsibility, the U.S. Navy remains oriented to the aircraft carrier, its escorts, mobile logistics, amphibious shipping and sealifted Marines. To police the sea lanes of the world, to support ground and air forces in limited wars, and to counter the Soviet submarine fleet has greatly taxed the Navy's resources, hence the number of major suface ships steadily declined due to budgetary constraints during the 1960s and 1970s. Indeed, the sheer number of Russian subs became so great that the Navy abandoned its specialized antisubmarine carriers in 1973 as woefully inadequate and depended for local antisubmarine protection on land-based P-3 Orion patrol planes and S-3 Viking sub hunters based aboard regular attack carriers. Sophisticated shipboard and fixed seabottom arrays also assist in the detection of Russian subs.

Soviet Russia since 1962 has sought to gain diplomatic leverage in the coastal regions of the world by enlarging its surface forces for diplomatic exposure in addition to continental defense. But being the police state that it is, its first priority remains the security of its land frontiers, with "reliable" buffer states, for internal as well as external security. The Red Army and satellite ground forces thus repressed uprisings in Czechoslovakia in 1968 and two years later in Poland, which became the most restive of the subject states again in the 1980s. The Kremlin has continued concentrating its greatest troop strength along the Chinese border and sent army forces into neighboring Afghanistan in 1980, there to be bogged down against guerrilla patriots. Dissention of even native Russians also requires constant vigilance, as in November 1975 when the crew of a Soviet Baltic destroyer, led by its political officer, mutinied and tried to reach Sweden before being forced back to Riga by a Russian submarine and helicopters!

Therefore, in spite of Admiral Gorshkov's veritable miracle in fashioning a powerful navy, he and his successors—like Colbert and Tirpitz before them—have faced the usual handicaps of continental naval leaders: subordination to the authoritarian political regime and its generals and a difficult geographical position unfavorable to oceanic operations. The Red Army has required the Navy to augment home defenses with large numbers of coastal and river vessels, minecraft, patrol boats, land-based naval aircraft, a Naval Infantry (reactivated in 1964) with amphibious shipping for coastwise operations, and the retention of many attack subs in coastal waters.

These ships, and the major surface combatants which have periodically operated on the high seas and visited distant lands, have been administered by four widely-separated area fleets: the Baltic based at Baltiisk, the Northern at the only ice-free port of Severomorsk (near Murmansk), the Black at Sevastopol, and the Pacific at Vladivostok. Because all four home bases are easily blockadable, forces operating from them have been deployed into three concentric "blue belt" defensive zones: the coastal waters out to 150 miles and covered by land-based naval aircraft; an intermediate zone up to another 150 miles offshore and partially covered by long-range planes; and the open sea dominated by far-ranging submarines. In addition to seafaring surface squadrons, the Russians have also created a very impressive merchant marine, oceanographic research fleet, and seagoing fishing factories—all of which however are highly vulnerable.

But the Russians have yet to establish advanced bases beyond their own shores, though they have used friendly and neutral ports world-wide. Early in the 1980s their major surface ship strength reached 300 vessels. Though occasionally coordinated in sprawling interocean "Okean" exercises since 1970, these ships do not operate in offensive fleets aimed at controlling distant seas and assaulting and holding overseas territories. Aside from the periodic appearance in the Mediterranean since 1963 of a large force, the normal squadron in other waters is comprised of three or four warships: one of the four *Kiev*-class VTOL carriers or one of the two helicopter carriers, one or more of the 36 cruisers, and perhaps a couple of the 70 destroyers or 170 frigates available. All these ships are charged with antiair and antisub defense and with killing enemy ships with cruise missiles, hence the carriers operate only short-range VTOL aircraft for local defense of the force. And the 400 land-based Russian Navy Backfire strike bombers have an extraordinary range of 3000 miles.

The primary active function of the Russian surface navy, short of war, is to exploit opportunities for backing up Kremlin diplomacy aimed at "showing the flag," and, wherever possible, to do it at the expense of the United States and its allies. This has occurred in areas where the Western alliances have had difficulty in maintaining peace between local rival states and between pro-Western and pro-Communist factions within nations.

The American-enforced *Pax* since 1962 has been most precarious in the southern peripheral regions of the Eurasian land mass—Southeast Asia, the Indian Ocean, and the Persian Gulf/Middle East. Hence the Soviet Union has operated its ships in these waters though without actively intervening against American forces. Indeed, as in the years before 1962, both superpowers continued to avoid direct confrontations by supporting client states in the latters' struggles. But only the Americans have been willing to commit their own forces to combat in limited overseas wars, giving them an incalculable advantage over the Russians in combat experience and the resulting self-confidence. In short, the United States has remained a true maritime state committed to an active maritime strategy.

In East Asia and Southeast Asia, the United States has continued to police the continental littoral against Soviet Russia, Communist China and North Korea by supporting and protecting the insular and peninsular areas of Japan, South Korea, Taiwan (Formosa), the Philippines and Malaysia, which achieved its independence in 1963. But the SEATO alliance lacked real teeth and gradually disappeared in the mid-1970s. So when pro-Communist Sukarno of Indonesia sent troops and guerrillas into Malaysian Borneo in 1963, the United States had no objection when Great Britain rallied to the side of Malaysia. Two British carriers, escorts, commandos, minesweepers, subs and hovercraft from Singapore isolated the battlefield by controlling the seas, then supported British, Malaysian, Anzac and Gurkha ground forces in turning the struggle against Indonesia. The British observed Indonesian territory and air space as sanctuaries and avoided bombing jungle targets for fear of hitting innocent natives, thereby winning their support. Sukarno dared not commit his Russian-built navy and even turned to China for help late in 1964. But the next year his generals overthrew him in an anti-Communist bloodbath and finally, in 1966, made peace with Malaysia. Both countries then turned to suppressing the ever-active pirates in their waters. Britain's classic use of a maritime strategy had been a resounding success.

By contrast, the United States' response to renewed North Vietnamese pressure against South Vietnam was politically ill-conceived, strategically unsound and tactically disjointed. The administrations of Presidents Eisenhower, Kennedy and Johnson all shored up several Asian nations under the Military Assistance Program, especially with military advisers in the Laotian and Vietnamese guerrilla wars of the late 1950s and early 1960s, while the five inshore squadrons of the Royal Thai Navy used American-built patrol boats and amphibious craft to police the long Gulf of Siam coast. Erroneously convinced from the Korean and Cuban experiences that the local Vietnamese struggle was linked to the Kremlin-led monolithic Communist bloc of the 1950s, the United States responded to intensified guerrilla attacks in 1963–64 with massive aid lest all Southeast Asia fall (the "domino" theory). And instead of focusing on the political questions raised by the main enemy, the indigenous National Liberation Front (Vietcong) of the South, the Americans viewed the crisis as primarily a military problem to be directed against North Vietnam, Russia and China, who were supporting the Vietcong. Strategically, therefore, the McNamara regime attempted to direct the military effort as closely as it did the missile effort against Russia, which meant a material strategy. Heavy military hardware was thus employed—naval support, aerial bombardment and finally troops—in uneven doses as part of the prevailing limited war doctrine of "controlled escalation" or "graduated response" of the early 1960s. Instead, this shortsighted strategy led to "gradualism" whereby the Vietnamese Communists were able to prepare adequate defenses and countermeasures for each gradual increase of American material force.

The Vietnam War (1965–73) exposed American ignorance of maritime strategy. Unlike the nineteenth-century British and their philosopher Corbett's teachings, unimaginative American strategists failed to recognize the prime military goals from the outset: total isolation of the battlefield by interdicting all enemy supplies by air attack and naval blockade and virtual total pacification and occupation of South Vietnam by ground forces. Since the country is not an island or peninsula like Malaya or Korea and thus not "interdictable," overland communications could never be cut by air bombing, and the United States and South Vietnam could never raise enough ground forces to occupy the long Laotian and Cambodian frontiers and thus prevent logistic and troop infiltration unless the United States decided to fight a major ground war in Asia. Furthermore, the World War II myths of strategic morale bombing led to attempts at intimidation by the bombing of selected targets in North Vietnam. Only the Navy was well-suited to meet its tasks: the long-term command of the waterways of and to South Vietnam, sealift and coastal support and naval blockade of the North— which was kept restricted until the very last months of the war. Consequently, the American armed forces tried to develop tactical doctrines on the foundations of an overall faulty strategy, and not surprisingly only the Navy fully succeeded. American participation went through three general stages: gradual involvement during 1964 and early 1965, gradual intervention and escalation between 1965 and 1968, and gradual disengagement 1968 to early 1973.

The gradual American involvement consisted of a series of naval incidents in addition to increased material aid and advisers. Overriding the advice of the Joint Chiefs, Secretary McNamara in February 1964 ordered American destroyer patrols into North Vietnamese waters, while South Vietnamese PT boats carried out commando raids against the North, and U. S. Navy and Air Force jets flew reconnaissance for Thai and Laotian air strikes on Laotian guerrillas near the North Vietnamese border. Fighter "flak suppressing" escorts joined after two Navy planes were shot down during the summer, and Seventh Fleet strength in the Gulf of Tonkin grew to four attack carriers plus one antisub carrier and escorts. On the night of July 30 South Vietnamese PT boats raided two North Vietnamese islands in the Gulf, and on August 2 counter-attacking enemy PT boats mistakenly engaged the American patrol destroyer *Maddox* which sank one and drove off the rest with the help of a carrier strike. The next night another raiding force from the South struck the North coast, leading to another confused encounter on the 4th during which carrier planes sank two more North PT boats. President Johnson used this "Gulf of Tonkin incident" to justify retaliatory carrier strikes which sank twenty-five North Vietnamese PT boats at their bases and destroyed the oil storage depot at Vinh. In September United States destroyers and North Vietnamese PT boats again skirmished, followed the next month by renewed South Vietnamese PT-commando raids. Vietcong guerrillas in the South finally attacked American advisers, leading Johnson to order carrier strikes north of the 17th parallel in February 1965 and the commitment of American ground forces.

The gradual intervention and escalation of the conflict involved Anzac, South Korean and Thai as well as South Vietnamese armed forces under general American command—till 1968 Admiral U. S. G. Sharp at Pearl Harbor and General William C. Westmoreland at Saigon. The three American armed services lacked overall philosophies for such an un-glamorous limited war, to the requirements of which they gave low equipment priorities. Their roles and missions overlapped and thus remained confused, fostering worse-than-usual interservice rivalries and competition. The Army viewed the struggle in Mao Tse-tung's terms as a problem for "counterinsurgency" but abandoned Clausewitzian notions of breaking the enemy's will in favor of ridiculous body-count statistics during halfhearted "search and destroy" patrols; took over the Marine Corps' vertical envelopment idea with "airmobile" divisions airlifted in helicopters, meaning that the Army had to build its own air force; and Regular Army units even found themselves operating as Marines in the waterways of the Mekong delta region. The Air Force stayed out of the tactical airmobility business altogether; refused to risk its B-52 bombers over North Vietnam against strategic targets (until very late in the war) but used them for—of all things—tactical air support with dubious effect in the South; and did not provide adequate close support until —as during the Pacific war and Korea—it used Navy and Marine techniques. The Marines were employed in positional Army-type operations near the 17th parallel ("Demilitarized Zone," DMZ) as during World War I and Korea instead of remaining a seagoing shock force. The Navy in its water element exercised its usual functions of commanding the sea, providing overall logistical sealift and amphibious mobility and naval bombardment of coastal targets North and South, while a good deal of its early strategic bombardment of the North with carriers was executed by piston-driven tactical A-1 Skyraider planes, which were thus kept from their more effective role of close air support in the South. The same was true of the one battleship employed. Also, the Navy often had to protect its own "riverine" forces in Army areas. Small wonder then that the armed forces had no better solution to the Vietnam problem than their equally confused civilian managers.

In the war of interdiction and supply, however, the Navy eventually completed all its assigned tasks. In addition to secondary coastal bases, Navy Seabees constructed major base facilities at Camranh Bay and Vung Tau in South Vietnam and Sattahip, Thailand, while the Military Sea Transportation Service called on its last mothballed Liberty and Victory ships to help meet the vast logistical requirements. Navy and Coast Guard river craft, monitors, helicopters, hovercraft, cutters and "Swift Boats" helped the South Vietnamese Navy's Junk Force and River Force cut off enemy waterborne supply along the coast and in the Mekong delta (Operations "Market Time" and "Game Warden"). Admiral Elmo R. Zumwalt extended this successful campaign to the Cambodian coast and inland "Parrot's Beak" sanctuary on the upper Mekong ("Sea Lords") during 1968–70, augmented by an Allied ground offensive thence during the spring of 1970. The Mobile Riverine Force similarly used new assault support patrol boats (ASPR) to clear the approaches to Saigon in the Rung Sat area in 1967–69, backed by off-shore helicopter carriers and bombardment forces. Gradually, successful anti-shipping patrols were extended up the North Vietnamese coast ("Sea Dragon") to the 20th parallel in 1966–68 with battleship, cruiser and destroyer fire and mining. Similarly, Task Force 77 carriers on "Yankee Station" struck selected North Vietnamese targets ("Rolling Thunder") during these years, their jets fighting off Russian-built Mig fighters but suffering heavily from Russian-made SAM missiles. The often politically interrupted naval air strikes, like those of the Air Force, had great success, especially in 1967 when they used deadly accurate television-guided air-to-surface Walleye glide bombs. Hanoi and Haiphong remained as sanctuaries, for fear of Russian and/or Chinese intervention to protect their freighters supplying the North. By the same token, Allied planes and ships assiduously avoided the Chinese border and air space, though the targeting was gradually extended to near the Chinese border in August 1967. Similarly, naval blockade was also absolutely forbidden.

Gradual disengagement followed from McNamara's growing realization of the uselessness of his "controlled escalation," the powerful Communist Tet offensive across the 17th parallel early in 1968, and violent anti-war sentiment in the United States. President Johnson gradually eliminated all bombing of the North throughout 1968 while seeking a negotiated settlement. His successor, Richard M. Nixon, continued the American withdrawal ("Vietnamization") as part of the Nixon Doctrine and the negotiations. The Doctrine, first officially enunciated in July 1969 and partly the work of Henry Kissinger, finally recognized the need for a maritime strategy by withdrawing American ground forces from the mainland of Asia, leaving such fighting to allied troops while the United States provides material aid and commands the sea and air. With most of the waterways successfully interdicted, the U. S. Navy in 1969–70 turned over some 825 inshore and river craft to the South Vietnamese Navy, a once faction-ridden service that had been stabilized by Commodore Tran Van Chon. American air strikes shifted to Laos and the still-open "Ho Chi Minh Trail" to keep up the pressure during the negotiations. The United States meanwhile achieved *rapprochement* with Russia and China, so that when North Vietnam launched a massive assault across the 17th parallel in the spring of 1972 the Nixon administration clamped an aerial mining blockade on Haiphong and six other harbors and ordered the most intensive bombing effort of the war, including planes from six carriers, against the North, this time including Hanoi and Haiphong. When the negotiations stalled late in the year, another aerial attack was launched. The settlement was finally reached in January 1973, freezing the *status quo.*

Its unhappy experience in Vietnam convinced the United States to quit the Asian land mass and remain content with policing the blue waters, islands and peninsulas. The unstable South Vietnam government thus finally collapsed in the spring of 1975, leading to the unification of all Vietnam under the victorious Communist regime, which lost little time in renewing ancient warring against its Indochinese neighbors. Early in 1976 the United States also withdrew from its bases in mainland Thailand, just as Great Britain quit Singapore after 157 years there—all part of its general economic retrenchment. But the Americans did nothing to lessen their policing of Asian waters, in spite of the seizure of the U.S. spy ship *Pueblo* by five North Korean patrol boats in their Wonsan Harbor in 1968 and similar incidents involving U.S. reconnaisance planes. American resolve to enforce international law on the high seas was dramatically illustrated in May 1975 when a Cambodian gunboat seized the U.S. merchant ship *Mayaguez* in the Gulf of Thailand. Two days later, covered by planes from the carrier *Coral Sea* striking Cambodian gunboats and airfields, U.S. Marines retook the ship and in a brisk firefight on Tang Island forced the release of the crew. Similarly, late in the decade and after, the Navy played a key role in saving Vietnamese refuguees fleeing their tyrannical overlords in open boats and subject to pirate attacks.

As part of the Nixon Doctrine, and indeed of any historical maritime strategy of concentration, the United States sought a continental ally in Asia to counter the Russians on land while America controlled the seas and air. The logical choice was mainland China, in spite of its communist system. Though it had broken with Russia in 1960, China had remained hostile to the United States through the Vietnam and Malaysian wars. In 1964, Admiral Hsiao undertook the development of three inshore fleets of antiquated coastal warships from the Yalu to the Gulf of Tonkin and centered on Peking, Shanghai and Canton. But having lost their technological support from Russia, the Chinese were receptive to President Nixon's overtures in the early 1970s to renew friendly relations with the United States. A decade of internal political chaos then wracked China, but the American connection has gradually improved, and by the 1980s China had begun—but only just begun—to recover internally and technologically, sending its first nuclear-powered submarines to sea. With American support, China thus becomes an ever greater threat to the Soviet Union, whose planes and warships have bracketed the Chinese coast by operating out of the Kamchatka peninsula in the north and from Camranh Bay in Vietnam to the south.

In the Indian Ocean, Great Britain continued its traditional policing role through the mid-1960s. In addition to the Malaysian intervention, the British assisted several new black nations of East Africa. In 1964 Britain air- and sealifted troops and commandos into Tanzanian Dar es Salaam, Kenya and Uganda and over the next four years carried out naval demonstrations as part of a U.N. arms embargo against the Portuguese (in Mozambique), Rhodesia and South Africa over these nations' apartheid policy. This was no idle activity, for South Africa had built up a formidable coastal navy, while Portugal operated the largest navy in African waters. Britain also continued supporting the Trucial System in the Persian Gulf. No longer able to afford these manifold responsibilities, however, Britain announced in the mid-1960s that it would withdraw all its military forces from the areas east of Suez by the end of 1971. It began by pulling out of Aden at the entrance to the Red Sea in 1967 and culminated, after some delays, by quitting its naval bases at Simonstown, South Africa in 1975 and Singapore early the next year.

The sudden development of a strategic vacuum in the Indian Ocean had monumental political and strategic effects on the nations bordering this sea. The Russians and Chinese were quick to give military and naval aid to many South Asian, Middle Eastern and East African states, thereby increasing their influence in that region. This prompted other underdeveloped nations in the Indian Ocean littoral to solicit arms and economic aid from the Western powers. The United States, at the time preoccupied in Vietnam and having no desire to be dragged into an Indian Ocean power struggle, complied. Most importantly, however, the oil-rich Persian Gulf states, suddenly freed from the British presence, drove up the global price of oil in the 1970s, thus alarming the NATO and Japanese Western allies dependent upon Middle Eastern oil.

India, key to the region but fiercely neutral in the Russo-American Cold War, nevertheless turned to the Soviets for aid in building up its surface navy against its rival neighbor, Pakistan, which country turned to France and Italy for submarines. India and Pakistan fought an inconclusive war in 1965, and then, six years later, when East Pakistan seceded as the new nation of Bangladesh, India blockaded the Pakistani coast and guaranteed Bangladesh independence. Between the British withdrawal and Pakistan's defeat, the old CENTO alliance evaporated. India's militancy frustrated Chinese attempts to help Pakistan but also gave the Kremlin cause to move a large force of 20 ships into the Indian Ocean for the first time, using anchorages at Socotra island and the Seychelles. These events of the late 1960s and early 1970s prompted both Britain and the United States to react. Britain delayed its departure and in 1974 allowed the United States to develop naval and air facilities at Diego Garcia in the middle of this ocean, while the Americans accepted Australia's invitation to establish a joint naval base at Cockburn Sound near Fremantle.

The sudden vulnerability of the Persian Gulf region to possible Russian incursion alarmed both the United States and Iran, leading the former during the 1970s to strengthen the latter as the key to Western defenses, Iran being the only stable and non-Arab nation in the region. Ever since 1958 Iran and Russian-backed Iraq had been in a localized naval arms race, so that instead of the now-departed single British frigate and five minesweepers to police the Gulf, Iran quickly purchased some 20 missile-armed vessels ranging from corvettes to destroyers from the West, along with trooplifting hovercraft, fighter planes, helicopters and tanks. The Iranians also enlarged their naval base at Khur-ramshahr opposite Iraqi Basra, built a hovercraft base further down the Gulf at Kharg Island, and established a new base at Bandar Abbas, commanding the vital Straits of Hormuz (Ormuz), where the Iranian navy seized three small islands late in 1971. The same year the United States was allowed to base a token 3-ship force at independent Bahrain in the Gulf and the next year agreed to supply Saudi Arabia with six missile corvettes and four landing craft.

America's Iranian ally became the ideal counterweight to Russian ambitions in the Persian Gulf during the decade of the 1970s, while the Trucial System was replaced by the Union of Arab Emirates which, along with the other coastal states of Saudi Arabia, Bahrain, Kuwait, Oman and Qatar, supplied oil to the West and utilized a few patrol boats to police the narrow Gulf. Practically overnight, these newly-powerful nations exerted immense power by placing an embargo on their oil exports in order to drive up prices in 1973. In strategic terms, however, these Gulf nations were pro-Western, with Iran being the dominant power. Iraq, now reduced to near naval impotence alongside Iran, turned again to Russia in 1972 to help build a new naval base at Umm Qasr in the vain hope she might regain her former strength against Iran. Increasing Russian naval activity in the Indian Ocean related to this was was finally matched by the appearance of major U.S. fleet units; late in 1974 the carrier *Constellation* led a task force into the Persian Gulf itself, the first American flattop to visit there since 1948. In addition, the United States and France supplied more arms to Saudi Arabia.

Suddenly, internal upheaval convulsed Iran and threatened the Western defensive arrangement in the Gulf. A fanatical Moslem religious movement overthrew the pro-Western monarch early in 1979 and that November seized the American embassy in Tehran. Then, at the turn of the new year, the Russians engineered a coup in neighboring Afghanistan and sent in army forces to back up the puppet regime. Thoroughly alarmed at these events in Iran and Afghanistan, the Jimmy Carter administration took action that very same month of January 1980. The President announced the "Carter Doctrine," whereby the United States would repel any outside power attempting to take over the Persian Gulf and its oil so valuable to the Western nations.

Carter's concern included the Red Sea region and East African coast, where the Russians had been establishing footholds since 1967 when the British withdrawal from Aden had resulted in the establishment there of two states, pro-Communist South Yemen and pro-Western Yemen to the north. South Yemen welcomed Russian naval and air units. Sudan provided the Soviets with the use of Port Sudan. Somalia allowed them to build a base at Berbera on the Gulf of Aden, and Ethiopia gave them use of Dahlak Island off the port of Massawa in the Red Sea. And even China had helped Tanzania develop naval facilities at Dar es Salaam. In West Africa, first Conakry in Guinea then Luanda in Angola became the main Russian naval and air base in the dark continent. And in 1978–79 Russian-backed Cuban troops operated in Ethiopia and Angola. On the eve of the Iranian crisis, the Strait of Bab el Mandeb at the apex of the Indian Ocean, Red Sea and Arabian peninsula appeared on the brink of coming under Russian domination, with only pro-Western north Yemen and the French at Djibouti (opposite South Yemen) holding out.

The events of 1979–80 changed all that. First, Somalia turned against the Russians late in 1979. Then, early in the new year, President Carter dispatched negotiators to the region to press for the use of naval and air base facilities. Encouraged by now three American carriers and 28 supporting ships on patrol in the Arabian Sea, Somalia, Oman and Kenya agreed, the latter making available to the U.S. Navy its great port of Mombasa. To replace Iran as the keystone of the West's defenses in the Persian Gulf, the United States increased its military and naval aid to Saudi Arabia, by then developing four naval bases in the Gulf to accommodate its expanded navy of missile and patrol boats, frigates, helicopters and amphibious craft. In addition to policing the Gulf, the Saudis also extended their naval patrols along the Arabian coast to the Red Sea. The United States gave more aid to Oman and the other friendly Gulf nations, particularly in the form of light naval craft, and obtained Britain's permission to enlarge the naval and air base at Diego Garcia.

The American initiative came none too soon. The fanatical Iranian regime was enraged when eight U.S. helicopters from the carrier *Nimitz* flew into Iran in April 1980 in a vain attempt to free its embassy hostages. However, the armed forces of Iran had virtually dissolved in the revolution, an open invitation for Soviet-backed Iraq to restore its naval supremacy in the Gulf. With 30 Russian warships demonstrating in the Indian Ocean and strengthened by new Soviet military aid, Iraq attacked Iran in September 1980, aiming to better protect its own naval base at Basra and to capture Iran's at Khurramshahr. Not only did Iraq fail, however, but in one battle in November determined Iranian warships sank eleven Iraqi vessels. The war then bogged down into a fierce regional struggle for control of the region. But neither nation could now match the growing strength of the U.S.-trained and equipped Royal Saudi Naval Forces and ground and air forces, backed up by American fleet units.

Aside from Iraq, Soviet naval presence in the Indian Ocean-Red Sea-African region was therefore reduced to the disparate nations of Angola, Ethiopia and South Yemen, from which aircraft and ships operate in scouting Western naval movements. The assertive projection of American sea power into the Indian Ocean in the early 1980s was a clear extension of the *Pax Americana* into the one remaining arena for superpower rivalry.

The ability of the Western navies to reach the Indian Ocean quickly has depended on their access to the Red Sea via the Suez Canal. This area has remained explosive simply because of the rampant Arab and Israeli nationalism of the adjacent nations, notably Egypt and Israel. In addition, the entire Eastern Mediterranean has become the closest point of direct contact between the rival superpower navies, for it is easily accessible to Soviet fleet units from the Black Sea and to NATO warships based in southern European ports. The Russians continued courting Arab and especially Egyptian favor after 1962, helping to build naval bases at Alexandria and two other places in Egypt. With the creation of the Soviet Mediterranean Fleet in 1963, Russian warships utilized auxiliary base facilities at Port Said and Syrian Latakia in supporting their own interests and those of their Arab allies.

In June 1967 the Arab-Israeli "Six Day War" erupted, in which pro-Western Israel's armed forces humbled those of Egypt, Syria, Iraq, Lebanon and Jordan. Israel's army and air forces pushed to the River Jordan and the Suez Canal, where the 15 Israeli destroyers and PT boats captured Egypt's naval base of Sharm el-Sheikh, repulsed a 12-submarine descent on the Israeli coast, and forced the Egyptians to quit Port Said and to close the Suez Canal. The powers became involved when a Russian squadron from the Black Sea entered Alexandria, and the Israelis severely damaged a U.S. reconnaisance vessel. The tense cease-fire was interrupted four months later when Egyptian PT boats sank an Israeli destroyer off Port Said with Styx cruise missiles—the first time in history of a warship being sunk by surface-to-surface missiles. The Russians kept a large surface force in the Med from then on to counterbalance the U.S. Sixth Fleet with its two or three aircraft carriers, enabling the Russians to actively use their surface force for gunboat diplomacy for the first time. But the United States and its NATO partners in 1968 strengthened their aerial surveillance of Soviet naval movements in the middle sea, and in the early 1970s the Americans deployed their own cruise missiles with the Sixth Fleet.

Unfortunately for the Russians, the Arab unity proved transitory, along with Egyptian friendship. In 1970 Syria attacked Jordan, and in 1972 Israel sealifted commandos which seized two unoccupied islets near the Strait of Bab el Mandeb to protect incoming Israeli oil tankers from Arab fedayeen guerrillas. That same year Egypt expelled the Russians and began to court favor with the United States, leaving Soviet warships to make-do in highly-vulnerable temporary anchorages wherever they could find them throughout the Mediterranean. Then in October 1973 the "Yom Kippur War" again pitted several Arab nations against Israel in mostly ground and air fighting. The enterprising Israeli navy operated under cover of night to avoid detection by Arab planes and with Gabriel cruise missiles sank several Syrian missile boats at Latakia and Tartus. Israeli ships also bombarded the coasts of Egypt and Syria before a truce ended hostilities. Both the United States and Russia reinforced their naval forces in the Med but, as usual, avoided participating in the fighting. The next year festering troubles on the island of Cyprus led to Turkish advances and naval demonstrations that resulted in Greece quitting the NATO alliance.

In the late 1970s the Soviet Union began deploying its VTOL carriers in the middle sea to balance the U.S. carriers there. The fragmented Arab world of the Middle East and North Africa became ever more tense over the Palestinian question and Israel, but the largest Arab state, now pro-Western Egypt, gradually shifted its naval equipment and doctrine from Russian to American. The fanatical Arab regime of Libya decided to challenge maneuvers of the U.S. carriers *Nimitz* and *Forrestal* in August 1981 with several of its Soviet-built SU-22 Fitter fighters 60 miles off the Libyan coast. When one of the Fitters fired an air-to-air missile at two F-14 Tomcat fighters from the *Nimitz*, the Tomcats intercepted and shot them down with Sidewinders. Three months later Egypt and the United States held joint amphibious exercises in a dramatic demonstration of Western strategic strength in the Eastern Mediterranean.

Beyond the constant vigilance over the Med, NATO concentrates on defending Western Europe and monitoring Soviet naval activity in the North Atlantic. Except for the U.S., only Britain and France (which remains independent of the NATO military command) have operated major naval units: carriers, nuclear-powered ballistic-missile and attack submarines, and cruisers. Canada, the Netherlands, Italy, Denmark, Norway and West Germany have specialized in antisubmarine destroyers, frigates, mine warfare craft, patrol planes and diesel subs. All the Western European navies have been aimed at the defense of convoys and of their own warships from Russian submarine attack, basically as adjuncts to the U.S. Navy. This strategy has been based on the (questionable) assumption of a future war on the continent of Europe a la World War II.

Of all non-superpower navies, Britain's has remained the most modern and sophisticated in the world, living up to its long reputation and traditions of over four centuries. The withdrawal of Royal Navy units from the Far East and Indian Ocean by the end of 1971 was designed to enable the fleet to focus on its two NATO missions—strategic deterrence with its ICBM subs and antisubmarine protection in the Eastern Atlantic. The decade of the 1970s was therefore devoted to strengthening the navy to meet these objectives and to phasing out its attack carriers in favor of antisub VTOL carriers and "through deck cruisers." But Britain's lingering global responsibilities required the presence of her warships outside their purely NATO roles. Repeated incidents in endless "cod wars" over Iceland's fisheries have kept her patrol boats policing those waters. The Iranian and Afghan crises called forth British naval demonstrations in the Indian Ocean to protect Britain's supertanker routes to the Persian Gulf. And Britain retains isolated possessions and bases around the world, not least Hong Kong on the Chinese coast, Gibraltar in the Mediterranean, and Diego Garcia in the Indian Ocean.

Economic difficulties and manpower shortages, however, led the British government to change its policy in 1980–81, halting the growth of the preceding decade and cutting back major surface units and escort vessels in favor of attack submarines and land-based patrol planes to counter Soviet subs. The alarm this caused NATO was minor compared to the shock of the British people when abruptly, early in April 1982, Argentina air- and sealifted ground forces into the British-owned Falkland Islands in the South Atlantic, claiming the territory to be rightfully Argentine. Having virtually rejected surface naval warfare in its new policy, Britain was hardpressed to mobilize an armada to retake the disputed islands.

The Falklands War, however, dramatically reaffirmed the efficacy of conventional offensive sea power in spite of modern tactical missiles. With an 8000-mile-long logistics "tail," the Royal Navy mounted an expeditionary force from Britain, covered by the antisub carriers *Invincible* and *Hermes,* fitted with "ski-ramps" for launching Sea Harrier VTOL attack "jump jets." To isolate the battlefield in true maritime strategic fashion, the British declared a 200-mile exclusion zone around the Falklands. And when this seemed inadequate, given the range of modern missiles, they extended this blockade to include all the South Atlantic save for the 12-mile offshore waters of the Argentine coast. This extension proved sound, for as the task force approached the islands at the end of April the small Argentine navy began a pincers movement to sink the two carriers; without air cover against the Argentine air force no landing could proceed. The northern Argentine force, built around its one World War II-vintage former British light carrier, was delayed by fog, though the southern one approached, centered on a pre-World War II ex-U.S. light cruiser, the *General Belgrano.*

Coordinated by Admiral Sir John Fieldhouse back home, the British went into action. The nuclear attack submarine *Conqueror* fired a salvo of World War II-era conventional torpedoes at the *Belgrano* on May 2, sending her to the bottom; her two escorting destroyers dropped depth charges, then fled, abandoning more than 300 survivors to perish. The sinking frightened the entire Argentine navy, including its carrier, back into port, rendering it impotent. The British task force then arrived off the islands to begin softening up the target, only to be savagely attacked over several weeks by Argentine Super Etendard, Mirage and A-4 Skyhawks from the mainland, 400 miles away. Lacking airborne early warning aircraft that a proper attack carrier would have provided, the British ''jump jets'' were unable to intercept all the low-flying attackers before they fired deadly Exocet cruise missiles and dropped iron bombs. Throughout May Argentine planes sank two British destroyers, two frigates, one assault ship, and one containership and damaged several other vessels. But of the some 500 combat sorties flown by the Argentines, half were turned back by the British and bad weather and 75 planes shot down by the Sidewinder-firing Harriers, SAM missiles and conventional gunfire—which crippled Argentina's only important means of retaliation.

In spite of the continuing attacks on their ships, the British masterfully executed their assault. Garrisons in outlying islands were isolated when Sea King helicopters from the carriers damaged and captured an Argentine submarine and destroyed eleven counterinsurgency planes in a surprise raid, and land-based bombers from Ascension Island over 3000 miles away destroyed the airfield and planes at Port Stanley, the Falklands' capital city. On May 22, in the midst of the Argentine air strikes, Royal Marines, Army troops and Gurkhas landed on the far side of the island from Stanley, well supported by the helicopter gunships. They moved overland and took the high ground over the port, 9500 troops and 100,000 tons of supplies coming ashore before the 12,000 Argentine troops surrendered on June 14. Great Britain had not lost her professional touch in effectively wielding her maritime strategy and tactics.

For the United States, the British experience in the Falklands affirmed the decision of the Ronald Reagan administration in the 1980s to undertake a major naval construction program. When President Reagan took office in 1981, he charged the new Secretary of the Navy, John H. Lehman, Jr., with restoring U.S. warship strength, down to 460, to 600 active ships by 1990. In addition to the growing Trident submarine inventory, Lehman planned an ever more powerful surface navy around 15 carrier battle groups and four surface action groups centered on the reactivated *Iowa*-class battleships—all to be escorted by new Aegis-missile cruisers, new destroyers and frigates and progressively fewer of the older ships. Mounted on board in various combinations are long-range Tomahawk antiship cruise missiles, short-range Harpoon cruise missiles, Phalanx close-in antiaircraft missiles, and the usual antisub systems. Thus tactically defended, the offensive carriers can launch their strike planes and the battleships their Tomahawks against naval and land targets, using conventional or nuclear warheads.

The rationale for this vast and powerful surface fleet is to command the seas in peacetime or war against the growing Soviet navy. In order to respond immediately and in strength to crises abroad which may only indirectly involve the Russians, the Reagan administration created the Rapid Deployment Joint Task Force of all the services in April 1981. Constructed to give it punch are new amphibious assault vessels with hovercraft and troop helicopters, new mine hunters and mine counter-measures ships, new hydrofoil patrol boats, and new Advanced Harrier VTOL planes to provide air support, while containerships and foreign-built merchantmen have been purchased to beef up logistical sealift for the joint force, reinforced by a Ready Reserve Fleet of dry cargo ships organized to be mobilized on ten days' notice. This amphibious mobility was first tested—successfully—in December 1981 when 1000 U.S. Marines landed ashore in Oman, operating in conjunction with Egyptian, Somalian, Omani and Sudanese forces and supported by carrier planes from the Arabian Sea. Large caliber 16-inch guns for fire support again became available in January 1983 with the recommissioning of the first of the battleships, the *New Jersey*.

America's global maritime strategy—halting, uneven, error-laden in the Vietnam era—was thus restored in the 1980s, creating ever greater obstacles for the Soviet Union to try to overcome. In spite of new cruisers and destroyers in the 1980s, all shorter-ranged but faster and mounting more antiship, antisub and antiair weapons launchers than its U.S. counterparts, the Russian navy remains oriented to the defensive. New 60,000-ton attack carriers may add much greater striking power for the Red fleet of the 1990s, but they remain no match for the several 92,000-ton American behemoths of the *Nimitz* class. A continual doctrinal debate thus proceeds within the Soviet high command over the need for carriers and whether to try to project them on a global scale. As so often in the past, the contending continental navy has awakened such fears in the prevailing maritime state that the latter has responded by outdistancing it with new construction and a strengthened resolve.

Thus, the Russo-American naval rivalry goes on but in the strategic environment of the *Pax Americana*—the active U.S. policing of the sea lanes of the world to enforce international law and the freedom of trade. Judging by the many nations which have rallied to the side of the United States in this endeavor during the late twentieth century, it is the policy and strategy most conducive to maintaining a stable balance of power and of preventing World War III.

Epilogue
World War III

. . . no empirical science, consequently also no theory of the Art of War, can always corroborate its truths by historical proof; it would also be, in some measure, difficult to support experience by single facts. If any means is once found efficacious in War, it is repeated; one nation copies another, the thing becomes the fashion, and in this manner it comes into use, supported by experience, and takes its place in theory, which contents itself with appealing to experience in general in order to show its origin, but not as a verification of the truth.

—CLAUSEWITZ

"Command of the sea" will continue to be a constant of historical maritime strategy as it has been in the past, up to the moment that a thermonuclear World War III breaks out—if it does. History continues to instruct in broad, strategic principles as well as in a continuum of development at lesser levels—tactical, administrative, logistical, material and command. Such general patterns of history, dependent always on geography, deserve summary notice here, especially as they reflect the preconditions and prerequisites for the emergence of thalassocracies and show why continental states have been prevented from such an evolution. By their several past examples, maritime- and non-maritime-centered national experiences suggest alternative courses of action for the future. And finally, stepping outside the strictures of his profession, the historian—or this one at least—can borrow from the political scientists, defense theorists and gamesmen to offer a "scenario" of a hypothetical World War III based on *current possibilities*. This last should at the very least round out the history of navies, since no historian likely to survive such a nuclear holocaust will have either the facts or the motivation to write the full naval history of World War III.

591

A very general evolutionary pattern of thalassocratic growth emerges from the histories of the Athenians, Venetians, Dutch, British and Americans (and possibly the Minoans), remembering always that each experience was unique in timing and details. First, from a favorable geographical position on an extensive coastline, the desire to trade fish, agricultural and manufactured goods for economic growth led to overseas merchant shipping. Second, the need for economic and thus political security to protect these vessels from pirates and rival maritime traders led to arming the merchantmen, then outfitting several as privateers or building a few cruisers especially for fighting. Third, a developing mercantilistic nation required a rudimentary navy of coastal gunboats to help defend the seaports and a fleet of cruisers and other warships to systematically protect shipping and to attack that of an enemy in wartime; this might be termed the *guerre de course* phase. Fourth and most crucial, shifting from the defensive to the offensive, the maritime nation acquired overseas colonies or trading stations for raw materials and for markets, and built and maintained a permanent superior navy of capital fighting ships designed to actively police the trade routes, to protect the merchant shipping and overseas stations, and to seek out and destroy the enemy's warships and merchant vessels in wartime battle and/or blockade. In other words, it achieved the ability to command the sea through a maritime strategy. Economically and militarily, it had become an integrated maritime empire, and it imposed order upon the seas—*pax*—with its navy in order to preserve its prosperity. It also supported the exploration of uncharted regions of the world both for profit and new knowledge. Finally, the vitality and affluence at work during this long process culminated in a golden age of enlightened government, human rights, high culture and artistic achievement. Usually seeking at least one major continental ally to help contain its jealous enemies, this thalassocracy enforced its *pax* by active "cold," limited and even total wars, leading it eventually to dominate world politics. This exalted status was usually lost only when emerging rival maritime powers and/or nearby continental enemies defeated the thalassocracy, aided by its internal decay caused partly by the greed and corruption of succeeding generations. Ultimately receding in grandeur and power, it then lived on the memories of its past glories.

By contrast, continental powers with long, exposed frontiers on land often aspired to thalassocratic greatness but usually never could get beyond the *guerre de course* stage, the fate of the Persians, Spartans, Phoenicians and Carthaginians, Arabs, Turks, Byzantines, Vikings, Spanish, Portuguese, French, Germans, Italians, Japanese and Russians. Alexander and Rome are very special cases of overland world conquest which thus absorbed all the seaports, but both had to borrow heavily from the conquered Greeks at sea. The geographic preoccupation with landward economies and defenses fostered autocratic, army- and/or church-dominated political systems that neither desired nor could afford equally strong armies and navies. Whatever cultural achievements such nations fostered, they rarely reached heights comparable to the thalassocracies in democratic government, free economic enterprise or intense artistic creativity. Many such nations tried to do these things by going to sea and even came close to such heights, but never quite succeeded, in the last analysis because of constant wars stemming largely from the heavy demands imposed by their geographic exposure and internal pressures. The industrial and technological revolutions of the past two centuries have enabled virtually all nations with any coastline to build more warships than previously, but technology can also be used to thwart thalassocratic growth as well as encourage it, of which the fascist and communist dictatorships are prime examples. Perhaps, by the twenty-first century, Russia's expansion upon the seas and exploration of space will modify the rigid Soviet system, but the geographic and political barriers are most formidable.

The last third of the twentieth century is unique, like any period in history, so that actual parallels are misleading, but the current *Pax Americana* does strongly resemble the *Pax Britannica* of a century ago. The American industrial capitalistic system dominates world markets, while American democratic government (for all its shortcomings) and material affluence provide the model for developing new nations, though the current level of American culture is more debatable. Strategically, the United States applies an oceanic maritime system that in any other time would have deserved the label imperial. The ballistic missile submarines are the chief agent for deterring nuclear aggression, while the surface navy enforces freedom of the seas and protects America's allies with their valuable bases. The anomalies in this system—by no means strange to earlier maritime states—are a disinterested and thus uninformed public about oceanic matters; conservative, apolitical admirals whose public relations and image still lag behind those of the generals; a professional naval and lay distaste for limited wars; a fleet of warships overaged because of governmental and public neglect; a dangerously deteriorating merchant fleet (though foreign flag carriers remain predominantly pro-American); and a quite normal Navy tendency to become alarmed, even panicky, over Russian naval and maritime growth—the type of alarm that a century ago generated unrealistic French "invasion scares" in Britain.

The United States Navy will, for the foreseeable future, strengthen its twofold capability of deterring nuclear war and policing the seas, more or less practicing an American maritime strategy alongside the Army and

Air Force to maintain its command of the sea. The current oceanic challenger, Soviet Russia—in the historical pattern of maritime and continental rivalries—has imitated Anglo-American maritime developments and has even contributed significant advances of its own to naval science. Ship for ship, many of its vessels are newer, faster and better than their American counterparts, like those of many of its continental predecessors over their maritime competitors; indeed, Russian oceanic trade, fishing and research are downright superior. But the Soviet Navy is still a parade fleet or "fleet-in-being," untried in battle and unrisked even in limited wars, and Russian diplomacy still remains too clumsy to make it an effective tool. Part of this diplomatic weakness is due to the unattractiveness of communism and Russian militarism to emerging nations. Indeed, any Russian East African bases will probably prove to be as relatively useless as were France's and Germany's colonies in the nineteenth century and for the same reasons. For Russia is not a thalassocratic nation, nor does it employ maritime strategy; the superior Red Army instead maintains a stranglehold over Central Europe and nervously patrols the long Chinese frontier. An ever stronger U. S. Navy can only force a Russia with naval delusions to commit even greater expenses on its own navy for really peripheral needs—a serious drain on any continental economy that must lead to continuing doubts by the Soviet's Party leadership, the predominant Army and the average consumer. Except in the nuclear arena, Russia remains the elephant to the American whale.

The Soviet Navy is developing a limited blue-water capability with its half-dozen or so medium-sized carriers and deadly cruise-missile ships, but it is doubtful whether these will ever seriously match the American attack carrier weapon system in quality or quantity. Amphibious vessels and the Naval Infantry will be increased, but largely for development around the periphery of Russia. The Russian fleets will thus remain defensive, relying upon the submarine both to provide strategic deterrence and to threaten American surface ships and subs, thereby defending the homeland from missile or amphibious attack. Russian diplomacy will continue to seek overseas facilities where the surface navy can "show the flag," but whether Russia will ever develop the logistical mobility and base network typical of a true blue-water navy is extremely doubtful. Of course, this analysis may be incorrect, especially if the United States creates power vacuums upon the seas by allowing its navy to deteriorate—an unlikely possibility.

Whatever the American and Russian navies do will depend upon the policies and decisions of their respective governments. Both countries have had such notoriously bad luck with some of their allies—the United States with France and South Vietnam, and Russia with China and

Egypt, for example—that both may tend to be drawn ever closer in resolving their differences. Both nations have traditionally fostered isolationistic tendencies, and the economic power centers of Western Europe and Japan offer formidable challenges. America and Russia may thus seek to progress from the initial SALT agreements of 1972 to reduce their—and others'—armaments and thus to compete more effectively in the economic sphere, thereby solving manifold internal problems. New reconnaissance satellites may force them to further limit land-based missiles, unless the latter have mobility as on railroads, while increasingly effective offensive weapons may lead to a total ban on ineffective and expensive defensive systems altogether. Indeed, such common interests and problems, along with the worldwide desire to reduce the chance of nuclear war, may drive the two superpowers into mutual economic dependence and—not inconceivably—into a defensive alliance by the end of the century, as in 1941 and as ancient rivals Britain and France did at the beginning of the century. Such a prospect, now less farfetched than ever, may well convince the United States to adopt a full-blown maritime strategy and the Soviet Union to be content with its defensive naval posture. Conversely, though, third parties like China or Israel could conceivably increase Russo-American tensions and even create a Sarajevo-like crisis to trigger a nuclear exchange.

Though rigid controls in any shooting situation between the United States and Soviet Russia are earnestly desired by both parties, such would be virtually impossible to enforce during the few minutes necessary for either side to gain the strategic advantage of the first strike, so that World War III—if it happens—will probably be a total thermonuclear war. Launching all their pre-targeted missiles, the subs should have little difficulty in obliterating every major city and port even if only relatively few of their missiles or warheads penetrate any anti-missile defenses. The qualitative edge of the U.S. Navy in ASW will enable its hunter subs, carrier planes and escort ships to sink many but surely not all of the numerous Russian subs and probably not before the latter have fired most of their missiles. Immediately, however, Soviet antiship attack subs and missile ships will sink as many American subs and surface ships as they can locate, despite defensive countermeasures. Manned bombers and land-based missiles will be launched on their one-way trips before their bases and silos are destroyed by the sub-launched missiles. Outside of the ballistic missile submarines, therefore, conventional naval forces will play an insignificant role. Amphibious forces, logistical ships, convoys and inshore craft will have virtually no function at all, for literally within, say, ninety minutes of the initial "button-pushing" the major political, transportation and communications centers will be wiped out, along with the important industrial and fuel complexes. Oil-burning vessels and all aircraft will be immobilized without more fuel, with most nuclear-powered ships being sunk. Any merchant and naval vessels already at sea that happen to survive this holocaust will return to gutted ports, there to drop anchor for the last time. If it matters, the United States will probably, militarily, have gotten the better of the short war, with the underdeveloped Third World nations escaping most of the direct destruction, if not the global fallout of radiation. But nobody will "win" World War III, for industrial civilization as we have known it will have ceased to exist.

Post-World War III civilization, whatever of it survives, will have to start all over again. Somehow, food will have to be produced, then goods traded on whatever vessels (sail?) can be fashioned; such craft will have to be protected from outlaws and pirates bent on their own survival, and so the need for armed warships, etc., etc. We will be back where the Minoans started, and the process will begin again. . . .

Bibliography

By the nature of this broad overview, secondary works provided most of the information, save for much primary and oral research the writer has done as part of his specialized work in twentieth-century naval history. In addition to books (naval and more general), several key dissertations, some theses and many articles have been consulted, along with newspaper items from the most recent years. Most sources consulted were in English, not surprisingly since maritime Britain has dominated the field of naval history, only sharing its lead with American scholarship since World War II—an obvious reflection of the strong national maritime and naval pursuits of both countries. Where non-English-language sources were necessary, the writer tended to rely on translators.

Works listed here reflect only those actually used in the writing of this book, so that this should not be considered as a definitive bibliography of the field. The literature of naval and maritime history is vast, but is catalogued best in Robert G. Albion, *Maritime and Naval History: An Annotated Bibliography,* 4th ed., Mystic, Conn., 1972. Other useful English-language bibliographies are:

Higham, Robin. *A Guide to the Sources of British Military History.* Berkeley; London, 1972. Listing of books, articles, private manuscripts and documents, official papers, British libraries, military booksellers and professional journals.

International Commission on Maritime History. *Bibliographie de l'Histoire des Grandes Routes Maritimes,* 4 vols. Lisbon, 1967–to date. Published first in the quarterly *Boletim Internacional de Bibliografia Luso-Brasileira* of the Calouste Gulbenkian Foundation, Volumes II (the United States) and IV (Great Britain) are in English, Volumes I (France, Denmark, Germany and Poland) and III (Spain and Portugal) are in French.

Manwaring, G. E. *Bibliography of British Naval History: Bibliographical and Historical Guide to Printed Manuscript Sources.* London, 1930, 1969.

Millett, Allan R. and B. F. Cooling. *Doctoral Dissertations in Military Affairs.* Manhattan, Kans., 1972. English language dissertations only; annual supplements in the journal *Military Affairs,* which also contains a bibliography of articles in each issue.

National Maritime Museum. *Catalogue of the Library,* 2 vols. Greenwich, 1968, 1970.

[Naval History Division]. *United States Naval History: A Bibliography*, 6th ed. Washington, 1972.

General sources are listed here first, then specific sources as they were first used in the writing of the book, though naturally many sources cover broad periods of time, overlapping in the chapters. Sources are otherwise listed alphabetically by author, being annotated only where the title fails to convey the subject matter. Abbreviations used for the *United States Naval Institute Proceedings* and the American *Naval War College Review* are *USNIP* and *NWCR* respectively.

GENERAL WORKS and BOOK ONE.
COMMAND OF THE SEA–AND THE ALTERNATIVES

Albion, Robert Greenhalgh and Jennie Barnes Pope. *Sea Lanes in Wartime: The American Experience, 1775–1945*, 2nd enl. ed. Hamden, Conn., 1968.
Allison, R. S. *Sea Diseases: The Story of a Great Natural Experiment in Preventive Medicine in the Royal Navy*. London, 1943.
Anderson, R. C. *Oared Fighting Ships, From Classical Times to the Coming of Steam*. London, 1962.
Anderson, Romola and R. C. *The Sailing Ship: Six Thousand Years of History*. New York, 1963.
Archibald, E. H. H. *The Metal Fighting Ship in the Royal Navy, 1860–1970*. New York, 1971.
———. *The Wooden Fighting Ship in the Royal Navy, 897–1860*. London, 1968.
Ballard, G. A. *Rulers of the Indian Ocean*. London, 1927.
Barraclough, Geoffrey. *An Introduction to Contemporary History*. New York, 1964. Recent history, 1890s to 1960s.
Barzun, Jacques, Paul H. Beik. George Crothers and E. O. Golob. *Introduction to Naval History*. New York, 1944.
Basch, Lucien. "Ancient Wrecks and the Archeology of Ships." *The International Journal of Nautical Archeology and Underwater Exploration*, I (1972), 1–58. An overview of the field.
Bass, George F., ed. *A History of Seafaring based on underwater archeology*. London, 1972.
Brodie, Bernard. *A Guide to Naval Strategy*, 5th ed. New York, 1965.
——— and Fawn Brodie. *From Cross-bow to H-Bomb*. New York, 1962. A short history of weapons.
Colomb, P. H., Vice Admiral. *Naval Warfare: Its Ruling Principles and Practice Historically Treated*. London, 1899.
Corbett, Julian S. *Some Principles of Maritime Strategy*. London, 1911, 1972.
Creswell, John, Captain, R.N. *Generals and Admirals: The Story of Amphibious Command*. New York, 1952.
Daly, R. W. "Russian Military and Naval Doctrines." Unpublished course narrative, U. S. Naval Academy. From the Scythians to the Revolution. See his "Russia's Ancient Ally: the Sea," *USNIP*, 98, no. 8 (August 1972), 60–67, for an example.
Dupuy, R. Ernest, Colonel USA (Ret), and Colonel Trevor N. Dupuy, USA (Ret). *The Encyclopedia of Military History*. New York, 1970.
Eccles, H. E., Rear Admiral USN (Ret). "Strategy," rev. essay. *Selected*

Readings in Evolution of Strategy Theory. Washington: mimeographed, 1968.

Fergusson, Bernard. *The Watery Maze: The Story of Combined Operations.* New York, 1961.

FitzGerald, C. P. *The Southern Expansion of the Chinese People.* London, 1972.

Gardiner, Leslie. *The British Admiralty.* London, 1968.

Hampshire, A. Cecil. *The Royal Marines, 1664–1964.* n.p. [1964].

Harrison, Richard Edes, and the Editors of *Fortune. Look at the World: The FORTUNE Atlas of World Strategy.* New York, 1944.

Hasslöf, Olof, *et al.*, eds. *Ships and Shipyards; Sailors and Fishermen: Introduction to Maritime Ethnology.* Copenhagen, 1972.

Hay, David and Joan. *No Star at the Pole: A History of Navigation from the Stone Age to the 20th Century.* London, 1972.

Hearnshaw, F. J. C. *Sea-Power and Empire.* London, 1940.

Huçul, Walter Charles. "The Evolution of Russian and Soviet Sea Power, 1853–1953." Ph.D., University of California at Berkeley, 1953.

Hyatt, A. M. J., ed. *Dreadnought to Polaris: Maritime Strategy Since Mahan.* Toronto, Ont., 1973.

Jameson, William. *The Most Formidable Thing: The Story of the Submarine from its earliest days to the end of World War I.* London, 1965.

Jane, Fred. T. *The Imperial Russian Navy: Its Past, Present, and Future.* London, 1899.

Knox, Dudley W. *A History of the United States Navy.* New York, 1948.

Kuykendall, Ralph S. *The Hawaiian Kingdom, 1778–1854: Foundation and Transformation.* Honolulu, 1947.

Landström, Björn. *The Ship: An Illustrated History.* Garden City, [1961]. Primitive to nuclear-powered vessels; all types.

Lewis, Michael. *The History of the British Navy.* Baltimore, 1957.

Lloyd, Christopher. *The Nation and the Navy: A History of Naval Life and Policy.* London, 1954. The British navy.

Macintyre, Donald, Captain, R.N. (Ret), and Basil W. Bathe. *The Man of War.* London, 1968. History of the warship.

McFee, William. *The Law of the Sea.* New York, 1950.

Marder, Arthur J. "From Jimmu Tennō to Perry—Sea Power in Early Japanese History." *American Historical Review,* LI, no. 1 (October 1945), 1–34.

Mitchell, Mairin. *The Maritime History of Russia, 848–1948.* London, 1949.

Nef, John U. *War and Human Progress.* New York, 1963.

Phillips-Birt, Douglas. *A History of Seamanship.* London, 1971.

[Pierce, P. K., Lieutenant Commander, USNR]. *Riverine Warfare: The U. S. Navy's Operations on Inland Waters,* rev. ed. Washington, 1969.

Potter, E. B. and Chester W. Nimitz, eds. *Sea Power: A Naval History.* Englewood Cliffs, N.J., 1960.

Potter, Pitman B. *The Freedom of the Seas in History, Law, and Politics.* London, 1924.

Ròbison, S. S., Rear Admiral, USN (Ret), and Mary L. Robison. *A History of Naval Tactics from 1530–1930.* Annapolis, 1942.

de la Roncière, Ch. and G. Clerc-Rampal. *Histoire de la Marine Française.* Paris, 1934. History of the French Navy.

Ropp, Theodore. *War in the Modern World,* rev. ed. New York, 1962. Since 1415.

Rose, J. Holland. *Man and the Sea: Stages in Maritime and Human Progress.* Cambridge, 1935. A catchall, but mostly exploration.

Rosinski, Herbert. *Power and Human Destiny.* New York, 1962. "Power" and "tension" as alternatives to "peace" and "war" through historical examples.

Roskill, S. W., Captain, R.N. (Ret). *The Strategy of Sea Power.* London, 1962. Historical overview with emphasis on Britain.

Russell, Sir Herbert. *Sea Shepherds: Wardens of our Food Flocks.* London, 1941. History of convoy.

Semple, Ellen Churchill. *Influences of Geographic Environment: On the Basis of Ratzel's System of Anthropo-Geography.* New York, 1911.

Stafford, Edward Perry, Commander, USN. *The Far and the Deep.* New York, 1967. History of submarines with bibliography.

Svenska Flottans Historia, 3 vols. n.p., 1942–45. A huge history of the Swedish Navy and thus Scandinavia in general.

Tavernier, Bruno (tr. by Nicholas Fry). *Great Maritime Routes: An Illustrated History.* Paris, 1970.

Taylor, E. G. R. *The Haven-Finding Art.* New York, 1971. History of navigation.

Tolkowsky, Samuel. *They Took to the Sea: A Historical Survey of Jewish Maritime Activities.* New York, 1964. Overstated.

Toussaint, Auguste (tr. by June Guicharnaud). *The History of the Indian Ocean.* Chicago, 1967.

Vagts, Alfred. *Landing Operations: Strategy, Psychology, Tactics, Politics, From Antiquity to 1945.* Harrisburg, 1946.

Weigley, Russell F. *The American Way of War: A History of United States Military Strategy and Policy.* New York, 1973.

Whitehouse, Arch. *Amphibious Operations.* Garden City, 1963. A history.

Williams, Neville. *Contraband Cargoes: Seven Centuries of Smuggling.* London, 1959.

Woodward, David. *The Russians at Sea: A History of the Russian Navy.* New York, 1965.

BOOK TWO. THE EARLY THALASSOCRACIES, 2000 B.C.–A.D. 1415

Adams, John, to Richard Rush, October 19, 1815. Adams papers, letter 148, on microfilm reel 122. Courtesy of John J. Kelly, Jr. A summary of international maritime law from 1075 to 1270.

Adcock, F. E. *The Greek and Macedonian Art of War,* Berkeley, 1962.

———. *The Roman Art of War Under the Republic.* New York, 1963.

Arrian (tr. by Aubrey de Sélincourt). *The Life of Alexander the Great.* Baltimore, 1958.

Ashe, Geoffrey, *et al. The Quest for America.* New York, 1971. The debate over prehistoric maritime contacts between Eastern and Western hemispheres.

Balcer, Jack M. "From Confederate Freedom to Imperial Tyranny: A Study of the Restrictions Imposed by Athens on the Political Self-Determination of the Members in the Delian Confederacy, 478–431 B.C." Ph.D. dissertation, University of Michigan, 1964.

Basch, Lucien. "Phoenician Oared Ships." *The Mariner's Mirror,* 55 (1969), 139–162, 227–245, 381–382.

Basham, A. L. *The Wonder That Was India.* New York, 1954. Early navies of India briefly recounted.

Bibby, Geoffrey. *Looking for Dilmun.* New York, 1969.

Boardman, John. *The Greeks Overseas.* Baltimore, 1964. Ancient Greek migrations and colonizations in the Mediterranean world.

Breasted, James Henry. *A History of Egypt.* New York, 1905; 1964.

Brooks, F. W. *The English Naval Forces, 1199–1272.* London, 1932; 1963.

Caesar, Julius (tr. by Jane F. Mitchell). *The Civil War.* Baltimore, 1967.

Carter, John M. *The Battle of Actium: The Rise and Triumph of Augustus Caesar.* London, 1970.

Cary, M. and W. H. Warmington. *The Ancient Explorers.* London, 1929; Baltimore, 1963.

Cassidy, Vincent H. *The Sea Around Them: The Atlantic Ocean,* A.D. *1250.* Baton Rouge, 1968.

Casson, Lionel. *The Ancient Mariners.* New York, 1959. A history of seafaring in the ancient world.

———. *Ships and Seamanship in the Ancient World.* Princeton, 1971.

Chambers, D. S. *The Imperial Age of Venice, 1380–1580.* London, 1970.

Charlesworth, M. P. *Trade-Routes and Commerce of the Roman Empire.* 1926; New York, 1970.

Cipolla, Carlo M. *Guns, Sails and Empires: Technological Innovation and the Early Phases of European Expansion, 1400–1700.* n.p., 1965.

Clark, Frederick William. *The Influence of Sea-Power on the History of the Roman Republic.* Menasha, Wisc., 1915.

Culican, William. *The First Merchant Venturers: The Ancient Levant in History and Commerce.* London, 1966.

Diehl, Charles. *Byzantium: Greatness and Decline.* New Brunswick, N. J., 1957.

Edwards, I. E. S., *et al.,* eds. *The Cambridge Ancient History,* 3rd ed., Vol. I, Pt. 2: *Early History of the Middle East.* Cambridge, 1971.

Eickhoff, Ekkehard. *Seekrieg und Seepolitik zwischen Islam und Abenland: Das Mittelmeer unter Byzantinischer und Arabischer Hegemonie (650–1040).* Berlin, 1966. Byzantine-Arab naval rivalry in the Mediterranean.

Fahmy, Aly Mohamed. *Muslim Sea-Power in the Eastern Mediterranean From the Seventh to the Tenth Century A.D.* London, 1950.

Fisher, Sir Geoffrey. *Barbary Legend: War, Trade, and Piracy in North Africa, 1415–1830.* Oxford, 1958.

Gomme, A. W. "A Forgotten Factor of Greek Naval Strategy." *Journal of Hellenic Studies,* 53 (1933), 16–24. A treatise on the interrelationships between Greek armies and naval squadrons.

Green, Peter. *Armada from Athens.* New York, 1970. The disastrous overseas expedition against Syracuse during the Peloponnesian War.

———. *The Year of Salamis, 480–479 B.C.* London, 1970.

Herman, Zvi (tr. by Len Ortzen). *Peoples, Seas and Ships.* New York, 1967. Ancient seafaring peoples.

Herodotus (tr. by Aubrey de Sélincourt). *The Histories.* Baltimore, 1964. The Persian invasion of Greece.

Hourani, George Fadlo. *Arab Seafaring in the Indian Ocean in Ancient and Early Medieval Times.* Princeton, 1951.

Hutchinson, R. W. *Prehistoric Crete.* Baltimore. 1962.

Irwin, Constance. *Fair Gods and Stone Faces.* New York, 1963. Argues for global-ranging seafarers in early times.

Johnstone, Paul. "Stern First in the Stone Age?" *The International Journal of Nautical Archaeology and Underwater Exploration,* II, no. 1 (March 1973), 3–11. Earliest Mediterranean seafaring.

Jones, Gwyn. *A History of the Vikings.* London, 1968.

Jordan, Borimir. "The Administration and Military Organization of the Athenian Navy in the Fifth and Fourth Centuries B.C." Ph.D., University of California at Berkeley, 1968.

Kienast, Dietmar. *Untersuchungen zu den Kriegsflotten der Römischen Kaiserzeit.* Bonn, 1966. The Roman imperial navy from Augustus through the fourth century A.D.

Laing, Donald R., Jr. "A New Interpretation of the Athenian Naval Catalog, IG 112, 1951." Ph.D., University of Cincinnati, 1965.

Landström, Björn. *Ships of the Pharaohs.* London, 1970.

Lane, F. C. "Venetian Ships and Shipbuilding of the Renaissance." Ph.D., Harvard University, 1934.

Lewis, Archibald R. "England as an Atlantic Maritime Power, 1100–1350 A.D." Unpublished paper, Medieval Academy Annual Meeting, Chapel Hill, N.C., 1971.

———. *Naval Power and Trade in the Mediterranean, A.D. 500–1100.* Princeton, 1951.

———. *The Northern Seas: Shipping and Commerce in Northern Europe, A.D. 300–1000.* Princeton, 1958.

Lo, Jung-pang. "The Emergence of China as a Sea Power during the Late Sung and Early Yüan Periods." *Far Eastern Quarterly,* XIV (August 1955), 489–503.

Luce, J. V. *Lost Atlantis: New Light on an Old Legend.* New York, 1969. Connects the Atlantis legends with ancient Minos, focusing on its collapse to volcanic eruption.

Ma Huan (tr. by J. V. G. Mills, ed.). *Ying-Yai Sheng-Lan* ["The Overall Survey of the Ocean's Shores"]. Cambridge, 1972. Contemporary accounts of Cheng Ho's voyages, early 1400s.

Marinatos, Spyridon. "Thera: Key to the Riddle of Minos." *National Geographic,* 141, no. 5 (May 1972), 702–726.

Marlowe, John. *The Golden Age of Alexandria . . . 331 B.C. to . . . 642 A.D.* London, 1971.

Meiggs, Russell. *The Athenian Empire.* Oxford, 1972.

Meirat, Jean. *Marines antiques de la Mediterranée.* Paris, 1964.

Mellersh, H. E. L. *The Destruction of Knossos: The Rise and Fall of Minoan Crete.* New York, 1970.

Merker, Irwin Loeb. "Studies in Sea-Power in the Eastern Mediterranean in the Century Following the Death of Alexander." Ph.D., Princeton University, 1958.

Miller, J. Innes. *The Spice Trade of the Roman Empire, 29 B.C. to A.D. 641.* Oxford, 1969.

Miller, Molly. *The Thalassocracies: Studies in Chronography II.* Albany, 1971. Sixth-century B.C. Aegean.

Morison, Samuel Eliot. *The European Discovery of America: The Northern Voyages, A.D. 500–1600.* New York, 1971.

Morrison, J. S. and R. T. Williams. *Greek Oared Ships, 900–322* B.C. Cambridge, 1968. Uses archeological evidence to clear up many problems about ancient Greek naval history.

Moscati, Sabatino (tr. by Alastair Hamilton). *The World of the Phoenicians.* New York, 1968.

Mylonas, George E. *Mycenae and the Mycenaean Age.* Princeton, 1966. "The Near East and the Aegean in the Second Millennium B.C." American Historical Association session, New York, December 1971.

Needham, Joseph. *Science and Civilisation in China,* Vol. 4, *Physics and Physical Technology,* Pt. III: *Civil Engineering and Nautics.* Cambridge, 1971. Ancient Chinese seafaring.

Ormerod, H. A. *Piracy in the Ancient World.* 1924; Chicago, 1967.

Page, D. L. *The Santorini Volcano and the Desolation of Minoan Crete.* London, 1971.

Renfrew, Colin. *The Emergence of Civilisation: The Cyclades and the Aegean in the Third Millennium* B.C. London, 1972. Argues for the unique development of Minoan and Greek civilization. Much on seafaring.

Riley, Carroll L., *et al.*, eds. *Man across the Sea: Problems of Pre-Columbian Contacts.* Austin, 1971.

Rodgers, W. L., Vice Admiral, USN (Ret). *Greek and Roman Naval Warfare.* Annapolis, 1937, 1964.

———. *Naval Warfare Under Oars, 4th to 16th Centuries.* Annapolis, 1939, 1970.

Sallust (tr. by S. A. Handford). *The Jugurthine War; The Conspiracy of Cataline.* Baltimore, 1963.

Sasson, Jack M. "Canaanite Maritime Involvement in the Second Millennium B.C." *Journal of the American Oriental Society,* 86, no. 2 (April–June 1966), 126–138.

Säve-Söderbergh, Torgny. "The Navy of the Eighteenth Egyptian Dynasty." *Uppsala Universitets Årsskrift 1946: no. 6.* Uppsala, 1946.

"The Search for Sunken Ships." *Surveyor* (August 1971), 22–28. Underwater archeology for the ancient Mediterranean.

Shepard, A. M. *Seapower in Ancient History.* Boston, 1924.

Snodgrass, A. M. *The Dark Age of Greece: An Archeological Survey of the Eleventh to the Eighth Centuries B.C.* Edinburgh, 1971.

Southworth, John van Duyn. *The Age of Sails.* New York, 1968.

———. *The Ancient Fleets.* New York, 1968.

Spencer, George Woolley. "Royal Leadership and Imperial Conquest in Medieval South India: The Naval Expedition of Rajendra Chola I, *c.* 1025 A.D." Ph.D., University of California at Berkeley, 1967. Includes a good overview of maritime activities in India and Southeast Asia, 2000 B.C. to A.D. 1100.

Starr, Chester G. "The Myth of the Minoan Thalassocracy." *Historia 3* (1954–5), 282–291.

———. *The Roman Imperial Navy, 31 B.C.–A.D. 324.* Ithaca, 1941.

Thiel, J. H. *Studies on the History of Roman Sea-Power in Republican Times.* Amsterdam, Holland, 1946.

Thompson, Edgar K. "Swiss Naval Wars." *Mariner's Mirror,* 59, no. 1 (February 1973), 99. 1300–1550 A.D.

Thucydides (tr. by Rex Warner). *The Peloponnesian War.* Baltimore, 1954.

Vegetius, [Flavius Renatus] (no tr.). "Military Institutions of the Romans." n.p., n.d. Book V of this classic work deals with the navies of imperial Rome.

Warmington, B. H. *Carthage.* Baltimore, 1964.

Watson, William. *Early Civilization in China.* New York, 1966.

Weir, Michael. "English Naval Activities, 1242–1243." *Mariner's Mirror,* 58, no. 1 (February 1972), 85–92.

Wheeler, Sir Mortimer. *Civilizations of the Indus Valley and Beyond.* New York, 1966.

Wiel, Alethea. *The Navy of Venice.* London, 1910.

Wilcken, Ulrich. *Alexander the Great.* 1931; New York, 1967.

Wilson, W. R., Captain, USN (Ret). "The Sea Battle of Dannoura." *The American Neptune,* XXVIII, no. 3 (July 1968), 206–222.

Yadin, Yigael. *The Art of Warfare in Biblical Lands,* 2 vols. New York, 1963.

BOOK THREE. THE OCEANIC AGE, 1415–1730

Albion, Robert Greenhalgh. *Forests and Sea Power: The Timber Problem of the Royal Navy, 1652–1862.* 1926; Hamden, Conn., 1965.

Anderson, R. C. "The First Dutch War in the Mediterranean." *Mariner's Mirror,* 49, no. 4 (November 1963), 241–265.

———. *Naval Wars in the Baltic during the Sailing Ship Epoch, 1522–1850.* 1910; London, 1969.

———. *Naval Wars in the Levant, 1559–1853.* Liverpool, 1953.

———. "The Thirty Years' War in the Mediterranean." *Mariner's Mirror,* 55 (1969), 435–451, and 56 (1970), 41–57.

Bamford, Paul W. *Fighting Ships and Prisons: The Mediterranean Galleys of France in the Age of Louis XIV.* Minneapolis, 1973.

———. *Forests and French Sea Power, 1660–1789.* Toronto, 1956.

Battick, John Francis. "Cromwell's Navy and the Foreign Policy of the Protectorate, 1653–1658." Ph.D., Boston University, 1967.

Beck, Horace P. *The American Indian as a Sea-Fighter in Colonial Times.* Mystic, 1959.

Bensusan, Harold Guy. "The Spanish Struggle Against Foreign Encroachment in the Caribbean, 1675–1697." Ph.D., University of California at Los Angeles, 1970.

Boxer, C. R. *The Dutch Seaborne Empire, 1600–1800.* New York, 1965.

———. *The Portuguese Seaborne Empire, 1415–1825.* New York, 1969.

Bradford, Ernle. *The Sultan's Admiral: The Life of Barbarossa.* New York, 1968.

Brandel, Fernand (tr. by Siân Reynolds). *The Mediterranean and the Mediterranean World in the Age of Philip II,* 2 vols. London, 1972–73.

Corbett, Julian S. *Fighting Instructions, 1530–1816.* London, 1905; New York, 1967.

Creswell, John. *British Admirals of the Eighteenth Century: Tactics in Battle.* Hamden, Conn., 1972.

De Meij, J. C. A. *De Watergeuzen en de Nederlanden, 1568–72.* Amsterdam, 1972. The Sea Beggars.

Earle, Peter. *Corsairs of Malta and Barbary.* Annapolis, 1970.

Ehrman, John. *The Navy in the War of William III, 1689–1697.* Cambridge, 1953.

Elliot, J. H. *Imperial Spain, 1469–1716.* New York, 1963.

———. *The Old World and the New, 1492–1650.* Cambridge, 1970.

Elridge, F. B. *The Background of Eastern Sea Power.* Melbourne, 1948. The navies of the Far East throughout history.

Gardiner, C. Harvey. *Naval Power in the Conquest of Mexico.* Austin, 1956. Cortez's inland fleet.

Geyl, Pieter. *The Netherlands in the Seventeenth Century.* London, 1961.

Goslinga, Cornelis Ch. *The Dutch in the Caribbean and on the Wild Coast, 1580–1680.* Gainesville, Fla., 1971.

Haley, K. H. D. *The Dutch in the Seventeenth Century.* London, 1972.

Hansen, H. A. "The Sound Trade and the Anglo-Dutch Conflicts, 1640–1654." Ph.D., University of California at Los Angeles, 1947.

Hess, Andrew C. "The Battle of Lepanto and its Place in Mediterranean History." American Historical Association unpublished paper, Boston, December 1970.

———. "The Evolution of the Ottoman Seaborne Empire in the Age of Oceanic Discoveries, 1453–1525." *American Historical Review,* LXXV, no. 7 (December 1970), 1892–1919.

Hoffman, Paul Everett. "The Defense of the Indies, 1535–1574. A Study in the Modernization of the Spanish State." Ph.D., University of Florida, 1969.

Huizinga, J. H. (tr. by Arnold J. Pomerans). *Dutch Civilisation in the Seventeenth Century, and other essays.* London, 1968.

Jamieson, Alan. "The Tangier Galleys and the Wars against the Mediterranean Corsairs." *American Neptune,* XXIII, no. 2 (April 1963), 95–112.

LeGuin, Charles A. "Sea Life in Seventeenth-Century England." *American Neptune,* XXVII, no. 2 (April 1967), 111–134.

Lisk, Jill. *The Struggle for Supremacy in the Baltic, 1600–1725.* London, 1967.

Mallett, Michael E. *The Florentine Galleys in the Fifteenth Century.* Oxford, 1967.

Marcus, G. J. *A Naval History of England,* Vol. I: *The Formative Centuries.* London, 1961. To the end of the American Revolution.

Monk, W. F. *Britain and the Western Mediterranean.* London, 1953.

Moore, Ronald Oury. "Some Aspects of the Origins and Nature of English Piracy, 1603–1625." Ph.D., University of Virginia, 1960.

Moses, Norton H. "The British Navy and the Caribbean, 1689–1697." *Mariner's Mirror,* 52, no. 1 (February 1966), 13–40.

Natharius, Edward William. "The Maritime Powers and Sweden, 1698–1702." Ph.D., Indiana University, 1959.

Oakeshott, Walter. *Founded Upon the Seas: A Narrative of Some English Maritime and Overseas Enterprises during the period 1550 to 1616.* Cambridge, 1942.

Ollard, Richard. *Man of War: Sir Robert Holmes and the Restoration Navy.* London, 1969.

Parry, J. H. *The Age of Reconnaissance.* New York, 1963. Covers the entire period of European exploration.

———. *The Spanish Seaborne Empire.* London, 1966.

Peckham, Howard H. *The Colonial Wars, 1689–1762.* Chicago, 1964. In North America.

Petersen, Charles W. "England and Danish Naval Strategy in the Seventeenth Century." Ph.D., University of Maine, 1975.

Pierson, Peter O'Malley. "A Commander for the Armada." *Mariner's Mirror,* 55 (1969), 383–400. The appointment of the Duke of Medina Sidonia.

Pilgrim, Donald George. "The Uses and Limitations of French Naval Power in the Reign of Louis XIV: the Administration of the Marquis de Seignelay, 1683–1690." Ph.D., Brown University, 1969.

Powell, J. R. *The Navy in the English Civil War.* Hamden, Conn., 1962.

Powley, Edward B. *The English Navy in the Revolution of 1688.* Cambridge, 1928.

————. *The Naval Side of King William's War.* London, 1972. Covers the years 1688–1690.

Richmond, H. W. *Statesmen and Sea Power: The Navy as an Instrument of Policy, 1558–1727.* London, 1946, 1953. The British navy.

Rogers, H. C. B., Colonel. *Troopships and Their History.* London, 1963. The British trooplifting transports from the mid-seventeenth to the mid-twentieth centuries.

Saunders, Roy. *The Raising of the Vasa: The Rebirth of a Swedish Galleon.* London, 1962.

Scheina, Robert Lewis. "Mass Labor: The Key to Spanish Maritime Construction in the Americas during the Sixteenth Century." *Mariner's Mirror,* 58, no. 2 (May 1972), 195–202.

Schurz, William Lytle. *The Manila Galleon.* 1939; New York, 1959. Spanish maritime commerce to the Philippines, 1565–1815.

Teneti, Alberto (tr. by Janet and Brian Pullan). *Piracy and the Decline of Venice, 1580–1615.* London, 1967.

Vere, Francis. *Salt in Their Blood.* London, 1955. A popular account of the Dutch navy during the seventeenth century and in World War II.

Williamson, James A. *The Age of Drake.* London, 1938.

Wilson, Charles. *The Dutch Republic.* New York, 1968.

————. *Profit and Power: A Study of England and the Dutch Wars.* London, 1957.

BOOK FOUR. BRITISH EMPIRE AND THE WORLD WARS, 1730–1815

Arthur, Charles Burton. "The Revolution in British Naval Strategy, 1800–1801." Ph.D., Harvard University, 1966. An overstated case for St. Vincent's close blockade of France.

Bird, Harrison. *Navies in the Mountains: The Battles on the Waters of Lake Champlain and Lake George, 1609–1814.* New York, 1962.

Brown, Wilbur S., Major General, USMC (Ret). *The Amphibious Campaign for West Florida and Louisiana, 1814–15.* Tuscaloosa, 1969.

Coggins, Jack. *Ships and Seamen of the American Revolution.* Harrisburg, 1969.

Darrieus, Gabriel, Captain, F.N. (tr. by Philip R. Alger). *War on the Sea.* Annapolis, 1908. Napoleon and sea power.

Forbes, Eric G. "Who Discovered Longitude at Sea?" *Sky and Telescope,* 41, no. 1 (January 1971), 4–6.

Glover, Richard. "The French Fleet, 1807–1814; Britain's Problem; and

Madison's Opportunity." *Journal of Modern History,* 39 (September 1967), 233–252. Napoleon's naval construction that forced the British to overextend their wartime fleet.

Graham, Gerald S. *Sea Power and British North America.* Cambridge, 1941. The demise of mercantilism after the American Revolution.

Gruber, Ira D. "Admiral, Lord Howe and the War for American Independence." Ph.D., Duke University, 1961.

Hayes, Frederic H. "John Adams and American Sea Power." *American Neptune,* XXV, no. 1 (January 1965), 35–45.

Howarth, David. *Trafalgar: The Nelson Touch.* New York, 1969.

Jackson, Melvin H. *Privateers in Charleston, 1793–1796.* Washington, 1969.

Kelly, John J., Jr. "The Struggle for American Seaborne Independence as Viewed by John Adams." Ph.D., University of Maine, 1973.

Kennedy, Ludovic. *Nelson's Band of Brothers.* London, n.d.

Knox, Dudley W. *The Naval Genius of George Washington.* Boston, 1932.

Kulsrud, Carl J. *Maritime Neutrality to 1780.* Boston, 1936.

Lester, Malcolm. "Anglo-American Diplomatic Problems Arising from British Naval Operations in American Waters, 1793–1802." Ph.D., University of Virginia, 1954.

Lewis, Emanuel Raymond. *Seacoast Fortifications of the United States: An Introductory History.* Washington, 1970.

Mackesy, Piers. *The War in the Mediterranean, 1803–1810.* Cambridge, Mass., 1957.

Mahan, Alfred Thayer. *The Influence of Sea Power upon History, 1660–1783.* Boston, London, 1890; New York, 1957.

————. *The Influence of Sea Power upon the French Revolution and Empire, 1793–1812,* 2 vols. Boston, 1892; New York, 1968.

————. *Naval Strategy.* Boston, 1911.

————. *Sea Power in its Relations to the War of 1812,* 2 vols. Boston, 1905; New York, 1968.

Marcus, G. J. *The Age of Nelson: The Royal Navy in the Age of its Greatest Power and Glory, 1793–1815.* New York, 1971. Volume II in an ongoing history of the British navy.

Masefield, John. *Sea Life in Nelson's Time,* 3rd ed. Annapolis, 1972.

Nasatir, Abraham P. *Spanish War Vessels on the Mississippi, 1792–1796.* New Haven, 1968.

Oglesby, J. C. M. "War at Sea in the West Indies, 1739–1748." Ph.D., University of Washington, 1963.

Parry, J. H. *Trade and Dominion: The European Overseas Empires in the Eighteenth Century.* New York, 1971.

Robertson, Sir Charles Grant. *Chatham and the British Empire.* London, 1946.

Rush, N. Orwin. *The Battle of Pensacola, March 9 to May 8, 1781.* Tallahassee, 1966.

Saul, Norman Eugene. "Russia and the Mediterranean, 1797–1807." Ph.D., Columbia University, 1965.

Stout, Neil R. *The Royal Navy in America, 1760–1775.* Annapolis, 1973.

Syrett, David. "The Methodology of British Amphibious Operations during the Seven Years and American Wars." *Mariner's Mirror,* 58, no. 3 (August 1972), 269–280.

Tunstall, Brian. *William Pitt, Earl of Chatham.* London, 1938.

BOOK FIVE. PAX BRITANNICA, 1815–1914

Allin, Lawrence C. *The United States Naval Institute: Intellectual Forum of the New Navy, 1873–1889.* Manhattan, Kansas, 1978.

Baker, Maury Davison, Jr. "The United States and Piracy during the Spanish-American Wars of Independence." Ph.D., Duke University, 1946.

Ballard, G. A. *The Influence of the Sea on the Political History of Japan.* London, 1921.

Bartlett, C. J. *Great Britain and Sea Power, 1815–1853.* Oxford, 1963.

Bauer, K. Jack. *Surfboats and Horse Marines: U. S. Naval Operations in the Mexican War, 1846–48.* Annapolis, 1969.

———. "The United States Navy and Texas Independence: A Study in Jacksonian Integrity." *Military Affairs,* XXXIV, no. 2 (April 1970), 44–48.

Baynham, Henry. *Before the Mast: Naval Ratings of the 19th Century.* London, 1971.

Belknap, George E., Rear Admiral, USN. "The Home Squadron in the Winter of 1860–61." *Papers of the Historical Society of Massachusetts,* XII: *Naval Actions and History, 1799–1898.* Boston, 1902, pp. 75–100.

Berghahn, Volker R. *Der Tirpitz-Plan.* Düsseldorf, 1972.

Bernath, Stuart L. *Squall Across the Atlantic: American Civil War Prize Cases and Diplomacy.* Berkeley, 1970.

Bidwell, Robert Leland. "The First Mexican Navy, 1821–1830." Ph.D., University of Virginia, 1960.

Bigelow, John. *France and the Confederate Navy, 1862–1868.* New York, 1888.

Billingsley, Edward Warner. *In Defense of Neutral Rights: The United States Navy and the Wars of Independence in Chile and Peru.* Chapel Hill, 1967.

Boatner, Mark Mayo, III, Lieutenant Colonel, USA. *The Civil War Dictionary.* New York, 1959.

Bourne, Kenneth. *Britain and the Balance of Power in North America, 1815–1908.* Berkeley, 1967. Includes navies.

———, and Carl Boyd. "Captain Mahan's 'War' with Great Britain." *USNIP,* 94, no. 7 (July 1968), 71–78. Mahan's war plans for a possible war with Britain in the 1890s.

Brainard, Alfred P. "Russian Mines on the Danube." *USNIP,* 91, no. 7 (July 1965), 51–56. The Russo-Turkish War of 1877–78.

Braisted, William Reynolds. *The United States Navy in the Pacific, 1897–1909.* Austin, 1958; New York, 1969.

———. *The United States Navy in the Pacific, 1909–1922.* Austin, 1971.

Bright, Samuel R., Jr. "Confederate Coast Defense." Ph.D., Duke University, 1961.

Brodie, Bernard. *Sea Power in the Machine Age.* Princeton, 1941. Covers the years 1814 to 1940.

Brooke, George M., Jr. "The Role of the United States Navy in the Suppression of the African Slave Trade." *American Neptune,* XXI, no. 1 (January 1961), 28–41.

Buhl, Lance Crowther. "The Smooth Water Navy: American Naval Policy and Politics, 1865–1876." Ph.D., Harvard University, 1968.

Buker, George E. *Swamp Sailors: Riverine Warfare in the Everglades, 1835–1842.* Gainesville, Fla., 1975.

Busch, Briton Cooper. *Britain and the Persian Gulf, 1894–1914.* Berkeley, 1967.

Cecil, Lamar J. R. "Coal for the Fleet That Had to Die." *American Historical Review,* LXIX, no. 4 (July 1964), 990–1005. Logistics of the Russian fleet voyage from the Baltic to Tsushima.

Challener, Richard D. *Admirals, Generals, and American Foreign Policy, 1898–1914.* Princeton, 1973.

Clowes, Sir William Laird. *Four Modern Naval Campaigns: Historical, Strategic, and Tactical.* London, 1902; 1970. Limited wars between 1866 and 1894.

Cornwall, Peter George. "The Meiji Navy: Training in an Age of Change." Ph.D., University of Michigan, 1970. Late nineteenth century Japan.

Cullen, Charles W., Lieutenant Commander, USN. "From the Kriegsacademie to the Naval War College: The Military Planning Process." *NWCR,* XXII, no. 5 (January 1970), 6–18. War colleges of the late nineteenth century.

Dallett, Francis James. "The Creation of the Venezuelan Naval Squadron, 1848–1860." *American Neptune,* XXX, no. 4 (October 1970), 260–278.

Daly, R. W. *How the Merrimac Won: The Strategic Story of the C.S.S. Virginia.* New York, 1957. That vessel's impact on McClellan's Peninsular Campaign.

Falk, Edwin A. *From Perry to Pearl Harbor: The Struggle for Supremacy in the Pacific.* Garden City, 1943. Japanese naval power from the 1850s to the 1940s.

Field, James A., Jr. *America and the Mediterranean World, 1776–1882.* Princeton, 1969. Includes the Mediterranean Squadron.

Fox, Grace. *Britain and Japan, 1858–1883.* Oxford, 1969. Naval relations included.

————. *British Admirals and Chinese Pirates, 1832–1869.* London, 1940.

Gebhard, Louis A. "The Development of the Austro-Hungarian Navy, 1897–1914: A Study in the Operation of Dualism." Ph.D., Rutgers University, 1965.

Gilbert, Benjamin Franklin. "Naval Operations in the Pacific, 1861–1866." Ph.D., University of California at Berkeley, 1951. Navies of all nations in the Pacific then.

Gough, Barry M. *The Royal Navy and the Northwest Coast of North America, 1810–1914.* Vancouver, 1971.

Gowing, Peter Gordon. "Mandate in Moroland: The American Government of Muslim Filipinos, 1899–1920." Ph.D., Syracuse University, 1968. Much background on Spanish naval pacification operations, then that by the United States.

Graham, Gerald S. *Great Britain in the Indian Ocean: A Study of Maritime Enterprise, 1810–1850.* Oxford, 1967.

————. *The Politics of Naval Supremacy: Studies in British Maritime Ascendancy.* Cambridge, 1965. Heaviest on the nineteenth century.

Grenville, John A. S. and George Berkeley Young. *Politics, Strategy, and American Diplomacy: Studies in Foreign Policy, 1873–1917.* New Haven, 1966. Much on the U. S. Navy.

Hagan, Kenneth J. "Admiral David Dixon Porter: Strategist for a Navy in Transition." *USNIP,* 94, no. 7 (July 1968), 139–143.

————. *American Gunboat Diplomacy and the Old Navy, 1877–1889.* Westport, Conn., 1973.

Halpern, Paul G. *The Mediterranean Naval Situation, 1908–1914.* Cambridge, Mass., 1971.

Hayes, John D., Rear Admiral, USN (Ret). "Sea Power in the Civil War." *USNIP,* 87, no. 11 (November 1961), 60–69.

————. "Stephen Bleecker Luce." *NWCR,* XXII, no. 1 (September 1969), 75–79.

Heffernan, John B. "The Blockade of the Southern Confederacy: 1861–1865." *The Smithsonian Journal of History,* II, no. 4 (Winter 1967–1968), 23–44.

Henson, Curtis Talmon, Jr. "The United States Navy and China, 1839–1861." Ph.D., Tulane University, 1965.

Hollyday, Frederic B. M. *Bismarck's Rival: A Political Biography of General and Admiral Albrecht von Stosch.* Durham, 1960. Early years of the Imperial German Navy.

Hough, Richard. *First Sea Lord: An Authorized Biography of Admiral Lord Fisher.* London, 1969.

————. *The Fleet That Had to Die.* New York, 1958. Tsushima.

————. *The Potemkin Mutiny.* New York, 1961.

Hovgaard, William. *Modern History of Warships.* London, 1920; Annapolis, 1971. The period 1860 through World War I.

Howeth, L. S., Captain, USN. *History of Communications-Electronics in the United States Navy.* Washington, 1963. Mostly the early years.

Huntington, Samuel P. *The Soldier and the State: The Theory and Politics of Civil-Military Relations.* New York, 1957. A historical view of the American situation.

Jane, Fred. T. *The Imperial Japanese Navy.* London, 1904.

Jenrich, Charles H. "The Papal Navy." *USNIP,* 89, no. 9 (September 1963), 74–79.

Johnson, Franklyn Arthur. *Defence by Committee: The British Committee of Imperial Defence, 1885–1959.* London, 1960.

Johnson, Ludwell H. "Commerce Between Northeastern Ports and the Confederacy, 1861–1865." *Journal of American History,* LIV, no. 1 (June 1967), 30–42.

Johnson, Robert Erwin. *Thence Round Cape Horn: The Story of United States Naval Forces on Pacific Station, 1818–1923.* Annapolis, 1963.

Jornacion, George W. "The Time of the Eagles: United States Army Officers and the Pacification of the Philippine Moros, 1899–1913." Ph.D., University of Maine, 1973. Includes Naval operations.

Kajima, Morinosuke. *The Emergence of Japan as a World Power, 1895–1925.* Tokyo, 1968.

Kelly, J. B. *Britain and the Persian Gulf, 1795–1880.* Oxford, 1968.

Kelly, Patrick James. "The Naval Policy of Imperial Germany, 1900–1914." Ph.D., Georgetown University, 1970.

Kiralfy, Alexander. "Japanese Naval Strategy." Edward M. Earle, ed. *Makers of Modern Strategy.* Princeton, 1941; New York, 1966, pp. 457–484. Mainly 1894–1942.

Laing, E. A. M. "Naval Operations in the War of the Triple Alliance, 1864–70." *Mariner's Mirror,* 54, no. 3 (August 1968), 253–279.

Langley, Harold D. *Social Reform in the United States Navy, 1798–1862.* Urbana, Ill., 1967.

Lass, William E. *A History of Steamboating on the Upper Missouri River.* Lincoln, Neb., 1962.

Lee, H. I. "Mediterranean Strategy and Anglo-French Relations, 1908–1912." *Mariner's Mirror,* 57, no. 3 (August 1971), 267–285.

Livermore, Seward W. "The American Navy as a Factor in World Politics, 1903–1913." *American Historical Review,* LXIII (July 1958), 863–879.

Lloyd, Christopher. *The Navy and the Slave Trade.* New York, 1949. The British navy, but others to some extent.

Long, David F. *Nothing Too Daring: A Biography of Commodore David Porter, 1783–1843.* Annapolis, 1970.

Makaroff [*sic*], S. J. [*sic*], Vice Admiral, I.R.N. (tr. by Lieutenant John B. Bernadou, USN). "Discussion of Questions in Naval Tactics." *Notes on Naval Progress.* Washington, 1898.

Marder, Arthur J. *The Anatomy of British Sea Power: A History of Naval Policy in the Pre-Dreadnought Era, 1880–1905.* New York, 1940.

—————. *From the Dreadnought to Scapa Flow: The Royal Navy in the Fisher Era, 1904–1919,* Vol. I. London, 1961.

La Marina Militaire Nel Suo Primo Secolo di Vita, 1861–1961. Rome, 1961. History of the Italian Navy.

McCleary, John William. "Anglo-French Naval Rivalry, 1815–1848." Ph.D., Johns Hopkins University, 1947.

McIntyre, W. David. *The Imperial Frontier in the Tropics, 1865–75.* London, 1967. The British.

Merli, Frank J. *Great Britain and the Confederate Navy.* Bloomington, Ind., 1970.

Miller, Harry. *Pirates of the Far East.* London, 1970. Heaviest on the nineteenth century.

Morgan, William Abraham. "Sea Power in the Gulf of Mexico and the Caribbean during the Mexican and Colombian Wars of Independence, 1815–1830." Ph.D., University of Southern California, 1969.

Naval History Division. *Civil War Naval Chronology, 1861–1865.* Washington, 1971.

—————. *The Texas Navy.* Washington, 1968.

Nish, Ian H. *The Anglo-Japanese Alliance: The Diplomacy of Two Islands, 1894–1907.* London, 1966.

Norton, Gary. "The Mississippi Marine Brigade, 1862–64." Uncompleted M. A. thesis, University of Maine.

O'Gara, Gordon Carpenter. *Theodore Roosevelt and the Rise of the Modern American Navy.* Princeton, 1943; New York, 1969.

Osborne, Milton E. *The French Presence in Cochinchina and Cambodia: Rule and Response (1859–1905).* Ithaca, 1969.

Padfield, Peter. *Aim Straight: A Biography of Admiral Sir Percy Scott.* London, 1966.

Parnell, Charles Lavelle, Lieutenant, USN. "Gunboats in the Desert." *USNIP,* 94, no. 11 (November 1968), 74–90. The British on the Nile, 1898.

Patterson, Andrew, Jr. "Mining: A Naval Strategy." *NWCR,* XXIII, no. 9 (May 1971), 52–66. Nineteenth and twentieth centuries.

Paullin, Charles Oscar. *American Voyages to the Orient, 1690–1865.* Annapolis, 1910–11; 1971.

Perry, John Curtis. "Great Britain and the Imperial Japanese Navy, 1858–1905." Ph.D., Harvard University, 1961.

Pocock, R. F. and G. R. M. Garratt. *The Origins of Maritime Radio*. London, 1972.

Preston, Antony and John Major. *Send a Gunboat! A Study of the Gunboat and Its Role in British Policy, 1854–1904*. London, 1967.

Preston, Richard A. *Canada and "Imperial Defense": A Study of the Origins of the British Commonwealth's Defense Organization, 1867–1919*. Durham, 1967.

Price, Marcus W. "Blockade Running as a Business in South Carolina During the War Between the States, 1861–1865." *American Neptune*, IX (1949), 31–62.

Priestley, Herbert Ingram. *France Overseas: A Study of Modern Imperialism*. New York, 1938. Includes the French Navy.

Prucha, Francis Paul. *The Sword of the Republic: The United States Army on the Frontier, 1793–1846*. [New York], 1969. Includes the waterborne support and river fortification network.

Pullar, Walter S., Lieutenant Colonel, USMC. "Abe Lincoln's Brown Water Navy." *NWCR*, XXI, no. 8 (April 1969), 71–88. The Civil War on the inland waters.

Rawlinson, John L. *China's Struggle for Naval Development, 1839–1895*. Cambridge, Mass., 1967.

Reynolds, Clark G. "The Civil and Indian War Diaries of Eugene Marshall, Minnesota Volunteer." M. A., Duke University, 1963. Includes waterborne pacification operations against Confederate guerrillas and the Sioux Indians, 1862–66.

————. "The Great Experiment: Hunter's Horizontal Wheel." *American Neptune*, XXIV, no. 1 (January 1964), 5–24. The leading challenger to the screw propeller.

———— and William J. McAndrew, eds. *1971 Seminar in Maritime and Regional Studies*. Orono, Me., 1972. Oceanic history and strategy in the nineteenth and early twentieth centuries.

Ropp, Theodore. "Anacondas Anyone?" *Military Affairs*, XXVII, no. 2 (Summer 1963), 71–76. Origins of the Union Civil War strategy.

————. "Continental Doctrines of Sea Power." Earle, ed. *Makers of Modern Strategy*, pp. 446–456. Mainly the French Navy.

————. "The Development of a Modern Navy: French Naval Policy, 1871–1914." Ph.D., Harvard University, 1937.

Ross, J. O'C. *The White Ensign in New Zealand*. Wellington, 1967. The Royal Navy in New Zealand, including the Maori wars.

Rossell, H. E. *Historical Transactions, 1893–1943: "Types of Naval Ships."* n.p., 1945.

Sandler, Stanley. "A Navy in Decay: Some Strategic Technological Results of Disarmament, 1865–69 in the U. S. Navy." *Military Affairs*, XXXV, no. 4 (December 1971), 138–142.

Scheina, Robert L. "Seapower Misused: Mexico at War 1846–48." *Mariner's Mirror*, 57, no. 2 (May 1971), 203–214.

Schonberger, Howard B. *Transportation to the Seaboard: The "Communication Revolution" and American Foreign Policy, 1860–1900*. Westport, Conn., 1971.

Schonfield, Hugh J. *The Suez Canal in Peace and War, 1869–1969*. Coral Gables, 1969.

Schurman, D. M. *The Education of a Navy: The Development of British Naval Strategic Thought, 1867–1914*. Chicago, 1965.

Seager, Robert, II. "Ten Years Before Mahan: The Unofficial Case for the New Navy, 1880–1890." *Mississippi Valley Historical Review*, XL, no. 3 (1953), 491–512.

Selby, John. *The Paper Dragon: An Account of the China Wars, 1840–1900*. New York, 1968.

Sokol, Anthony E. *The Imperial and Royal Austro-Hungarian Navy*. Annapolis, 1968.

Soley, John C., Lieutenant, USN. "The Naval Brigade." *Military Historical Society of Massachusetts*, XII [1890], 245–268. Early landing forces in the U. S. Navy.

Spector, Ronald. *Professors of War: The Naval War College and the Development of the Naval Profession*. Newport, 1977.

Sprout, Harold and Margaret. *The Rise of American Naval Power, 1776–1918*. Princeton, 1939, 1967.

Sprout, Margaret. "Mahan: Evangelist of Sea Power." Earle, ed. *Makers of Modern Strategy*, 415–445.

Steinberg, Jonathan. *Yesterday's Deterrent: Tirpitz and the Birth of the German Battle Fleet*. London, 1965.

Still, William N., Jr. *Confederate Shipbuilding*. Athens, Ga., 1969.

―――. *Iron Afloat: The Story of the Confederate Ironclads*. [Nashville], 1971.

Stokesbury, James Lawton. "British Concepts and Practices of Amphibious Warfare, 1867–1916." Ph.D., Duke University, 1968.

Stoll, Ronald M., Midshipman, USN. "A Ship There Was, But It Flew the White Ensign." Undergraduate research paper, United States Naval Academy, 1966. The British navy in the Boer War.

Taylor, George Rogers. *The Transportation Revolution, 1815–1860*. New York, 1951. Land, sea, canal, river, etc.

Turk, Richard Wellington. "Strategy and Foreign Policy: The United States Navy in the Caribbean, 1865–1913." Ph.D., Fletcher School of Law and Diplomacy, 1968.

Utley, Robert M. *Frontiersmen in Blue: The United States Army and the Indian, 1848–1865*. New York, 1967.

Vale, Brian. "The Creation of the Imperial Brazilian Navy, 1822–1823." *Mariner's Mirror*, 57, no. 1 (January 1971), 63–88.

―――. "Lord Cochrane in Brazil. I. The Naval War of Independence, 1823." *Mariner's Mirror*, 57, no. 4 (November 1971), 415–442.

―――. "Lord Cochrane II: Prize Money, Politics and Rebellion, 1824–25." *Mariner's Mirror*, 59, no. 2 (May 1973), 135–159.

Ward, W. E. F. *The Royal Navy and the Slavers*. London, 1969.

[Webber, Richard H., Lieutenant, USNR]. *Monitors of the U. S. Navy, 1861–1937*. Washington, 1969.

Wells, Tom Henderson, Commander, USN. *Commodore Moore and the Texas Navy*. Austin, 1960.

―――. *The Confederate Navy: A Study in Organization*. University, Ala., 1971.

White, Donald G., Ensign, USNR. "The Misapplication of a Weapons System: The Battle Cruiser as a Warship Type." *NWCR*, XXII, no. 5 (January 1970), 42–62.

Williamson, Samuel R., Jr. *The Politics of Grand Strategy: Britain and France Prepare for War, 1904–1914*. Cambridge, Mass., 1969.

Willock, Roger, Colonel, USMCR. *Bulwark of Empire: Bermuda's Fortified Naval Base 1860–1920.* Princeton, 1962.

―――. "Gunboat Diplomacy: Operations of the North America and West Indies Squadron, 1875–1915." *American Neptune,* XXVIII, no. 1 (January 1968), 5–30, and XXVIII, no. 2 (April 1968), 85–112. The British.

Wiswall, F. L., Jr. *The Development of Admiralty Jurisdiction and Practice Since 1800: An English Study with American Comparisons.* Cambridge, 1970.

Woodward, E. L. *Great Britain and the German Navy.* Oxford, 1935. The Anglo-German naval rivalry, 1898–1914.

Worcester, Donald E. *Sea Power and Chilean Independence.* Gainesville, Fla., 1962.

Wyckoff, Don P. "The Chilean Civil War, 1891." *USNIP,* 88, no. 10 (October 1962), 58–63.

BOOK SIX. ERA OF THE TOTAL WARS, 1914–1945

Albion, Robert G. *Makers of Naval Policy 1798–1947.* Annapolis, 1980.

Anderson, Edgar. "An Undeclared Naval War: The British-Soviet Naval Struggle in the Baltic, 1918–1920." *Journal of Central European Affairs,* XXII (April 1962), 43–78.

Andrade, Ernest, Jr. "The Ship That Never Was: The Flying-Deck Cruiser." *Military Affairs,* XXXII, no. 3 (December 1968), 132–140. Aspects of the 1930 London naval conference.

―――. "Submarine Policy in the United States Navy, 1919–1941." *Military Affairs,* XXXV, no. 2 (April 1971), 50–56.

―――. "United States Naval Power in the Disarmament Era, 1921–1937." Ph.D., Michigan State University, 1966.

Ansel, Walter. *Hitler and the Middle Sea.* Durham, 1972. German strategic designs on the Mediterranean, 1940–41.

―――. *Hitler Confronts England.* Durham, 1960. The German mobilization and plan to invade England in 1940.

Auphan, Paul, Rear Admiral, F.N. (Ret), and Jacques Mordal. (tr. by Captain A. C. J. Sabalot, USN [Ret]). *The French Navy in World War II.* Annapolis, 1959.

Barker, A. J. *The Bastard War: The Mesopotamian Campaign of 1914–1918.* New York, 1967. Includes river operations.

Bauer [Hermann], Admiral [G.N., Ret] (tr. by Lieutenant H. G. Rickover, USN). *The Submarine.* Berlin, 1931; Newport, 1936. World War I impact of submarines.

Baxter, James Phinney, 3rd. *Scientists Against Time.* Boston, 1946. American scientific-weapons research and development, World War II.

Beitzell, Robert. *The Uneasy Alliance: America, Britain and Russia, 1941–1943.* New York, 1972.

Belote, James Hine. "The Development of German Naval Policy, 1933–1939." Ph.D., University of California at Berkeley, 1954.

Bennett, Geoffrey. *Cowan's War: The Story of British Naval Operations in the Baltic, 1918–1920.* London, 1964.

Berg, Meredith William. "The United States and the Breakdown of Naval Limitation, 1934–1939." Ph.D., Tulane University, 1966.

Berg, Sigval M., Jr., Midshipman, USN. "A Period of Crucial Development, 1920–1940." Undergraduate research paper, United States Naval Academy, 1967. Interwar American submarines.

Bidlingmaier, Gerhard. *Seegeltung in der Deutschen Geschichte.* Darmstadt, 1967. Sea power in modern German history.

Buell, Thomas B., Lieutenant Commander, USN. "Admiral Raymond A. Spruance and the Naval War College." *NWCR,* XXIII, no. 7 (March 1971), 30–51 and no. 8 (April 1971), 29–53.

Bulkley, Robert J., Jr., Captain, USNR (Ret). *At Close Quarters: PT Boats in the United States Navy.* Washington, 1962. World War II.

Burdick, Charles B. *Germany's Military Strategy and Spain in World War II.* Syracuse, 1968.

———. " 'Moro': The Resupply of German Submarines in Spain, 1939–1942," *Central European History,* III, no. 3 (September 1970), 256–282.

Bureau of Supplies and Accounts [USN]. *Special Report on Operations and Organization of the German Naval Supply System During World War II.* Washington, 1953.

Burns, Richard Dean. "Inspection of the Mandates, 1919–1941." *Pacific Historical Review,* XXXVII (November 1968), 445–462.   ,

———. "Regulating Submarine Warfare, 1921–41: A Case Study in Arms Control and Limited War." *Military Affairs,* XXXV, no. 2 (April 1971), 56–63.

Bush, Vannevar. *Pieces of the Action.* New York, 1970. Direction of American scientific-weapons activity in World War II.

Caldwell, Robert C., Major, USMC. "The Role of the Tracked Amphibian in Modern Amphibious Warfare." *NWCR,* XXII, no. 5 (January 1970), 68–99.

Christman, Albert B. *History of the Naval Weapons Center, China Lake, California,* Vol. I: *Sailors, Scientists, and Rockets.* Washington, 1971. Early rocket and missile research.

Clark, Admiral J. J., USN (Ret) with Clark G. Reynolds. *Carrier Admiral.* New York, 1967. Autobiographical account of American naval aviation, 1925–1953.

Davis, George T. *A Navy Second to None: The Development of Modern American Naval Policy.* New York, 1940.

Douglas, Lawrence H. "Submarine Disarmament, 1919–1936." Ph.D., Syracuse University, 1970.

Dreyer, Sir Frederick C., Admiral, R.N. *The Sea Heritage: A Study in Maritime Warfare.* London, 1955. Autobiographical.

Duroselle, Jean-Baptiste. "Le conflict stratégique anglo-american de juin 1940 à juin 1944." *Revue d'Histoire Moderne et Contemporaire,* X (July–September 1963), 161–184. Traces roots of American continental strategic tradition.

Dyer, George Carroll, Vice Admiral, USN (Ret). *The Amphibians Came to Conquer: The Story of Admiral Richmond Kelly Turner,* 2 vols. Washington, 1972. American amphibious leadership, World War II.

———. "Naval Amphibious Landmarks." *USNIP,* 92, no. 8 (August 1966), 50–60. 1920s to middle of World War II.

Enders, Calvin W. "The Vinson Navy." Ph.D., Michigan State University, 1970.

Fergusson, Bernard. *The Watery Maze: The Story of Combined Operations.* London, 1961. British amphibious operations, World War II.

Frank, Willard Chabot. "Sea Power, Politics and the Onset of the Spanish War, 1936." Ph.D., University of Pittsburgh, 1969.

Fuchida, Mitsuo and Masatake Okumiya. *Midway, The Battle That Doomed Japan.* Annapolis, 1955.

Garthoff, Raymond L. "Soviet Naval Operations in the War with Japan— August, 1945." *USNIP,* 92, no. 5 (May 1966), 50–63.

Genda, Minoru, General, JASDF (Ret). "Tactical Planning in the Imperial Japanese Navy." *NWCR,* XXII, no. 2 (October 1969), 45–50.

Gilbert, Nigel John, Lieutenant Commander, R.N. "British Submarine Operations in World War II." *USNIP,* 89, no. 3 (March 1963), 73–81.

Gordon, Arthur, Commander, USNR (Ret). "The Day the *Astral* Vanished." *USNIP,* 91, no. 10 (October 1965), 76–83. An aspect of German-American quasi-war, 1941.

Grant, Robert M. *U-Boats Destroyed: The Effect of Anti-Submarine Warfare, 1914–1918.* London, 1964.

Greenfield, Kent Roberts, ed. *Command Decisions.* Washington, 1960. World War II.

Golovko, Arseni G., Admiral, Soviet Navy. (ed. by Sir Aubrey Mansergh; tr. by Peter Broomfield). *With the Red Fleet.* London, 1965. Autobiographical; the Northern Fleet in World War II.

Grenfell, Russell, Commander, R.N. *The Art of the Admiral.* London, 1937. Naval strategy from 1900 to 1937.

Gretton, Sir Peter, Vice Admiral, R.N. *Winston Churchill and the Royal Navy.* New York, 1968.

Groeling, Dorothy Trautwein. "Submarines, Disarmament and Modern Warfare." Ph.D., Columbia University, 1935.

Hayes, John D., Rear Admiral, USN (Ret). "Admiral Joseph Mason Reeves. USN (1872–1948)." *NWCR,* XXIII, no. 3 (November 1970), 48–57 and XXIV, no. 5 (January 1972), 50–64.

Herwig, Holger H. "Admirals *versus* Generals: The War Aims of the Imperial Germany Navy, 1914–1918." *Central European History,* V, no. 3 (September 1972), 208–233.

Hezlet, Sir Arthur, Vice Admiral, R.N. *The Submarine and Sea Power.* London, 1967. The twentieth century.

Higham, Robin. *The Military Intellectuals in Britain: 1918–1939.* New Brunswick, N. J., 1966.

Historical Section, Office of the Chief of Staff of the Royal Italian Navy. *The Italian Navy in the World War, 1915–1918.* Rome, 1927.

Holmes, W. J. *Undersea Victory: The Influence of Submarine Operations on the War in the Pacific.* Garden City, 1966. American and Japanese.

Hood, Ronald Chalmers, III. "The Crisis of Civil-Naval Relations in France, 1924–1939: No *Concorde* Between Them." M. A., University of Maine, 1972.

Horn, Daniel. *The German Naval Mutinies of World War I.* New Brunswick, N. J., 1969.

Isely, Jeter A. and Philip A. Crowl. *The U. S. Marines and Amphibious War.* Princeton, 1951. Through World War II.

Ito, Masanori, with Roger Pineau. *The End of the Imperial Japanese Navy.* New York, 1962.

Jane's Fighting Ships, 1919. London, 1919; New York, 1969.

Kennedy, Malcolm D., Captain. *The Estrangement of Great Britain and Japan, 1917–35.* Berkeley, 1969.

Koginos, Manny T. *The Panay Incident: Prelude to War.* Lafayette, Ind., 1967.

Kumao, Baron Harada (tr. by Thomas Francis Mayer-Oakes). *Fragile Victory: Prince Saionji and the 1930 London Treaty Issue from the Memoirs of Baron Harada Kumao.* Detroit, 1968.

LeMasson, Henri. *Navies of the Second World War: The French Navy,* 2 vols. Garden City, 1969. Prewar period too.

Lenton, H. T. *Navies of the Second World War: Royal Netherlands Navy.* London, 1967. Prewar period too.

Lewis, Wallace Leigh. "The Survival of the German Navy 1917–1920: Officers, Sailors and Politics." Ph.D., University of Iowa, 1969.

Lockwood, Charles A., Vice Admiral, USN (Ret). *Down to the Sea in Subs.* New York, 1967. Autobiographical; 1900 through World War II.

Lott, Arnold S., Lieutenant Commander, USN. *Most Dangerous Sea: A History of Mine Warfare, and an Account of U. S. Navy Mine Warfare Operations in World War II and Korea.* Annapolis, 1959.

Louis, William Roger. *British Strategy in the Far East, 1919–1939.* Oxford, 1971.

Lundeberg, Philip K. "The German Naval Critique of the U-boat Campaign, 1915–1918." *Military Affairs,* XXVII, no. 3 (Fall 1963), 105–118.

———. "Undersea Warfare and Allied Strategy in World War I." *The Smithsonian Journal of History,* I, no. 3 (Autumn 1966), 1–30 and no. 4 (Winter 1967), 49–72.

Macintyre, Donald, Captain, R.N. (Ret). "Shipborne Radar." *USNIP,* 93, no. 9 (September 1967), 70–83. Prewar and World War II development in all navies.

Marder, Arthur J. *From the Dreadnought to Scapa Flow: The Royal Navy in the Fisher Era, 1904–1919,* Vols. II–V. London, 1965–1970.

———. "The Influence of History on Sea Power: The Royal Navy and the Lessons of 1914–1918." *Pacific Historical Review,* XLI, no. 4 (November 1972), 413–443.

———. "The Royal Navy and the Ethiopian Crisis of 1935–36." *American Historical Review,* LXXV (June 1970), 1327–56.

———. "Winston is Back: Churchill at the Admiralty." *The English Historical Review.* Supplement 5, 1972.

Martienssen, Anthony. *Hitler and His Admirals.* New York, 1949.

Maugeri, Franco, Admiral, Italian Navy. *From the Ashes of Disgrace.* New York, 1948. The Italian Navy before and during World War II.

Maund, L. E. H., Rear Admiral, R.N. *Assault From the Sea.* London, 1949. British amphibious warfare in World War II.

McHugh, Francis J. "Gaming at the Naval War College." *USNIP,* 90, no. 3 (March 1964), 48–55.

Milkman, Raymond H. "Operations Research in World War II." *USNIP,* 94, no. 5 (May 1968), 78–83.

Monroe, Elizabeth. *Britain's Moment in the Middle East, 1914–1956.* Baltimore, 1963.

Moorehead, Alan. *Gallipoli.* London, 1956.

Morison, Samuel Eliot. *History of United States Naval Operations in World War II,* 15 vols. Boston, 1947–62.

———. *Strategy and Compromise.* Boston, 1958. Allied strategic decisions.

Morton, Louis. "War Plan *Orange:* Evolution of a Strategy." *World Politics,* XI, no. 2 (January 1959), 221–58.

O'Connor, Raymond, ed. *The Japanese Navy in World War II*. Annapolis, 1969. Articles by former Japanese naval officers.

Okumiya, Masatake, Lieutenant General, JASDF (Ret). "For Sugar Boats or Submarines?" *USNIP*, 94, no. 8 (August 1968), 66–73. Japanese interwar development of the mandated islands.

Oyos, Lynwood E. "The Navy and the United States Far Eastern Policy, 1930–1939." Ph.D., University of Nebraska, 1958.

Piterskij, N. A. [Rear Admiral, Soviet Naval Reserve]. *Die Sowjet-Flotte im Zweiten Weltkrieg*. Oldenburg, 1966. The Soviet Navy in World War II.

Preston, Richard A. "The R.C.N. and Gun-Boat Diplomacy in the Caribbean." *Military Affairs*, XXXVI, no. 2 (April 1972), 41–44. The Canadian navy in the early 1930s.

Raeder, Erich, Grand Admiral, German Navy. *My Life*. Annapolis, 1960.

Reynolds, Clark G. "Die Entwicklung des Flugzeugträgers in Amerika, 1919–1945." *Marine Rundschau*, 60, no. 6 (December 1963), 337–48. Development of the aircraft carrier in the United States.

————. *The Fast Carriers: The Forging of an Air Navy*. New York, 1968. Anglo-American-Japanese carrier development, prewar and World War II; emphasis on attack carriers in the Pacific.

————. "Hitler's Flattop—The End of the Beginning." *USNIP*, 93, no. 1 (January 1967), 41–49.

————. "Sea Power in the Twentieth Century." *Journal of the Royal United Service Institution*, CXI (May 1966), 132–39. An interpretative updating of Mahan.

————. "Submarine Attacks on the Pacific Coast, 1942." *Pacific Historical Review*, XXXIII, No. 2 (May 1964), 183–93. Japanese.

Ropp, Theodore. "The Modern Italian Navy." *Military Affairs*, V (Spring 1941), 32–48 and (Summer 1941), 104–116. Early twentieth century.

Roscoe, Theodore. *United States Submarine Operations in World War II*. Annapolis, 1949.

Roskill, Stephen. *Naval Policy Between the Wars*, 2 vols. London, 1968; Annapolis, 1976.

————, Captain, R.N. *The War at Sea, 1939–1945*, 3 vols. London, 1954–62. The Royal Navy in World War II.

Ruge, Friedrich, Vice Admiral, F.G.N. (tr. by Commander M. G. Saunders, R.N.) *Der Seekrieg: The German Navy's Story, 1939–1945*. Annapolis, 1957.

Sachar, Howard M. *The Emergence of the Middle East: 1914–1924*. New York, 1969. Includes the naval aspects of confrontation.

Saville, Allison Winthrop. "The Development of the German U-Boat Arm, 1919–1935." Ph.D., University of Washington, 1963.

Schilling, Warner R. "Admirals and Foreign Policy, 1913–1919." Ph.D., Yale University, 1953. United States.

Schofield, B. B. *British Sea Power: Naval Policy in the Twentieth Century*. London, 1967.

Socas, Roberto E. "France, Naval Armaments and Naval Disarmament: 1918–1922." Ph.D., Columbia University, 1965.

Spigai, Virgilio, Vice Admiral, Italian Navy. "Italian Naval Assault Craft in Two World Wars." *USNIP*, 91, no. 3 (March 1965), 50–59.

Sprout, Harold and Margaret. *Toward a New Order of Sea Power: American Naval Policy and the World Scene, 1918–1922*. Princeton, 1943; New York, 1969. Global postwar naval realignments.

Sweetman, Jack. *The Landing at Veracruz: 1914.* Annapolis, 1968.

Toland, John. *The Rising Sun: The Decline and Fall of the Japanese Empire, 1936–1945.* New York, 1970.

Tolley, Kemp, Rear Admiral, USN (Ret). "Our Russian War of 1918–1919." *USNIP,* 95, no. 2 (February 1969), 58–72.

Trask, David F. *Captains & Cabinets: Anglo-American Naval Relations, 1917–1918.* Columbia, Mo., 1972.

Tuleja, Thaddeus V. *Statesmen and Admirals: Quest for a Far Eastern Policy.* New York, 1963. The Pacific area, 1931–41.

Turnbull, Archibald D. and Clifford L. Lord. *History of United States Naval Aviation.* New Haven, 1949. To 1941.

Von der Porten, Edward P. *The German Navy in World War II.* New York, 1969.

Walter, John C. "The Navy Department and the Campaign for Expanded Appropriations, 1933–1938." Ph.D., University of Maine, 1972. United States.

Watt, Donald C. "Stalin's First Bid for Sea Power, 1933–1941." *USNIP,* 90, no. 6 (June 1964), 88–96.

Wheeler, Gerald E. *Prelude to Pearl Harbor: The United States Navy and the Far East, 1921–1931.* Columbia, Mo. [1963].

———. "William Veazie Pratt, U. S. Navy: A Silhouette of an Admiral." *NWCR,* XXI, no. 9 (May 1969), 36–61.

White, Donald G., Ensign, USNR. "The French Navy and the Washington Conference." *NWCR,* XXII, no. 3 (November 1969), 33–44.

Wilds, Thomas. "How Japan Fortified the Mandated Islands." *USNIP,* 81, no. 4 (April 1955), 400–407. Pre-World War II.

Williams, Ann. *Britain and France in the Middle East and North Africa.* London, 1968. Twentieth century.

Winton, John. *The Forgotten Fleet: The British Navy in the Pacific, 1944–1945.* New York, 1969.

Woodward, David. "The High Seas Fleet—1917–18." *Journal of the Royal United Service Institution,* 113 (August 1968), 244–250. Germany.

BOOK SEVEN. PAX AMERICANA. AND EPILOGUE: WORLD WAR III

Abel, Elie. *The Missile Crisis.* New York, 1966. Cuba, 1962.

Ackley, Richard T., Commander, USN (Ret). "The Soviet Navy's Role in Foreign Policy." *NWCR,* XXIV (May 1972), no. 9, 48–65.

Alden, John D., Commander, USN. "A New Fleet Emerges: Combat Ships." *Naval Review, 1964.* Annapolis, 1963.

Allen, Scott, Lieutenant Commander, USN. "China: Nuclear Dragon." *USNIP,* 98, no. 6 (June 1972), 43–49.

Auer, James E., Lieutenant Commander, USN. "Japan's Maritime Self-Defense Force: An Appropriate Maritime Strategy?" *NWCR,* XXIV, no. 4 (December 1971), 3–20.

Baker, R. K. "Tropical Africa's Nascent Navies." *USNIP,* 95, no. 1 (January 1969), 64–71.

Baldwin, Hanson W. "After Vietnam—What Military Strategy in the Far East?" *The New York Times Magazine* (June 9, 1968), 36–37 and *passim.*

———. *Strategy for Tomorrow.* New York, 1970.

Barber, James A., Commander, USN. "The Nixon Doctrine and the Navy." *NWCR,* XXIII, No. 10 (June 1971), 5–15.

de Bazelaire, Yves, Rear Admiral, F.N. "The French Navy." *Naval Review 1965.* Annapolis, 1964, 118–137.

Beavers, Roy, Commander, USN. "The End of an Era." *USNIP,* 98, no. 7 (July 1972), 18–25. Shifting power balances and naval requirements.

Bird, Thomas C., Lieutenant Commander, USN. "British East of Suez Policy: A Victim of Economic Necessity." *NWCR,* XXII, no. 8 (April 1970), 54–70.

Blixt, Melvin D., Captain, USN. "Soviet Objectives in the Eastern Mediterranean." *NWCR,* XXI, no. 7 (March 1969), 4–27.

Borgese, Elisabeth Mann. "The Prospects for Peace in the Oceans." *Saturday Review* (September 26, 1970), 15–22.

Bradley, David. *No Place to Hide.* Boston, 1948. Early A-bomb tests.

Breyer, Siegfried (tr. by Lieutenant Commander M. W. Henley, R.N.). *Guide to the Soviet Navy.* Annapolis, 1970.

Brittin, Burdick H., Captain, USN. "Piracy—A Modern Conspectus." *USNIP,* 91, no. 5 (May 1965), 71–81.

Brodie, Bernard. *Strategy and National Interests: Reflections for the Future.* New York, 1971.

———. *Strategy in the Missile Age.* Princeton, 1959, 1965.

Bull, Hedley. "The New Balance of Power in Asia and the Pacific." *Foreign Affairs,* 49, no. 8 (July 1971), 669–681.

Bussert, J. C., Master Chief Sonar Technician, USN. "The Navy Gap in the Seventies." *USNIP,* 98, no. 6 (June 1972), 18–26. Partly fiction.

Cagle, Malcolm W., Commander, USN and Commander Frank A. Manson, USN. *The Sea War in Korea.* Annapolis, 1957.

Cagle, Malcolm W., Vice Admiral, USN. "Task Force 77 in Action Off Vietnam." *USNIP,* 98, no. 5 (May 1972), 66–109.

Carlson, Verner R., Major, USA. "Rebuilding Norway's Navy." *USNIP,* 92, no. 1 (January 1966), 55–65.

Casey, Ralph E. "Political and Economic Significance of the World's Merchant Marines into the 1980s." *NWCR,* XXI, no. 8 (April 1969), 4–13.

The Center for Strategic and International Studies. *Soviet Sea Power.* Washington, 1969.

Christol, Carl Q. and Charles R. Davis (and Quincy Wright). "Maritime Quarantine: The Naval Interdiction of Offensive Weapons . . . to Cuba, 1962." *American Journal of International Law,* 57 (July 1963), 525–565.

Cliff, Donald K., Lieutenant Colonel, USMC. "Soviet Naval Infantry: A New Capability." *NWCR,* XXIII, no. 10 (June 1971), 90–101.

Cohen, Paul. "The Erosion of Surface Naval Power." *Foreign Affairs,* 49, no. 2 (January 1971), 330–349.

Colestock, Edward E., Rear Admiral, USN (Ret). "A Naval Appreciation of Brazil." *Naval Review 1967.* Annapolis, 1966, pp. 160–179.

Collins, Frank C., Jr., Commander, USN. "Maritime Support of the Campaign in I Corps," *USNIP,* 97, no. 5 (May 1971), 156–179.

Colvin, Robert D., Commander, USN. "Aftermath of the *Elath.*" *USNIP,* 95, no. 10 (October 1969), 60–67. Trends in PT boats.

Cottrell, Alvin J. and R. M. Burrell, eds. *The Indian Ocean: Its Political, Economic, and Military Importance.* New York, 1972.

Cox, Donald V., Rear Admiral, USN. "The Sea Control Ship System." *USNIP,* 98, no. 4 (April 1972), 113–115.

Coye, Beth F., Lieutenant Commander, USN, *et al.* "An Evaluation of U. S. Naval Presence in the Indian Ocean." *NWCR,* XXXIII, no. 2 (October 1970), 35–52.

Craft, James Pressley, Jr. "The Role of Congress in the Determination of Naval Strategy in Support of United States Foreign Policy 1956–1966." Ph.D., University of Pennsylvania, 1969.

Crowe, William James, Jr. "The Policy Roots of the Modern Royal Navy, 1946–1963." Ph.D., Princeton University, 1965.

Cummings, E. J., Captain, USN. "The Chinese Communist Navy." *USNIP,* 90, no. 9 (September 1964), 64–73.

Cunliffe, Marcus, ed. *The London Times History of Our Times.* New York, 1971. An overview, 1945–70.

Davies, John Paton. "The U. S. Invented the 'Imbalance of Power.' " *The New York Times Magazine* (December 7, 1969), pp. 50 and *passim.*

Davis, Vincent. *The Admirals Lobby.* Chapel Hill, 1967. USN, twentieth century.

"Details of Indo/Pakistani War Reported in *Marine Rundschau." USNIP,* 99, no. 3 (March 1973), 127–128.

Dewenter, John R. "China Afloat." *Foreign Affairs,* 50, no. 4 (July 1972), 738–751. The Chinese Navy.

Eccles, Henry E., Rear Admiral, USN (Ret). *Military Concepts and Philosophy.* New Brunswick, N. J., 1965. Contemporary.

———. "Suez 1956—Some Military Lessons." *NWCR,* XXI, no. 7 (March 1969), 28–56.

Eller, Ernest McNeill, Rear Admiral, USN (Ret). *The Soviet Sea Challenge: The Struggle for Control of the World's Oceans.* n.p., 1971.

Emery, S. W., Jr., Lieutenant (j.g.), USN. "The Merchant Marine Act of 1970." *USNIP,* 97, no. 3 (March 1971), 38–43.

Fairhall, David. *Russian Sea Power.* Boston, 1971.

Fall, Bernard B. *The Two Viet-nams: A Political and Military Analysis.* New York, 1963.

Feis, Herbert. *From Trust to Terror: The Onset of the Cold War, 1945–1950.* New York, 1970.

Field, James A., Jr. *History of United States Naval Operations: Korea.* Washington, 1962.

Fontaine, André (tr. by Renaud Bruce). *History of the Cold War: From the Korean War to the Present.* New York, 1969.

Freitag, Robert F., Captain, USN. "The Effect of Space Operations on Naval Warfare." *Naval Review 1962–63.* Annapolis, 1962, pp. 173–195.

Galvin, John R. *Air Assault: the Development of Airmobile Warfare.* New York, 1969. World War II through Vietnam.

Garrett, William B., Lieutenant Commander, USN. "The U. S. Navy's Role in the 1956 Suez Crisis." *NWCR,* XXII, no. 7 (March 1970), 66–78.

Gorshkov, Sergei G., Admiral of the Fleet, Navy of the U.S.S.R. "The Development of Soviet Naval Science (Excerpts)." *NWCR,* XXI, no. 11 (February 1969), 30–42.

Gretton, Sir Peter, Vice Admiral, R.N. (Ret). *Maritime Strategy.* New York, 1965.

Gullion, Edmund A., ed. *Uses of the Seas.* Englewood Cliffs, N. J., 1968. An overview, naval and non-naval.

Hagan, Kenneth J. and Jacob W. Kipp. "U.S. and U.S.S.R. Naval Strategy," *USNIP,* 99, no. 11 (November 1973), 38–44.

Hale, Richard W. "The Fledgling Navies of Black Africa." *NWCR,* XXIV, No. 12 (June 1972), 42–55.

Halperin, Morton H. *Limited War in the Nuclear Age.* New York, 1963.

Hankinson, David K., Commander, R.N. (Ret). "HMS *Centaur* at Dar es Salaam." *USNIP,* 95, no. 11 (November 1969), 57–66.

Harllee, John, Rear Admiral, USN (Ret). "Patrol Guerrilla Motor Boats." *USNIP,* 90, no. 4 (April 1964), 70–79. Inshore vessels.

Harrigan, Anthony. "Inshore and River Warfare." *Orbis,* X, no. 3 (Fall 1966), 940–946.

Hayes, John D., Rear Admiral, USN (Ret). "Patterns of American Sea Power, 1945–1956: Their Portents for the Seventies." *USNIP,* 96, no. 5 (May 1970), 337–352.

————. "Sea Power and Sea Law." *USNIP,* 90, no. 5 (May 1964), 60–67. The Cold War aspects.

Herrington, Arthur C. "U. S. Navy Policy." *NWCR,* XXII, no. 1 (September 1969), 4–13.

Hessler, William H. "Blue Water Around Red China." *USNIP,* 89, no. 2 (February 1963), 27–39.

Hewlett, Richard G. and Francis Duncan. *A History of the United States Atomic Energy Commission,* Vol. II: *Atomic Shield, 1947–1952.* University Park, Pa., 1969.

Hezlet, Sir Arthur, Vice Admiral, R.N. (Ret). *Aircraft and Sea Power.* New York, 1970. Twentieth century, but used for the Cold War.

Hooper, Edwin Bickford, Vice Admiral, USN (Ret). *Mobility, Support, Endurance: A Story of Naval Operational Logistics in the Vietnam War, 1965–1968.* Washington, 1972.

Hoopes, Townsend. *The Limits of Intervention.* New York, 1969. High-level American planning during the Vietnam War.

Huan, Claude, Lieutenant Commander, F.N. "The French Submarine Force." *USNIP,* 92, no. 2 (February 1966), 42–53.

Hunt, George P. "The Four-Star Military Mess." *Life* (June 18, 1971), 50–68.

Jane's Fighting Ships, 1969–70. London, 1970.

Joshua, Wynfred. *Soviet Penetration into the Middle East,* rev. ed. New York, 1971.

Kaul, R., Lieutenant Commander, I.N. (Ret). "India's Russian Navy." USNIP, 96, no. 8 (August 1970), 38–45.

————. "The Indo-Pakistani War and the Changing Balance of Power in the Indian Ocean." *USNIP,* 99, no. 5 (May 1973), 172–195.

Kotsch, W. J., Captain, USN. "The Six-Day War of 1967." *USNIP,* 94, no. 6 (June 1968), 72–81.

Laforest, T. J., Captain, USN. "Strategic Significance of the Northern Sea Route." *USNIP,* 93, no. 12 (December 1967), 56–65.

Littauer, Raphael and Norman Uphoff, eds. *The Air War in Indochina.* Boston, 1972.

Little, Ivor C., Commander, SAN. "Sea Trials for South Africa." *USNIP,* 98, no. 12 (December 1972), 78–83.

Lowe, George E. *The Age of Deterrence.* Boston, 1964. The nuclear arms race and strategic theory, 1953–64.

————. "The Case for the Oceanic Strategy." *USNIP,* 94, no. 6 (June 1968), 26–34.

————. "The Only Option?" *USNIP*, 97, no. 4 (April 1971), 18–26. The Nixon Doctrine as oceanic strategy.

MacDonald, Scot. *Evolution of Aircraft Carriers*. Washington, 1964. Twentieth century, but used for post-World War II aspects.

Margaritis, C., Vice Admiral, Hellenic Navy. "The Future Roles and Problems of Small Countries' Navies." *NWCR*, XXIV, no. 5 (January 1972), 35–40.

Martin, L. W. *The Sea in Modern Strategy*. New York, 1967.

Masson, Philipe and J. Labayle Couhat. (tr. by G. G. and K. K. Sick). "The Soviet Presence in the Mediterranean: A Short History." *NWCR*, XXIII, no. 5 (January 1971), 60–66.

MccGwire, Michael, ed. *Soviet Naval Developments: Context and Capability*. Halifax, 1973.

McCleave, Robert E., Jr., Major, USA. "The National Defense Requirement For a U. S.-Flag Merchant Marine." *NWCR*, XXI, no. 12 (June 1969), 64–79.

McClintock, Robert. "The American Landing in Lebanon." *USNIP*, 88, no. 10 (October 1962), 65–79.

————. "Latin America and Naval Power." *USNIP*, 91, no. 10 (October 1965), 30–37.

————. "The River War in Indochina." *USNIP*, 80, no. 12 (December 1954), 1303–11. The years 1945–54.

McCutcheon, Keith B., Lieutenant General, USMC. "Marine Aviation in Vietnam, 1962–1970." *USNIP*, 97, no. 5 (May 1971), 122–155.

McDevitt, Joseph B., Rear Admiral, USN. "Current International Law Problems of the Navy." *NWCR*, XXII, no. 9 (May 1970), 41–49.

McDonald, David L., Admiral, USN. "Carrier Employment Since 1950." *USNIP*, 90, no. 11 (November 1964), 26–33.

McKnew, Thomas W. "Four-Ocean Navy in the Nuclear Age." *National Geographic*, 127, no. 2 (February 1965), 145–187.

Merdinger, Charles J., Captain, USN. "Civil Engineers, Seabees, and Bases in Vietnam." *USNIP*, 96, no. 5 (May 1970), 254–275.

Moulton, J. L., Major General, Royal Marines (Ret). "The Defense of Northwest Europe and the North Sea." *USNIP*, 97, no. 5 (May 1971), 80–97.

————. "The Indonesian Confrontation." *Naval Review 1969*. Annapolis, 1969, pp. 143–171.

Murphy, Frank M., Captain, USN. "Seapower and the Satellites." *USNIP*, 95, no. 11 (November 1969), 75–83. Warsaw Pact navies.

Murphy, R. P. W., Lieutenant, USNR, and Colonel Edwin F. Black, USA. "The South Vietnamese Navy." *USNIP*, 90, no. 1 (January 1964), 52–61. The early years, to 1963.

Naval History Division. *Keeping the Peace*. Washington, 1966. Cold War naval operations.

"New Nuclear Strategy for America?" *U. S. News and World Report* (April 13, 1970), 32–34. The sea-based missile option.

The New York Times. *The Pentagon Papers*. New York, 1971. High-level planning and prosecution of the American intervention in the Vietnam War, 1964–68.

————. *United States Foreign Policy in the Nixon Administration*. New York, 1971.

Paolucci, Dominic A., Captain, USN (Ret). "The Development of Navy Strategic Offensive and Defensive Systems." *USNIP*, 96, no. 5 (May 1970), 204–223. The period 1945–70.

Parson, Nels A., Jr. *Missiles and the Revolution in Warfare*. Cambridge, Mass., 1962.

Petersen, Charles W. "The Military Balance in Southern Africa." C. P. Potholm and Richard Dale, eds., *Southern Africa in Perspective*. Glencoe, Ill., 1972, 298–317.

Petersen, Henrik M., Captain, Royal Danish Navy. "Maritime Denmark." *USNIP*, 94, no. 1 (January 1968), 37–49. Cold War naval buildup.

Petrov, Victor P. "Soviet Canals." *USNIP*, 93, no. 7 (July 1967), 32–44.

Polaris Fleet Ballistic Missile Weapon System Fact Sheet. [Washington], June 1, 1966.

Polmar, Norman. *Soviet Naval Power: Challenge for the 1970s*. New York, 1972.

Popham, Hugh. *Into Wind: A History of British Naval Flying*. London, 1969. Used for post-1945 aspects.

Porath, Reuben, Lieutenant Commander, IDFN. "The Israeli Navy," *USNIP*, 97, no. 9 (September 1971), 33–39.

Prina, L. Edgar. "The Navy First Used Think Tanks During World War II," *Armed Forces Journal* (September 28, 1968). Mainly the 1960s.

Ramage, Lawson P., Vice Admiral, USN. "The Military Sea Transportation Service." *NWCR*, XXI, no. 9 (May 1969), 4–11.

Ravenal, Earl C. "The Nixon Doctrine and Our Asian Commitments." *Foreign Affairs*, 49, no. 2 (January 1971), 201–217.

Roberts, Chalmers M. *The Nuclear Years: The Arms Race and Arms Control, 1945–70*. New York, 1970.

Rogers, Robert B., Commander, USN. "Trends in Soviet Naval Strategy." *NWCR*, XXI, no. 11 (February 1969), 13–29.

Rosecrance, R. N. *Defense of the Realm: British Strategy in the Nuclear Epoch*. New York, 1968.

Ruge, Friedrich, Vice Admiral, GFN (Ret). "The Reconstruction of the German Navy, 1956–1961." *USNIP*, 88, no. 7 (July 1962), 52–65.

"Russia: Power Play on the Oceans." *Time* (February 23, 1968), 23–28.

Saar, C. W., Commander, USN. "Offensive Mining as a Soviet Strategy." *USNIP*, 90, no. 8 (August 1964), 42–51.

Schneider, Mark Bernard. "SABMIS and the Future of Strategic Warfare." *USNIP*, 95, no. 7 (July 1969), 26–34.

Schratz, Paul R. "A Commentary on the *Pueblo* Affair." *Military Affairs*, XXXV, no. 3 (October 1971), 93–95.

Schreadly, R. L., Commander, USN. "The Naval War in Vietnam, 1950–1970." *USNIP*, 97, no. 5 (May 1971), 180–209.

———. "Sea Lords." *USNIP*, 96, no. 8 (August 1970), 22–31. Waterborne interdiction in the Mekong delta, Vietnam War.

"Seapower in the Space Age." *Air Force/Space Digest* II, no. 4 (April 1966) [entire issue].

Sharp, U. S. G., Admiral, USN. "Report on Air and Naval Campaigns Against North Vietnam and Pacific Command-Wide Support of the War, July 1964/July 1968." *Report on the War in Vietnam (as of 30 June 1968)*. Washington, 1969.

Sherrill, Robert. "SCRAM, SCAD, ULMS and other aspects of the $85.9-

billion defense budget." *The New York Times Magazine* (July 30, 1972), pp. 7 and *passim.*

Sherwood, [M.] Lee. "The Seventh Fleet in Limited War: From Theory to Practice." Undergraduate research paper, University of Maine, 1969.

Sick, Gary G., Lieutenant Commander, USN. "Russia and the West in the Mediterranean: Perspectives for the 1970s." *NWCR*, XXII, no. 10 (June 1970), 49–69.

Simpson, Howard R. "Offshore Guerrilla War." *NWCR*, XXII, no. 2 (October 1969), 17–20. Surface-to-surface missile boats.

Smith, Robert H., Captain, USN (Ret). "ASW—The Crucial Naval Challenge." *USNIP*, 98, no. 5 (May 1972), 126–141.

Sokol, Anthony E. *Sea Power in the Nuclear Age.* New York, 1961.

"Soviet Union: Reaching for Supremacy at Sea." *Time* (January 31, 1972), 28–33.

Spanier, John W. *American Foreign Policy Since World War II,* 4th rev. ed., New York, 1971.

Steel, Ronald. *Pax Americana,* rev. ed. New York, 1970.

Stewart, James, Lieutenant Commander, R.N. (Ret). "East of Suez." *USNIP*, 92, no. 3 (March 1966), 41–51. British policy.

———. "The Suez Operation." *USNIP*, 90, no. 4 (April 1964), 37–47. The 1956 affair.

Swarztrauber, S. A., Commander, USN. "River Patrol Relearned." *USNIP*, 96, no. 5 (May 1970), 120–157. River warfare, Vietnam.

Symington, Stuart, Senator. "Laos: The Furtive War." *World* (August 29, 1972), 34–37. American involvement, 1964–72.

Theberge, James D. *Soviet Seapower in the Caribbean: Political and Strategic Implications.* New York, 1972.

Uhlig, Frank, Jr. "Some Speculations on the Navy at the End of the 1970s." *NWCR*, XXIV, no. 9 (May 1972), 9–15.

"U. S. Naval Operations Against North Vietnam, August 1964–November 1968." *Naval Review 1969.* Annapolis, 1969, pp. 359–363.

Valentine, Andrew J., Commander, USN. "℞: Quarantine." *USNIP*, 89, no. 5 (May 1968), 38–50. Cuban missile crisis and blockade.

Van Horssen, D. A., Lieutenant Commander, USN. "The Royal Thai Navy." *USNIP*, 92, no. 6 (June 1966), 77–83.

Vito, Albert H., Jr., Captain, USN. "Developing the Fleet's Aircraft." *USNIP*, 92, no. 9 (September 1966), 69–77. Post-1945.

Waskow, Arthur I., ed. *The Debate over Thermonuclear Strategy.* Boston, 1965.

Weyer's Warships of the World, 1969. Annapolis, 1968.

Wettern, Desmond. "The Royal Navy and the Continuing Commitments." *USNIP*, 97, no. 8 (August 1971), 18–25.

Windchy, Eugene G. *The Tonkin Gulf.* New York, 1971. In August 1964.

Xydis, Stephen George. "The American Naval Visits to Greece and the Eastern Mediterranean in 1946—Their Impact on American-Soviet Relations." Ph.D., Columbia University, 1956.

Much material on the post-1945 period was derived from standard press accounts and numerous interviews and conversations with many U. S. Navy and Marine Corps officers, former midshipmen students and colleagues during and since the writer's years on the faculty at the U. S. Naval Academy

(1964–68) and as coordinator of the U. S. Naval Institute's Distinguished Visitor Program (1967–69).

Key works published between the publication of the 1973 and 1983 editions:

Abbazzia, Patrick. *Mr. Roosevelt's Navy: The Private War of the U.S. Atlantic Fleet, 1939–1942*. Annapolis, 1975.

Akawa, Hiroyuki. *The Reluctant Admiral: Yamamoto and the Imperial Navy*. New York, 1979.

Barrow, Clayton R., Jr., ed. *America Spreads Her Sails: U.S. Seapower in the 19th Century*. Annapolis, 1973.

Blair, Clay, Jr. *Silent Victory: The United States Submarine War Against Japan*. Philadelphia, 1975.

Bryson, Thomas A. *Tars, Turks, and Tankers: The Role of the United States Navy in the Middle East, 1800–1979*. Metuchen, N.J., 1980.

Cable, James. *Gunboat Diplomacy, 1919–1979*. New York, 1981.

Coletta, Paolo E. *The American Naval Heritage in Brief*. Washington, 1978.

————, Robert G. Albion and K. Jack Bauer, eds. *American Secretaries of the Navy*, 2 vols. Annapolis, 1980.

————. *A Bibliography of American Naval History*. Annapolis, 1981.

————. *The United States Navy and Defense Unification, 1947–1953*. Newark, Del., 1981.

Cooling, Benjamin Franklin. *Gray Steel and Blue Water Navy: The Formative Years of America's Military-Industrial Complex, 1881–1917*. Hamden, Conn., 1979.

Coote, John O., Capt., RN (Ret.). "Send Her Victorious. . . ." *USNIP* (January 1983), 34–42. The Falklands War.

Dictionary of American Naval Fighting Ships, 8 vols. Washington, 1959–1981.

Dingman, Roger. *Power in the Pacific: The Origins of the Naval Arms Limitation, 1914–1922*. Chicago, 1976.

Dismukes, Bradford, and James McConnell, eds. *Soviet Naval Diplomacy*. New York, 1979.

Dull, Jonathan R. *The French Navy and American Independence: A Study of Arms and Diplomacy, 1774–1787*. Princeton, 1976.

Dull, Paul S. *A Battle History of the Imperial Japanese Navy, 1941–1945*. Annapolis, 1978.

Ekoko, A. E. "British Naval Policy in the South Atlantic, 1874–1914," *Mariner's Mirror* (August 1980), 209–223.

Fioravanzo, Admiral Giuseppe. *A History of Naval Tactical Thought*. Annapolis, 1979.

Fowler, William M., Jr. *Rebels Under Sail: The American Navy during the Revolution*. New York, 1976.

Friedman, Norman. *Carrier Air Power*. Annapolis, 1981.

————. *U.S. Naval Weapons*. Annapolis, 1983. 1883–1983.

Glover, Richard A. *Britain at Bay: Defence Against Bonaparte, 1803–1814*. New York, 1973.

Gorshkov, Admiral Sergei G. *The Sea Power of the State*. Annapolis, 1979. Updating of his original *Red Star Rising at Sea*.

Graham, Gerald S. *The China Station: War and Diplomacy, 1830–1860*. Oxford, 1978.

Guilmartin, John F. *Gunpowder and Galleys: Changing Technology and Mediterranean Warfare at Sea in the Sixteenth Century*. London, 1974.

Herwig, Holger H. *The German Naval Officer Corps . . . 1890–1918*. Oxford, 1973.

———. *"Luxury Fleet": The Imperial German Navy, 1888–1918*. Boston, 1980.

Hewlett, Richard G. and Francis Duncan. *The Nuclear Navy, 1946–1962*. Chicago, 1974.

Herzlett, Arthur. *Electronics and Sea Power*. New York, 1975.

Hoffman, Paul E. *The Spanish Crown and the Defense of the Caribbean, 1535–1585*. Baton Rouge, 1980.

Hooper, Edwin B., Dean C. Allard and Oscar P. Fitzgerald. *The United States Navy and the Vietnam Conflict*, I. Washington, 1976.

Horsfield, John. *The Art of Leadership: The Royal Navy from the Age of Nelson to the End of World War II*. Westport, Conn., 1980.

Howarth, David. *The Voyage of the Armada: The Spanish Navy*. London, 1981.

Howse, Derek and Michael Sanderson. *The Sea Chart*. London, 1973.

Hunt, Barry D. *Sailor–Scholar: Admiral Sir Herbert Richmond 1871–1946*. Waterloo, Ontario, 1982.

Jenkins, E. H. *A History of the French Navy*. London, 1973.

Johnston, Robert E. *Far China Station: The U.S. Navy in Asian Waters, 1800–1898*. Annapolis, 1979.

Johnstone, Paul. *The Sea-craft of Prehistory*. Cambridge, Mass., 1980.

Kennedy, Paul M. *The Rise and Fall of British Naval Mastery*. New York, 1976.

Kilmarx, Robert A., ed. *America's Maritime Legacy*. Boulder, Colo., 1979.

Laffin, Jean. *Fight for the Falklands*. New York, 1982.

Lane, Frederick C. *Venice: A Maritime Republic*. Baltimore, 1973.

Love, Robert W., ed. *The Chiefs of Naval Operations*. Annapolis, 1980.

Marder, Arthur J. *From the Dardanelles to Oran: Studies of the Royal Navy in War and Peace, 1915–1940*. Oxford, 1974.

May, W. E. *A History of Marine Navigation*. London, 1973.

MccGwire, Michael and John McDonnell. *Soviet Naval Influence*. New York, 1977.

McLynn, F. J. "Sea Power and the Jacobite Rising of 1745," *Mariner's Mirror* (May 1981), 163–172.

McNeill, William H., Jr. *The Pursuit of Power: Technology, Armed Force and Society Since A.D. 1000*. Chicago, 1982.

Millett, Allan. *Semper Fidelis: The History of the United States Marine Corps*. New York, 1980.

Morris, James M. *Our Maritime Heritage*. Washington, 1979. U.S.

Niven, John. *Gideon Welles*. Oxford, 1973.

Padfield, Peter. *Tide of Empires*, I, II. London, 1980, 1982.

Peattie, Mark R. "Akiyama Saneyuki and the Emergence of Modern Japanese Naval Doctrine," *USNIP* (January 1977), 60–69.

Pelz, Stephen. *Race to Pearl Harbor.* Cambridge, Mass., 1974.

Pemsel, Helmut. *A History of War at Sea.* Annapolis, 1978.

Polmar, Norman. *The American Submarine.* Annapolis, 1981.

Reed, Rowena. *Combined Operations in the Civil War.* Annapolis, 1978.

Reynolds, Clark G. "American Strategic History and Doctrines: A Reconsideration," *Military Affairs* (December 1975), 181–190.

————. "The Continental Strategy of Imperial Japan," *USNIP* (August 1983).

————. *Famous American Admirals.* New York, 1978.

————. "MacArthur as Maritime Strategist," *NWCR* (March-April 1982), 79–102.

————. "The Sea in the Making of America," *USNIP* (July 1976), 36–51.

Rossler, Eberhard. *The U-Boat: The Evolution and Technical History of German Submarines.* Annapolis, 1981.

Ruge, Friedrich, Vice Admiral. *The Soviets as Naval Opponents, 1941–1945.* Annapolis, 1979.

Ryan, Paul B. *First Line of Defense: The U.S. Navy Since 1945.* Stanford, 1981.

Sandler, Stanley. *The Emergence of the Modern Capital Ship.* Newark, Del., 1979. The 1860s.

Saul, Norman. *Sailors in Revolt: The Russian Baltic Fleet in 1917.* Lawrence, Kansas, 1978.

Scammell, G. V. "European Seamanship in the Great Age of Discovery," *Mariner's Mirror* (November 1982), 357–376.

————. *The World Encompassed: The First European Maritime Empires, c. 800–1650.* Berkeley, 1981.

Schurman, Donald M. *Julian S. Corbett, 1854–1922.* London, 1981.

Seager, Robert, II. *Alfred Thayer Mahan: The Man and His Letters.* Annapolis, 1977.

Still, William N., Jr. *American Sea Power in the Old World: The United States Navy in European and Near Eastern Waters, 1865–1917.* Westport, Conn., 1980.

Swanson, Bruce. *Eighth Voyage of the Dragon: A History of China's Quest for Seapower.* Annapolis, 1982.

Symcox, Geoffrey. *The Crisis of French Sea Power, 1688–1697.* The Hague, 1974.

Symonds, Craig L. *Navalists and Antinavalists: The Naval Policy Debate in the United States, 1785–1827.* Newark, Del., 1980.

Tarpey, John F. "Uncle Carl," *USNIP* (January 1982), 38–45. Vinson.

Till, Geoffrey, *et al. Maritime Strategy and the Nuclear Age.* London, 1982.

Trask, David. *The War With Spain in 1898.* New York, 1981.

USNIP (March 1982). International navies issue.

Valle, James E. *Rocks & Shoals: Order and Discipline in the Old Navy, 1800–1861.* Annapolis, 1980.

Vlahos, Michael. *The Blue Sword: The Naval War College and the American Mission, 1919–1941.* Newport, 1980.

Yerxa, Donald A. "The United States Navy and the Caribbean Sea, 1914–1941." Ph.D., University of Maine, 1982.

Note: Index for both volumes.

Index

Place names indexed only when relating to specific naval action.

629